CRIME IN PROGRESS

CRIME IN PROGRESS

INSIDE THE STEELE DOSSIER AND THE FUSION GPS INVESTIGATION OF DONALD TRUMP

GLENN SIMPSON
and
PETER FRITSCH

RANDOM HOUSE
NEW YORK

Published in the United States by Random House,
an imprint and division of Penguin Random House LLC, New York.

RANDOM HOUSE and the HOUSE colophon are
registered trademarks of Penguin Random House LLC.

Hardback ISBN 978-0-593-13415-3
Ebook ISBN 978-0-593-13416-0

Printed in the United States of America on acid-free paper

randomhousebooks.com

2 4 6 8 9 7 5 3 1

FIRST EDITION

Glenn:

For Mary, Max, and Charlie

Peter:

For Mom, Dad, Lynn, and the kids

CONTENTS

PREFACE

This book was made possible by Donald Trump and his supporters in Congress. For more than two years, they pursued multiple legal avenues to pry into the private client work of Fusion GPS, even as they labored to hide the Trump campaign's dealings with Russia. Their baseless allegations about Fusion's work, which at their core attacked the constitutional right to free speech, ultimately forced the firm and some of its clients to provide documents and testimony about its research efforts—information Fusion would have otherwise been contractually obligated to keep confidential. Congress's assault on Fusion provided the firm with an unexpected opportunity to tell the true story of its investigations into Trump and its work with Christopher Steele.

CRIME IN PROGRESS

CHAPTER ONE

"I THINK WE HAVE A PROBLEM"

THE SUREST SIGN THE DAM WAS ABOUT TO BURST CAME IN THE form of an encrypted call, on the afternoon of January 4, 2017, from a number in the 646 area code. A New York cellphone. Glenn Simpson and his business partner at Fusion GPS, Peter Fritsch, had been getting their share of blind calls since Donald Trump's election.

The inauguration was just weeks away, and reporters from all the major media outlets were desperate to catch up on a story many had fumbled or simply ignored: how to explain the bizarre relationship between Trump and Russia.

By then, Simpson and Fritsch were deep into that story. Few outside of a small group of journalists and lawyers knew of their work during the campaign, but word had started seeping out after Trump's upset victory. Their Washington-based research firm had been digging into Trump's ties to criminal elements in the United States and Russia since September 2015. Month after month the project had grown in scope, starting with a review of his business record and expanding to a full excavation of his many dubious real estate projects, from Panama to Azerbaijan. Fusion worked with a global network of sources and subcontractors to examine Trump's dealings with an array of oligarchs and convicted criminals from the former Soviet Union as well as his decades of mysterious trips to Russia in pursuit of real estate deals that never got off the ground.

Fritsch swiped his phone to answer. "Hello, Peter?" a voice said. "This is Carl Bernstein." The legendary former *Washington Post* Watergate reporter was now working with CNN. He had something urgent to discuss. Bernstein was polite and affable, far from the aggressive, take-no-prisoners reporter Fritsch imagined from *All the President's Men.*

After exchanging a few pleasantries, Bernstein said he wanted to discuss some information he came across that suggested Trump might be entangled with Russian president Vladimir Putin in ways virtually no one knew or even suspected. If true, Bernstein said, this was a situation as dire as Watergate—maybe more so. He was also eager to get to a former British spy working at a company based in London called Orbis. He asked if Fritsch could help put him in touch.

Fritsch, a former *Wall Street Journal* reporter and editor, fished a bit, trying to figure out how Bernstein had known to call Fusion. Hardly one to give up a source, Bernstein made vague reference to mutual friends. "I'm pretty sure what I'm hearing is more than just rumor," he said.

Then he got to the point. He had heard some documents existed that painted an alarming portrait of the ways in which Russia may have compromised the incoming president. Could Fritsch help flesh out his understanding, off the record? Could he help him get in contact with the ex-spy who had produced the documents? Fritsch answered in general terms that, yes, Trump's relationship with Russia was important, but he begged off any deeper discussion. At least for now.

After hanging up, Fritsch called Simpson on an encrypted line. Simpson was wrapping up a year-end holiday in Mexico. "Hey, I think we have a problem," Fritsch said. "I think Carl Bernstein may have Chris's reports."

Chris was Christopher Steele, a former intelligence officer with Britain's MI6 who once served in Moscow and went on to run the spy service's Russia desk. A highly respected but low-profile Russia expert, Steele was about to become famous in ways he never expected. "Ugh," Simpson said. "That's not good."

After delving into Trump's Russia dealings for nearly nine months, Fusion had hired Steele in May 2016 to supplement its research. By then, Fusion had many reasons to harbor suspicions about the Trump campaign. Months earlier, they had uncovered court filings in Virginia seeming to show that Trump's campaign chairman, Paul Manafort, owed tens of millions of dollars to Oleg Deripaska, a Russian oligarch who wanted his money back and had close ties to Putin. Simpson and Fritsch had also gotten wind of a closely guarded secret: The FBI suspected that the Russian government had hacked into the computer system of the

Democratic National Committee. Fusion began to wonder if these events were related.

Steele's task was to tap his Russian source network to answer some nagging questions arising from the information on Trump that Fusion had already gathered: Why had Trump made so many trips to Russia over the years, without ever getting a single development project off the ground? Why did so many threads in the Trump story lead to Moscow and figures close to Putin? And why was Trump so smitten with Putin, who seemed fond of Trump in return?

Simpson had spent fifteen years in Washington and Europe as a *Wall Street Journal* investigative reporter, focusing much of his work on the emerging scourge of transnational crime. To his surprise, some of the characters from the ex–Soviet Union who surfaced in the initial phase of Fusion's investigation of Trump were people he had written about a decade earlier while investigating Russian corruption and organized crime for the *Journal,* stories Fritsch had edited while the two worked in Brussels.

Simpson wasn't completely surprised by the news of the Bernstein call. He told Fritsch that he had recently heard from a friend at *The Washington Post* that Fred Hiatt, the paper's editorial page editor, was talking about some sensational memoranda that sounded a lot like Steele's work.

Someone was leaking—that was clear. This had the potential to be a big problem.

The Steele reports—soon to be known as "the dossier"—were field intelligence from one of the West's most senior Russia watchers. The memos he produced were never meant to be viewed outside of a tiny circle of people, much less shared with the public. In unredacted form, the reports could expose Steele's sources and jeopardize lives. Steele took great care to mask those sources in his reports to Fusion. Still, the information clearly came from people with extraordinary access in Russia, and Russian intelligence could figure out who they were and track them down. Those sources included a number of people inside Russia and field operatives outside the country who needed protecting at all costs. Unredacted memos flying around among the Washington press corps risked exposing people to real danger.

Given the control Fusion had maintained over the memos, there was only one likely suspect for the leak: David Kramer, a longtime adviser to Republican senator John McCain.

At Steele's urging, Simpson had provided a set of the memos to Kramer a few weeks after the election. This was done for the sole purpose of passing them to McCain, who would then provide them to the head of the FBI. Steele had been secretly working with FBI agents for months, trying to sound the alarm, while Simpson had provided updates to a longtime contact at the Justice Department. Still, the feds seemed to be slow on the uptake, and Steele, Simpson, and Fritsch were concerned that the information was not getting through to the top brass. An alarmed McCain had promised to fix that.

Senator McCain, still many months from a dire brain cancer diagnosis, wanted to put a copy of Steele's memos in front of FBI Director James Comey—a decision his friend and fellow Republican senator Lindsey Graham encouraged. McCain wanted to know if the FBI was doing anything about credible information from a trusted ex–intelligence official in the U.K. that a hostile foreign power might have influence over the U.S. president-elect.

Simpson agreed to entrust Kramer with a copy of the Steele memos, for McCain's eyes only, because he knew that Kramer's dislike of Putin ran deep. While still a reporter, Simpson had turned to Kramer as a source a decade earlier for stories on Russia's growing political influence in Washington. But Kramer's alarm was so acute that he could easily do something rash. Lately, he had been telling associates that he still hoped to find a way—any way—to stop Trump from being inaugurated. He thought that exposing Trump's Russia ties might just be the answer. How he planned to do that was unclear.

Kramer's theory was about to be tested.

The story blew open at 5:10 P.M. on the afternoon of January 10, 2017, in a live broadcast by CNN that revealed just how far up the chain the Steele reporting had traveled. Above the chyron "INTEL CHIEFS PRESENTED TRUMP WITH CLAIMS OF RUSSIAN EFFORTS TO COMPROMISE HIM," a phalanx of three top CNN correspondents, plus Carl Bernstein, announced that senior intelligence officials had appended a two-page synopsis of some disturbing information to a classified briefing presented to both President Obama and President-elect Trump.

Jim Sciutto, CNN's longtime national security correspondent, delivered the overview: "Classified documents on Russian interference in the 2016 U.S. election," he said, had been presented to Obama and Trump.

And those documents reportedly included "allegations that Russian operatives claimed to have compromising personal and financial information about Mr. Trump."

And then, for the first time, he spoke of what would become known as the dossier, saying the allegations were based on memos "compiled by a former British intelligence operative whose past work U.S. intelligence officials consider credible." Barely a year earlier, Steele's information had played a role in the U.S. government's successful prosecution of corruption inside FIFA, soccer's worldwide governing body. He had U.S. and British government contacts at the highest levels. CNN said the information had been commissioned by an unnamed political research outfit.

Simpson and Fritsch and their team of researchers stood rapt in front of the big-screen TV in their Dupont Circle office, a fifteen minute walk up Connecticut Avenue from the White House. "The intel chiefs briefed Obama on Chris's memos?" Fritsch said. "That is beyond big."

What the CNN report didn't note was something Simpson and Fritsch knew from their experience as journalists: There is no way "opposition research" or field intelligence from a private foreign source reaches the desk of the president of the United States without senior officials in the U.S. government ascribing at least some credibility to those findings.

For Fusion, news of the leak caused alarm because of the potential risk to Steele's sources. But it also provided a validation of the research. For months, Simpson, Fritsch, and Steele had all tried, in different ways, to discreetly point reporters and authorities to a growing body of information indicating that Trump had a litany of troubling ties to Russia—with only limited success. Now, it seemed, some of that information had shot to the highest levels of the federal government.

If Trump was truly beholden to Putin, or susceptible to being manipulated by him, the implications were chilling. Just as scary, both houses of Congress were under the control of a Republican Party that now seemed ready to put all its chips on Trump. The possible consequences of Trump's unchecked friendliness toward Putin included the lifting of sanctions on Russia, the weakening or even demise of NATO, the spread of Russian-style corruption and kleptocracy to the West, and, more immediately for Fusion, the threat of retaliation from an incoming regime eager to even the score against its critics and whistleblowers.

As the CNN panel dissected what this all might mean, Bernstein and his colleagues appeared to do their best to walk a fine line: balancing the public's right to know with the need to protect sources involved in ongoing matters of national security. *Where had this shocking information come from?* moderator Jake Tapper wondered. The protection Bernstein offered was pretty thin.

"It came from a former British MI6 intelligence agent who was hired by a political research—opposition research—firm in Washington who was doing work about Donald Trump for both Republican and Democratic candidates opposed to Trump," he said.

Bernstein and CNN didn't name Steele or Fusion, but they certainly sprinkled some bread crumbs that could easily lead to their doors. And because neither Fusion nor Orbis had given the memos to CNN, the network had no obligation to grant them the kind of blanket anonymity that *The Washington Post* had bestowed upon Deep Throat during Watergate.

The CNN scoop was so explosive and authoritative in its sourcing that Simpson and Fritsch knew it would set off a fevered chase among competitors to not only match the story but advance it. What details in the "dossier" could be verified? Who was the former spy? What was the research firm that had hired him, and who had paid for it all? Not only would the media and the government relentlessly pursue the truth about Trump's ties to Russia, they would also hunt down his accusers.

Simpson, Fritsch, and Steele, who were all accustomed to working behind the scenes, had ventured into treacherous territory. They had done the work under contract with a law firm paid by Hillary Clinton's presidential campaign and the Democratic National Committee. That law firm technically "owned" the work product, including the Steele reports. But the discovery of so many hair-raising allegations of a conspiracy between the Kremlin and the Trump campaign to swing an election was "potentially a crime in progress," as Simpson later testified, a possible national security emergency that needed to be reported immediately to the authorities. Put simply, they had become gravely concerned that a hostile foreign adversary had compromised the incoming president.

As the post-9/11 mantra went: *If you see something, say something.*

Soon after the CNN report broke, Simpson and Fritsch called Steele by their preferred communication method, an encrypted voice application. Steele, whose view of U.S. politics and media could be surprisingly naive, was shocked but also elated by the story. Surely now, he reckoned, the U.S. government would do something to stop Trump from taking office. Right? Simpson and Fritsch said that was unlikely. They warned him that their names were now all but sure to come out. Being exposed as whistleblowers on the incoming leader of the free world would be bad, but tolerable, they concluded. The most important thing was to protect the underlying sources. They agreed to say nothing and hope the focus remained on Trump and Russia, at least initially, and not on the mysterious messengers.

That hope would prove to be short-lived.

Disaster struck at 6:20 P.M., barely an hour after the first CNN report aired. *BuzzFeed,* a website known for promoting viral Internet content but with bigger journalistic ambitions, published Steele's reports to Fusion virtually unredacted. The seventeen reports the firm had received over seven months were embedded in a *BuzzFeed* report that made repeated reference to their "unverified" nature and stated, inaccurately, that "the documents have circulated for months and acquired a kind of legendary status among journalists, lawmakers and intelligence officials who have seen them."

Within hours, hundreds of thousands of readers were devouring the dossier, and its highlights clogged Twitter. The dossier's shocking main thesis—that the Russians had significant leverage over Trump and had worked alongside his election team to enhance his odds in November—was soon swamped by its raciest allegation: that Russian spies had videotaped Trump in 2013 enjoying a "golden shower" show of prostitutes urinating on the bed in a Moscow hotel suite once occupied by President and Michelle Obama.

Inside the Fusion office, panic ensued. Fritsch ran to find Simpson, who was already screaming into the phone at Ken Bensinger, the lead reporter on the *BuzzFeed* story. "Take those fucking reports down right now!" Simpson yelled. "You are going to get people killed!"

Simpson was furious. Bensinger, who was on a trip with his wife and kids to Disney World, sounded sympathetic but said the matter was out of his hands: He had argued against publication but was overruled by his editors. Simpson and Fritsch had met Bensinger by happenstance barely a month earlier. Bensinger was a friend of their Los Angeles–based Fusion colleague Jason Felch. Felch had invited Bensinger to drop by a year-end Fusion retreat at a house high in the hills of California's Sonoma County one night in early December. Bensinger got lost en route and had backed into a ditch on a meandering dirt road high above Geyserville. A Fusion search party later found him and freed his car.

Later, over drinks, they discussed—off the record—Trump's documented ties to Russia, setting Bensinger on a reporting trail that ultimately brought him to the Washington office of one David Kramer.

Simpson hung up and dialed *BuzzFeed* editor in chief Ben Smith. Smith had been lured away from *Politico* in 2011 to run *BuzzFeed,* with a mandate to make it a more serious news outfit. This was not what pros do, Simpson screamed. "Take down those reports *right now!*"

Smith was implacable. The dossier had been briefed to the incoming and outgoing presidents, he said. President Obama had ordered a massive investigation of Russian interference in the election. This was all a matter of national importance that deserved to be vetted and scrutinized. It was the first version of the high-minded journalistic argument he would make repeatedly in coming days to defend his decision to publish source intelligence on the Internet.

Simpson argued that Smith was missing the more immediate point. The reports could help Putin track down the sources—not just Steele, but the sources he had relied on *within Russia.* There were lives at risk. Smith said he hadn't pondered that, but he said he had no intention of taking the post offline. It was too late for that anyway.

Simpson and Fritsch again reached Steele on an encrypted line. It was late in England. Steele was angry but calm. He, too, suspected that the McCain camp had acted irresponsibly and betrayed them. Fusion and Orbis would figure that out later. Right now, Steele had higher priorities. He was already making plans to, as he put it, "go to ground"— spy-speak for going into hiding. "Let's reassess in the morning," Steele said.

His preparations were put to use almost immediately. The following day, January 11, Steele's longtime partner in Orbis, a former British agent named Christopher Burrows, received an unannounced visit at his home outside London from a reporter for *The Wall Street Journal.* Could Burrows confirm that Christopher Steele was the author of the memoranda published in *BuzzFeed?* The reporter said he was on deadline and urgently needed a comment. Burrows politely declined. A flurry of calls ensued between Burrows, Simpson, Steele, Fritsch, and eventually Kramer.

While Kramer claimed not to know how the *Journal* had obtained Steele's name, he also said he had interceded with the *Journal*'s editors in an attempt to persuade them not to publish Steele's name, for security reasons. Later that day, the paper where Simpson and Fritsch had spent most of their careers—and which had done little reporting on the Trump-Russia story throughout the campaign—ignored those warnings and identified Steele as the author of the already famous dossier.

The next to be outed later that day was Fusion. The greatest threat there was from *The New York Times*.

Over the previous year, Simpson and Fritsch had taken extreme care not to give copies of the Steele reports to the media. But a few weeks after the election, they had decided to make an exception. They gave an off-the-record briefing and a redacted copy of the reports to the *Times*'s national security team in Washington. The *Times* had published a now infamous story at the end of October 2016 saying the FBI had looked into suspected Russia ties to Trump and found "no conclusive or direct link between Mr. Trump and the Russian government." The Kremlin's hack attack "was aimed at disrupting the presidential election rather than electing Trump." Within weeks of Trump's shocking victory over Clinton, both statements had begun to seem increasingly questionable. The paper was anxious to figure out whether it had gotten it wrong. They knew Fusion had information on that, and asked for help.

Despite the *Times*'s fateful pre-election miscue, Simpson and Fritsch agreed that no other publication had the sources and global reach needed to follow up on the underlying information in the Steele reports, so they gave the documents to the *Times* with strict instructions: They were on "deep background," a term of art that meant they were to be used solely to inform other reporting; they couldn't be reproduced or quoted from under any circumstances; and Fusion could not be identified as the source. Fusion knew and trusted the leader of that reporting team, Mark Mazzetti. There was no way he would break that promise, let alone share the reports' contents outside the *Times*.

Fusion knew that the minute its name was out, it would come under attack from the incoming White House and likely face retribution against the firm and its clients. But now, in the wake of the *BuzzFeed* leak, the competition for scoops about "the dossier" was at a fever pitch. Another *Times* reporter decided he was not bound by the paper's agreement to not identify Fusion, on the grounds that the firm's exposure was inevitable either way. On January 11, the *Times* published a front-page story putting Fusion and Steele together for the first time—a story with details the reporter could include only by breaking the confidential source agreement the paper had made with Simpson and Fritsch.

In twenty-four hours, Steele and Fusion had gone from no-profile to front-page news—something they neither sought nor wanted. Steele and his family went into hiding as the media—most menacingly, Russia's state-owned propaganda arm, RT—staked out his home in a leafy village in the London suburbs.

Simpson and Fritsch were worried for themselves but were more concerned about Steele and stayed in constant contact with him. He was nervous but safe, and implied that he had some help from his former colleagues. Experience had taught him that the threat to his personal safety was minimal: Putin was ruthless when it came to perceived traitors but was loath to attempt the assassination of a foreign national on foreign soil.

The reaction to the dossier hit every imaginable extreme. Republicans and a large contingent of the political chattering class churned out incredulity and outrage. Many pundits focused on purported spelling errors that were actually variants in transliterations between Russian and English. But pros in the Intelligence Community accurately recognized the material for what it was: a series of contemporaneous human intelligence reports—notes from conversations with well-placed sources—intended to inform additional investigation, not to be publicly released and read as a finished product. Fusion had decided it would be best to give McCain the complete Steele reporting to avoid tainting or diluting the agent's work in any way.

Trump weighed in, attacking *BuzzFeed* as a "failing pile of garbage" and adding, bizarrely, that the golden shower incident had to be bogus because he was "very much a germaphobe." His surrogates took to Twitter and the airwaves to pile on. One of their key points: Obviously the document was flawed, since it was paid for by "operatives" presumably working for his opponent, Hillary Clinton. What none of them knew was that Steele, in fact, did not know whom Fusion's client was when he compiled his first report, dated June 20, 2016, or that Fusion had not drafted, edited, or dictated a word of Steele's reporting. They also could not have known that the Steele memos were but a tiny subset of a vast cache of disturbing information Fusion had accumulated about Trump and Russia over the previous sixteen months.

But even on their own, Steele's memos made for a solid body of work. His sources were deep and well placed. And Steele was trained to filter out information that bore the hallmarks of possible disinformation or was otherwise not credible, an important skill in the world of professional intelligence collection. Fusion's researchers found nothing in the public record that contradicted the reporting.

Bob Woodward, Bernstein's Watergate reporting partner, was among the many members of the pundit class all too ready to talk first and report later. On *Fox News Sunday* that weekend, January 15, he called the dossier "a garbage document." Woodward, who at the time was seeking access to Trump for a book, said Trump's "point of view" was being "underreported," a nonsensical statement, given the blanket coverage of Trump's every utterance. Minutes later, as if on cue, Trump tweeted, "Thank you Bob Woodward."

In the months to come, one side of the commentariat would seek to hold the Steele memos to the impossibly high standards of a court filing or a front-page article in *The Washington Post,* while the other would interpret them as they were intended: disturbing leads outlining a dark international political conspiracy. Amid all the noise about "salacious" this and "unverified" that was the fact that the Steele dossier offered a series of findings that provided insights into Trump's persistent adulation for a regime in Moscow that has sought to undermine U.S. goals around the world since Putin took office in 1999.

The dossier and its exposure just ten days before Trump's inauguration triggered a cascade of events that disrupted a secret rapprochement brewing between the incoming Trump administration and the Kremlin, and eventually led to years of congressional investigations and hearings, the firings of National Security Adviser Michael Flynn and FBI Director James Comey, the appointment of special counsel Robert Mueller to what became a nearly two-year criminal investigation, an ongoing counterintelligence investigation, and a swirling brawl between the two political parties that plagued Trump's term in office from the very first day.

All of that would take months—years—to adjudicate. What was clear in January 2017 was that Fusion GPS, a tiny investigative research company tucked above a Starbucks and a used clothing store in Washington, D.C., was now in the middle of a dizzying political drama that seemed like something drawn from a Hollywood screenplay. The odds it would survive were not good.

CHAPTER TWO

PROJECT BANGOR

PROJECT BANGOR, WHICH WAS TO BECOME FUSION'S MOST complex and fateful assignment, began with a one-line email.

It was late August 2015, and the 2016 presidential campaign could not have been younger, nor the candidacy of Donald Trump more far-fetched. Trump had jumped in the polls since getting into the race in June, provoking the first stirrings of disbelief among establishment Republicans. His bombastic appearance in the first GOP debate, on August 5, catapulted the broadcast to the most watched primary debate ever, with more than twenty-four million viewers. But the idea of a Trump nomination still seemed outlandish, considering all his garish flaws and the supposed strengths of seasoned competitors like Jeb Bush, Chris Christie, and Marco Rubio.

As absurd as Trump seemed, Simpson sensed a rich research and business opportunity. "Trump" was the subject heading in the email he sent that Sunday morning to a longtime Republican politico. "Couple interesting threads that might be worth a look if you know anyone who might be interested in funding."

"Yes," came the reply. "Let's discuss. Can I call you this eve?"

Based on that suggestion of interest, Simpson then reached out to a couple of reliable contractors who might lend a hand, part of a stable of freelance specialists—lawyers, former journalists, linguists, archivists, data crunchers—that Fusion routinely turned to when assembling its research teams.

Their response was swift: *We're in.*

At that point, neither Simpson nor Fritsch knew much about Trump. Simpson was a longtime denizen of political Washington, a former *Roll Call* reporter turned investigative sleuth. Fritsch, a former foreign correspondent for the *Journal* who had spent more than fifteen years in Latin America, Southeast Asia, and Europe, knew Trump from his years in New York mainly as the rakish star of tabloid columns by Liz Smith and Cindy Adams. Trump had been a marginal figure, at best, in national politics. A couple of brief flirtations with a presidential run, frequent fulminations over trade or immigration policy, and a lot of potshots, some racially tinged, at President Obama—that was about it. His presence in Washington wasn't much more fulsome: a few turns of congressional testimony, an occasional appearance at the White House Correspondents' Dinner, and a big hotel project under way on Pennsylvania Avenue, a few blocks from the White House.

A quick check of Simpson's own reporting archive showed that in the course of publishing hundreds of articles about American campaigns, elections, and lobbying, he had mentioned Trump fewer than five times.

But Trump was climbing in the early polls, and Simpson's Republican acquaintance had begun to fret that his bombastic and xenophobic message might actually appeal to just enough nativist Republican primary voters to give him an edge in a fractured field.

Trump's Achilles' heel was probably his own troubled record in business, a subject most traditional "opposition research" firms weren't as well equipped to handle. Simpson had an inkling that establishment Republicans might be willing to fund a deep look at Trump's business past and finances for the stories that often hid in the small print of footnotes.

When they spoke that night, Simpson told the Republican operative that there were plenty of preliminary indications that Trump would be a fertile subject for investigation, and that some of the lines of inquiry would probably resonate with the media or primary voters. The operative said he was interested but needed to secure funding for Fusion's fee—about $50,000 for the first month.

After hanging up, Simpson banged out a quick email to an old journalistic acquaintance, the legendary *Village Voice* investigative reporter Wayne Barrett. Simpson was a longtime admirer of Barrett's reporting, which he began reading as a journalism student in college. Two of Barrett's biggest lifelong foes, Simpson knew, were Donald Trump and former New York City mayor Rudolph Giuliani. Barrett had written biographies on both. He also knew Barrett was struggling with lung cancer.

"Hey Wayne," he wrote. "Hope you are hanging in there. It's that time in America we all await with a curious mix of morbid anticipation and dread. Got some time to chat?" Simpson didn't bother mentioning Trump. They'd compared notes during the 2012 presidential campaign, and he knew Barrett would get it.

Barrett replied the next morning: "i've been feeding every reporter in america on donald," he wrote, "but most can't report like you. on vacation at ocean city house, where all my old trump files reside."

While Barrett's claim to be "feeding every reporter in America on Donald" was hyperbole (as was his flattery), the truth wasn't too far off: Barrett literally wrote the book on Trump with his 500-page 1992 exposé, *Trump: The Deals and the Downfall*. One of Barrett's earliest Trump pieces for *The Village Voice* in the 1970s had led to a grand jury investigation, while his book's details on Trump's organized crime ties nearly cost Trump his Atlantic City casino license. "While I was reporting that book in 1990, I was muscled out of Trump Castle and handcuffed overnight to a wall at the Atlantic City jail," Barrett later recalled.

Any researcher or reporter who wanted to know about Trump would naturally call Barrett, who was a strong believer in the necessity of collaboration among journalists when investigating politicians. He had trained, mentored, counseled, or otherwise encouraged dozens of talented investigative reporters over the years, many of whom went on to become some of the best in the business.

After updating Simpson on his ongoing health struggles, Barrett briefed him on Trump. Not nearly as rich as he claims. Terrible toward women. Serial liar. Lousy businessman. Ties to organized crime. What's more, Barrett added that he had a huge pile of old Trump documents he would be happy to share. Simpson was encouraged, and soon asked a New York–based colleague to go dig through the boxes of files Barrett brought back to his Brooklyn brownstone as summer ended. There would be plenty of material to sift.

By Labor Day weekend, Trump had carved out a solid lead over the pack of more than a dozen candidates, garnering the support of more than a quarter of Republicans, according to the rolling average compiled by RealClearPolitics. Many Republican elites figured he would soon hit his ceiling, but the jitters were rising. Ever since the commentator Pat Buchanan fatally wounded President George H. W. Bush's re-election chances by challenging him in the 1992 Republican primary on an anti-trade, anti-immigrant "America First" platform, establishment Republicans lived in fear of the party's nativist wing. Free trade was part of Republican orthodoxy, and it was an article of faith among Republican elites that a populist Republican nominee would get crushed in a general election matchup with virtually any Democrat. On September 4, 2015, the *Times* reported that top Republican strategists and donors were combining efforts in a still nascent campaign to stop Trump.

Less than a week later, Fusion had put together the outline of a draft plan to investigate Trump. The pitch was basic, and the investigation was meant to last just a month or so. The checklist of specific areas they intended to cover was also short: "Research Donald Trump's long-standing connections to organized crime, receipt of questionable tax abatements in New York City, overall record of tax avoidance, use of bankruptcies to victimize workers and small businessmen, and overall litigation history." The foundation of the research would be the collection and compilation of a large stash of news articles, books, and corporate, legal, and tax records, the beginnings of what was to become a vast repository of Trump data.

Reporters would later portray Fusion as a political "oppo research" shop, but the Trump job actually marked a dramatic departure from its usual line of work. With a stable of reliable clients—law firms, big corporations, hedge funds—Fusion specialized in complex and often expensive corporate and legal investigation. What it offered was simple: Its researchers traced assets, dug through investments, and read the fine print of court and regulatory filings to help clients understand a complicated situation or get an edge on a competitor. Few political races lent themselves to that sort of work, and few campaigns cared to invest in real investigative work, opting instead to pour their money into TV ads.

After nearly a decade in business, Fusion had dipped into national campaign politics only once before: in 2012, when the Republicans nominated Mitt Romney, a private equity tycoon with a long history in complicated deals and convoluted personal tax shelters. Romney was an ideal subject for Fusion research. Fusion spent more than a year deconstructing his decades-long history of opaque deals and easily accumulated wealth, findings that fed well into Barack Obama's case against Romney as an out-of-touch plutocrat.

Trump was an even more tantalizing target. Absent from that first outline to the potential Republican client, though, was any mention of Russia or any focus on the racier side of Trump's record, which is to say his reputedly rich past with myriad women. Looking into people's sex lives wasn't Fusion's strength.

The final go-ahead to begin research on Trump came in a call from the client on Friday, September 11, while Simpson was in London. Fusion would be hired by *The Washington Free Beacon,* a conservative online publication backed by the hedge fund billionaire Paul Singer. He had been a big backer of Rudolph Giuliani and then George W. Bush but was reportedly no fan of Trump. Fusion's Republican contact gave just a verbal thumbs-up, with no specific marching orders. That was how Fusion liked it. Some research clients try to dictate the objectives (and thus the outcome) of the research process, but Fusion prefers not to work that way. Better to have no preordained thesis and instead gather up *everything* at the beginning—on the theory that if you decide what you are looking for before you begin, you risk blinding yourself to unexpected things that come up and prove to be important.

After just a few hours of cursory research, Simpson was struck by the scale of the task. The sheer abundance of lawsuits alone was mind-boggling. Fusion had done a lot of legal research over the years, and it had never encountered a person who had initiated or been the target of as much litigation as Donald Trump. A litigation search of a prominent businessman in his sixties or seventies might turn up a page or two of entries on a federal court database. When Simpson searched Trump's name, his computer spat back two dozen pages of cases that ran the gamut from allegations of fraud to unpaid bills.

Simpson ordered a used copy of Barrett's long-out-of-print *The Deals and the Downfall,* the first of ten Trump books that, by the end of the month, formed the beginnings of a digital archive on Trump. As the books arrived at Fusion's office, the spines and bindings were carefully removed using a sharp blade, and the loose pages were scanned and converted into text that could be easily searched: An instant library of thousands of pages of digitally searchable Trump literature.

The negative news stories on Trump were almost as abundant as his lawsuits. His aborted 2012 presidential run had caused a few journalists to compile hurried overviews of his business past, cataloging a pattern of questionable business partners and interactions with the mob. A spurt of stories from years earlier, concerning Trump's relationship to a convicted felon named Felix Sater, stood out from everything else. The earliest article, published on B1 in the local news section of *The New York Times* in December 2007, carried a mundane headline, "Real Estate Executive with Hand in Trump Projects Rose from Tangled Past." It detailed Sater's ties to the Mafia and his reinvention as a real estate executive working with Trump. Wayne Barrett had also penned a 2011 follow-up on Trump's ties to Sater for *The Daily Beast.* The piece sought to explain why Trump didn't run for president in 2012: "With lawsuits pending and shady partners, Trump's business empire could not withstand the scrutiny of a presidential campaign."

Simpson's interest was piqued. Sater did not appear to be your average criminal. The feds had accused him of large-scale money laundering and stock manipulation involving Italian organized crime. He was Russian-born and grew up in the rough-and-tumble émigré neighborhood of Brighton Beach, and his dad was a convicted extortionist with ties to local criminal gangs.

Simpson went back on Amazon and ordered a copy of *The Scorpion and the Frog: High Times and High Crimes,* a lightly fictionalized 2003 memoir penned by Sater's erstwhile business partner Salvatore Lauria. The book contained passages recounting Trump making boorish passes at women and told how Lauria and Sater ran stock scams out of an office located in a Trump-owned building at 40 Wall Street.

More intriguing were several lawsuits that had been filed against Sater's real estate firm, Bayrock Group, in Florida and several other states. Trump had done several projects with Bayrock and was named in the suits. Sater worked out of an office just one floor below the Trump Organization, in Trump Tower. Simpson pored over hundreds of pages of court records—from Fort Lauderdale to New York City. In depositions, Trump seemed to grow vague and evasive when asked about Sater and Bayrock, claiming he did not know Sater well and "never really understood who owned Bayrock." These statements seemed like they must be lies, potentially provable lies, and they were made under oath. Lying under oath, particularly about unsavory activities or associates, is a major problem for candidates running for high office. Or at least it used to be. Simpson made a mental note to check whether they could prove Trump had lied.

All this just on day one of the Trump work, or what became the newly christened Project Bangor, in keeping with Fusion's practice at the time of naming projects for random cities. (While some firms and investigative agencies make sly allusions to the underlying subject of an investigation when naming cases, Fusion follows the more anodyne naming conventions of the British police.)

Though it wasn't clear at the time, the focus on Trump's relationship to Sater would prove to be an early milestone in the Fusion project, as it began to orient the research toward Russia. But these early finds didn't require much sophisticated sleuthing, just basic, early-stage homework.

The following week, Simpson and Fritsch began to assemble Project Bangor's investigative team, with Jacob Berkowitz as the lead researcher. Berkowitz, a Maine native with a master's degree in international relations, would come to serve as the project's human hard drive. Insert into Berkowitz's brain the name of a Russian oligarch and his three layers of barely connected offshore LLCs and the information stayed there, ready for instant retrieval. He was also an agile connector of dots, able to construct mental link charts showing relationships among various characters. Berkowitz would eventually become one of the foremost repositories of all things Trump and a sort of reference librarian for investigative journalists looking to untangle the mysteries.

At the Republican debate on September 16, Trump declared his admiration for Putin and predicted that he would be on the warmest of terms with the former KGB officer. "I would talk to him. I would get along with him," Trump said, pledging that if he became president, "we won't have the kind of problems that our country has right now with Russia." Trump's comments stirred immediate interest within Fusion, because the more the team read up on Trump's past, the more his expressions of fondness toward Moscow fit a pattern. For decades, Trump had shown a starry-eyed fascination with Russia, and he had been lured to travel there by the Soviet government in 1987, ostensibly to scout a potential Moscow project that never got off the ground. George W. Bush and Barack Obama had both boasted, at least for a while, of their ability to see the good hidden within Putin. But Trump had often shown a genuine admiration for Putin's leadership style and a desire to be friendly with, and respected by, the Russian leader. This pattern would become even more glaringly obvious in the months ahead.

The following day, Simpson and Berkowitz engaged in a bit of Sater one-upmanship via email, tossing back and forth little findings as they combed through public filings and social media. Berkowitz: "He likes

Trump on Facebook." Simpson: "Nice house on Long Island." Berkowitz: "Appears to be using a UPS box for his business address." Sater also had a business card listing himself as "senior advisor to Donald J. Trump."

The sheer enormity of the Trump project raised the obvious challenge of where to start. Trump's business past sprawled across decades and continents. The Fusion team quickly designed a research program that involved half a dozen people, both in-house and contractors, with an emphasis on people who knew their way around court records. Simpson and Fritsch would direct traffic and do their own digging. Berkowitz and another researcher were the main document collectors. Two outside specialists, including a lawyer and a professional archivist, began to dig through the national digital search engine for federal court cases, known as PACER, and to seek out other state and local court filings with promptings from Simpson and Berkowitz.

The cases covered the gamut and included a plethora of material on Sater and Bayrock. They also went back well into the 1980s and Trump's tumultuous years in the Atlantic City casino world. Many of the court files were stashed in remote archives or existed only on microfilm. In some cases, court clerks insisted that records had long been purged—which didn't always turn out to be the case. But within a week or so, the tedious work of amassing the full repository of relevant court records was well under way.

Team Bangor also began to delve into other curiosities that would crop up repeatedly in the months to come. For one, Trump's legally required candidate financial disclosure forms raised many questions. There was one company listed in Delaware corporate records, "Chicago Unit Acquisition," that appeared to be a vehicle for stashing debt or avoiding taxes. The forms also showed that most of Trump's bank loans came from a single institution, Deutsche Bank. And Trump attributed huge round-dollar valuations to many of his properties, which struck researchers as made-up. Trump claimed in his filings to be worth more than $10 billion, but the evidence he proffered to support this was notably flimsy. It looked like a possible con job and potential violation of the Ethics in Government Act and the law prohibiting knowingly making false statements to the federal government.

Trump's reputation as a savvy billionaire was further belied by his creation of Trump University, a for-profit, unaccredited real estate training school that had drawn a raft of lawsuits and regulatory scrutiny before it shut down in 2010 after five years of operation. The school was an obvious scam. Why would a supposed mega-billionaire set up a fake university to con a few thousand strivers out of their meager life savings? There were really only two possible explanations, neither of them comforting: Either Trump wasn't nearly as rich as he claimed to be and needed the money, or he was a pathological cheat who could not resist preying on the weak.

As Fusion prepared a series of memos from public records on everything from Trump's bankruptcies to his history of stiffing contractors, the Republican client latched on to the subject of Trump University, which was colorful and easy to understand. The *Free Beacon* wanted more on that. There were numerous ongoing fraud cases against the Trump Organization, with hundreds of scorned attendees and "students" as plaintiffs. Fusion harvested dozens of names to find anyone who wanted to speak out about their relationship with the business side of Trump. Among the victims of the school scam were a police sergeant, a former U.S. Army officer, and a Liberty University graduate. In all, the names of seventy victims possibly willing to speak went to the client. By October 4, Berkowitz and his colleagues had completed a first draft of a comprehensive twenty-page memo on the fraud allegations against the Trump Organization.

Meanwhile, Fusion embarked on another task, assembling the first of its many timelines for Trump—a chronology of his bankruptcy cases and other litigation that would run to seventeen pages. At Fusion's behest, a New York–based lawyer spent an afternoon at Barrett's Brooklyn house, combing through sheaves of notes and old press clippings. The lawyer gathered up what seemed relevant and shipped it to the Fusion office via overnight mail.

Among the cache was information gathered by Barrett regarding Trump's alleged ties to the Philadelphia mob, his drafts, notes, and emails from various reporting projects, and filings from Trump's $5 billion libel suit against one of Barrett's journalistic disciples, Timothy L. O'Brien, for daring to write in his 2005 book, *TrumpNation: The Art of Being the Donald,* that Trump was not a billionaire. Trump had lost the case. That outcome was significant, as it suggested that Trump was either unwilling or unable to produce credible evidence in court that proved his claims about his wealth. Notably, one of Trump's own witnesses in the O'Brien case was none other than convicted felon Sater, who in a deposition recounted taking trips with Trump and his children around the United States and abroad and being asked personally by Trump to testify in his case against O'Brien. Sater also acknowledged his own colorful criminal past, which didn't make him much of a witness for Trump.

The emerging picture of a faux billionaire scam artist who consorted with criminals caused Fusion to kick the paper chase into high gear. The accumulated lawsuits all began to sound somewhat the same, indicating an increasingly obvious pattern. A Trump development would begin with great fanfare, Trump and his children proudly proclaiming their extensive personal involvement and the Trump Organization's stake in the project, as well as extolling the intense early buyer interest and sales. Eventually, the project would fail, the sales claims would turn out to be hype, and the investors and partners would sue Trump. Then Trump would claim he was not the developer, merely a licensor. This happened from New York to Florida to Panama.

The forty-six-story hotel and condo complex in Manhattan known as Trump SoHo, developed with Sater starting in 2006, followed this pattern. In 2011, amid a fraud investigation by the Manhattan district attorney, Trump and his co-defendants agreed to settle a civil suit by Trump SoHo customers and refunded most of the project's more than $3 million in deposits. The plaintiffs had alleged that Trump, along with his son Donald Jr. and daughter Ivanka, had defrauded buyers by exaggerating early sales figures in an effort to lure more buyers to the failing development. The use of dubious "pre-sales" hype as a pretext to secure more buyers and financing was a hallmark of Trump projects, Fusion would come to learn.

A classic example was Trump's Fort Lauderdale project, in which Trump initially said he was an investor in the project but then later claimed under oath that he couldn't remember saying any such thing. So was he an investor? "Well, not an investor per se," Trump said. "They gave me an interest that allowed them to pay me fees." Asked if he'd been an investor in any of his many other projects, Trump insisted he was not. "I can't think of any," he claimed. "I mean, in Miami we're a licensor . . . in Toronto, we're a licensor." That would have been news to many people who had bought Trump's condos in those places.

This sort of pattern recognition is one of the core methods in an investigation based on public records. All data and documents have a story to tell. But understanding what that story means can be a challenge. Was Trump's string of failures just a run of bad luck, or was it in some way orchestrated? Did Trump care if his projects all failed? Did he actually intend to fail? Did he care who he did business with? To Fusion, it had begun to appear that Trump either was oblivious to possible fraud in his projects or may have adopted systematic fraud as his late-career business model. In either case, it was disturbing behavior for a possible future U.S. president.

Telling the difference between a series of coincidences and a conspiracy is tricky. But as time went by, the intentional-fraud scenario began to seem increasingly possible, given the mounting evidence of Trump's career-long history of dealings with people associated with organized crime. In many organized crime business ventures, insiders plan from the start for the business to fail, using the venture as merely a means of tapping and then absconding with lines of credit or bank loans, diverting the company's assets, or simply fleecing investors who come along later. These recurring failures had the hallmarks of many Mafia schemes in New York in the 1980s and '90s, when Trump did business with Italian organized crime figures.

Trump's criminal ties were explored at length in an October 16, 2015, *Washington Post* story that married some of the material accumulated by Fusion on Trump's Mafia ties to the paper's own research and interviews with former FBI agents. "No serious presidential candidate has ever had Trump's depth of documented business relationships with mob-controlled entities," the story observed. The report featured prominently in the paper but made barely a ripple in the increasingly heated primary campaign. Trump's Republican opponents ignored it, as did other news outlets. The client was frustrated the story didn't get more pickup but thought it was a good start.

Fusion's partners were surprised by the lack of reaction. In normal elections, revelations of this kind usually spark days of coverage and attacks by rivals. You had to go back to John F. Kennedy to think of a candidate with such close ties to organized crime. Fusion, though, knew from its contacts that more on that front was coming as other reporters began to dig into Trump's transition in the 1990s from ties to the Italian Mafia to links to the Russia mob. As the power and influence of La Cosa Nostra in New York City waned in the 1980s and '90s under relentless law enforcement pressure, organized crime figures from the former Soviet Union increasingly took over rackets like prostitution and drugs and also moved in on the casinos of Atlantic City. This shift was chronicled by another *Village Voice* investigative reporter, the late

Robert Friedman, in his book *Red Mafiya: How the Russian Mob Has Invaded America.* First published in 2000, the book would become a reference for Fusion researchers working to understand and map Trump's milieu.

While it would have seemed to be in their self-interest for Trump's Republican opponents to jump on the *Post* report, by mid-autumn of 2015 a sort of game-theory dynamic had begun to develop in the seventeen-person GOP primary field. The campaigns were beginning to realize they needed to unload on Trump, but no one wanted to go first, for fear of drawing his withering return fire. Nor did Trump's opponents want to earn the ire of his fervent followers. The result: The issue of Trump's relationship to organized crime never really made it to voters in a way that stuck.

Another dynamic was at play that would blunt the effectiveness of the Trump research project all the way through to Election Day 2016 and help pave his path to the presidency. Unlike most previous presidential candidates, Trump had a level of celebrity that meant he was already known to the vast majority of Americans. Some knew him as a buffoonish New York real estate developer with a history of splashy divorces and casino bankruptcies. Others knew him as the cocky billionaire boss on *The Apprentice*. But the point was that everyone knew him, or at least thought they knew him.

As a result, media outlets either steered away from the usual string of meet-the-candidate revelations that could rock the public's view of an up-and-comer, or, when they did do pieces about Trump's mob ties or his business failures, the coverage had a desultory tone and seemed to evaporate on contact. Trump's unusual ability to make noise and respond to attacks with immediate counterattacks also deflected attention and blunted the impact—as the Democrats, the Washington press corps, and the public later came to see during his presidency.

Another set of lawsuits turned up by Fusion's researchers revealed still more questions about what Trump and his properties were really worth. These were protests filed by the Trump Organization against various local tax authorities. Trump, who had claimed in his presidential candidate forms that all of his projects were fabulously successful and incredibly valuable, insisted in his tax lawsuits that his properties barely made any profits and were practically worthless.

"Trump is either lying in his tax filings or lying on his federal candidate disclosure forms," Simpson said in a note to team Bangor.

Deepening the mystery was the disconnect between Trump's business failures and the huge sums of money flowing through his projects. No project illustrated that more vividly than the Trump SoHo development involving Felix Sater and Bayrock. A lawsuit filed in New York federal court that Fusion retrieved alleged that Bayrock and other developers that did business with Trump and Sater had been involved in laundering hundreds of millions of dollars in hot money from the Central Asian nation of Kazakhstan, a remote, corruption-riddled dictatorship sandwiched between Russia and China.

The new allegations indicated that there was something not just sleazy but possibly criminal about Trump's partners in the deal.

Simpson recognized some of the players involved from his days covering financial fraud at *The Wall Street Journal*. The laundered money, like a lot of laundered money, was flowing into New York real estate projects, with American partners. For a cash-starved developer, money in need of washing was a godsend.

"Sounds like we are onto something," Simpson said to the team. "Yeah, Trump's the perfect host for parasites looking to launder money," Fritsch replied. The emerging theory of the case was that Trump's repeated bankruptcies had left him unable to raise money from banks and ordinary investors, so he'd replaced them with illicit sources of foreign cash. The theory grew out of prior Fusion money-laundering investigations, including one in which the proceeds of suspected narcotics trafficking and political corruption in Latin America landed in South Florida condominium projects.

Bayrock appeared to have links to powerful Russian interests. By the end of October, Fusion had acquired a set of court documents filed by a former Bayrock executive that alleged that $50 million had flowed into Bayrock from a shadowy financial firm in Iceland called the FL Group—an arrangement orchestrated by Sater. According to the court complaint, all the other Bayrock executives knew was that the company had chosen the firm as an investor because an unnamed oligarch behind it was in favor with the Kremlin at the time. Who could that be? Did the $50 million go to Trump? At a minimum, there was little question that Trump benefited from the capital injection, which records showed was earmarked by Bayrock for several of his projects. FL Group folded shortly afterwards, amid Iceland's financial meltdown, leaving little solid information behind. Even today, after the company's bankruptcy and countless Bayrock lawsuits, no one has been able to figure out who is behind the FL Group.

Trump would continue to deny familiarity with Sater all through the fall and early winter. Only much later, in 2018, would it emerge that the Trump Organization had been secretly pushing ahead all along with a proposed Trump Tower in Moscow—a 100-story skyscraper with 250 luxury condos, at least 150 hotel rooms, and a "Spa by Ivanka Trump." Handling that deal was Sater and Trump's own right-hand man, a one-time personal-injury lawyer and New York taxi entrepreneur named Michael Cohen. Trump had hired Cohen in 2007 to act as his in-house enforcer against all antagonists, be they reporters or business rivals. Cohen, through his wife's family, also had ties to the former Soviet Union and had mixed with Sater in New York's circles of émigrés. On October 13, 2015, Sater forwarded a letter to Cohen signifying their intent to go ahead with the Moscow deal, which Trump reportedly signed two weeks later.

The Russia coincidences continued to pile up. On October 29, Trump's primary remaining bank lender—Deutsche Bank—announced it was setting aside $1.3 billion to cover legal expenses related to global allegations that it had laundered billions of dollars in dirty money from Russia in a complex case unrelated to Trump.

By November, as Trump rose in polls and the client approved additional months of work, it was clear that the questions about Trump, particularly his ties to the former Soviet Union, merited far deeper investigation. At the time, this wasn't an obvious line of inquiry; it would be months before Russia's cyberattacks on the Democrats became known and a year before its manipulation of social media came to light. Fusion was now taking the story where the research led, much as journalists do.

As luck would have it, some highly qualified help appeared at a critical juncture. In October 2015, Simpson received an unsolicited query from a distant acquaintance, a former Central Intelligence Agency analyst named Nellie Ohr.

Simpson and Ohr had first met in 2010 at a two-day private symposium sponsored by the National Institute of Justice—the research arm of the U.S. Justice Department—on the growth of international organized crime. Since then, her résumé had grown even more impressive. She had an undergraduate degree from Harvard in Russian history and literature and an MA and PhD from Stanford in Russian history. Between 2008 and 2014 she had worked for "various US government clients" on "developments in Russia, Central Asia, and Ukraine, focusing on politics, cyber issues, business, crime, corruption, and other areas."

Nellie Ohr was at the 2010 conference with her husband, Bruce Ohr, who at the time was chief of the Organized Crime and Racketeering Section of the Justice Department. Attending the conference were a smattering of other academics and intelligence and law enforcement officials, part of a group tasked with assessing the state of knowledge about international organized crime and coming up with some recommendations for addressing this growing scourge.

Nellie Ohr had recently seen a reference to Fusion in an August 27 *New York Times* story about the firm's work for Planned Parenthood. Fusion had worked to expose the digital manipulation of abortion clinic sting videos secretly recorded by an anti-abortion-rights group called the Center for Medical Progress. In an email, Ohr noted that she had admired Simpson's investigative work on Russian corruption when he was at the *Journal*. She noted her "extensive experience as a Eurasia analyst and multilingual researcher" and said she specialized in "profiling individuals and companies, both legitimate and criminal . . . to disentangle their relationships—especially any possible ties with the Russian military or special services or with Eurasian crime groups." Might Fusion, she asked, have "any projects in the Russia/Eurasia field that could use my skills, experience and passion for research?"

Fusion first hired Ohr in October to research the use of Bitcoin by Russian criminals.

A month later, it asked her to assist Fusion in looking into Trump's ties to Russia. She came back swiftly with a pitch to do an extensive search of all Russian-language online sources for mentions of Trump's business connections in Russia and Central Asia. In addition, she would dig into Trump's ties to a number of his associates, including Sater.

Fusion hired Ohr for a month of work, renewable by mutual agreement. It was a decision that fit perfectly with Fusion's practice to seek and hire the best experts in the field to execute specialized research. Ohr could not have been a better candidate. She was a fluent Russian speaker who knew well the universe of questionable characters from the former Soviet sphere who had entered the Trump orbit, and she was highly trained in open-source collection.

The hiring of Nellie Ohr made perfect sense for Project Bangor, but it would later help fuel an elaborate right-wing conspiracy theory. In this version of events, the effort to research and understand Trump's curious interactions with the Russian underworld was actually a nefarious liberal plot—reaching from the Clinton campaign to career officials and Nellie's husband at the Justice Department—to undermine the future Trump presidency. A presidency not even Donald Trump himself thought would happen.

CHAPTER THREE

THE CHARLATAN

WITH THE BOMBAST OF P. T. BARNUM, TRUMP ON THE STUMP promoted a mythical image of himself as a self-made, ultrapatriotic, owned-by-no-one tycoon. Many of his most fervent Republican supporters were middle- and working-class voters attracted to his apparent business success, his hard-line positions on immigration, and his frequent denunciations of American companies that moved manufacturing jobs overseas.

As tantalizing as the Russia leads seemed, Russia wasn't yet Fusion's overriding focus—not in these early months. The myriad leads on that front were piling up, to be sure, but the first order of business was to better understand the man's hypocrisies and failures—and the multiple myths he used to disguise his flaws. These were the things they believed would ultimately matter most to voters.

The more Fusion dug into Trump, the more he appeared to fit the textbook definition of a charlatan. Here was a supposed business genius whose career was littered with bankruptcies and failures. A purported multibillionaire who was almost certainly worth a fraction of what he claimed. A supposed self-made entrepreneur whose wealth actually sprang from an accident of birth. An immigrant basher who employed countless immigrants—and was even married to one. A "Buy American" proponent whose own clothing line was made in Mexico. A proud straight-talker with a long history of prevarication and outright fabrications—including under oath.

It was Fusion's job to catalog all these contradictions, exaggerations, and utter lies into research reports with clear documentation. In commercial engagements, these reports would be solely for the client, but in political campaigns their purpose can be threefold: to expose an opponent's vulnerabilities, provide source material for the media, and feed attack ads. A typical Fusion memo was essentially a lengthy treatise on a single subject, covered in fine detail and meticulously sourced. These products provided clients with a smorgasbord of material, to be deployed any way they pleased. Fusion also made many of its findings available to interested reporters as background material that could be confirmed and expanded with their own reporting.

The issue that most neatly seemed to capture the hypocrisy at the heart of Trump's xenophobic campaign was immigration. From the first, Trump had staked his presidential hopes on stoking voter anxieties about immigration. But that also made the issue his greatest liability if it could be shown that he didn't practice what he preached: Voters tend to dislike hypocrites even more than liars and cheaters. So Fusion set its drilling rig atop Trump's record as an employer, knowing that both the construction and hospitality industries are rife with undocumented immigrants. Sure enough, Trump's record revealed him to be a longtime, avid, and quite deliberate bulk consumer of illegal immigrant labor. "He likes illegals and criminals for his workforce because he can pay them under the table," Simpson said in a note to the team. "That's a foundation of his success as a developer—his costs are lower because he cheats."

Trump viciously bashed immigrants, but it was immigrants—many hired illegally—who built his tall towers, fed his country club members, mowed his lawns, and cleaned his hotel rooms. You could sum it up another way: Donald Trump hated immigrants . . . unless they worked for him.

Trump also had a long record of recruiting workers from abroad and importing them to the United States. Fusion collected Labor Department records showing the Trump Organization had sponsored at least 1,494 foreign worker visas since 2000. His Palm Beach estate and private club, Mar-a-Lago, was the largest of his properties to import immigrant labor, with at least 872 visas to its name. Fusion wasn't the only one to come across this data. Reuters published its own report that ran in numerous publications, but Trump's Republican rivals and many other media organizations took little notice.

Like many big developers, Trump hired "illegals" despite his recent adoption of inflammatory rhetoric against the practice of employing them. A Trump Taj Mahal casino worker was arrested in October 2012 for being an undocumented immigrant. More recently, workers at two Trump projects—the hotel at the Old Post Office Pavilion, in D.C., and the Trump SoHo in New York City—admitted to reporters that they were undocumented. Later reporting, well after his election, found that nearly all of his U.S. facilities relied heavily on undocumented workers.

With the first primaries just months away, Republican voters barely knew of these hypocrisies. Fusion's job was to supply the research that could change that.

No building captured the hypocrisy of Trump's immigration stance like his signature Trump Tower, on New York's Fifth Avenue. The building embodied Trump's gilt-encrusted image of glamour and success, which is why he used its lobby as the backdrop for his showy campaign launch on June 16, 2015. But the story of its construction was, from the outset, a tale of illicit labor practices that could be reconstructed in detail.

As was well documented in multiple court cases, construction began in 1980, sneaking around zoning laws blocking high-rises with the addition of a five-story atrium fronting Fifth Avenue, offered originally as a public passageway, that immediately became a commercial space. Trump had moved swiftly to demolish the famed Bonwit Teller building, using a company previously known for its window washing. Much of the hazardous work was done by a team of some two hundred non-union Polish workers, who earned less than unionized workers, slept at the work site, and became known as the "Polish Brigade."

These illegal labor practices had ended up in court when union members discovered that Trump and his contractor, Kaszycki & Sons, weren't making required payments to union insurance and pension funds. Union members sued both Kaszycki and Trump. They alleged that Trump knowingly used illegal immigrants because he was short of cash and desperate to meet deadlines required by his lenders.

Fusion dug up Trump's testimony in the case from federal court archives. The court record showed that Trump engaged in numerous evasions, some of them outright laughable. Asked if he was familiar with the phrase "working off the books," Trump replied, "I don't believe so, no . . . I have not heard that phrase, I am not familiar with it." Presented with a business certificate bearing his own signature, Trump claimed not to know what it was. Even though the building was the signature project designed to put him on the map in New York real estate, Trump claimed he rarely visited the site himself. He said he had no recollection of expressing satisfaction with his Polish workers or reading local news coverage of their alleged exploitation. In all, he claimed some forty-eight times that he couldn't remember important details of the long-running controversy.

Fusion's researchers, reviewing the case files some twenty-five years later, were astonished at the audacity of Trump's fabrications. His own longtime business associate Danny Sullivan, a mob-linked labor consultant, testified that Trump "knew about the undocumented workers." The court ultimately endorsed Sullivan's version of events, with a federal judge saying in 1991, "There is strong evidence of tacit agreement by the parties (Kaszycki . . . and the Trump defendants) to employ the Polish workers."

While the Trump Tower case was old, it suggested a comfort with inexpensive illegal labor that Trump would have a hard time squaring with his campaign rhetoric. It was also easy to envision the story in a devastating attack ad. More recent reporting showed that Trump's use of illegal immigrants in his building projects continued up through 2015. *The Washington Post* found that illegal immigrants were among the construction workers refurbishing the Trump International Hotel in Washington. In that case, the Trump Organization placed the onus for checking the workers' employment status on Bovis Lend Lease, the project's contractor. That was not a particularly strong defense, since Bovis and the Trump Organization had a long-standing business relationship, and Bovis also allegedly recruited foreign labor for hazardous duty on the Trump SoHo project.

Trump, of course, wasn't the only real estate developer in his immediate family. Jared Kushner, Trump's son-in-law, ran Kushner Companies, which he took over in 2005 following his father's conviction on charges of tax evasion and witness tampering. Fritsch and Simpson decided that company was also worth a look for labor violations and the financing behind his family's projects. One afternoon, while watching soccer in the office and surfing the Net, two Fusion researchers stumbled onto some interesting marketing materials for a condo complex in Jersey City being developed by Trump and Kushner. The two men planned to finance construction of the project using a government program known as EB-5, which allows foreign citizens to obtain U.S. residency if they invest more than $500,000 in the United States. Kushner's target market was China, the very country Trump was out hammering in his stump speeches, blaming Beijing for an industrial policy based on cheap labor and an undervalued currency that had harmed the economy of the industrial Midwest. The researchers found that Kushner had partnered with a company based in Shanghai to assist in the visa-selling operation. His sister was actively marketing the scheme, even though U.S. authorities have long suspected that China used the EB-5 program to place spies in the country.

Stories highlighting the arrangement ran in multiple outlets in early March 2016, some pointing out how Trump's use of the program exposed his hypocrisy on the China front. Trump, as *Bloomberg* put it, "has called for a revamping, even a freezing, of the immigration system, but says he would make an exception for the highly skilled. Yet no skills are required of the wealthy Chinese being courted by a Chinese-subtitled video to help finance a huge Trump-branded tower in New Jersey."

Immigration came up again and again during the GOP debates, with the candidates tussling over who had the tougher plan to crack down on undocumented workers. Trump reveled in the severity of his zero-tolerance policy. "People that have come into our country illegally, they have to go," he said at the debate in Las Vegas in mid-December. But his challengers rarely blasted Trump directly for the rank hypocrisy embodied in his rhetoric on immigration and his long history of using illegal and low-wage immigrant labor—a vulnerability no other candidate had.

The glaring contradiction between his public rhetoric and his private use of foreign workers finally began hitting the major media in early 2016, with *The New York Times* weighing in on February 25: "Donald Trump to Foreign Workers for Florida Club: You're Hired." But by then it was too late for Republican primary voters in Iowa, New Hampshire, South Carolina, and Nevada, all of whom had already cast their votes—and put Donald Trump well on the path toward becoming president of the United States.

Trump's double standards when it came to immigrant labor and his offshore sourcing of apparel paled in comparison with the mass of information Fusion was simultaneously collecting on Trump's ties to organized crime. Through the end of 2015 and into 2016, the Bangor team rounded up thousands of pages of law enforcement documents and court records testifying to Trump's dealings with mobbed-up lawyers, dope dealers, and "labor consultants." The various strands of the project were parceled out to subcontractors, one tasked with getting casino investigation records, another pulling Trump's labor disputes, a third scanning court cases and old clips for allegations of criminal connections.

Among the most damning of the documents that turned up was a December 1992 investigative report by the New Jersey Casino Control Commission's Division of Gaming Enforcement. The confidential thirty-six-page report, prompted by Wayne Barrett's reporting, avoided drawing conclusions about many of the allegations it investigated on behalf of the commission, whose job it was to make the ultimate determination about whether Trump was fit to hold casino licenses. But in numerous areas, the report provided official confirmation of some of the most serious allegations Barrett and other journalists had made about Trump's dealings with a rogues' gallery of criminals.

One section of the report was devoted to Trump's relationship to convicted narcotics trafficker Joseph Weichselbaum, who owned a helicopter company that worked for Trump's casinos, ferrying high rollers from New York to Atlantic City. Among other things, Barrett had alleged that Trump wrote a letter to a federal judge in 1986 pleading for a lenient sentence for Weichselbaum after he was convicted of large-scale drug smuggling—a remarkable favor for a prominent businessman to provide, especially since it was Weichselbaum's third major criminal conviction.

Gaming investigators had long probed Trump's ties to Weichselbaum and already knew that Trump had personally leased one of his own apartments to him and his brother. They also had confirmed that an alleged girlfriend of Weichselbaum's had bought two adjoining condo units in Trump Tower in 1988 for $2.25 million. When asked in a 1990 sworn interview with casino regulators whether he had indeed written a letter of support for Weichselbaum, Trump made the improbable claim that he could not remember doing so. Trump and his lawyers also claimed they had no copies of such a letter. When later shown a copy bearing his signature, Trump acknowledged it was his signature.

Another disturbing section of the report addressed Trump's dealings with Philadelphia's dominant Mafia family and a politically connected Atlantic City lawyer named Paddy McGahn. In 1982, Trump used McGahn to negotiate with the city and with several organized crime families that owned the plots he coveted for his boardwalk casino. Barrett, in his reporting, had described the Trump-McGahn relationship as "behind-the-scenes" and reported that McGahn had boasted that he "controlled the City Commission."

According to gaming investigators, Trump instructed McGahn to broker an all-cash deal for a corner parcel in Atlantic City owned by members of a notorious Philadelphia mob family. McGahn reportedly had a paralegal from his firm purchase the plot from Philly gangster Salvatore Testa (later executed by some of his colleagues and dumped on the side of a dirt road). The property was then transferred to Trump, allowing Trump to maintain distance from the transaction in the eyes of casino regulators. The closing was handled in McGahn's office and was attended by both Testa and Chris Scarfo, the son of top Philly mob boss Nicodemo "Little Nicky" Scarfo.

McGahn was already a mover and shaker in Atlantic City at the time, having led the effort to legalize gambling in New Jersey in 1979. McGahn, who also represented Trump during his casino bankruptcy proceedings in 1990, was once the subject of a state investigation into charges of influence peddling with his older brother, a state senator. McGahn's nephew Donald F. McGahn II later became Trump's campaign lawyer and first White House counsel.

Another mobbed-up figure close to Trump was Robert LiButti. In 1991, Trump was fined by casino regulators for giving millions in illegal gifts to LiButti, an Atlantic City high roller who claimed to have ties to the Mafia. Regulators determined that Trump had handed LiButti cash himself, and that the two were close. Casino regulators also charged Trump with discrimination after LiButti ordered him to remove all female and black dealers. LiButti was considered by regulators to have ties to mob boss John Gotti.

The Trump-LiButti relationship would be chronicled early in the presidential campaign, in searing detail, by *Yahoo News,* but once again Trump's political opponents were largely mum. Without other candidates willing to give stories like this oxygen by bringing them up on the record in attacks on Trump, and without other news outlets amplifying them, the stories tended to sputter quickly.

Based on the New Jersey gaming report and piles of other government records, Fusion summarized its research on Trump's criminal connections in stark terms: "During the entire span of his career, Donald Trump has done business with at least 25 individuals and companies with documented mob ties, including various powerful Italian and Russian syndicates. Casino regulators in at least three states have extensively investigated Trump for his dealings with organized crime. Two of those states, Missouri and Pennsylvania, refused to grant Trump a casino license with little explanation."

As alarming as this history was, many in the press wrote it off as old news and the by-product of a career spent in New York real estate development. "I mean, who *isn't* mobbed up in Manhattan who ever got anything built," one television news producer told Fritsch. "Besides, wasn't this all a long time ago?" True, Trump had been beset by allegations of mob connections for many years, but most of that coverage concerned the early years of his career and traditional Italian Mafia families. Changing tack a bit, the Fusion researchers began to focus on the myriad ways that Trump's more recent business deals appeared to connect him with figures from the former Soviet Union suspected by U.S. federal authorities to have ties to organized crime.

Some of these connections had been dug out and reported in the press a decade earlier, when people like Felix Sater popped up in the Trump orbit, but in the intervening years, the media seemed to have lost interest. Despite the wide coverage of Trump and his business past in 2015, few of these reports concerned his organized crime ties.

At the center of these relationships was the Bayrock Group, which had invested in the Trump SoHo project in New York. The firm's principals included Sater, who claimed to have co-founded Bayrock and was described as the company's majority owner by its former chief financial officer. But his involvement in the company was not disclosed to other investors in several Bayrock-Trump projects.

Bayrock was awash in allegations of serious criminality. The former chief financial officer of the company alleged in court papers, first filed in 2010, that it was a criminal enterprise used for money laundering and tax evasion. While Trump was trying to distance himself from Bayrock, plenty of evidence showed that both he and two of his children had dealt directly with the firm, particularly during the building of the Trump SoHo project. Bayrock appeared to have potentially violated New York's so-called Martin Act by not disclosing Sater's criminal past to potential buyers of Trump SoHo condominiums.

Crime ran in the Sater family. His father was a convicted extortionist and allegedly involved with Russian organized crime. In 1991, Felix got into a bar fight and plunged the stem of a broken margarita glass into a fellow stockbroker's neck. In 1998, he was charged with securities fraud and pleaded guilty to a one-count criminal charge for his involvement in a wide-ranging "pump and dump" scam that benefited from the assistance of the Italian Mafia. In return, mob families "received compensation in the form of securities and the proceeds of fraudulent sales of securities."

Sater then extricated himself from these troubles by becoming a U.S. government informant, which delayed his sentencing until 2009. He had faced up to twenty years' imprisonment and $60 million in restitution, according to his cooperation agreement. Sater's criminal past had been concealed by federal prosecutors, with all relevant records sealed, apparently as a reward for his work as a cooperating witness in stock fraud cases. His cooperation was said to have included attempting to buy missiles on the black market and helping the U.S. government track Osama bin Laden. He never served any time for the stock fraud conviction.

Sater's connections to Trump went well beyond Bayrock. He also claimed to have had an intimate role in the Trump Organization itself, including employment during 2010—more than two years after a December 2007 *New York Times* article revealed his criminal past. Checking his LinkedIn page, Fusion discovered that he had recently altered his profile to remove all references to Trump.

In that same 2007 *Times* article, Trump admitted to knowing and meeting Sater at Bayrock and acknowledged that Sater may have brought him the idea of embarking on an ambitious condominium project in Fort Lauderdale, which got under way in 2005. Trump took his name off the project four years later when it became embroiled in legal troubles. Trump told the *Times* that he conducts "very tough" due diligence, and he did not believe Sater was connected with organized crime.

To Fusion, that seemed like yet another flimsy claim. Sater's organized crime links were a matter of public record.

Sater and Bayrock exemplified the emergence of the organized crime wave migrating west after the collapse of the former Soviet Union. In New York, Russian gangs began to compete and then merge with remnants of the Italian Mafia. Many who would end up in Trump's world were not ethnic Russians but hailed from the outer reaches of the empire, particularly Central Asia.

Bayrock Group underscored this international shift. The company was founded by Tevfik Arif, a Central Asian émigré and former Soviet tourism minister in Kazakhstan. Arif was arrested in Turkey in 2010 for allegedly running an underage prostitution ring aboard his yacht, a charge for which he was later acquitted. Among the others arrested on Arif's yacht were several high-ranking officials from the government of Kazakhstan. The court determined that none of the women were underage. According to federal court records in New York, Bayrock's executives were allegedly linked to a company involved in a multibillion-dollar bank fraud in Kazakhstan that laundered money through the Trump SoHo project and other New York developments.

Simpson had written stories at *The Wall Street Journal* chronicling the corruption seeping into the West from Central Asia, particularly Kazakhstan. The Central Asia crime wave had also come up in a handful of cases Simpson and Fritsch had handled since founding Fusion, cases involving fraud and money laundering. So Simpson took note when Ivanka Trump, in her book *The Trump Card,* mentioned how she had traveled to Kazakhstan in the mid-2000s to "meet with business partners." Kazakhstan is a famously corrupt autocratic state, and the Fusion team wondered whether illicit funds from the former Soviet Union might have ended up in some of Trump's building projects. "What are the chances these guys are clean?" Simpson asked Fritsch rhetorically. "Yeah, seriously," Fritsch replied.

One former Bayrock executive claimed in New York federal court filings that millions of dollars had flowed into Bayrock from Arif's brother in Russia, "who had access to cash accounts at a chromium refinery in Kazakhstan, and that Bayrock was acting as a conduit hiding those funds." Bayrock denied the allegations.

Court records from the libel case Trump filed against journalist Tim O'Brien in New Jersey shed additional light on Trump's ties to Bayrock. In a deposition, Trump praised Arif's "international connections" and detailed half a dozen "phenomenal" prospective tower deals with Arif, including ones in Moscow, Yalta, Warsaw, Istanbul, and Kiev.

This was the kind of world Fusion contractor Nellie Ohr knew well, and she dove in fully. Working from her home office in suburban Virginia, Ohr stumbled upon a nugget in the Russian publication *Izvestia* that gave color to the Trump-Arif relationship: a video that had Trump offering a remote toast for Arif's birthday party, in which he says, "Tevfik is my friend! Let's drink to Tevfik!"

Other connections between Trump and Sater came from two depositions the Fusion team had dug out of the case files. The suits were brought by condominium purchasers in Florida alleging deceptive sales practices. One of them, *Taglieri v. SB Hotel Associates,* directly alleged that condo buyers had been harmed by nondisclosure of Sater's criminal record.

Trump told the *Times* in its 2007 story that he was surprised to learn the details of Sater's past. "We never knew that," he said of Sater. "We do as much of a background check as we can on the principals. I didn't really know him very well." Trump said that most of his dealings with Bayrock "had been with its founder, Tevfik Arif, and that his son Donald and his daughter Ivanka were playing active roles in managing the project."

Trump's evasions about Sater became the subject of a long quest by Fusion to find every instance in which Trump was asked about Sater under oath and lied about their work together. Figuring that out would involve a close review of thousands of pages of court records.

The excavation finally hit pay dirt in court papers filed in Florida. In November 2013, Trump had been deposed as part of a suit brought by a dissatisfied Florida condominium buyer named Matthew Abercrombie. When asked about Sater, Trump claimed to barely know him. "If he were sitting in the room right now, I really wouldn't know what he looked like," he testified. That was a lie, pure and simple. In late 2015, a Fusion researcher obtained a high-resolution video of the deposition from the lawyer who brought the case. The video eventually made its way to ABC News, where a story on Trump's dubious denials ran on *Good Morning America* and was seen by millions of viewers.

In the early weeks and months of its Trump research, Fusion had cast an intentionally wide net to catch all aspects of Trump's sordid business past. No matter what the subject, this was always the company's methodology: Make no prior assumptions, and follow the evidence where it leads. But the Bayrock research served to reorient Fusion's compass. It raised serious issues about Trump's character, truthfulness, and business practices. It also hinted that a primary explanation for Trump's surprising late-career comeback as a real estate developer was investment money coming from Russia and other parts of the former Soviet Union, a region renowned for its official corruption and hundreds of billions of dollars in new wealth seeking safe harbor—and cleaning—in investments abroad.

In the fall of 2015, Trump started to make a rapprochement with

Putin's Russia one of his main foreign policy talking points on the presidential campaign trail. By then, Putin had invaded two of Russia's neighbors and ordered a state-sponsored murder in central London. No one in official Washington was talking anymore about making friends with Vladimir Putin.

Yet Trump talked as if none of that recent history had occurred. "I will get along—I think—with Putin," Trump claimed during a televised Republican debate in September. "I think I would get along very well with him," he told CNN twelve days later. Then, in a November 10 debate, Trump boasted that he and Putin were pals. "I got to know him very well because we were both on *60 Minutes*. We were stablemates, and we did very well that night." It was an odd statement—and also complete fiction. Trump and Putin were never on *60 Minutes* together; the show merely carried interviews with both on the same Sunday broadcast.

The warm words for Putin would make sense only in hindsight, when it became clear that, just as Trump was making his comments, his lawyer and Sater were in the midst of talks for a Trump Tower in Moscow, a project that could move forward only with help from higher-ups in the Russian government.

A couple of weeks after that November debate, Nellie Ohr came back with her first big memo on Trump and his Russia ties, a copious sweep through Russian-language media. Among other things, Ohr noted the importance of Trump's holding the 2013 Miss Universe pageant in Moscow, and how he had talked about plans for a Trump Tower there. "Possible partners included the Crocus Group of Aras Agalarov, which had helped organize and provide the venue for the beauty pageant," Ohr wrote in one memo. Over the following months, Trump's connections to the Agalarovs piled up, and Aras Agalarov would become a figure in the Steele dossier.

On December 14, 2015, Ohr supplied Fusion with a second batch of findings in which she dug deeper into the lesser-known history of Trump's ties to Russia. She had unearthed a number of puzzling statements, such as when Trump supposedly told a Russian reporter in 2015 that he had donated $5,000 to RT, the Russian government's propaganda machine, "to fight against the American evil in the form of Senator John McCain and other idiots."

Far more significant to Fusion's emerging theory of the case, she found a 2008 article in Russian in which Trump said that Russians were his favorite customers because they always paid in cash and did not need mortgages. The article also stated that Trump had invited a group of Russian reporters to the United States to see the Trump SoHo and even paid some of their travel expenses. The story lent support to the idea that sometime in the mid-2000s, Trump revived his business enterprise with hot cash from the former Soviet Union—something that Fusion now set out to attempt to document.

"I have a very good business relationship with the Russians," Trump told the Russian magazine *Seagull*. "A Russian recently bought a house in Florida from me for $100 million. Some Russians buy homes for $50 million. Great shoppers! People with good taste and good money understand the value of the Trump brand. It is always a guarantee of quality and a win-win location. By investing in Trump, you invest for sure. By the way, I really like Vladimir Putin. I respect him. He does his job well. Much better than our Bush."

The Russian buyer in Florida was Dmitry Rybolovlev, a Russian billionaire from Perm who ditched a career in alternative medicine to build potash producer Uralkali into a global player in the fertilizer industry. Rybolovlev spent eleven months in jail in 1996 in Russia under indictment for racketeering, including the suspected murder of a competitor. Later, his legal problems mysteriously cleared up, allegedly with the help of some high-level contacts in Moscow. Moscow's modus operandi for years has been to identify Russians in legal jeopardy who can redeem themselves by using their wealth abroad to advance the Kremlin's influence-buying operations. Rybolovlev eventually emigrated to Monaco, where he acquired the local soccer club and a taste for overpriced fine art.

In July 2008, at the height of the financial crisis, he purchased a Palm Beach mansion from Trump for $95 million, more than twice what Trump had paid for it in 2005. At the time, it was the most expensive single-family home sale ever in Palm Beach County. The purchase price was well above the going market rate—by some estimates, double the rate. The massive profit helped Trump out of a hole at a crucial moment in his career. The transaction smelled fishy, to put it mildly. To Fusion, it looked like it could be a Russian payoff that got Trump out of another liquidity jam.

By early 2016, Fusion had prepared its own lengthy survey of Trump's many mysterious connections to the former Soviet Union. All of the disparate threads were beginning to come together into a disturbing picture. Some in the media had also begun to catch on.

"Before he was a presidential candidate, Trump's hunger to be popular in Russia was less troubling," *Bloomberg* columnist Josh Rogin wrote in March 2016. "Now it is a conflict of interest. At minimum, there is the appearance of wrongdoing: The candidate's foreign-policy positions are conveniently aligned with his long-standing business agenda. But what's good for the Trump Organization isn't necessarily good for America."

That feeling would be cemented among a small group of Trump watchers as his path to the nomination cleared and his team added an ominous figure from Simpson's and Fritsch's journalistic past: a political consultant named Paul Manafort.

CHAPTER FOUR

THE FIXER

BY LATE MARCH 2016, DONALD TRUMP HAD SOLIDIFIED HIS front-runner position and his path to the nomination was beginning to look assured. Jeb Bush was out. So were Marco Rubio, Ben Carson, Chris Christie, and all but three of the original stampede of candidates that had entered the race the previous summer. Now it was just Trump, Texas senator Ted Cruz, and Ohio governor John Kasich, the last of the vehement Trump foes, still standing.

The more headway Trump made, the more the ranks of the Never Trump movement swelled. A number of well-known Republicans were determined to deny him the nomination. The clamor to stop Trump did not appear to be motivated primarily by heartburn over his policy positions, his ties to criminals and dubious Russian oligarchs, or even a fear that a Trump presidency could destroy the Republican Party. The primary motivation appeared to be the widely held conviction among political pros that Trump was a sure loser in November. "Hillary would beat him from jail," predicted one former Jeb Bush adviser.

In an effort to quell these concerns and put down a brewing internal GOP revolt, Trump turned to an old political pro, Paul Manafort.

The move set off shock waves among a small group of loosely affiliated Republican operatives whose primary candidates had already dropped out of the race and were now aiding the GOP's Never Trump effort and talking to Fusion.

"Trump just hired this guy Paul Manafort," one Republican operative working with Fusion's client wrote to Simpson on March 29, 2016. "Has ties to Oleg Deripaska, Russian tycoon and Putin crony. Do we have anything on this?"

"Tons," Simpson replied. "He is super close to the Russians."

As it happened, Fusion was already looking into Manafort for a legal client in a matter unrelated to the presidential campaign and had recently obtained fresh evidence of his ties to Deripaska, a Russian billionaire long banned from entering the United States for his alleged ties to organized crime.

Manafort's emergence as an adviser to Trump seemed unlikely to be a coincidence and in fact added fuel to the smoldering concerns within Fusion that Russians were trying to get their hooks into Trump. When you combined Trump's many unexplained links to Russia and the history of foreign attempts to sway U.S. elections, it wasn't that big a stretch.

To Fusion, Manafort wasn't just another Beltway bandit from yesteryear. He was a seminal figure in the annals of Washington consulting, a famously avaricious and venal operative who was close to the late GOP strategist Lee Atwater and a former business partner of Richard Nixon's old dirty trickster Roger Stone. Here was a consultant who had a history of blending foreign lobbying with his work on presidential campaigns and, more recently, had spent more than a decade working actively against U.S. interests in Europe, in furtherance of Putin's goal of driving a wedge through the NATO alliance.

The son of a Connecticut mayor, Manafort climbed up through the Republican ranks during the Reagan era as a slick young operative who could control a room and manipulate party factions with uncanny skill. He parlayed his success wrangling delegates at the 1980 Republican National Convention into what soon became Washington's most mercenary lobbying firm: Black, Manafort and Stone. It was a firm, *The Atlantic*'s Franklin Foer would later write, that "exuded the decadent spirit of the 1980s." Manafort carved out a very lucrative niche burnishing the reputations of and seeking favor for some of the least savory of world leaders, people like Ferdinand Marcos of the Philippines and Jonas Savimbi of Angola.

For the past decade, he had worked extensively for the Ukrainian politician Viktor Yanukovych, a Kremlin pet, reaping millions in consulting fees that he poured into his increasingly lavish lifestyle. But by the time Trump came calling, Manafort had hit a rough patch in both his professional and personal lives—just how rough, Fusion would soon find out.

Trump cast the hiring of a veteran operative like Manafort as proof that the campaign was swiftly moving to acquire the right kind of talent to assure all went well at the GOP convention in Cleveland as fears of a delegate fight mounted. Manafort would be the adult in the room, the guy who had been there before. *The New York Times* described the long-time operative as "among the few political hands in either party with direct experience managing nomination fights."

The *Times* and others noted his recent work in Ukraine, but his ties to Russian oligarchs and his questionable PR and political consulting work over the prior decade received only cursory coverage. The hire shocked those who knew the full story, but didn't make a big news splash. It was as if most of Washington had forgotten who Manafort was.

Simpson and Fritsch didn't fall into that camp. The two had pursued very different paths through the *Journal* over the years before coming together as reporter and editor for the first time in Brussels in 2006. Fritsch had spent years as a foreign reporter and editor before arriving from Singapore as *Journal* bureau chief for Northern Europe. Simpson had spent most of his career in Washington investigating political corruption, including cases of illicit foreign influence. He had been a European investigative reporter since coming over from Washington in late 2004, writing about the organized crime and kleptocracy seeping westward from the lawless states of the former Soviet Union. He quickly discovered that escaping Washington wouldn't be so easy: There was a gold rush under way of sketchy Washington political consultants seeking to service the nouveau riche of ex-Communist nations, who had lots of political and legal problems and plenty of cash to pay for top-dollar American talent.

Simpson and his wife, Mary Jacoby, also a *Journal* reporter, had written several articles in 2007 and 2008 exploring this phenomenon. Those stories, edited by Fritsch, starred none other than Paul Manafort. By that point, Manafort had faded from the D.C. scene and resurfaced as a big-ticket political Svengali in the endemically corrupt and dysfunctional Ukraine—Russia's largest western neighbor and the object of deep historical Kremlin obsessions. Ukraine was a big story in Europe and occasionally also in Washington. For much of the 2000s, Putin's efforts to dominate Ukraine politically and squeeze it economically generated big headlines, because Europe depended on Russian natural gas piped across Ukraine to fuel its factories and heat millions of homes. Every time Putin threatened to cut off gas to Ukraine, Washington's key European allies shuddered.

Their reporting had thrown a spotlight on how Manafort, while representing clients involved in those fierce geopolitical struggles over Ukraine, had not seen fit to comply with a lobbying law called the Foreign Agents Registration Act (FARA)—the very law that Robert Mueller and his team would come to rely on years later to help pry open Manafort's years of criminal activity.

FARA is one of those federal laws known largely to a small cadre of PR executives, specialty lawyers, and lobbyists who have to register under its auspices. It exists, though, for compelling reasons. Congress passed the law in 1938 in response to the rise of Adolf Hitler and a flood of Nazi propaganda and subversion. Anyone conducting political activities in the United States on behalf of a foreign power now had to register and report their spending. The felony statute was used in twenty-three criminal prosecutions during World War II.

The tactics the Nazis used to influence Washington in the years before World War II weren't much different from the Kremlin's modern-day methods. One case under FARA brought in 1941 involved fake news produced by a Nazi-controlled wire service called Transocean News Service. While posing as a legitimate news organization, Transocean was in reality "nothing more nor less than a propaganda arm of the Nazi regime," according to a congressional report.

Over several months in 2007, Simpson and Jacoby reported on Manafort's PR and lobbying efforts on behalf of Yanukovych. They concluded, based on what they found, that Manafort might be in violation of the foreign agent law, a serious crime. They wrote a letter to Manafort seeking his comment. He didn't reply. His apparent failure to register under FARA was included in a story in *The Wall Street Journal* that laid out how a who's who of Washington players—from Bob Dole to former FBI Director William Sessions—were lining up to help controversial clients from the former Soviet Union. Many of those clients had run afoul of the law and wanted help cleaning up their reputations so that they could travel to and bank in the United States. In other cases, the lawyers and lobbyists brokered deals with the U.S. government under which oligarchs with suspected criminal ties would obtain visas to visit the United States on the condition that they help law enforcement better understand Putin's Russia—a promise that often fell short of U.S. officials' hopes and expectations.

The story also delved into a Washington lobbying campaign by Deripaska, then a little-known Russian oligarch close to Putin and a veteran of Russia's "Aluminum Wars"—violent battles for control of the country's vast bauxite mines and aluminum smelters after the fall of Communism. Deripaska emerged from those fights with a fortune estimated at over $6 billion and a reputation scarred by his battles with competing oligarchs.* Simpson and Jacoby had come across filings made by lobbyists for Deripaska involving "US Department of State visa policies and procedures," an indication that the U.S. government was reluctant to let him into the country.

They followed up and Jacoby eventually came across a Republican political appointee at the State Department named David J. Kramer, who said he knew a lot about the matter from his previous senior post there working on European affairs. Kramer told Jacoby that Deripaska's visa had actually been revoked by State at the request of the FBI, which suspected he wasn't telling the truth about his possibly criminal background.

Simpson and Kramer would cross paths intermittently over the coming years as they compared notes on Putin's Russia. They never dreamed their paths would cross again, in dramatic fashion, nearly a decade later when Kramer would become the one to leak the Steele dossier to the media.

The first *Journal* story in 2007 caused barely a ripple in Washington, as stories on lobbying violations there were common fare, and Deripaska was far from a household name. But the scoop that Deripaska was being blackballed by the State Department at the behest of the FBI made a splash in official circles both in the United States and in Europe. The report had trade, foreign policy, and national security implications and contributed to early signs of a dark turn under way in Russia. The story caught the eye of, among others, CIA analyst Nellie Ohr.

What Simpson and Fritsch didn't know yet was that the Manafort

---

* Especially troublesome was a 2001 court battle in the United States over an alleged "massive racketeering scheme" involving "an international Russian-American organized crime group" fighting over a huge aluminum factory in southwest Siberia. The case alleged that Deripaska and his rivals and associates "committed numerous criminal acts, including, but not limited to, murder, bribery, extortion, mail and wire fraud, and money laundering." Antony Barnett and Nick Kochan, "Chelsea Boss Faces £2bn Court Battle," *Guardian,* October 25, 2003.

and Deripaska stories overlapped. That only became apparent nearly a year later, after Manafort's Russian connections resurfaced at the start of the 2008 U.S. presidential campaign.

In a follow-up to the original *Journal* story, *The Washington Post* reported in January 2008 that Manafort and his longtime consulting partner Rick Davis—working then as a firm known as Davis Manafort—had arranged a meeting in Switzerland in 2006 between Deripaska and Senator John McCain that was described as a social occasion including drinks and dinner. At the time, Deripaska was trying to drum up support in Washington for an independence referendum in Montenegro, and Davis and Manafort were angling to snag a fat contract running the pro-independence campaign.

"Part of the warm Manafort embrace of sleaze," Fritsch wrote in an email to Simpson and Jacoby, both of whom by this time had moved back to Washington.

The story was big news in the United States, because Davis was no longer just a lobbyist; he was on leave from Davis Manafort, managing McCain's campaign for the Republican presidential nomination. The inference was that one of Putin's more notorious cronies could potentially have influence over McCain via Manafort and Davis.

This concern seemed hypothetical at the time. In reality, it had more validity than anyone but Manafort and Davis knew: Manafort had secretly been hired by Deripaska in 2006 for a whopping $10 million a year after pitching the oligarch on a confidential plan to "greatly benefit the Putin government."

This history would later prove critical to Fusion's understanding of Trump's relationship with Russia and aspects of the Steele dossier.

Simpson and Jacoby broke the story in May 2008 that Manafort and Davis were working for both McCain's campaign and a pro-Putin party in Ukraine at the same time. The story recounted in detail how Davis and Manafort had avoided registering under FARA for years but had finally done so retroactively in January 2008. The issue came roaring back weeks before the 2008 election when other media accounts detailed more connections between Davis Manafort, McCain, and Deripaska.

Years later, Simpson would look back on the Manafort and Deripaska controversies from that period as the first inklings of an emerging Kremlin program to win sway in Washington through a network of captive oligarchs and their well-connected—mostly Republican—fixers.

———

Manafort's entanglements with foreign clients were well known among top GOP operatives. "We dealt with this in '08 because Rick Davis was constantly getting the campaign dinged over his ties to Manafort," one anti-Trump Republican consultant recalled to Simpson at the time. "No one is eager for a replay of that."

Further clues to the depths of Manafort's ties to Russia's oligarchs continued to accrue. In London, Simpson met with a Republican power broker at the Dorchester Hotel on Park Lane. Over martinis, the talk turned to Trump's recent promotion of Manafort to chairman of his campaign. Simpson mentioned that Manafort might have received upwards of $20 million from Deripaska. "I think it's more like $100 million," the Republican shot back. Court records later showed that Manafort's firm had "vanished more than $18.9 million" of Deripaska's investments—an odd phrase that would later become clear.

Simpson wasn't guessing about Manafort's financial entanglements with Deripaska. Weeks before Trump tapped Manafort to run his campaign, Christopher Steele had hired Fusion for help investigating Manafort. The matter had nothing to do with politics and was a typical commercial assignment. Orbis had recently been queried by an American law firm about finding Manafort's assets. The firm's unidentified client claimed that Manafort owed him millions of dollars and was seeking to collect by locating Manafort's property. Orbis wanted to procure a copy of Fusion's Manafort archive and have Fusion check for any new information about Manafort in public records in the United States—just the kind of routine American public records task that Orbis farmed out to Fusion from time to time rather than attempt to do the work itself from across the Atlantic.

Steele didn't have much to offer in terms of leads, but he did say that Manafort appeared to have spent huge amounts at a Manhattan tailor known in the corporate records as Fortunato & Venanzi. Owing to a clerical mistake, F&V was classified in business records as an ice cream shop, prompting Steele to theorize that Manafort must be using it to launder money. (The truth ultimately turned out to be more prosaic, but also more telling: This was one of the places where Manafort squandered his Russian oligarch money, eventually dropping $1.3 million on fancy clothes, including a $15,000 ostrich jacket.)

Orbis did not disclose the ultimate client for the job, and Fusion didn't press the issue. Most assignments of this nature, known as "asset recovery" in the legal field, are quite routine, and the identity of the client is not particularly relevant or important, since the work is straightforward, if not easy.

At the time Manafort first surfaced in the Trump campaign, Fusion and Orbis had inked that small deal to research Manafort's finances for Steele's client. (Steele did not know at the time that Fusion's Republican clients for the Trump work were also becoming interested in Manafort.) Manafort's reappearance in American politics seemed like an odd, but happy, gift for Fusion and the Never Trump operation. In the research business, it is not unusual for cases to intersect or for investigative subjects to resurface. So there was nothing suspicious to Fritsch and Simpson about the interest in Manafort from two different quarters. They did debate whether the situation presented a possible conflict but ultimately decided there wasn't one, since the parties were not adverse to each other.

Not everyone would see it that way. Farther down the road, Trump supporters in Congress and the media would seek to portray the convergence of these two projects as a Kremlin conspiracy.

In early April 2016, Fusion's Manafort investigation, which was still being paid for by *The Washington Free Beacon,* was going full speed when Michael Isikoff of *Yahoo News,* a friend of Simpson's from the days of the Clinton scandals, called with a question. What did Simpson make of a 2014 court case in the Cayman Islands that suggested that Manafort and his partner Rick Gates were on the run from a huge bankruptcy case and some unidentified creditor? One Cayman Island filing stated that "Paul Manafort and Rick Gates have simply disappeared."

The financial machinations in the case were "pretty wild," Isikoff said. "Deripaska invests $18.9 million in some cable-telecommunications deal and then, I gather, the money disappears and they can't get in touch with Manafort."

Indeed, Manafort's whereabouts had been something of a mystery for the two years before he resurfaced at the Trump campaign. In May 2014, *Politico* ran a long piece under the headline "Mystery Man: Ukraine's U.S. Fixer," in which it described the once omnipresent D.C. operative as the Invisible Man.

The story quoted an email sent by Manafort's former business partner and longtime Trump ally Roger Stone. "Where is Paul Manafort?" Stone asked a group of mutual friends. It then offered a jokey multiple choice that included "chauffeuring Yanukovych around Moscow" and "loading gold bullion on an Army Transport plane from a remote airstrip outside Kiev and taking off seconds before a mob arrived."

Intrigued by the Isikoff query, Simpson went hunting for more information to help solve the mystery of what Manafort had been doing in recent years and why he had become a ghost. On April 19, 2016, Simpson began rummaging through the PACER court records database looking for litigation in Northern Virginia—Manafort's home—that might shed new light on Manafort's financial problems. The logic was basic, if not obvious: People who don't or can't pay their bills tend to get sued.

There was nothing fresh on the docket under Manafort's name. Knowing that foreign courts sometimes file cases in the United States under obscure titles, he decided to try a favorite trick and tapped in a special PACER code for a search of the Virginia docket for all evidence requests emanating from foreign courts. Maybe lawyers in the Cayman bankruptcy had made such a filing in their pursuit of Manafort.

It wasn't long before he came across a blandly captioned filing from the previous year on behalf of the Grand Court of the Cayman Islands: "In re: Application of Kris Beighton and Alex Lawson, in their capacities as Joint Official Liquidators of Pericles Emerging Market Partners LP, for assistance pursuant to 28 USC 1782." The mention of Pericles caught Simpson's attention. That was the name of the fund mentioned in the Cayman Islands bankruptcy case involving Manafort.

The text of the document was astonishing. Over nineteen pages, it alleged in scorching detail how Manafort and Gates had apparently made off with tens of millions of dollars that they had promised to invest in Ukraine on behalf of a mysterious company in Cyprus called Surf Horizon Limited. The filing described an elaborate series of transactions involving some $37 million and a long chain of offshore shell companies. The whole thing reeked of fraud and possible money laundering.

While a private investigator had eventually tracked down and subpoenaed Gates, it appeared from the court record that the PI had a great deal of trouble finding Manafort. That almost certainly meant that Manafort, the big-shot political consultant, had spent much of his time in 2015 hiding from process servers.

Simpson and Fritsch were both incredulous. The Republican front-runner for president of the United States had recruited to help run his campaign an alleged international fraudster who appeared to be on the run from one very wealthy, very angry, and almost certainly foreign fraud victim. It was as if Manafort had boarded the Trump campaign plane with baggage stuffed with explosives. Within Fusion, researcher Jacob Berkowitz initiated a $5-per-entry When Is Manafort Gone? office pool. Most people gave the new hire a month or two at best. Simpson was the least sanguine. Trump would fire him by May 1, he predicted. Fritsch took the opposite view: "Never—Trump don't capitulate to no one!"

The Virginia filings and other documents on the Surf Horizon affair soon surfaced in various articles about Manafort in the national media, but they had no discernible impact, either on the race or on Manafort's job security. Manafort and the Trump campaign simply shrugged them off, and the press moved on.

Fusion did not. The re-emergence of Manafort was simply too weird and disturbing. Why would he take such a high-profile job without pay if he was in hock and on the run? And who owned the bizarrely named Surf Horizon? Trump's campaign manager owed someone a great deal of money, that was clear. What if it really was a foreign oligarch? Wouldn't that mean the person managing a major presidential campaign was dangerously compromised by someone—whoever that someone might be?

Fusion decided to try to unravel Surf Horizon's ownership mystery on its own, ordering the corporate records from Cyprus. While many of the documents were in Greek, a few contained some company names in the Latin alphabet. One document seemed to show that in 2013, one of the directors of Surf Horizon was actually not a person but rather another offshore company, this one based in Panama, called Sarvangasana Holdings Limited.

A records search turned up some securities filings in Hong Kong, where the owner of Sarvangasana had been required by law to identify himself. It was none other than . . . Oleg Deripaska. The very same Putin-allied Russian oligarch whom Simpson and Fritsch had published stories about nearly a decade earlier.

Once again, Deripaska appeared to have found a way to exert leverage over a presidential campaign via Manafort and his partner Gates. Months before anyone learned of Russia's hacking of Democrats, it seemed to be a sign that the Russians were seeking ways to influence Trump.

CHAPTER FIVE

NEW CLIENT

FRITSCH WOKE UP ON THE MORNING OF MARCH 1, SUPER TUES-
day, knowing a Trump nomination was now all but inevitable, even if a
Trump presidency still seemed far-fetched. He figured the funders of the
Free Beacon would soon resign themselves to a Trump candidacy and
pull the plug on their opposition research efforts. Even the most fervent
of Never Trump billionaires would be reluctant to turn their opposition
to him into support for Hillary Clinton. It seemed obvious that demand
for information on Trump would soon shift to the Democrats.

At 7:44 that morning, he fired off an email to a senior figure in the
Democratic Party establishment. The subject line was simple: "Trump."
So was the message: "Ok he has to be stopped," Fritsch wrote. "We have
done the most on him."

Nine minutes later, Fritsch received a reply: "Yes. Let's talk."

Inside Fusion, Fritsch was out on a limb. Simpson wasn't a big fan
of the Clintons, having covered them as a journalist: the Whitewater
mess, the Monica Lewinsky scandal, and, most important, Bill Clinton's courtship of Chinese campaign contributions during the 1996
race for president—a race that posed some parallels to what would
play out through the rest of 2016. The river of foreign money that later
coursed through the Clinton Global Initiative suggested to Simpson
that the Clintons presided over a twenty-first-century political machine built on peddling influence to foreign oligarchs and other foreign interests, many of whom benefited in one way or another from
Secretary of State Hillary Clinton's actions in office.

Fritsch and Fusion partner Tom Catan sympathized with Simpson's wariness of the Clintons, but they ultimately took a different view as Trump ascended. Fritsch made a lesser-of-two-evils argument in support of approaching the Hillary camp. In a head-to-head with Trump, there was only one evil, he'd argue. Catan would remind Simpson that continuing the Trump research was also a business decision: They'd be stupid not to capitalize on all the work they'd done.

By March 1, Simpson had begun to reconsider. At 10:25 that morning, he emailed Catan and Fritsch. "The only way I could see working for HRC is if it is against Trump," he wrote. "We should make sure [the Democrats] know we have a big book on Trump. Lest they try to buy it someplace else."

As expected, Trump romped on Super Tuesday, winning seven of the eleven states. The next day, March 2, Fritsch had a preliminary chat with Fusion's Democratic contact, who promised to make some inquiries inside the Hillary campaign and get back ASAP.

The partners' growing knowledge of Trump's troubling Russia ties and his questionable business practices had fed a collective sense of concern as Trump racked up primary wins. When Fritsch finally told Simpson about his side conversations about working for the Clinton campaign, Simpson barely looked up from his computer. "Guess we have no choice," he muttered.

There was now unanimity inside Fusion on the need to do what they could to keep Trump out of the White House, and also unanimity as to why. Many of his traits disqualified him for the job, and his political rhetoric was loathsome, but his ties to the criminal underworld, his reliance on hidden flows of Russia money, and his record of chicanery in business topped the list.

On March 15, Trump all but put the nomination away, driving Senator Marco Rubio from the race by drubbing him in his home state of Florida. The state's governor, Rick Scott, endorsed Trump the next day and said it "is now time for Republicans to accept and respect the will of the voters." The candidate himself said that if the party somehow conspired to deny him the nomination, "I think you'd have riots."

Fusion's move to the Hillary campaign would take some time; the firm was more than a month from signing on. In the meantime, the work for the *Free Beacon* would keep going, at least for now. Their patrons had apparently not given up hope of somehow stopping Trump before the Republican convention in July. One reason appeared to be that they had been persuaded by Fusion's research that Trump was vulnerable on his ties to Russia.

That view solidified with Manafort's arrival on the scene at the end of the month. The *Free Beacon* team was initially eager to expose Manafort's Russian entanglements and his adventures in Ukraine. Two days after Manafort joined the Trump campaign, the *Beacon* posted a story on a theme that others in the mainstream media would write about only later: "Lawsuit: Trump Aide Funneled Mob-Linked Ukrainian Oligarch's Fortune into U.S. Real Estate." Soon, the *Free Beacon*'s appetite for attacking Trump began to wane as Trump's nominating position grew stronger, which suggested to Fusion that even Trump's most ardent conservative critics were unlikely to abandon the Republican banner if Trump emerged as their standard-bearer. Email queries slowed to a trickle, and there was no longer the same hunger for fresh material.

On April 19, Trump took the New York primary with 59 percent of the vote.

The next day, Simpson and Fritsch sat down in Washington with Marc Elias, an attorney at Perkins Coie, a Seattle-based law firm with a large political practice in D.C. on the Democratic side of the aisle. Fusion's Democratic contact had made the introduction to Elias, arguably the most powerful attorney in Democratic politics. He served as general counsel to both the Democratic National Committee and the Hillary for America campaign. He was also personal counsel to many Democratic senators. As a voting rights specialist, he had argued—and won—multiple cases before the U.S. Supreme Court.

Despite his résumé, Elias is a supremely informal character. He is a large, balding man who looks like he could have played on the offensive line of his favorite NFL team, the New York Giants. His shoes are sensible, his sentences short. He is as happy talking about his dog, Bode, as he is discussing election law or politics. A dog bed shares space in his office with Giants swag and framed letters of appreciation from every Democratic senator you can name, and a few you can't.

Elias didn't need much convincing. He had heard of the research Fusion had done on Mitt Romney and Bain Capital during the 2012 campaign and said he needed that kind of deep research on Trump. The existing in-house research at the DNC and the campaign was incomplete. The campaign wanted a belt-and-suspenders approach to its research efforts; redundancy was tolerable if that meant the campaign ended up with the very best information at its disposal.

Money wouldn't be a problem, Elias said. Clinton, the Democratic Party, and related PACs would go on to raise over $1.2 billion for her campaign.

Elias said the campaign knew what it needed to know about Trump on a lot of the issues—Trump's cynical flip-flops to a pro-life stance on abortion rights and his latter-day opposition to a ban on assault weapons. Less understood, he said, was how Trump had managed to recover from a string of bankruptcies that should have ruined him. Where did his money come from, how much did he really have, and who helped him? "We know what he says," Elias said. "We need you guys to figure out who he *is*."

Fritsch disclosed that Fusion was currently engaged by an unnamed Republican client to do research on Trump but expected that engagement to end soon. Simpson said the firm couldn't share the written reports it had done for the Republicans but had a wealth of knowledge and promising leads gleaned from public records that could be drawn upon in new, general-election-focused research. Elias didn't see a conflict or a problem.

Elias said Fusion would be reporting only to him, which sounded great to Fritsch and Simpson. They didn't want to have any contact with the campaign brass. Elias wanted it that way for legal reasons: If Fusion's communications were with a lawyer, they could be considered privileged and kept confidential. Political work like this can be perilous, provoking lawsuits down the road—as this job would later prove. Elias also didn't want Fusion drawn into the daily fire drill of a presidential campaign, forced to respond to the jack-in-the-box demands of political operatives. He wanted Fusion to focus on the big picture, and Trump himself.

For all the conspiracy theories and accusations that came later, that rule was strictly applied. As far as Fusion knew, Clinton herself had no idea who they were. To this day, no one in the company has ever met or spoken to her.

"Okay, what do you guys got?" Elias said, turning the conversation back to the substance of the case. "Plenty," Simpson replied.

Fritsch and Simpson ran through some highlights of Fusion's Trump public record research thus far: the Trump University scam, his history of not paying his debts, his hypocrisy on immigration, and the mounting evidence that he was lying about his wealth. The most perplexing element of the work to date, they told him, was Trump's intense and long-lasting fascination with Russia—and his failure to consummate any meaningful deal there. His business world intersected repeatedly with the Russian Mafia in New York, while the sudden re-emergence of Manafort—a consultant who had remade the Kremlin's favorite Ukrainian politician in Manafort's own image—was a major red flag.

"We think you guys will really want to pay attention to the Russia angle," Fritsch said. It was obvious from Elias's reaction that the Russia element was new to him. "Can you tell me more?" he said.

Trump's affiliations with Russians of all kinds, Simpson said, went way back to the opening of Trump Tower in the early 1980s, when known Russia-connected mobsters like David Bogatin began scooping up units, often to obscure the source of criminal profits. The five luxury condos Bogatin bought in 1984 were later seized by the feds as part of a massive money-laundering case. This would soon emerge as a distinct pattern, they told Elias. In project after project, from Florida to Panama to Toronto, Russians with dubious résumés and questionable pasts turned out in great numbers to buy Trump-branded units.

Elias was intrigued, if a bit befuddled by all the names and dates. He wasn't in a hurry, and his face said: *Keep going.* Simpson cracked open his MacBook to walk him through some documents.

As Trump's own financial travails grew in the late 1980s, so did his outreach and ties to Russia. In 1987, he took an all-expenses-paid trip to Moscow at the invitation of the Soviet ambassador to the United States. While there, he and his then-wife, Ivana, toured several sites for a proposed Trump Tower. No deal seemed likely, but soon after he came back Trump spoke of running for the White House and took out a full-page ad in several U.S. papers arguing that the United States should stop spending so much to defend foreign countries, foreshadowing the pro-Russian, anti-NATO stance he would take on the campaign trail thirty years later.

Trump tried again in 1996 to cook up a big Moscow project, Simpson and Fritsch told Elias, this time with the help of Howard Lorber, one of Trump's only true friends and a broker for wealthy Russians seeking real estate investments in the United States. That project, too, fell flat. The Trumps kept trying to kindle something, making repeated trips to Moscow to view potential sites or talk to possible partners.

While Trump hadn't succeeded in investing in Russia, they said, the Russians had definitely begun making an investment in Trump. Many had troubling backgrounds, and they highlighted the criminal record of Felix Sater and Trump's history of lying about their relationship. By 2008, Donald Trump Jr. was boasting that Russians "make up a pretty disproportionate cross-section of a lot of our assets." Five years later, in Moscow for the Miss Universe pageant, Trump again suggested that he was deep into talks for a Trump skyscraper. (Only much later would investigators uncover that his own representatives were trying to cook up a Trump project in Moscow even as he campaigned to be president.)

In other words, Fritsch and Simpson stated what seemed obvious: The party of Ronald Reagan, whose antipathy to the Soviet Union had helped precipitate its collapse, might have real qualms about a nominee with such close ties to the remnants of what Reagan had called the Evil Empire.

This angle was all new to Elias, and he loved it. The research book the DNC had put together on Trump, he said, contained none of this stuff. Fusion's research team would soon be hired and given wide latitude to go where the story led it.

Formalizing the engagement with Perkins Coie, Elias's firm, would take weeks.

The biggest sticking point was the matter of indemnification. In 2013, Fusion had been drawn into a defamation lawsuit against *Mother Jones* by a rich Romney donor and campaign finance official who had concluded—wrongly—that Fusion was behind an unflattering article about him published the previous year. *Mother Jones* eventually won that suit, but Fusion had to defend against a third-party subpoena that sought to expose its client and its work. That had cost the company tens of thousands of dollars in legal fees—costs its client declined to cover. If something like that happened again, Fusion wanted to know it wouldn't again be stuck with the legal fees. Trump was famously litigious, and the last thing Fusion wanted was a legal fight with a vindictive tabloid figure with a long history of aggressive litigation.

The potential for an ugly, public fight is one big reason most private consultants like Fusion eschew political work. (A pay scale below that of commercial work is the other.) In a political battle with high stakes, there is a huge incentive to attack the credibility of anyone bearing bad tidings about a candidate or elected official, however well substantiated.

In the end, Perkins Coie would not guarantee to cover Fusion's costs in a legal fight. That realization was the point when Fusion might have said to Elias: *Thanks, but no thanks.* Fusion's partners, in fact, discussed bailing on the project but eventually decided the risk was worth it. The Trump project was just too important and interesting a research subject.

The costliest component of the work, they told Elias, would be some on-the-ground reporting they envisioned doing outside the United States. They ran through Trump's many trouble-plagued projects in developing countries and business dealings abroad; the budget would need to include funding for foreign investigators in Mexico and other countries. The riskiest bit of fieldwork, which they didn't yet share with Elias, would be in Russia. They knew just the guy for the job: a Russian-speaking former spy. They figured they could do that work discreetly. No one would ever find out about it.

CHAPTER SIX

CALLING AGENT STEELE

BY THE TIME FUSION DECIDED TO TURN TO CHRISTOPHER Steele in May 2016, the firm had amassed a mountain of research about Trump's business past, his ties to Russia, and his reliance on questionable investors. Manafort's arrival had magnified the sense that Russia might be seeking inroads into the Trump campaign.

To take stock of where the work stood, Simpson and Fritsch asked Berkowitz, the lead researcher on Project Bangor, to draft a document that would round up all the various strands of their work to date. "Donald J. Trump—Research Summary" ran to 105 single-spaced pages with 665 footnotes. The word "Russia" appeared twenty-eight times, and "mafia" twenty-five times. Trump, the document noted in the last line of its executive summary, "has significant associations to the Russian and Italian mafia at home and abroad."

In early May, Fritsch asked Berkowitz to expand on the Russia angle. The result was a fifteen-page memorandum Fritsch described in a May 19 email to Berkowitz as "a true tour de sleaze." Its first line: "Donald Trump's connections to Vladimir Putin's Russia are deeper than generally appreciated and raise significant national security concerns." The memo went on to describe the work done by Trump advisers Manafort and Carter Page and other players on behalf of Russian oligarchs and companies, and cataloged Manafort's financial dealings with Deripaska. It also highlighted the preponderance of Russian money coursing through Trump projects in New York, Toronto, and Panama—most notably the signature Trump Tower in midtown Manhattan.

The memo recounted Trump's many trips to Russia in search of real estate investment deals and left many questions unanswered. How to explain the Russian fascination with a New York developer who kept slipping into bankruptcy and was constantly scrambling for new lenders willing to support his next project? Why did Russians keep dangling business deals that never seemed to go anywhere? Why was Felix Sater so close to the Trumps, even traveling to Moscow with Ivanka and Don Jr. in 2006?

Maybe Trump did this out of desperation, or maybe it was just a failure to vet his business partners properly. Or, quite possibly, there was a more sinister explanation. Either way, Fusion had the sense that it couldn't answer some of the crucial questions surrounding Trump's conduct through open records alone. It needed a new avenue of inquiry to get a better feel for what was happening within Russia itself, where open-source research left much to be desired.

Simpson and Fritsch needed to hire someone to talk to people inside Russia—a risky enterprise, especially in the context of a presidential campaign. They needed someone they could trust to be ultra-discreet. As important, they needed someone who wouldn't rip them off. Human reporting from distant locales was shot through with fraud; many in the private consulting world just made stuff up.

There was only one firm that checked those boxes: Orbis. Simpson put in a call to Steele: *Let's meet soon.*

Christopher Steele was back on his heels when he first met Simpson in 2010, at a noisy Italian restaurant called Franco's in the tony London neighborhood of St. James. The year before, Steele had retired after two decades of government service and set out with a fellow MI6 colleague, Christopher Burrows, to create Orbis, a private consulting firm specializing in the collection of intelligence from a network of sources around the world. But that fall, Steele had lost his wife of twenty years, Laura, a death that devastated him and their three young children. Two mutual friends of Steele and Simpson, knowing of their shared interest in Russian organized crime and their common struggles as newly minted entrepreneurs, had arranged the meeting.

Steele's official government biography described him as a Foreign Office diplomat. But it was well known (at least in investigative circles) that his real employer was the United Kingdom's Secret Intelligence

Service—better known as MI6. He'd had prestigious postings in Moscow and Paris and, as head of the Russia desk at HQ, was considered one of Britain's foremost Russia hands by a shrinking circle of Kremlinologists in the United States and the U.K. who had done battle with the Soviets during the Cold War.

Steele was now a forty-five-year-old, recently bereaved widower working out of a serviced office in Mayfair during the day and rushing home in the afternoons to care for his three children. Steele didn't wear his grief on his sleeve. Over lunch with Simpson, he was mostly interested in talking business opportunities and exchanging stories about various Russian oligarchs in the court of Vladimir Putin.

Steele literally couldn't afford to wallow in grief. Unlike many of his peers at Cambridge University and MI6, Steele didn't come from money. He had earned his way to the elite university through hard work and a determination that came through subtly in conversation. He looked you square in the eye in meetings and listened more than he spoke, which he did with a somewhat flat affect and an accent that was firmly middle class; he smiled at the right prompts but wasn't one to tell a joke. In short, he was a brain. Yet there were moments when he seemed to exhibit a certain melancholy that hinted at something more than just British reserve or the caution of a former spy.

"Pete, it's critical that we all stick together," he once told Fritsch at the height of the furor over the dossier. "Our friendship absolutely must prevail."

Steele and Simpson had much in common. Born barely a month apart in 1964, both had left their longtime employers at almost the exact same time to strike out on their own in the world of private research. They shared an interest in corruption in the former Soviet Union and the movements of its oligarchs. They also knew enough about each other's worlds to bond over mutual acquaintances and war stories seen from different perspectives. By the end of lunch, Steele and Simpson had agreed to try to do business together if possible and to refer potential clients to each other.

On his occasional visits to Washington over the next few years, Steele would swing by Fusion's office and trade gossip about who was up and who was down among Russians currying favor with Putin.

Those sessions sometimes ended with pints at Maddy's Bar & Grille, conveniently located below Fusion's first office. In London, Steele would reciprocate at a local pub. After a beer or two—but never three—Steele would drop talk of how to gin up business and reveal a genuinely deep and warm laugh while speaking of his nature walks and a budding interest in bird-watching.

For years, the relationship was more kinship than commerce.

Steele was born in Yemen in 1964, on the ebb tide of the British Empire. His father, Perris, was then stationed in Aden, a British protectorate near the mouth of the Red Sea, working as a meteorologist for the military. The British would leave Aden for good in late 1967.

The Steele family moved frequently between postings in the U.K. and Cyprus, eventually settling southwest of London in the county of Surrey, where the younger of Steele's two sisters was born. Steele speaks proudly of his family's roots in the Welsh coal mines. In truth, his parents were comfortably middle class. An excellent student, Steele aced his A levels, the British equivalent of the SATs, and won admission to Cambridge University, matriculating in 1982.

In the U.K., an Oxford or Cambridge education can help burnish one's standing in the upper class, but Steele had something of a chip on his shoulder when it came to his privileged peers. That chip and a cold determination helped him work his way to the presidency of the Cambridge Union, the university's renowned debating society. There, he poked at the conservative core of the institution by inviting a member of the Palestine Liberation Organization to speak and taking on Margaret Thatcher's fondness for Ronald Reagan.

Steele graduated from Cambridge in 1986 with a degree in political science and toyed with a career in journalism, of all things. One day, he answered a blind newspaper ad promising adventure and work abroad. "It just sounded like good fun," Steele recalled.

The mystery employer was in fact MI6, which quickly pegged him as a candidate for its prestigious Russia training program. The Cold War was still in full swing in those days, and the Soviet sphere still drew the best and brightest. Administratively, he became an employee of the Foreign and Commonwealth Office, spending the next several years in London gaining fluency in Russian and studying the country's history and politics. In reality, he had joined Her Majesty's secret service.

In the spring of 1988, Steele went on a blind date with Laura Hunt, a young woman working for an accounting firm who happened to be the daughter of a Russian-speaking nuclear physicist. He chased her as relentlessly as he had the presidency of the Cambridge Union.

In April 1990, the young couple, now engaged, moved to Moscow for MI6, returning to the U.K. to marry in July. For the next three years Steele would watch over the messy dissolution of the Soviet Union from the diplomatic cover of a post at the British embassy along the Moskva River. That cover wasn't too deep: Steele would laugh when recalling the dopey mind games the KGB would play to remind him that he and Laura were under constant surveillance, once stealing her favorite dress shoes before a diplomatic dinner.

When the Soviet Union finally collapsed, the suffocating surveillance of Western diplomats and suspected intelligence officers suddenly ceased—which for a brief moment seemed like a possible harbinger of a new, less authoritarian future for Russia. But the surveillance started again within days. The intrusive tails and petty harassment were indistinguishable from Soviet practices and have continued to this day. To Steele, that told him all he needed to know about the new Russia: The new boss was the same as the old boss.

The Steeles returned to England in 1993 and had two boys. In 1998 they moved to Paris and then the French village of Bougival, where Steele worked on a variety of subjects, this time under the diplomatic cover of first secretary for financial affairs. There, they had a daughter in 2000. Steele recalls the period as among the happiest in his life.

Much of Steele's work during his years with MI6 remains classified, and he refuses to discuss it, even with friends. But some details are known. After returning to Britain, he was dispatched to post-invasion Iraq to work with U.S. forces setting up the new government. This was a period when Western intelligence agencies made a hard pivot to countering Islamic terrorism. Russia and the former Soviet satellite states moved to the back burner.

But Steele's head stayed in Moscow. He watched from afar as Putin consolidated power and presided over an organized kleptocracy that stripped the Russian state of its wealth to enrich those close to the Kremlin. Steele, a person with a deeply held and binary view of good and evil, took corruption personally. His dislike for Putin's Russia became far more intense after the 2006 murder in London of Alexander Litvinenko, a former KGB officer turned MI6 source, who was poisoned with radioactive polonium.

"Despite all the decay and dysfunction, the Russians remain and probably always will be very formidable adversaries, and it is perilous to underestimate them," Steele would say. "They also know how to play things long." The Russian gift for deception, he would add, is perhaps one of their greatest assets. "But that's a corollary of their greatest weakness: They are incapable of trust, which makes it impossible to have a healthy economy."

In 2009, Steele and Burrows decided that after decades of public service it was time to branch out on their own and make some money. They gave their notice to MI6 and launched Orbis in September. Two weeks later, Steele's wife died, just two days after Burrows's wife gave birth prematurely to a son. The partners would work from a small office in Farnham so they could be near their children.

Their business would service companies throughout Western Europe on how to compete for business in emerging markets, particularly in Russia, the former Eastern Bloc states (Burrows had been stationed in Berlin at one point), and other countries in which they had served, like France and Greece. Like many firms, they would also do whatever work they could conducting due diligence research and litigation support. By 2010, a steady book of business had begun to flow their way, and they hired several junior analysts as the company grew.

From the outset, Steele and Burrows agreed that they would strictly adhere to the legal obligations they had accepted when they left government service: If they ever came across information they believed threatened national security, they were duty-bound to report it, whether their clients liked it or not.

That credo would be put to the test on one of Orbis's very first assignments, investigating corruption in soccer's global governing body, FIFA, on behalf of England's Football Association. After a months-long investigation, tapping his sources in Russia and elsewhere, Steele determined that Russia had won the right to host the 2018 World Cup through bribery of FIFA officials. Igor Sechin, the head of Putin's kitchen cabinet and the state oil company Rosneft, appeared to be involved. Steele also learned from his source network that Russia's bribery program had spread money across the globe.

His contract with the English association was over, but Steele thought Russia should be exposed. He was offended by the idea that the Russians might get away with it. He just couldn't let it go. In 2011, he contacted Michael Gaeta, an FBI agent he met at a conference in Oxford in 2009, who headed the Bureau's Eurasian Joint Organized Crime Squad. Later, he would work with Gaeta on one of the FBI's longest-running and highest-priority cases: the hunt for fugitive Russian Mafia don Semion Mogilevich, whom Orbis eventually established was hiding out in a small village north of Moscow under Russian government protection.

He briefed Gaeta on what Orbis had learned. The result was one of the Obama administration's most successful organized crime prosecutions: the 2015 federal indictment in Brooklyn of fourteen people, mainly from Latin America, in a massive FIFA bribery scheme. Ironically, Steele's contributions to the FIFA case have remained under wraps, because the Russians suspected of orchestrating and executing the worst acts of bribery have all remained inside Russia, beyond the reach of international law enforcement. Until one is apprehended and extradited to the United States for trial, the Russian element of the FIFA case—presumed to be the centerpiece of the entire investigation—will remain outside the public view.

Fusion and Orbis found it easy to work together because they occupied two very different spaces in the private research world. Steele specialized in the collection of human intelligence developed from a confidential source network, an approach that's a must in countries like Russia, where information is severely restricted. Fusion generally operated in places with good access to public records, working on the premise that documents properly collected could tell a tale as reliable as even the best human source, and were much easier to use for law firms, which made up a large portion of Fusion's client base.

These different approaches also mirror the different intelligence-gathering strengths of the United States and the U.K. The U.S. government has by far the best capabilities in data collection, while the British have always excelled in "humint"—human intelligence. Britain's aptitude for humint owes much to its historical administration of a far-flung empire. From India to South Africa, boots on the ground were an essential tool for governing often huge, unruly colonies. The United States, meanwhile, excels at technological innovation and the creation of electronic surveillance systems.

Bound by language and a shared history confronting aggression in two world wars, the United States and the U.K. form the core of the "Five Eyes" intelligence alliance with Canada, New Zealand, and Australia. The common trust in that group is so high that many secrets, sources, and methods are shared freely.

Orbis's cultural roots in the national security space made them averse to working on assignments they considered contrary to the interests of the U.K. or its allies. Steele and Burrows tended to work at the direction of large international law firms, as Fusion did—oversight that helps ensure that projects are carried out legally and professionally.

The quality of Orbis's clientele reflected that, tending toward big European multinational companies and the global law firms. Some were sophisticated businessmen and women with experience operating in Russia and other ex-Communist countries with weak or nonexistent legal systems. Steele's flat affect and neutral gaze, which could sometimes come across as lacking in charm, enhanced his credibility in professional settings.

Steele spoke of his children often and was fastidious in his diet and attire. He was very much the opposite of his London competitors, a cynical crew who worked for the scariest of Russian oligarchs without qualm. One competitor who had long ago sold out to the Putin kleptocracy once told the Fusion partners that he "absolutely loved being caught in honey traps"—Russian intelligence operations seeking to ensnare Westerners in compromising sexual situations. "They already own me so why not have a bit of fun?"

None of this was of concern to Steele, because he couldn't go to Russia anymore. In 1999, a disgruntled former MI6 colleague posted on the Internet a list of 116 supposed MI6 agents. Most of the names were indeed spies operating under "light cover" in British embassies overseas, as Steele had in Moscow in the early nineties. Steele's name was on the list, along with those of Burrows and their mentor and former MI6 chief Sir Richard Dearlove.

The upshot of this twist of fate was that Steele, a Russia specialist who preferred fieldwork, was forced to become a desk officer. In the following years, he rose to oversee all of MI6's covert operations in Russia. He oversaw its inquiry into one of the most sensitive matters involving Putin's Russia, the 2006–2008 investigation of Litvinenko's murder. This was an assassination on British soil carried out by Russia's Federal Security Service (FSB), Steele believed, at Putin's behest.

By 2012, Orbis was firmly established, and Steele's personal life took a happy turn. He'd gotten married to a British diplomat named Katherine, and their combined brood included four children, three cats, and a comfortable home in the village of Farnham, Surrey. They settled into a routine: He would take the train to Orbis's offices in London and return to the quiet of the countryside each evening.

Simpson traveled to the U.K. in mid-May of 2016 to broach the Trump work to Steele. They met at a branch of the Italian restaurant chain called Carluccio's, in Heathrow Airport's Terminal 5. Steele was already waiting when Simpson arrived, dragging his carry-on bag. Over lasagna, Simpson told Steele that Fusion had been investigating Trump for about eight months on behalf of an unnamed client. That work had ended, but a new client had come along that had deep pockets. Simpson had just come down from Edinburgh, where he had lined up some local help investigating Trump's money-losing collection of golf courses in Scotland and Ireland. The courses were an inviting target for Fusion's efforts to document Trump's dismal business record and the fake valuations of his properties in his official candidate disclosure filings: Unlike in the United States, private companies in the U.K. and Ireland are required to file detailed financial statements for public inspection.

"He seems to lie about pretty much everything," Simpson told Steele, describing how the work in Scotland aimed to disprove Trump's claim that his two courses there were each worth over $50 million. "These figures are beyond exaggerated," he told Steele. "They're fictional."

Simpson said they had unearthed numerous connections between Trump and various characters from the former Soviet Union, as well as a series of mysterious trips Trump had made over the years to explore building projects in Russia. Now that the primaries were coming to an end, he said, Fusion expected to soon have a new budget to pursue some of its leads in Russia. Would Steele be interested? The project he had in mind was a modest one, he said. Just a month of inquiries with his Russia sources to see if there were any interesting leads on Trump.

Steele confessed to not knowing very much about Trump. That didn't really matter. He was interested.

Fusion thought there might be information in Russia to indicate that Trump had unsavory dealings with corrupt politicians or businessmen. Another possibility, Simpson said, was that Trump was merely going to Russia to chase women, and his pursuit of business deals in the country was just a cover story. If that was all it was, he added, "no one will give a shit."

To the contrary, said Steele, if Trump was engaged in sexual dalliances in Moscow, he'd probably been taped by the FSB. "*Kompromat* is a serious issue," he said. "It still happens all the time."

Steele suggested the Russians might have taken a political interest in Trump, and mentioned that he had recently completed a similar project on Russian meddling in the politics of European countries for another client. Project Charlemagne, as Orbis called it, had chronicled signs of extensive Russian electoral interference in support of right-wing parties all across Western Europe.

The work had been undertaken for a private client, he said, but the findings were so troubling that he had voluntarily provided copies of his Charlemagne reports to the U.S. government. The Kremlin, he claimed, had "a secret black budget of several tens of millions of dollars" earmarked for populist nationalist politicians in Europe who were opposed to the European Union.

Steele said he was unable to travel to Russia himself and had even received what appeared to be veiled threats from the Russians via intermediaries. However, he added, the vast Russian diaspora in the West made it possible to build and manage productive networks of sources on the ground in Moscow.

Steele came back quickly with a proposal to conduct a one-month inquiry for about $30,000. He and Fritsch, who normally handled budget matters, hammered out the terms verbally. Simpson gave Steele the simplest of tasking instructions: *Find out what you can about what Trump and his circle have been up to in Moscow over the years.*

Fusion didn't share with Steele any of its reports on Trump, nor did it identify its new client beyond eventually saying that it was a law firm. This was important from an operational standpoint. Contractors, even professionals, have a natural tendency to tailor their finds to what they think clients want to hear. Fusion didn't want to infect Steele's inquiry with any preconceived goals or even basic theories of the case, much less the political context of the engagement.*

Steele set out to find what he could on Donald Trump and Russia.

---

* The exchange was later captured by the FBI in a classified submission to a special court in Washington that deals exclusively with intelligence matters: "Source #1," a.k.a. Steele, "was approached by an identified U.S. person, who indicated to source #1 that a U.S.-based law firm had hired the identified U.S. person to conduct research regarding candidate #1's ties to Russia. . . . The identified U.S. person never advised Source #1 as to the motivation behind the research into candidate #1's ties to Russia."

As Steele went to work on his new assignment, Simpson briefly turned his attention to another of Fusion's long-standing projects, a lawsuit that was winding down involving an obscure Russian company called Prevezon.

Fusion didn't know it then, but its involvement with Prevezon and its lawyer Natalia Veselnitskaya would later collide in dramatic and unforeseeable ways with Fusion's Trump investigation—a collision that has reverberated for years after.

Fusion did not engineer that collision, which some still find hard to believe: As with the Deripaska case, the coincidence of two work streams coming together would fuel wild conspiracy theories and color congressional inquiries into the whole of the Trump investigation.

Understanding how it did happen is important to the broader story.

Since early 2014, Fusion had been doing research for a team of American lawyers in a complex civil case. Its ultimate client, Prevezon, wanted to stop the U.S. Justice Department from seizing its property in New York. By 2016, the case seemed to be on its last legs: A federal judge had removed Fusion's client, the law firm BakerHostetler, from the case over a possible conflict of interest. A prestigious firm with deep Republican ties, BakerHostetler was appealing that decision.

On June 9, Simpson went to New York to attend the hearing with the BakerHostetler lawyers and Veselnitskaya, the Russian lawyer representing Prevezon.

After the hearing, Simpson dashed to Penn Station to catch a train home. As he did so, unbeknownst to him, Veselnitskaya was heading uptown for a far more consequential appointment: a meeting in Trump Tower with Donald Trump Jr., Paul Manafort, and Jared Kushner to deliver what the Russians had promised the Trump campaign would be Kremlin dirt on Hillary Clinton.

This session between the Russian lawyer and the top brass of the Trump campaign would remain unknown to Fusion, the press, and investigators until news of it broke more than a year later, in July 2017. When it did, Trump's defense team quickly pointed out that the Trump Tower meeting had come about soon after Fusion hired Steele. For the conspiracy minded, the ties between Fusion and Prevezon were even more evidence of a plot to frame Trump.

It was anything but.

Simpson had met Veselnitskaya but a handful of times, almost always with her U.S. lawyers present. They talked little, divided as they were by language. Fusion had been working on the Prevezon case sporadically for more than two years, initially trying to help the lawyers decipher a pile of bank records. Veselnitskaya had little to do with that spadework.

After meeting the Trump campaign brass that Friday, Veselnitskaya traveled to Washington to meet with her American lawyers, who had organized a social dinner at a tapas restaurant called Barcelona Wine Bar, in the neighborhood of Cathedral Heights. Simpson attended. So did an impish, Russian-born, D.C.-based lobbyist named Rinat Akhmetshin, who, it was later revealed, had accompanied Veselnitskaya to the Trump Tower meeting.

Incredible as it would later seem to Republican investigators, neither Veselnitskaya nor Akhmetshin ever mentioned to Simpson that they had sandwiched an encounter with the brain trust of the Trump campaign between that New York court date and their D.C. dinner.

Fusion's work on the Prevezon case began in late 2013 with a call from Moscow—John Moscow, a legendary former prosecutor who broke open some of the biggest financial scandals of the 1980s and '90s and had been a journalistic source for both Simpson and Fritsch. After retiring from the Manhattan DA's office in 2005, he became a partner at BakerHostetler.

Moscow told Simpson that he was representing a Russian firm in a complex case. Federal prosecutors in New York were trying to seize some $14 million in money and Manhattan real estate controlled by Prevezon, alleging that the assets were the proceeds of a massive tax fraud in Russia. Eventually, the Justice Department alleged, some of the money wound up in New York.

John Moscow's reputation outweighed whatever skepticism Simpson harbored about the law firm's client. To understand the government's case, Moscow eventually deposed the federal agent who had led the investigation. He revealed that much of his information on Prevezon came from documents supplied by William Browder, a wealthy, American-born hedge fund manager based in London.

This came as a surprise to Fusion, which had been researching another aspect of the case. Simpson and Fritsch knew a good bit about Browder from their time at the *Journal*. After working as an investment banker, Browder had moved to Russia in the 1990s and established a hedge fund called Hermitage Capital Management. He amassed a fortune in the Russian stock market during Putin's rise. Along the way, he gave up his U.S. citizenship and stopped paying American income taxes on his profits from Russia.

Long an outspoken Putin fan—*The Economist* called him a "loyal Putinista" in 2006—Browder eventually fell out with the Kremlin in a dispute over unpaid taxes and was later expelled from Russia. Russian authorities had accused Hermitage of tax fraud and arrested the hedge fund's outside tax accountant, a man named Sergei Magnitsky, as a party to the alleged fraud. The thirty-seven-year-old Magnitsky died in 2009 while in custody awaiting trial—retribution, Browder said, for the accountant's having blown the whistle on official Russian corruption.

Magnitsky's wrongful death and Browder's expulsion from Russia seemed to flip a switch in Browder, who remade himself as a human rights crusader. Putin did his part, killing and jailing critics and invading Russia's neighbors.

None of that had direct bearing on the Prevezon case. But on a political level, it made Browder a more credible Putin critic in the public eye—especially among lawmakers in Congress. At Browder's urging, Congress passed a law in 2012 to sanction Russian officials involved in Magnitsky's death—a law that came to be known as the Magnitsky Act.

Browder was always eager to testify before Congress or appear on TV, but he did not want to answer questions from BakerHostetler lawyers about his role as a whistleblower in the Prevezon case. So the lawyers asked Fusion to figure out how they could get Browder's testimony. What ensued was a legal game of cat and mouse in which Fusion developed information that would help BakerHostetler subpoena Browder multiple times, forcing him to testify about his business activities in Russia and earning Fusion his everlasting enmity.

The U.S. government had staked its case against Prevezon on the credibility of Browder. Yet he was reluctant to explain under oath where he had obtained his evidence. It was an odd position for a human rights crusader to take.

By 2016, Browder's long-running battle to avoid testifying was beginning to generate sparks in the media and threatened to undermine his credibility. That apparently didn't go unnoticed in the sanctions-battered Kremlin, increasingly on the lookout for ways to fight back against its critics in the West.

———

Fusion had always thought of Veselnitskaya, the Prevezon lawyer, as a minor figure on the periphery of Russian power. But she was now on the front lines of a pitched battle with Putin's archenemy, Browder. That was sure to get her noticed in high places—if she didn't already have friends there.*

Veselnitskaya was perfectly positioned to attack Browder at a time when Russia's need to discredit him had increased exponentially. In early 2016, Congress took up a major expansion of the Magnitsky Act that would allow the government to impose harsh sanctions on any foreign government officials implicated in human rights abuses.

In the spring of 2016, Veselnitskaya launched an effort to dilute the expanded Magnitsky Act. Part of that job was to diminish Browder's credibility in the eyes of Congress. Veselnitskaya worked with Baker-Hostetler and Akhmetshin to point to contradictions in Browder's story of his past in Russia.

Fusion never did a dollar's worth of business with Akhmetshin, and no one ever asked Fusion to conduct research for him, but Akhmetshin eventually testified that some of Fusion's Browder findings for the Prevezon litigation were "later recycled for some of the work" on Capitol Hill. That was not up to Fusion, whose research for BakerHostetler was legally the property of Prevezon. Fusion had no say in the matter if Prevezon decided to take evidence from a court case and repurpose it.

But all this would come back to haunt Fusion, long after the Prevezon work ended and even before the news broke of Donald Trump Jr.'s meeting with the Russians.

In his new assignment, Steele wasted no time digging into Trump's Russia connections. In mid-June, just days after the still-secret Trump Tower meeting, Steele called Simpson with concern in his voice. His sources had come back to him with astonishing reporting, information he wasn't comfortable sharing over the phone, even on an encrypted line. He was assembling the information in a report he didn't want to transmit electronically.

---

*Perhaps they should have figured it out sooner, but only much later did it become clear to Fusion that Veselnitskaya did indeed have high-level contacts in the Russian government. According to a 2019 federal indictment of her for obstruction of justice, as early as 2014 she was secretly working with a senior prosecutor in Moscow to hamper U.S. prosecutors investigating the Prevezon matter.

The moment was already fraught. Not long before, Fusion had learned that the Democratic National Committee's computer systems had been thoroughly breached by Russian hackers in March 2016, a fact later reported by *The Washington Post* on June 14, 2016. Around the same time, a new website emerged called DCLeaks that promised the real truth about Hillary Clinton and her backers. Fusion also heard that in April the DNC had hired a cyber-investigations firm called Crowd-Strike to look into the hack, and it quickly determined that at least one of the digital break-ins had been committed by a group of hackers for Russia's Foreign Intelligence Service (SVR).

Fusion's in-house cyber ninja, Laura Seago, was asked to analyze the DCLeaks site. Her assessment came back quickly. "The poor English and amateurish site architecture—no SSL encryption, open downloads folder—screams 'Russian hackers' to me," she said.

The same day Steele was writing up his first memo, he and his countrymen were going to the polls to vote in a referendum on whether the United Kingdom should get a divorce from the European Union. All spring, advocates for remaining in the EU had warned that Russia was quietly pulling for Brexit, a claim that Brexit supporters mocked. The surveys all seemed to indicate that the question was immaterial, since voters appeared to favor remaining in the EU by a small but solid margin of four percentage points. Yet when the votes were counted that night, the percentages came out reversed. The British far right had scored a huge, shocking victory, one that was sure to thrill Putin, who was intent on undermining both the EU and NATO.

Something weird was going on. And now here was Steele saying he had something alarming to report from Russia.

Prior to this moment, Fusion didn't really have a need for a heightened level of operational security. Email was fine. Fusion had moved to encrypted telephone communications as a precaution but didn't have a reliable system in place to ensure the secure transmission of sensitive documents. A human courier was the safest way to go, but that was expensive and time-consuming and carried its own risks.

So Steele called FedEx.

The first memo almost didn't make it to Washington.

Steele's FedEx package was due to arrive at Fusion's office on June 23, but it didn't turn up as scheduled. A frazzled Simpson assumed it was missing and emailed Steele and Fritsch at 3:45 A.M. on June 24, urging Orbis to take the shipment "to United Airlines at Heathrow first thing in the morning and have it delivered via the United Airlines same-day package delivery service."

Two hours later, Steele replied that FedEx had tried to deliver it twice the previous day, at 11:21 A.M. and 2:22 P.M. That set off a mad scramble to figure out what had gone wrong. It turned out Fusion's intercom was broken—again. Their office manager soon tracked down the package.

The FedEx sleeve was addressed to Simpson. He went into his office, closed the door, and ripped it open. Inside was a blank envelope. There was no cover letter or other marking to indicate who had written what was inside, or why. The document's header read CONFIDENTIAL/SENSITIVE SOURCE. Below was a simple two-and-a-half-page document of text with a four-paragraph summary and six bullet points. At the end, it was dated "20 June 2016," European style.

The opening assertion of "Company Intelligence Report 2016/080" was written in the eccentric, telegraphic style of a British intelligence report. It was as hard as they come: "Russian regime has been cultivating, supporting and assisting Trump for at least 5 years. Aim, endorsed by PUTIN, has been to encourage splits and divisions in the western alliance."

That was a big claim, but the report pulled no punches. Russia's main spy service, the report said, "has compromised TRUMP through his activities in Moscow sufficiently to be able to blackmail him." The Russians had also amassed a mound of compromising material on Hillary Clinton, which they had yet to share with the Trump campaign. "Russian intentions for its deployment still unclear."

The memo went on to recount a bizarre episode that allegedly took place in the presidential suite of Moscow's Ritz-Carlton hotel in 2013. Steele's sources said that Trump's hatred of the Obamas ran so deep that he had asked "a number of prostitutes to perform a 'golden showers' (urination) show in front of him," to defile the bed in which the Obamas had slept years earlier. The report said Russian intelligence had it on videotape for potential use as a tool of blackmail. Steele would later point out that one of his sources was a hotel staffer who had been on duty at the time.

Fusion had expected Steele to come back with information about Trump's many failed business deals in Russia, perhaps explaining how the Trump Organization had run afoul of some corruption agency or bungled some bribe. Or perhaps some information that would help Fusion fill out the picture of Trump's odd associations with Sater and other criminals. Simpson later told congressional investigators: "We threw a line in the water and Moby Dick came back."

After reading the memo, Simpson walked a copy over to Fritsch's office and closed the door behind him. Fritsch read it, too. Once he was finished, he looked up at Simpson, aghast. "What the fuck?" he said. "I know," Simpson said. They called Steele and had a brief conversation about sourcing. They kept things vague and understated over the phone, even on an encrypted line.

"Chris, Peter's here with me," Simpson said. "We read your report. Very interesting, to say the least. You feel pretty good about the sourcing here?"

Steele was elliptical but firm. The sources were good: Source A was "a senior Russian Foreign Ministry figure"; source B "a former top-level intelligence officer still active in the Kremlin"; source C "a senior Russian financial official"; source D "a close associate of Trump"; sources E and F were inside the Ritz; and source G was "a senior Kremlin official."

Steele offered a bit more detail on the specific placement of these sources, which only confirmed their credibility in the Fusion partners' minds. That was all he wanted to say over the phone.

Stylistically, the memo was typical of a field intelligence report: a sober recitation of what sources had said, without much elaboration or context. As with the other fifteen memos that Steele would file over the course of the summer and fall, it didn't purport to be flawless or 100 percent accurate, but it did purport to be credible, a crucial distinction. His memoranda, like all such humint products, are designed to pass along meaningful tips from credible sources to help flesh out or buttress other reporting. And, equally important, they are meant for an intentionally small audience who understands their context and purpose but also their idiosyncrasies and limitations.

Steele and Burrows had agreed between themselves to include the "golden showers" incident, Steele said, since it seemed to reflect a political statement about Trump's hatred for Obama and its availability as a potential weapon of blackmail, not because of its salaciousness. But Burrows objected to Steele's characterization of the act as "perverted." He believed that was subjective and imposed a value judgment that didn't belong in a client report.

As an intelligence specialist, Steele was trained to filter out disinformation and never relied on a single source for any one claim. He also took care to avoid the echo chamber effect of one source having picked up information from another source.

For Simpson, the possibility that a foreign government was seeking to influence an American presidential election was not hard to accept. He'd written at the *Journal* about Chinese efforts to help Bill Clinton win re-election, and he also knew that the FBI quietly devotes substantial counterintelligence resources to the threat in every national election. Fritsch, too, understood what Russia was capable of, having covered Russia's war on Georgia in 2008. But this was another order of magnitude, an allegation that the Russians had gotten inside a U.S. presidential campaign.

Initially, few inside Fusion knew of the Steele memoranda. Much was beyond its ability to verify. At the same time, the June 20 memo did offer a coherent explanation for the disparate data points Fusion had assembled over the past ten months pointing to a special relationship between Trump and Russia.

Fusion needed to know more.

CHAPTER SEVEN

SAY SOMETHING

WITHIN DAYS OF SENDING FUSION HIS FIRST MEMO, CHRISTO-pher Steele called Simpson to say he'd reached a startling conclusion: He needed to inform the FBI of what he had found. This was just one memorandum, but if the thrust of it was correct, Steele said, the United States and its allies were facing a potential national security emergency. He believed he had a duty to act.

Simpson was taken aback. His first thought was that Fusion's client would likely object to such a move. Steele didn't know it at the time, but the client was the Clinton campaign, whose standard-bearer was still under investigation by the FBI. It would be unusual practice for a contractor working for the Clinton campaign to turn around and send the FBI information about Trump. But from where Steele sat, his concern was security, not politics.

In any event, Simpson added, he didn't know anyone at the FBI that he could report something like this to and be believed. Steele told Simpson not to worry. He could handle it. He knew the perfect person. Simpson asked for time to mull it over.

The following day, Steele called again. This time he was even more insistent.

Simpson still didn't think the matter was of great urgency. For one, the information was quite fresh and needed more consideration. For another, the most eye-popping element of the memos was a sex story that would probably be difficult to prove or disprove. Allegations of sex tourism against Trump were not particularly surprising or significant and likely to cause nothing but trouble if they surfaced during the campaign.

Steele had a very different view. There was cause to believe that a leading candidate for president of the United States was under the sway of Russia, he told Simpson. He explained the importance of sexual *kompromat* in espionage and Russia's long history of using the practice against Western officials. He'd spent much of his career dealing with the issue. Both the U.S. and U.K. governments, he said, invest huge sums to vet high government officials to assure they're not harboring any dark secrets, sexual or otherwise, that would render them susceptible to blackmail. The alleged Trump tape Steele had heard about was exactly the sort of blackmail material that counterintelligence officials feared.

This was above Fusion's pay grade, they agreed. Steele was the national security professional. Simpson and Fritsch were former journalists. Besides, these were Steele's findings, not Fusion's, so it made sense for Steele to escalate the matter if he felt the need to.

Simpson told Steele he wouldn't object. Fritsch agreed. The reasoning went like this: The allegations outlined a criminal conspiracy involving a hostile foreign power. If the allegations turned out to be true, there was no question that the government needed to know what was happening. If they didn't prove true, probably nothing would come of it—so long as Fusion didn't involve the client or itself in the matter and risk politicizing the reporting.

Simpson and Fritsch decided not to tell Elias, the Clinton campaign's attorney, that Steele was going to the FBI. In fact, Elias had never even heard of Steele. While Elias was aware that Fusion had engaged someone outside the United States to gather information on Trump's ties to Russia, he did not ask who it was or what the person's credentials were. In this case it was better to ask forgiveness than permission, they reasoned.

The decision to keep Elias in the dark about Steele's outreach to the FBI put Fusion in a bind. In legal engagements, investigators work at the direction of attorneys and are essentially their agents. Yet Simpson and Fritsch knew there was also a competing ethical and legal obligation under the law to report a possible felony. The potential crimes outlined in Steele's memos included possible violations of the Federal Election Campaign Act, the Computer Fraud and Abuse Act, and, not least, the Espionage Act. Later on, Republicans in Congress—many of whom are lawyers and former prosecutors—would behave as if they were oblivious to this well-known legal concept.

Meanwhile, Steele made plans to go to the FBI.

His own sense of urgency was animated by the alarming nature of the intelligence, but the political calendar was also relevant. This was the end of June, and the Republican National Convention was a couple of weeks away. Once confirmed as the nominee, Trump would become eligible to receive a national security briefing from the Intelligence Community. Steele thought that community needed urgently to know—if it didn't already—that the next possible U.S. president was potentially under the sway of Russia.

In what had by then become a persistent, unsettling pattern, the newspaper headlines reinforced Steele's deep concerns. On June 17, Putin told the St. Petersburg International Economic Forum that he would "welcome" a Trump presidency, saying Trump was "ready to fully restore Russian-American relations." Three days later, Trump fired campaign manager Corey Lewandowski and handed over his duties to Manafort, who had already assumed the role of campaign chairman and chief strategist on May 19. On June 25, a hacker named Guccifer 2.0, strongly suspected of being tied to Russia, published thousands of emails stolen from the DNC.

In Washington, Simpson and Fritsch agreed they had to keep going. And Steele needed to keep working his sources, regardless of what he did with the FBI.

Understanding the quality of those sources was Fusion's first order of business. Steele believed he had enough to go to law enforcement. But Fusion knew that the minute they shared Steele's explosive reports with Elias, even verbally, they would get a lot of questions they might not be able to answer, at least right then. If they were going to share this field intelligence, they wanted to understand as best they could why Steele found it so credible. Simpson and Fritsch pressed Steele for details that would help them evaluate that.

After reviewing the first month's findings with them, Steele ran through a separate report he called a "source key" that listed and described his "sub sources"—people who had existing relationships with Orbis's sources. That key identified, sometimes by name, no fewer than seven sources for the report's shocking hotel scene. It also detailed the relationships of numerous other sources to senior people close to the Kremlin and Putin. It was an impressive roster of people in and out of government.

Steele said that one of his collectors was among the finest he had ever worked with, an individual known to U.S. intelligence and law enforcement. Neither Simpson nor Fritsch was told the name of this source, nor the source's precise whereabouts, but Steele shared enough about the person's background and access that they believed the information they planned to pass along was credible.*

But just because the source was credible did not mean everything the source produced would turn out to be true. In intelligence, as journalism, all sources merely pass along what they see, hear, or think—not all of which turns out to be correct. Eyewitnesses to a car accident routinely give strikingly different versions of how it happened. That's why news organizations require reporters to have two sources for every key claim in a story. But having two sources in intelligence is oftentimes a luxury.

Steele added that his team had identified a U.S.-based Russian American in the Trump orbit. This person purported to know a good deal about Trump's activities in Russia and the Kremlin's alleged support for the Trump campaign, and was prone to talking about it with others outside his circle. His role in the events of 2016 remains underappreciated, even today. His name was Sergei Millian, though he has had others.

Millian had popped up in Nellie Ohr's early reporting in November 2015 for his ties to Trump, but Fusion had yet to research him in depth. Within days of Steele telling Fusion his name, researchers at the firm began digging deeper into Millian, a self-promoter whose record suggested a background entirely consistent with that of some sort of state intelligence asset. A linguist by training, Millian was the head of an obscure trade group with a grandiose name, the Russian American Chamber of Commerce in the U.S.A. He had changed his name at some point in the 2000s from Siarhei Kukuts, around the time one of his associates got into legal trouble. Millian was from Belarus, a small neighboring Russian satellite state sometimes adopted as a cover for Russian operatives seeking to distance themselves from Russia proper.

Just two months earlier, Millian had boasted of his business ties to Trump and extolled Trump's virtues in an interview with a Russian-government-controlled "news" outlet, RIA Novosti, that Putin converted to a Kremlin propaganda outlet in 2013. The article carried a

---

* Steele and Burrows have vowed to never reveal the source's identity. That anonymity "is a bit of a shame, really," Steele later told friends. "This is a remarkable person with a remarkable story who deserves a medal for service to the West."

photo of Millian and Trump along with the billionaire real estate developer Jorge Pérez. Dozens of other articles regurgitated the interview across other Russian-government-controlled press outlets under headlines such as "President Trump Is Capable of Saving Ukraine and Coming to Agreement with Moscow."

Millian claimed to be working with Trump's fixer, Michael Cohen, on a variety of real estate projects. He displayed knowledge of other projects as well, including bits of information that, while public, were not well known, such as the identity of Trump's main partner in the Trump SoHo project. He also seemed to be familiar with the status of Trump's real estate ambitions in Russia and even claimed that he had helped Trump study the Moscow real estate market. Trump, he added, was "keeping Moscow in his sights and is waiting for an appropriate time" to launch a new project there. In retrospect, Millian's cryptic statement about "keeping Moscow in his sights" was eerily on target. At the same time Millian was making these comments, Trump and Cohen were in the thick of a secret project to build a giant new tower in Moscow.

It went without saying that Steele, when he met with the FBI, would be asked where his information came from and who had engaged him. Fusion expected Steele to disclose the little he then knew about his clients—that they were working for some Democrats opposed to Trump. But he would not be able to tell them that the ultimate clients were the Democratic National Committee and Hillary for America, because he didn't know that yet.

That was a big reason Fusion raised no objection to Steele going to the FBI and felt no burning need to loop Elias in on his plans. The less politics entered into Steele's discussions with the FBI, the better.

Steele, like all contractors, had signed a strict nondisclosure agreement with Fusion. But his intel had created an exceptional situation. As Simpson would tell Senate investigators a year later, "This was not considered by me to be part of the work that we were doing. . . . This was like, you know, you're driving to work and you see something happen and you call 911."

At the end of June, Steele reached out to Michael Gaeta, the veteran FBI agent he had worked with to blow the whistle on corruption in the global governing body for soccer, FIFA. Gaeta was one of the Bureau's most knowledgeable experts on Russian organized crime and understood the nexus between the Kremlin and the Mafia. He had even had some tangential dealings with Trump's world; for years, he had pursued a notorious Russian gangster known as Taiwanchik who ran his operations out of Trump Tower in New York. It was Gaeta's pursuit of Taiwanchik that first led him to Steele in 2010. Gaeta was now working at the U.S. embassy in Rome as the Bureau's legal attaché to the Italian police and security services.

Gaeta showed up in London on Tuesday, July 5. In a meeting with Steele and Burrows at the Orbis offices, near Victoria Station, Steele briefed Gaeta on both his findings and sources for his early reporting to Fusion. Gaeta reacted much the way Simpson and Fritsch had—"flabbergasted," as Steele later put it—and remarked that such matters were far above his pay grade. He thanked them for the information and said he would pass word up the ladder.

Steele told Simpson that he gave the information to a contact at the FBI, whom he didn't identify.

Neither Fusion nor Orbis knew exactly what Gaeta did with Steele's information, but James Comey later revealed that the FBI had in fact opened an investigation into the Trump campaign's possible coordination with Russia a few weeks later. As it happened, Steele met with Gaeta the day Director Comey announced an end to the FBI's Clinton email inquiry, declining to charge her but saying her conduct had been "extremely careless"—an unusual rebuke of a politician from an FBI director.

Unbeknownst to Steele or Fusion, the FBI was also getting word of possible Russian coordination with the Trump campaign from a separate track. In the wake of the hacking revelations, Australia's then-top diplomat in the U.K., Alexander Downer, reported to his own government a May 2016 meeting he'd had with Trump campaign foreign policy adviser George Papadopoulos in which Papadopoulos claimed Russia had compromising information on Clinton. After tense internal discussions about how to proceed, the Australians decided to share that information with U.S. investigators. The FBI then flew two agents to London to get the details of the conversation from Downer. This meeting, unknown to the outside world at the time, would later become another element in the bitter partisan feud over the origins of the FBI's inquiry into Russian meddling in the 2016 election. Republicans would come to insist it was Steele's dossier, which they saw as a political hit piece, that sparked the inquiry, while Democrats (and the FBI) asserted that the real trigger was a chatty junior Trump adviser running his mouth over drinks in London.

On July 7, two days after Steele and Gaeta met, another Trump foreign policy adviser engaged in an odd form of outreach to Moscow that would also soon catch the FBI's attention. Carter Page delivered an address at the city's New Economic School—a privilege that had been extended to Barack Obama in 2009 when he was a sitting U.S. president. Page was, to put it mildly, a highly unusual choice for such an honor. He was a virtual unknown in the field of international relations who had a brief and undistinguished career as an investment banker. It was a shock when Trump revealed to *The Washington Post* in March 2016 that Page was part of his foreign policy brain trust. His only previous stint in politics had been a minor role with McCain's failed presidential bid in 2008.

Page's rambling talk seemed to channel the talking points of the Kremlin, surprising Russia watchers in the foreign policy establishment and echoing remarks he had made the previous month praising Putin at a closed-door foreign policy roundtable at Blair House, across the street from the White House, for visiting Indian prime minister Narendra Modi. "Washington and other Western capitals have impeded potential progress through their often hypocritical focus on ideas such as democratization, inequality, corruption, and regime change," Page said in his remarks in Moscow. Those words must have been music to the ears of many Russians in attendance.

Political observers reacted with increasing suspicion toward Page. One *Washington Post* columnist noted that Page "has close ties to Gazprom, the Russian energy company under Putin's thumb." Russia hawks also later pointed to the speech as the moment when they became truly alarmed. "It scares me," McCain adviser David Kramer told the *Post*, foreshadowing the concern that would cause him to take dramatic action at year end.

A subsequent Steele memo, landing just as the Republican convention was getting under way in Cleveland in mid-July, reported that Page had met on the sidelines of his Moscow visit with a close Putin adviser, Igor Sechin, who was currently under U.S. sanctions. The memo said the two had discussed a quid pro quo: If a Trump administration was prepared to drop Ukraine-related sanctions, Russia had energy deals and dirt on Clinton to offer in return.

Suddenly there seemed to be a wave of Russia-related news that pointed to a close relationship between the Kremlin and the Trump camp. Political conventions are notoriously news-free zones. Yet revelations coming out of the Republican gathering exacerbated the growing fear inside Fusion and Orbis that there was something nefarious going on.

No sooner had the festivities begun on July 18 than *Washington Post* columnist Josh Rogin—who had been among the first to question Trump's weirdly consistent embrace of Putin back in March—reported that the Trump campaign had quietly intervened to gut the party's policy platform on Ukraine, removing a call for the provision of weapons to rebels fighting Russian aggression in the country. The move was a total break with GOP policy orthodoxy and notable for being the only position in the party platform that the Trump campaign sought to change. In pushing for the change, Rogin wrote, the Trump camp was "contradicting the view of almost all Republican foreign policy leaders in Washington."

This development pointed to the work of political mercenary Paul Manafort, Simpson and Fritsch suspected, and was likely a sop to the Kremlin.

That same day, *Yahoo News* reporter Michael Isikoff, whom Simpson had encouraged to investigate the Trump campaign's Russia ties, interviewed Lieutenant General Michael Flynn, a Trump adviser later to be named his first national security adviser, at the convention and asked him why he had agreed to sit next to Putin at an event the previous December celebrating the tenth anniversary of Russian state television network RT, a blatant Kremlin propaganda arm. Flustered, Flynn denied having been paid by Russia to speak at the event. That turned out to be a lie.

The constant drip, drip, drip of Trump campaign moves favorable to Russia—combined with Russia's hacking efforts and ever more frightening details coming from Steele's memos—led Simpson and Fritsch to conclude that they were on to something big, if not yet fully understood. The flurry of events suggested that their research needed to look even harder at the intersection of Trump and Russia, almost to the exclusion of all else. The Democratic National Convention in Philadelphia was due to begin July 25, and it seemed all but certain the Russians would look to make more mischief there.

Sure enough, on July 22, three days before the Democratic convention, WikiLeaks released thousands of DNC emails that were later determined to have been stolen by Russian hacking groups linked to

Russian intelligence. The dump was designed to create maximum havoc, and political reporters dutifully covered it with not much thought as to its source or purpose. The juiciest emails were the ones that showed the party brass's preference for Clinton over Bernie Sanders of Vermont. Sanders backers, convinced of a DNC plot to sabotage their candidate, were up in arms. Protests broke out decrying a rigged convention. The news dominated coverage in the days leading up to the convention, and two days later forced the resignation of DNC chairwoman Debbie Wasserman Schultz just as the party's gathering was about to begin.

Suddenly, the whispers of a Russian interference campaign to boost Trump began playing out under klieg lights on the evening news.

"Experts are telling us that Russian state actors broke into the DNC, stole these emails, and other experts are now saying that the Russians are releasing these emails for the purpose of actually helping Donald Trump," Clinton campaign manager Robby Mook told CNN's Jake Tapper in the wake of Wasserman Schultz's resignation. At the time, such comments were widely dismissed as Clinton spin.

Trump responded via Twitter early the next morning: "The new joke in town is that Russia leaked the disastrous DNC emails, which should never have been written (stupid), because Putin likes me."

This was no joke. It was time for a new plan of action.

For many months, Simpson and Fritsch had quietly assisted the media with its inquiries into Trump. Fusion's offices had become something of a public reading room for journalists who wanted to know more about Manafort, Sater, and others in Trump's orbit. Other reporters wanted Trump's bankruptcy records or the U.K. filings that showed his Scottish golf courses bleeding money. Berkowitz, by now a human encyclopedia of Trump facts, had become a go-to resource for news organizations now playing catch-up on a candidate they hadn't taken seriously.

Before now, Fusion's role with the media had been largely passive: Reporters they knew came to Fusion looking for background information or documents, which they provided. They had a big head start and were so steeped in the material that they were an easy stop for reporters looking to truncate the reporting process with meticulously sourced research they could flesh out and confirm as they pleased on their own. None of this included the information streaming in from Steele.

Much as Steele believed he needed to blow the whistle with his peers,

Simpson and Fritsch thought it was now time to become more active with the media, the people they knew best.

The combination of the work on the Trump team's odd affinity for Russia, Steele's reporting, and now the WikiLeaks dump was starting to persuade Simpson and Fritsch that the country might in fact be in the middle of a Russian active measures campaign—the kind of vicious dirty tricks operation pioneered by the KGB during the days of the Soviet Union. As one major network television reporter put it to Fritsch in an email with the subject line "Russia" on Sunday afternoon, July 24, in the wake of the WikiLeaks release: "OMG. Can we talk tomorrow? U warned me."

On July 25, Simpson and Fritsch decided to make an impromptu trip to Philadelphia, where the political and media elite were gathered for the Democratic convention. They wanted to have some discreet conversations with a few reporters to let them know they might be able to help with stories about Trump, particularly on Russia. Under the circumstances, many reporters would be looking into whether the Russians were really behind the WikiLeaks dump.

Upon arrival at Amtrak's 30th Street Station in Philadelphia, they grabbed a cab to a hotel near Rittenhouse Square. Waiting for them there, tucked in a small, round booth at the back of the lobby restaurant, were two of the most powerful editors in American journalism: *Times* executive editor Dean Baquet and his deputy in charge of investigative projects, Matthew Purdy. The paper had done some solid work on Trump in recent months but had yet to fully get out of bed when it came to the Russia angle.

Simpson knew Purdy a bit from investigative reporting conferences, and they would grab an occasional cup of coffee when Simpson was in New York. Simpson had reached out to him a few days earlier with a simple offer: He and Fritsch would be in Philly for the convention and knew a lot about Trump's fascination with Russia. *Care to get together to hear more?* Simpson said. *Sure,* Purdy wrote back, asking if he could bring his boss along. *No problem,* Simpson said.

The group exchanged pleasantries and chatted about mutual friends from Baquet's time at the *Los Angeles Times.* They then established the ground rules for the conversation. Everything Simpson and Fritsch said would be off the record. Baquet and Purdy agreed. Over the next ninety minutes the Fusion partners laid out everything they knew about Trump's ongoing flirtation with Putin's Russia—a version of the rundown they had given Elias months earlier. They parsed Trump's real estate developments and his ties to Russian organized crime. They explained how Russian money had given Trump a crucial boost coming out of bankruptcy. They laid out what they knew about Manafort's ties to Russia and his work in Ukraine on behalf of Yanukovych. They left behind no documents. Nor did they mention or discuss Steele's dossier—or even inform the *Times* that they were working with him.

The editors took handwritten notes and said their reporters would look into a number of angles Simpson and Fritsch had highlighted. The next morning, Simpson sent Purdy the public files from the court in Virginia detailing Deripaska's allegations against Manafort and the Russian billionaire's efforts to track Manafort down: Manafort had stood on the stage during Trump's acceptance of the Republican nomination, but two years earlier Virginia court records suggested he was in hiding from Deripaska. The editors asked for a follow-up meeting the next morning.

When they got together again, Simpson gave Purdy more about the Trump campaign's Russian connections. Purdy said he would put Simpson in touch with Mike McIntire, one of the paper's best investigative reporters, and that one of their best Russia reporters was already on the case: former Moscow bureau chief Steven Lee Myers, who had relocated to Washington.

They discussed how one might go about reporting the Manafort story and the likelihood that there would be information available in Ukraine from the pro-Western political coalition that took power in 2014. Simpson said there was a lot of bitterness toward Manafort in Kiev for his work propping up the corrupt Yanukovych. Purdy said they were sending one of their best Moscow-based reporters to ask around in Kiev and he'd make sure they reached out to the people involved in investigating Yanukovych's thievery. Later that day, Berkowitz sent Purdy pages of court documents outlining Manafort's work for Yanukovych and his business dealings with Russian oligarch and Putin favorite Oleg Deripaska. The *Times* published its first big story on Manafort's activities in Ukraine on July 31: "How Paul Manafort Wielded Power in Ukraine Before Advising Donald Trump." But it was datelined out of Washington and short on specifics about Manafort's financial machinations. Still, the *Times* had planted its flag. Anyone with information about Manafort's dealings in Ukraine knew whom to call.

Simpson and Fritsch met with a number of other journalists in Philadelphia during the convention as well. Chief among them was *Post* investigative reporter Tom Hamburger. The three were all *Journal* alums and friends. Simpson and Hamburger had spent years together in the Washington bureau. Hamburger was, and is, among the most seasoned, hardworking, and honorable reporters in the business. Simpson and Fritsch trusted him completely.

Hamburger, like every other reporter in Philadelphia, was wrestling with multiple reporting threads all at the same time. The WikiLeaks dump had forced every publication to devote multiple reporters to dig through the cache of emails. The Russia element was beginning to snap into focus, and Hamburger was eager to learn all he could. But he didn't have a lot of time; he was busy trying to match a *Times* story reporting that U.S. intelligence officials had concluded that Russian military intelligence was behind the DNC hack.

Still, knowing he could be trusted, Simpson decided to tell Hamburger about the Steele work on a promise that he would keep it mum. Simpson laid out the basic allegations in the first Steele report. He mentioned the alleged golden shower episode at the Ritz-Carlton but played down its significance. Hamburger reacted with shock. The information, Simpson told him, had been collected by a "senior former Western intelligence official." Hamburger was intrigued. "Can I talk to him?" he asked. "Probably not, not now anyway," Simpson told him. "But tuck that away for future reference."

While Simpson briefed Hamburger, Fritsch headed back to Washington. He was sitting in the 30th Street train station watching actress Susan Sarandon sign autographs when he got a call from an old friend who knew Carter Page from his years as a journalist in Moscow. "Carter is a climber who never really got anywhere," the friend said. "He'd be a perfect target for Russian intelligence." He said Page had been particularly interested in pursuing deals in the energy business. Interesting, Fritsch thought, in the context of Steele's report of Page's clandestine meeting with oil giant Rosneft in which the Russians allegedly dangled energy deals in return for lifting economic sanctions against Russia if Trump won the election.

The next day, Trump gave a press conference in Florida in which he trashed assessments that put the blame for the DNC hacks squarely on Russia. He then made his now famous plea. "I will tell you this: Russia, if you're listening, I hope you're able to find the thirty thousand emails that are missing," he said of the Clinton emails that had been lost from a private server she had kept at home while secretary of state, a supposed security breach that was a favorite far-right bugaboo. "I think you will probably be rewarded mightily by our press."

Five hours later, federal investigators would later reveal, hackers for Russia's military intelligence service, the GRU, launched at least fifteen spear-phishing attempts on Clinton's personal office email accounts.

Here was a candidate for president encouraging a hostile foreign power to commit espionage. Fritsch called Steele.

"Did you see what Trump just said?" Fritsch asked.

"Fucking hell," Steele replied.

Steele was becoming increasingly agitated by the accelerating revelations tying Trump to Russia. But this was too much. It had been nearly a month since his meeting in London with the FBI and he hadn't heard anything. He wanted to come to Washington to confer.

He also had a few other meetings on his agenda.

CHAPTER EIGHT

BREAKFAST AT
THE MAYFLOWER

IT WAS A SULTRY FRIDAY IN LATE JULY, TOPPING NINETY DE-grees, when Christopher Steele slipped back into Washington on a hastily arranged two-day trip. He had come to confer with Fusion and meet some of his closest contacts in government. The city was dead: It seemed everyone was at the conventions, on the hustings campaigning, or at the beach.

Steele was now sitting on fresh intel that there was a growing nervousness in the Kremlin that the political fallout from Putin's efforts to help Trump was, as his report filed the next day said, "spiralling out of control." Pundits and the press were now all over Russia and the DNC hack. The executive summary on Steele's newest memo said it all: "Extreme nervousness among TRUMP's associates as a result of negative media attention/accusations. Russians meanwhile keen to cool situation and maintain 'plausible deniability' of existing/ongoing pro-TRUMP and anti-CLINTON operations."

Three weeks had gone by since Steele's meeting with Gaeta, and there was no sign that anyone in the U.S. government was doing anything with his information. At the meeting in London, Gaeta had told Steele he didn't want to receive copies of Steele's reports, because the material was so explosive, and he needed to take instructions from his superiors. There was little doubt a report like Steele's would give heartburn to people inside the FBI in the heat of a presidential election. Steele understood that sensitivity but had a hard time understanding why no one had followed up yet. To Steele, this was an emergency that needed to be dealt with swiftly. Trump, now the Republican nominee, was due to get his first classified briefing in a matter of days.

Fusion's original deal with Orbis was a one-month engagement to end in July. Simpson asked Steele to extend that into the fall at a minimum. Simpson also wanted to brief Steele on all the other information Fusion had accumulated over the previous nine months. Steele had seen little of that work. Fusion also needed to discuss in person how to continue gathering information safely and transmit it securely back and forth across the Atlantic.

While in Washington, Steele and an Orbis colleague added another event to their schedule. Unbeknownst to Fusion, Steele had arranged to have breakfast at the Mayflower Hotel the next morning, a Saturday, with Bruce Ohr, a senior official in the Justice Department's Criminal Division. In addition to being old colleagues who had dealt with each other in government in the 2000s, Steele and Ohr had recently worked together on a National Security Council project to cultivate Russian oligarchs as sources of intelligence about Putin.

Over the years, Steele had become personal friends with Ohr and his wife, Nellie, and exchanged Christmas cards with them.

Bruce Ohr, a native of Oak Ridge, Tennessee, was the epitome of a top-level, low-profile bureaucrat with an elite education and an intellectual bent. His father and mother were immigrants who came to the United States after the Korean War. His father worked as a scientist at Oak Ridge National Laboratory, the U.S. Energy Department's largest nuclear research facility, for twenty-two years. Ohr himself earned a degree in physics from Harvard before deciding to go to Harvard Law School and joining the Justice Department. A genial and unassuming man, he had spent virtually his entire professional life pursuing some of the world's worst criminals.

"If you are in town it would be good to meet up, perhaps for breakfast tomorrow morn?" Steele wrote Ohr, offering no hint that it would be anything but a friendly get-together. "Happy to see Nellie too if she's up for it."

An expert in Russian language and history, Nellie Ohr had met Steele years earlier, during a stint working as a CIA analyst. A Harvard graduate like her husband, she was the farthest thing from a lefty partisan warrior. Nellie was a specialist in the rural history of Stalinism; her 428-page doctoral dissertation at Stanford was titled "Collective Farms and the Russian Peasant Society, 1933–1937: The Stabilization of the Kolkhoz Order." While they came across as quiet and reserved, the Ohrs were stone-cold realists when it came to Russia. As Nellie put it later in congressional testimony, "I view myself as part of a community of people who are interested in Russia, and Chris Steele was part of that community."

Steele was vaguely aware that Nellie had done some Russian media research for Fusion, while Nellie had no idea that Steele was also working for Fusion. But the breakfast would come to dog the Ohrs' careers once congressional Republicans learned of it.

Once settled in at a quiet table at the Edgar Bar & Kitchen—named for FBI Director J. Edgar Hoover—Steele eased into some of his recent findings. He described to the Ohrs how the former head of Russia's Foreign Intelligence Service, the SVR, had told a source that the Kremlin "had Donald Trump over a barrel." Steele also recounted his information about Page's meetings earlier that month with Sechin, and Manafort's business dealings with Deripaska.

After recounting some recent intelligence Orbis had received about the FSB's role in rigging doping tests in sporting competitions, Steele said he'd already provided his first two reports on the Russia-Trump ties to FBI agent Gaeta, whom Bruce Ohr knew from working together for many years on Russian cases. Simpson, he added, could provide the Justice Department with the others he'd filed.

Bruce Ohr, who knew that Steele had been a paid informant for the FBI and had provided "actionable" information about the Russians to the FBI and made significant contributions to criminal cases, was stunned. Steele hadn't given him any hint that the breakfast agenda was anything more than another collegial catch-up session. "So I think I was in a little bit of shock at that point," he recalled later.

For most of the breakfast, Nellie Ohr simply sat and listened. But in the course of the discussion, Steele mentioned that he was working with Fusion. Nellie would later call this an "aha moment"—Fusion had never told her of its work with Steele. It appears that Bruce Ohr also first learned at that breakfast that Steele was working for Fusion. Nellie said nothing about her work with Fusion.

Later that afternoon, four members of the Fusion team sat down with Steele and his associate over lunch at the Dupont Circle Hotel. They wanted to discuss various aspects of the investigation and protocols for exchanging information through encrypted channels. In retrospect, it was an odd choice of venue: Nine months earlier, the Kremlin's former propaganda chief Mikhail Lesin had been found dead of blunt force trauma in the hotel's penthouse suite. The coroner said it was a drunken accident, but Steele had provided the FBI with a report from his own sources claiming that Lesin had been beaten to death by Russian thugs in a murky Kremlin dispute over graft. It was later revealed that Lesin's hotel bill was being covered by the Justice Department, with whom he had been scheduled to meet the next day.

The talk of Lesin's mysterious demise in the heart of downtown Washington prompted them to reflect on the increasing gravity of their own situation. "It's getting pretty terrifying, isn't it?" said Steele. If Trump really was having secret dealings with the Kremlin, he said, people in the West whom the Kremlin considered to be enemies, such as Steele, should no longer assume they were welcome—or secure—in the United States. "If this guy wins, I may never be able to come to America while he's in office," he said grimly.

Late that afternoon, Steele and his colleague went to Simpson's house to kill some time before their flight back to London. Sitting around a backyard goldfish pond, Steele recounted his breakfast with the Ohrs. Simpson was surprised to learn that Nellie had been there. Simpson decided to bring him into the loop about her work. Simpson explained Nellie's role doing Russian-language research for Fusion and some of her discoveries about Sergei Millian and other Russians close to Trump. Steele was pleasantly surprised to learn she was on the team. He held Nellie in high regard.

Waiting to board his overnight flight back to London that evening at Dulles International Airport, Steele penned one of his ritual thank-you notes to the Ohrs. "Great to see you and Nellie this morning Bruce. Let's keep in touch on the substantive issue/s. Glenn is happy to speak to you on this if it would help."

Steele didn't know it at the time of his breakfast with the Ohrs, but the FBI had already woken up to connections between the Russians and the Trump campaign and started to dig into its files on Manafort and Page, both of whom the FBI knew had engaged in curious dealings with Russians for years. The FBI had already received the Papadopoulos intelligence from the Australian ambassador through the U.S. embassy in London. Steele was putting the spurs to a horse that was already running.

Indeed, as Steele was sweating it out in Simpson's backyard, FBI counterespionage chief Peter Strzok sent this text to his colleague and lover Lisa Page, a top FBI lawyer: "Hey if you discussed new case with [FBI Deputy Director Andrew McCabe] would appreciate any input/ guidance before we talk to Bill [Priestap, Strzok's boss] at 3."

Strzok had been tasked with following up on the tip from the Australians. A major new counterespionage case was under way. The timing of that text indicates that Strzok's "new case" likely was not a result of the Ohrs' breakfast that morning with Steele at the Mayflower Hotel.

Based on Bruce Ohr's testimony and other records, however, it could only have been several days, at most a week, before Ohr passed the substance of his discussions with Steele along to McCabe, Page, and Strzok.

This chronology would become important later, when Trump and his allies in Congress tried to trash the FBI's Russia investigation as an invention of Steele, Fusion, and the Clinton campaign. The FBI's Lisa Page later said that the agents working the Trump-Russia investigation hadn't seen Steele's reports until mid- to late September, but it's clear that Ohr began providing the FBI with information he'd gleaned from Steele at the Mayflower breakfast shortly afterward.

On Sunday, July 31, Steele arrived back in England, hoping Ohr would get the higher-ups at the FBI to take an interest in his information. What Steele didn't know was that Strzok was in his office at the FBI that same day, assigning a case name to the probe that would soon morph into the Trump-Russia investigation. He called it "Crossfire Hurricane." "And damn this feels momentous," he texted Lisa Page that evening, shortly before midnight.

Immediately after opening the case, Strzok and another FBI agent headed to London to interview Downer, who recounted Papadopoulos's claims for the agents. This meeting occurred outside normal diplomatic channels, to keep the inquiry quiet at the height of the campaign.

Sometime in this period—he couldn't remember precisely when— Bruce Ohr reported his conversation with Steele to McCabe at his FBI office. Lisa Page, McCabe's counsel, was there. Suddenly there was a lot of talk about Trump and Russia at the top of the FBI.

While Steele continued to plug away with his contacts in Russia and to communicate on his own with U.S. officials, Simpson and Fritsch were managing their own sprawling Trump-Russia investigation.

One priority was learning more about one of the key intermediaries between Trump and the Russians whom Steele had identified, Sergei Millian. The more Fusion pulled at his story, the odder it seemed. Address records linked him to a Soviet émigré in Florida who was the head of something called the Spiritual Diplomacy Foundation and claimed to be a religious refugee, but also said he had gone back to Russia in 1991 to conduct prayers in the Kremlin and at KGB headquarters.

Fusion's research into property records showed that many of the Trump-branded properties Millian claimed to be pushing on Russian investors were located in New York and three huge condo towers north of Miami Beach in a community called Sunny Isles Beach, a.k.a. "Little Moscow." Like Brighton Beach in Brooklyn, the area has been known to the FBI since the mid-2000s as ground zero for the Russian Mafia. That's where Fusion decided to dedicate considerable research muscle.

A look inside those buildings revealed some interesting characters. One Sunny Isles investor, Vladimir Popovyan, was a former colonel in the Russian army. Roman Sinyavsky, a realtor who had worked with Trump, was one of the first brokers to gain access to Sunny Isles in 2002. The Russian version of Sinyavsky's website said that his clients included Russian businessmen, athletes, and performers; Sinyavsky's website displayed photos of him with various VIPs and offered a hint at who might have bought Trump or Sinyavsky properties.

Social media and newspaper clips suggested that Millian was something of a self-promoter who was chatty with the press. Fusion doesn't usually interview people, so Simpson decided to alert a major television news network about Millian's ties to Trump to see if it could get Millian on camera. Simpson reached ABC News producer Matthew Mosk, a friend and former *Post* reporter, and described what Fusion had learned about Millian's work with the Trump Organization, making no mention of Steele. The Trump-Russia theme was hot, and Mosk saw the potential news value. On July 29, Millian sat down with veteran correspondent Brian Ross at ABC News for an on-camera interview with Millian.

The "Trump team," Millian explained in his Russian-inflected English, "realized that we have lots of connection with Russian investors. . . . And they needed my assistance, yes, to sell properties and some of the assets to Russian investors." He estimated that, "overall, Trump has done significant business with Russians. And the level of business amounts to hundreds of millions of dollars that he received as a result of interaction with Russian businessmen."

Ross pressed on. "So he likes Russia because there's money to be made there?"

"He likes Russia because he likes beautiful Russian ladies," Millian replied with a smirk. He also predicted that Trump "has a lot of other tricks up his sleeve" to use against Clinton.

As the interview seemed to be winding down, Ross asked Millian about his multiple names and other oddities in his background. "Because some people," Ross said, "wonder whether you are working for the Russian government secretly." Millian insisted he was not a spy, saying he was merely a real estate guy who happened to be politically connected in Russia and kept his friends in the Kremlin informed about American politics.

According to the Mueller report, the day after the interview was taped, Millian met with Trump campaign adviser Papadopoulos. They met again the following day, even as Strzok was in London trying to find out more about Papadopoulos's alleged claims that the Russians had Hillary Clinton's emails.

Millian had contacted Papadopoulos a few weeks earlier, claiming that he had "insider knowledge and direct access to the top hierarchy in Russian politics," Mueller would later find. Millian promised he could mobilize Russian immigrants to vote for Trump. A few weeks later he followed up with a Facebook message promising to "share with you a disruptive technology that might be instrumental in your political work for the campaign."

The Mueller report later concluded that Millian, a U.S. citizen otherwise happy to talk to the press, apparently fled the country once the special counsel investigation was launched. Millian spurned the Mueller team, the report said, "despite our repeated efforts to obtain an interview." His whereabouts are unknown.

On August 3, Simpson and Fritsch took the Acela train to New York for a meeting with *New Yorker* editor David Remnick and features editor Daniel Zalewski at the Condé Nast offices in 1 World Trade Center. Remnick had been a foreign correspondent in Moscow for *The Washington Post* in the late eighties and had written the Pulitzer Prize–winning book *Lenin's Tomb,* an eyewitness account of the collapse of the Soviet Union. Much as Steele thought it was time to escalate his efforts to get the attention of higher-ups in the U.S. law enforcement establishment, Fritsch and Simpson decided it might be useful to engage with a wider circle of journalists, especially those with particularly sensitive Russia antennae.

Remnick was certainly under no illusions about Putin's intentions toward the West. Much as they had with Baquet and Purdy at the *Times* the previous week, Simpson and Fritsch spent ninety minutes reviewing the myriad ties between Trump and Russia beyond what had been reported publicly. They repeated their briefing later that day for two senior editors at Reuters. Fusion left Steele out of its presentation but let on that credible sources thought Trump had been compromised by Moscow.

These were smart editors who got it. Remnick had no doubt Putin was up to no good and agreed that Trump was a perfect target for the Russian spy state. He later asked a couple of his reporters to follow up on some of Fusion's leads about Manafort and the cast of sketchy Russians orbiting Trump World. Fusion was skeptical that a magazine with a long gestation period like *The New Yorker* would commit to stories the daily papers were likely to get to first. Wire services like Reuters, meantime, had all they could do to keep up with the avalanche of news during the campaign. To Fusion, these were consciousness-raising encounters, and it was worth getting a reality check from savvy, skeptical journalists. While neither revved up coverage before the election, *The New Yorker* would later become among the most aggressive outlets in covering the Russia story.

As Simpson and Fritsch saw it, there were too many obstacles, some practical, but also failure of imagination that stopped reporters from chasing the bigger story. It was just hard to believe that Putin would invest big in Trump or dare to provoke the United States on its home turf, the thinking went. And even if you did think something like that might be true, it would be a nearly impossible story to report out before Trump inevitably lost and went back to reality television and selling frozen steaks and fake college degrees. In that context, some editors doubted the wisdom of chasing a vague set of tips about a sprawling counterintelligence story in the final weeks of a raucous presidential campaign.

Over at *The Washington Post,* Steele's allegations about Page's secret meetings with high-level officials in Moscow got an incredulous reception from the paper's Russia team. "It's bullshit. Impossible," one correspondent said to a colleague at the paper.

Simpson wasn't surprised. "No worries, I don't expect lots of people to believe it," he replied. "It is, indeed, hard to believe."

———

The Intelligence Community, as later became clear, was finally beginning to imagine the worst. The Kremlin's propaganda outlets were spewing increasingly disturbing content, including segments in early August about Clinton's supposedly debilitating secret health problems, her imminent arrest over her emails, and various other messages that appeared to echo or complement Trump campaign messaging. This rang alarm bells within the Obama administration.

In early August 2016, CIA Director John Brennan emerged from an internal intelligence review convinced that Russia had launched an audacious attack to not only hack the Clinton campaign but use the information to help Trump win the election. He said nothing publicly, but he was also worried about repeated contacts between Trump campaign officials and Russians. As he testified later to Congress, "Frequently, people who go along a treasonous path do not know they are on a treasonous path until it is too late."

On August 4, Brennan held a call with Alexander Bortnikov, the head of Russia's FSB intelligence agency, and warned him against further interference with the election. Bortnikov denied Russia's involvement, a denial Brennan later called "hogwash." The Kremlin was now officially on notice.

With President Obama's approval, Brennan then decided to brief the so-called Gang of Eight—the party leaders in Congress and the chairs and ranking members of the Senate and House intelligence committees. The group included House Speaker Paul Ryan, who was already aware of suspicions from inside his own leadership that Trump had some sort of corrupt relationship with Russia. The Republicans, led by Senate Majority Leader Mitch McConnell, were openly hostile to Brennan, accusing him of a ploy to help Clinton.

In fact, some of them appear to have already had a pretty good idea of what was going on. On June 15, the day that Guccifer 2.0 leaked internal DNC research on Trump to *Gawker* and a website called the Smoking Gun, Republican House leaders gathered privately and discussed Russia's malign activities and intentions in a meeting that was secretly recorded by someone in attendance.

In the recording, Speaker Ryan recounted a meeting he'd just had with the new prime minister of Ukraine and recited a warning he had received from the Ukrainian leader: "What Russia is doing to us, financing our populists, financing people in our governments to undo our government, you know, messing with our oil and gas energy, all the things Russia does to basically blow up our country, they're just going to roll right through us and go to the Baltics and everyone else."

Another Republican, Cathy McMorris Rodgers, then recalled a recent visit to the region. "My big takeaway from that trip was just how sophisticated the propaganda is coming out of Russia and Putin," she said.

"It's very sophisticated," Ryan agreed. "This isn't just about Ukraine."

"It's a propaganda war," Rodgers said.

"Maniacal," Ryan agreed.

Ryan's number two in the house, California representative Kevin McCarthy, then chimed in. "I'll *guarantee* you that's what it is," he said, noting that there was no question the Russians were trying to help Trump. "The Russians hacked the DNC and got the opposition research that they had on Trump," he said with a chortle. "There's two people, I think, Putin pays: Rohrabacher and Trump," he declared, referring to longtime California congressman Dana Rohrabacher. "Swear to God."

It was an extraordinary claim. But no one at the meeting, which wasn't known publicly until it was reported by the *Post* eleven months later, raised any suggestion they might want to inform the FBI of these concerns. Instead, Ryan elected to put a cork in it. The discussion, he decreed, was off the record. "No leaks!" he ordered. "What's said in the family stays in the family."

Steele's memos kept coming in at a steady pace, with three more in July that detailed Russia's offensive cyber operations, its use of WikiLeaks as a platform for hacked material, and Carter Page's activities in Russia. His sixth report landed on August 5, the day after Brennan gave his warning to the Russians. The Russians, it said, were feeling a bit like the dog that caught the ambulance. Their operation had been partially exposed, and they were pointing fingers at one another over whom was to blame for the heat now coming from Washington. Steele's report said that Kremlin chief of staff and Putin confidant Sergei Ivanov thought the U.S. operation, led by Putin spokesman Dmitry Peskov, "had gone too far in interfering with foreign affairs with their 'elephant in a china shop black PR.'" This was high-level Kremlin-speak suggesting a rift at the top over the hack.

The report said Peskov feared for his job. One week later, however, Putin instead sacked his longtime friend Ivanov. Steele's report may have misread the outcome, but it was prescient regarding turmoil at the top. To Steele, this signaled that Putin had decided to go all in on the campaign to disrupt the election and help Trump.

By now, there was a daily drumbeat of Russia-related news. On August 8, Roger Stone, the colorful pro-Trump agitator and former Manafort business partner, told a Republican conference in Florida that he had "actually communicated with [WikiLeaks leader Julian] Assange" and had intel on what WikiLeaks would dump next. The implication was that Stone knew what the Russian hackers were up to.

For reporters, and for Fusion, there was a bread-and-circuses quality to Stone's theatrics. It was hard to take seriously and easy to ignore. Dirty trickster that he was proud to be, Stone also excelled at playing the buffoon. But, like Trump, he was dangerous precisely because he was so easy to dismiss.

The Stone slapstick nearly drowned out a much more consequential bit of news that same day, one that would lead Fusion down another important research path. Late that night, *Bloomberg* filed a story from Spain about a Russian named Alexander Torshin under the headline: "Mobster or Central Banker? Spanish Cops Allege This Russian Is Both." The story described how a former senator from Putin's political party who had gone on to run the Central Bank of the Russian Federation was the subject of an investigation in Spain into money laundering by a Russian organized crime syndicate called the Taganskaya Gang. Torshin insisted in an interview with the reporter that it was all a big misunderstanding. He had high-powered friends in many countries, he insisted.

Halfway through the story, tossed in almost as an aside, was a tantalizing line: "Torshin . . . said his network of contacts extends to the United States, where he's a member of the National Rifle Association. He said he's met Republican presidential nominee Donald Trump and in May shared a dinner table with the billionaire's son, Donald Trump Jr., at the gun lobby's annual convention in Louisville, Kentucky."

Simpson circulated the story around the Fusion office first thing the next morning, highlighting that sentence.

"Wild, looks like he has been close to the NRA for many years," Berkowitz said after doing some quick digging.

One key aspect of the story made no sense, though. Supposedly, Torshin was leading a movement to put guns in the hands of ordinary Russians, which would somehow fix Russia's many problems. And yet gun ownership is tightly regulated there, far more than in the United States, and few Russians can own guns legally.

This had the appearance of a Trojan horse—a Kremlin-backed ruse to cozy up to Trump and open a back door to the Republican establishment through the NRA. That was the kind of lead Fusion could run down. The partners worked to track down a report from the Spanish prosecutor leading Operación Dirieba, the case looking at Torshin and Russian money laundering. Simpson also had extensive files on Torshin's alleged crime family, the Taganskaya Gang. Torshin had attracted attention in late 2004 for his role in supporting rigged elections designed to put Russia's favored candidate, Manafort client Viktor Yanukovych, into power in Ukraine, an election he said comported with "democratic principles and election legislation."

For Fusion, it was the beginnings of a unified-field theory of Russian venality. In sum, the Kremlin had a guerrilla army of oligarchs, spies, and gangsters—some of whom were all three—spread across the free world. They were now working in concert to destabilize the West by infiltrating and corrupting right-wing political parties and their affiliated social issue groups, like gun rights groups and the Christian right. "God, it all seems so crazy," Berkowitz said to Fritsch one afternoon.

If there was a Kremlin plot to influence Republican Party politics, it made sense that they would try to infiltrate the NRA. It would be a perfect cover for cultivating relationships with influential conservatives or even possibly funneling campaign money to Republican candidates without detection. The Russians could also use it to promote Russian small-arms exports to the United States and lobby to reverse import-export regulations imposed by the Obama administration. The NRA had publicly opposed Obama's ban on Kalashnikov imports in 2014. Torshin also was a close friend of Kalashnikov's late founder and had promoted the brand in the United States.

The Russia-NRA story would take many more months to unwind, work that took Fusion researchers well past the election.

Fusion's NRA research had barely gotten off the ground when, in mid-August, the *Times* produced the results of its latest reporting in Ukraine: "Secret Ledger in Ukraine Lists Cash for Donald Trump's Campaign Chief." Manafort had received more than $12 million working for the pro-Russia party in Ukraine. This was even wilder than what Simpson and Fritsch had suspected when they met with the *Times* brass several weeks earlier in Philadelphia. The paper had worked its sources in Kiev to track down a ledger that kept a record of the illicit payments to Manafort. Some of the records came from a muckraking former journalist in the Ukrainian parliament. In text messages, Manafort had recently claimed that "the renewed interest by reporters is being generated by the HC campaign." Trump's other defenders would make the same claim repeatedly over the next three years. In fact, while Simpson recalled mentioning the Ukrainian parliamentarian to Purdy as a source the *Times* might want to try, Fusion didn't know the lawmaker.

Manafort was unable to persuade Steve Bannon and other Trump advisers that the *Times* report was merely a groundless hit job by the Clinton campaign. Under rising pressure and scrutiny, Manafort resigned as Trump's campaign chairman five days later. On the same day, August 14, Roger Stone started messaging with Guccifer 2.0, the front for the Russian hackers who had penetrated the DNC.

The presidential campaign was now heading into the homestretch. Fusion was running flat out, and having a hard time keeping up with all the Trump-Russia angles. Each headline had the effect of making Steele's reporting that much more credible in their minds, reinforcing the sense that Trump was indeed compromised by the Russians. For voters and the press, the blur of events made it nearly impossible to spot the underlying patterns or to give each development its proper attention.

Even the FBI seemed to be having a hard time processing everything they were seeing. Early on August 11, Strzok texted Lisa Page in all caps: "OMG I CANNOT BELIEVE WE ARE SERIOUSLY LOOKING AT THESE ALLEGATIONS AND THE PERVASIVE CONNECTIONS." A moment later he added, "What the hell has happened to our country!?!?!??"

Fusion and Steele still had no idea whether the FBI was on the case. So Steele asked Simpson to share some of their combined findings with Bruce Ohr, their mutual acquaintance in the Justice Department. On August 22, Simpson and Ohr met at a Peet's Coffee near the Justice Department headquarters in Washington. The meeting lasted less than an hour. Simpson tried to fill out the picture Steele had begun to paint for Ohr three weeks earlier, describing possible intermediaries between the Russian government and the Trump campaign, including Manafort, Carter Page, and Sergei Millian. He thanked Simpson and headed back to work, making no mention of any active FBI investigation.

By the end of August, the soon-to-retire Senate minority leader, Harry Reid, had received private briefings on the Russian interference, as had other senior members of Congress, and he was frustrated with Republican reluctance to call out Russia's hostile activity. He had also learned of Russian efforts to infiltrate the computers of state election systems and was frustrated by the Obama administration's slowness to react.

Reid sent a letter to Comey calling for an investigation. The August 27 letter issued a blunt assessment of the situation: "The prospect of a hostile government actively seeking to undermine our free and fair elections represents one of the gravest threats to our democracy since the Cold War."

Many journalists wrote the letter off as partisan politicking. But at Fusion's office, ears perked up. Fusion thought it was evidence that Reid had been briefed by Brennan and probably knew a lot more than he was saying. So did Strzok, it turned out. He texted Page a link to the *Times* account of the letter, saying, "Here we go."

Polls at the end of August still showed Clinton ahead by anywhere from 4 to 9 percentage points. The prospect that Russia could tamper with voter rolls was a serious concern to Obama and his team, more so even than a bunch of leaked emails that basically confirmed what everyone knew about the DNC's distaste for Bernie Sanders. That possibility caused Obama to task Homeland Security Secretary Jeh Johnson with working with state voting officials to make sure systems were secure. Once again, the effort broke down along party lines; Republican state attorneys general said they didn't want the feds poking around in their voting systems.

By early September, Obama had decided he needed to intervene. He did so in private, a move later criticized by a frustrated Clinton campaign. The president pulled Putin aside on the sidelines of the G20 summit in Hangzhou, China, said the United States knew what Russia was up to, and warned of retaliation. Obama hinted at what retaliation might look like at a subsequent press conference, telling reporters, "Frankly, we've got more [cyber] capacity than anybody, both offensively and defensively."

The administration, in fact, had worked up a series of possible responses that included everything from leaking details of Putin's hidden wealth to booting diplomats out of the country and imposing deeper economic sanctions on Putin's cronies. But in the end, the White House thought those steps too provocative. A dogfight with Russia over election meddling could be seen as partisan in a heated election season.

Upon his return to Washington, Obama instead pushed congressional leaders for a bipartisan declaration blaming Russia for its attacks on the electoral process. The administration laid all its intel cards on the table for congressional leaders in a meeting on September 8.

The Democrats agreed. But once again, Mitch McConnell staunchly refused, going so far as to threaten that if the White House made such a declaration, he would put out his own statement accusing Obama of playing politics.

By the first week of September, it had been two months since Steele first sat down with the FBI's Gaeta in London, and a month since he met with Ohr. No one had followed up with him. Steele would ask Simpson and Fritsch again and again: Is maintaining the appearance of impartiality in this election so important to you Americans that you are willing to risk electing a Russian asset?

CHAPTER NINE

HAIL MARY TIME

THE STEADY STREAM OF FRESH RUSSIA INTELLIGENCE FROM Steele's sources fed his growing anxiety. On September 14, he sent Fusion another report, his seventh, and one that would prove to be among his most prescient. "Russians do have further 'kompromat' on CLINTON (e-mails) and considering disseminating it after Duma [legislative elections] in late September," he wrote. The stolen emails would be released through "plausibly deniable" channels, he added. Channels like WikiLeaks.

That same day, it would later emerge, Russian military intelligence officers posing as tipsters began contacting American reporters over Twitter to give them passwords to protected sections of the DCLeaks website that housed hacked DNC information. The next day, the Russians reached out to WikiLeaks to begin arranging the transfer of yet another huge cache of emails. The emails had been stolen by the Russians from the personal account of Clinton campaign chairman John Podesta.

By now, Steele had become alarmed about what he perceived to be the FBI's foot-dragging. He reached out to a mentor, Sir Andrew Wood, Britain's former ambassador to Moscow, to seek his advice and share the intelligence he had gathered. He also messaged his contact at the State Department, Jonathan Winer, to let him know he had developed disturbing information about Trump's ties to Russia. Steele asked to meet in person the next time he was in Washington.

In mid-September, Steele heard from the FBI's Gaeta via Skype.

Would Steele be willing to meet with the FBI team in Rome and share his reporting on Trump? Gaeta and Steele immediately established a secure system for transmission, and the reports began flowing. This sudden flash of interest by the FBI made it clear to Steele and Fusion that the Bureau was indeed now investigating Trump—and they had apparently picked up something that suddenly made Steele's memos seem a lot more urgent and relevant. Operation Crossfire Hurricane had finally caught up with Steele. He would go to Rome on his own dime two weeks later.

Fusion had no way of knowing how serious the FBI probe was, and warned Steele that it was doubtful anything dramatic would be done before the election, thanks to long-established Justice Department rules about refraining from any overt enforcement actions that could affect an election in the homestretch of a campaign. Steele was always annoyed by this explanation. Surely, he would say, national security trumps politics.

The Fusion team said nothing about the FBI's outreach to anyone. Simpson and Fritsch decided that if Hillary's campaign operatives got wind of a possible FBI investigation, it might be unable to resist the temptation to leak it to the press. That could compromise the investigation (by alerting the targets) and subject the FBI to political attacks from Republicans that would undermine the probe's credibility. To the Republicans, with their own history of misusing the government's legal powers to smear and punish their political opponents, that explanation later seemed impossible to believe.

Steele was encouraged by the FBI's outreach. Still, he was losing faith that the Bureau would move quickly enough to put a stop to whatever the Trump campaign and the Russians were planning.

Despite Simpson and Fritsch's skepticism, they agreed it was important to at least try to make people aware of what was happening, even if the truth about Trump and Russia only came out after the election. Sooner or later, the American national security establishment was going to have to clean up the Russia mess. And the best way to make sure the government did its job, they thought, was to involve the media as a watchdog.

Christopher Steele was about to break cover.

Fusion wanted Steele to come to Washington and meet the press, face-to-face. The idea of briefing the American media was a novel proposition for Steele, who had had little contact with reporters and eyed them skeptically. Journalists often behaved irresponsibly, he believed, and were capable of mishandling sensitive information or selling out a source for a good story. He had never confirmed to anyone that he had worked for MI6, even after he was outed in 1999, and he didn't want to start now.

Trust us, Simpson and Fritsch said. There was some risk to the strategy, for sure, but it could be managed. They would introduce him to a handful of reporters they knew and could trust to protect sources. All were seasoned national security or investigative reporters who dealt regularly with confidential whistleblowers and former intelligence and law enforcement officials.

Steele wouldn't have to mention MI6 or name a single source, they told him. His name and nationality will be off-limits.

"Do you think they'll write stories based on what I say?" Steele wanted to know.

Probably not, they said.

Much like the Justice Department's policy against taking overt investigative steps against candidates in the sixty days before an election, reporters try to begin wrapping up their investigative work on the presidential campaigns soon after Labor Day, to avoid the risk of being manipulated by one side or the other into an unfair or untrue "late hit."

The idea, Simpson told Steele, was to alert some leading journalists in the national security community to a potential crime in progress in the hope that they would investigate it, whether or not Trump won. Multiple signs pointed to active cooperation between the Trump team and Moscow. At a minimum, Putin's men were openly aiding the campaign in ways that violated U.S. law. If the two sides weren't working hand in hand, then at the very least the Russians were manipulating top aides and advisers to the Republican candidate. All of this warranted scrutiny, even if it seemed unlikely that the story would become public before Election Day. That shouldn't matter: Clinton seemed almost certain to win.

Steele flew to Washington on September 21.

Fritsch reserved two private rooms at 10 A.M. the next day at the Tabard Inn, a quiet, discreet, and charmingly shabby spot a bit removed from Washington's power corridors. The meetings were organized in one-hour sessions, with breaks staggered between the rooms to prevent journalists from bumping into one another as they came and went. The guest list included Jane Mayer of *The New Yorker*, Michael Isikoff of *Yahoo News*, Matthew Mosk of ABC News, and Eric Lichtblau and David Sanger of the *Times*. Later, the Fusion partners took Steele to the offices of *The Washington Post*, where they met with Tom Hamburger and Dana Priest. Collectively, these reporters boasted more than 150 years of experience reporting in Washington and had won virtually every award the news profession has to offer.

Fusion laid the ground rules. Steele would speak only on background, meaning any information the reporters wished to quote could only be attributed to a "former senior Western intelligence official." His name and nationality were off-limits. Fusion, they explained, had hired Steele to look into Trump's business dealings with Russia. But he had developed information along the way that pointed to a more sinister relationship, one with serious national security implications. The information was Steele's, not Fusion's. Yes, Fusion was working for a client opposed to Trump. No, Fusion would not identify that client. If that meant the reporters didn't want to hear from Steele, no problem.

The reporters all agreed to those terms. The Steele memos that would later come to be known as the dossier were not shown or given to any of the reporters.

Fusion explained Steele's background as a reliable source of intelligence to U.S. law enforcement and invited them to check his reputation with their sources. Many of the reporters wanted to know if the U.S. government was aware of what Steele had found and whether it was investigating. Not wanting to compromise the FBI's investigation, Simpson and Fritsch kept it vague: It would be fair to assume the U.S. government was aware of Steele's information, they said. Only Isikoff pressed the question aggressively, eventually squeezing out of Steele an admission that he had briefed the FBI about Carter Page and other matters.

Steele did almost all the talking. Simpson and Fritsch would interject occasionally for context and explain how Steele's conclusions jibed with what was in the public record.

In the meetings, Steele ran through his key findings. He played down the hard-to-confirm details of Trump's alleged nocturnal exploits during the Miss Universe pageant in 2013 and emphasized his reporting on Page's mysterious Moscow mission and meetings with people from the

Kremlin and Rosneft—the fattest hog in Putin's kleptocratic corporate pigsty. He noted that his sources had mentioned discussions between Page and Russian officials about Trump lifting U.S. sanctions on Russians in return for other favors. The sourcing there was particularly solid.

In a *New Yorker* article, Jane Mayer would later describe her session with Steele. "Despite Steele's generally cool manner, he seemed distraught about the Russians' role in the election. He did not distribute his dossier, provided no documentary evidence, and was so careful about guarding his sources that there was virtually no way to follow up." Mayer's published account was faithful to her real-time reaction: *Interesting, but what is the point of this if none of it can be confirmed?*

Isikoff decided to see what, if anything, he could run down with his own law enforcement sources. After verifying Steele's bona fides, he got through to a senior law enforcement official who confirmed investigative interest in Page's supposed meetings with Sechin and other Kremlin types. The day after his encounter with Steele, Isikoff published a story under the headline "U.S. Intel Officials Probe Ties Between Trump Adviser and Kremlin." The story recalled Senator Reid's blind reference to what must have been Page in his letter to Comey and reported the alleged Sechin meeting Steele had described. The story also mentioned another alleged meeting Page had with a top Kremlin official, Igor Divyekin.

Isikoff's September 23 story made a modest splash for a day or two. A few days later, Page told the *Post* that he would be taking a "leave of absence" from the Trump campaign and trashed Isikoff's story as "complete garbage." The core allegation of the story, that Page was being investigated for allegations that he had "opened up private communications with senior Russian officials—including talks about the possible lifting of economic sanctions if the Republican nominee becomes president," was later proven to be accurate by congressional investigations.

The campaign's swift moves to distance itself from Manafort and Page limited the fallout and contained the story, but at least Fusion and Steele felt satisfied that their work had helped lead to two of the Trump campaign's suspected intermediaries with the Russians being taken off the field.

"The primary objective of most counterintelligence operations is disruption, so we're not doing badly," Steele pointed out.

The following month, the Foreign Intelligence Surveillance Court approved a wiretap of Page—a fact that wouldn't emerge until well after the election. A highly redacted copy of the court's order said that Page had "established relationships with Russian government officials, including Russian intelligence officers," and that the FBI thought "the Russian government's efforts are being coordinated with Page and perhaps other individuals" tied to the Trump campaign. Still later, it came out that Russian intelligence had tried to recruit Page in 2013. The FBI had even asked him about his Russian contacts in March 2016—the month Trump introduced him to the editorial board of the *Post* as part of his foreign policy team. And this was all long before Steele had ever heard of Carter Page, much less put his name in a report.

Trump defenders would later try to advance the notion that the briefings at the Tabard Inn had led to a spate of oppo-driven stories in the final weeks of the campaign. The truth is, the story in *Yahoo News* was the only one that emerged from the Steele sessions.

After making the rounds with journalists, Steele met with longtime former State Department official Jonathan Winer in a Washington hotel and gave him a rundown of the intel he'd gathered, akin to the one he had just given reporters.

Simpson and Fritsch had known Winer for years. The lawyer and diplomat knew a lot of journalists in town, dating back to his days as an Iran-contra investigator for Senator John Kerry. He was a specialist in money laundering and transnational crime. After leaving government in 1999 for private consulting, he developed a specialty in the countries of the former Soviet Union. He met Steele soon after Orbis was founded in 2009.

Winer returned to government in 2013 at then–Secretary of State Kerry's request as special envoy for Libya. On the side, he acted as an informal pipeline between Steele and State Department official Victoria Nuland for Orbis's reporting on Russia. Again, Steele shared that work for free, in the interest of helping an ally augment its understanding of a place where good source intelligence was hard to come by, increasingly so since the shift in the Intelligence Community's focus to Islamic terror after 9/11.

Winer was stunned by Steele's Trump findings and vowed to do what he could to bring the matter to Secretary Kerry's attention. As a lawyer and veteran of many D.C. political scrapes, Winer was also sensitive to the optics of the situation: Here was a former British spy working for some former journalists who, he knew, were probably working for the Democrats.

Soon after his meeting with Steele, Winer called Fritsch and asked to talk. Winer and Fritsch live in the same neighborhood in the Washington suburbs. One evening in late September, Fritsch went to Winer's house with a copy of all the reports Steele had produced to date. Fritsch allowed Winer to read them and take notes, for the express purpose of making Kerry aware of the substance of Steele's reporting.

Winer then pulled out a document of his own for Fritsch to review. It was a report that appeared to be written by some kind of investigator, but it was sloppy and unformatted; it looked like a reporter's raw notes. Its findings, however, were explosive: They echoed Steele's own reporting that the Russian FSB spy service had tapes of Trump having sex with prostitutes in Moscow. It was now Fritsch's turn to be stunned.

This appeared to be a totally different reporting stream, providing a measure of corroboration for Steele's reporting. But was this report legitimate? It made reference to conversations with journalists, including the *Journal*'s former Moscow correspondent Alan Cullison. Was this all just hearsay or reporter gossip? There was no way to know. Winer would only say that it came from a trusted friend. Fritsch had a few suspicions about who that was. Winer had long been friends with Sidney Blumenthal, a former journalist who had gone on to work in the Clinton White House and become very close to both Bill and Hillary. Fusion knew that Blumenthal worked with a Los Angeles–based freelance journalist named Cody Shearer to generate opposition research for the Clintons. Fritsch asked if his hunch was right, but Winer would neither confirm nor deny.

When Fritsch returned to the office and described the document to his colleagues, Simpson sighed and said, "We don't want to get within a thousand miles of that." But the parallels to the dossier were admittedly intriguing. Fusion's suspicions later proved correct. Shearer was, in fact, the author of the document, and Blumenthal had indeed passed it to Winer, who also shared a copy with Steele.

Steele had no idea who Blumenthal was and had trouble accepting Fusion's warnings to him that anything the Clinton operative touched, no matter how legitimate, was destined to be branded as hopelessly partisan. Winer had explained to Steele the origin and chain of custody of the document. Even still, Steele believed the parallels to his own reporting to be potentially germane, especially since the information seemed to come from an entirely different source network.

The FBI's Gaeta had asked Steele to share *anything* he deemed potentially relevant. The Shearer memo qualified, in Steele's mind. He provided a copy of the memo to the FBI at meetings in Rome on October 3, with a handwritten note on the front—scrawled in the back of a Roman taxi—explaining his understanding that the document had been written by Shearer and that he had no knowledge of its sourcing and couldn't vouch for its veracity. Copies of the report and Steele's note were dutifully recorded in the FBI's file documenting its dealings with Steele.

Steele's Rome meeting, which took place in a secure facility, was attended by a phalanx of FBI agents, one of whom Steele already knew from the Litvinenko case. Burrows had been expected to attend but had other commitments, so Steele felt outnumbered and a bit under siege. The atmosphere was charged, the urgency now palpable. Steele and Burrows had always thought of their FBI relationship as cordial and contractual, but now Steele was being bombarded with intrusive questions and insistent requests for Orbis to gather more information on various subjects. "They were unusually demanding," he told Simpson afterwards. Steele promised to do what he could. The assumption that emerged from the meeting was that after Trump lost the election and its contract with Fusion ended, Orbis would go back to working directly for the FBI.

The session yielded an important bit of intelligence for Fusion. FBI agents surprised Steele by asking him what he knew about Trump adviser George Papadopoulos. Nothing, it turned out; none of Steele's sources had ever reported on him. Steele inferred that Papadopoulos was somehow important within the overall inquiry, but they didn't say exactly why they thought that, only that they had additional source reporting to back that up. (Downer's name wouldn't surface until much later, and the FBI didn't share it with Steele.)

This was important information in its own right, suggesting that there was an active Bureau investigation that relied on sources other than Steele. It was also a sign of the FBI's regard for Steele that it would query him regarding such an important lead.

Steele passed that important tidbit on to Simpson, who found it reassuring: The FBI had developed information that independently corroborated Steele's own reporting, and they seemed to trust him enough to run it by him.

"My understanding was that [the FBI] believed Chris at this point . . . because they had other intelligence . . . and that one of those pieces of intelligence was a human source from inside the Trump Organization," Simpson later told congressional investigators.

When Steele briefed him on what had happened at the meeting, Simpson reacted with alarm. "This is starting to scare the shit out of me," he told Steele. Once again, he felt like they were in way over their heads. There was now more reason to suspect an active conspiracy between the Russians and the Trump campaign.

Fusion knew a bit about Papadopoulos. Research analyst Berkowitz had already determined that he had made up or inflated virtually every detail of his résumé. He was like Carter Page: an overeager, gullible wannabe with access to the hierarchy of the Trump campaign. In other words, another ideal mark for Russian intelligence. What Fusion couldn't work out was why the FBI might be interested in Papadopoulos, but what they did understand now was that Steele's reporting was looking a lot more reliable.

By the time Clinton and Trump faced off in their first debate, on September 26, virtually everyone in the national security community believed that Russia had hacked the DNC. But the Obama administration's stubborn silence on the matter gave Trump the space to declare that no one really knew who had hacked his opponents. "She's saying Russia, Russia, Russia, but I don't—maybe it was," Trump told debate moderator Lester Holt. "I mean, it could be Russia, but it could also be China. It could also be lots of other people. It could also be somebody sitting on their bed that weighs four hundred pounds, okay?"

Any doubt about the identity of the culprit—at least in the real world—was soon to be removed once and for all. At about 3:30 P.M. on October 7, the Obama administration put out a statement timed to dominate the evening news cycle. "The U.S. Intelligence Community (USIC) is confident that the Russian Government directed the recent compromises of e-mails from US persons and institutions, including from US political organizations. The recent disclosures . . . are intended to interfere with the US election process."

Three and a half months after Steele's first memo raising the alarm over Russia's efforts to interfere in the November election, the U.S. government had finally stepped up and raised its own alarm, with just a month left before Election Day. The statement was notable for its lack of comment from the White House or the president, who was still worried about being seen as tipping the scales or playing politics. It was also immediately drowned out by other news.

Barely a half hour after that statement hit the wires, the *Post* dropped a bombshell. Trump had been caught on an *Access Hollywood* videotape boasting about being so famous he could hit on married women and grab them by the genitals. There was no doubt that it was Trump's voice, and the campaign didn't deny it, writing off the remarks as "locker room banter." Here was a presidential nominee boasting about assaulting women. It would have been death to any other candidate. Even Mitch McConnell and Paul Ryan were forced to express their disgust. "It is over," Fritsch declared confidently to a friend. "Trump is done." Simpson popped open a celebratory beer.

But the day's insane news cycle hadn't yet come to an end. Minutes later, WikiLeaks released the trove of emails Russia had pilfered from Clinton campaign chairman John Podesta's account. The emails themselves were largely anodyne. Good Beltway dish, to be sure, and unflattering to both Clinton and her staffers, but hardly the kind of stuff that would hold back the *Access Hollywood* tsunami. Still, the impeccable timing wasn't lost on Fusion. Outside forces were doing what they could to trample on a story doing damage to Trump. The Russians were riding to Trump's rescue.

By the third week of October, most polls still had Hillary Clinton winning by 7 points—not a blowout, but at least outside of the margin of error.

That edge was about to be destroyed.

The last four days of October would see a series of events that, taken together, amounted to the mother of all October surprises and inflicted what political insiders and many outside experts would later describe as a mortal blow to the Clinton campaign.

Barely a month earlier, FBI Director Comey had batted aside congressional queries over whether the FBI was investigating Trump campaign ties to Russia. "Our standard is we do not confirm or deny the existence of investigations," Comey told the House Judiciary Committee, "except in certain exceptional circumstances."

Comey would soon abandon that standard. An FBI investigation of former New York congressman Anthony Weiner's sexually explicit texts with an underage girl had found that his laptop contained work emails belonging to his wife, a close Clinton aide named Huma Abedin. Agents in New York alerted FBI headquarters about the Weiner laptop find and said those emails might constitute new evidence that needed to be analyzed.

So on October 28, eleven days before the election, Comey sent a letter to congressional leaders saying there was new information that obligated the FBI to effectively reopen the Clinton email probe, with no predicted end in sight. Republicans leaked the letter instantly, causing an uproar among both Democrats and Republicans, for very different reasons.

A boisterous crowd at a Trump rally that evening in Cedar Rapids, Iowa, burst into chants of "Lock her up, lock her up!" Democrats were furious. Some saw the hidden hand of Trump lawyer Rudolph Giuliani, who presumably had friends in the New York FBI office and only two days earlier had told Fox News that Trump had "a surprise or two you're going to hear about in the next two days." Senator Harry Reid accused Comey, a Republican, of springing an October surprise on Clinton while sitting on "explosive information about close ties and coordination between Donald Trump, his top advisers, and the Russian government."

The reaction from across the Atlantic was one of sheer apoplexy. Steele recalls being at a pet store buying crickets for his family's pet lizard when he heard the news. He called both Fritsch and Simpson separately, complaining that he'd been misled. The Fusion partners had assured him the FBI wouldn't do anything big in the last weeks before an election, and now Comey had weighed in to inflict damage on the Clinton campaign. And Comey had said absolutely nothing about what Steele *knew* was an ongoing FBI investigation of the Trump campaign. "Unconscionable," Steele said. "Treasonous, really." He was so fed up he didn't even bother to call Gaeta in Rome to ask him what was going on.

The Fusion partners were also alarmed. They weren't sure what Comey was up to, but it sure seemed like he was putting his thumb on the scale. "They are going to cover up the Russia investigation, aren't they?" Simpson said. Fritsch sometimes looked sideways at Simpson's conspiratorial musings. Not this time. Comey's bombshell prompted the Fusion partners to decide they needed to do what they could to expose the FBI's probe of Trump and Russia.

It was Hail Mary time.

Steele and the Fusion partners exchanged a flurry of calls over the week-end and entertained a variety of options, including bringing Steele back to the United States to speak publicly about his findings and dealings with the FBI. Perhaps a press conference on the steps of the Capitol? That was quickly ruled out as too silly and likely to backfire.

No, the best route was to find a reporter who trusted Fusion and who just might have the aggressiveness to write a story this explosive in the final days of a presidential campaign. David Corn, the Washington cor-respondent for *Mother Jones,* fit the bill. He was an old acquaintance of Simpson's and occasionally reached out to him for news leads.

After the Comey letter was released, it occurred to Simpson that Corn was an espionage buff who'd written a well-researched biography of a notorious former CIA official. He would be capable of evaluating Steele and his information much more quickly than a typical political reporter. Simpson texted him and suggested they meet.

That weekend, Corn and Simpson met at the Pain Quotidien off Du-pont Circle. Simpson described the contents of the dossier and then, when they were done eating, walked Corn back to the Fusion office and, later, let him review a copy. "This is crazy stuff," said Corn. "But how am I supposed to know if any of it is true?" Simpson explained that it had come from MI6's former lead Russianist. Corn lobbied to speak with the author as soon as possible.

The next day, October 31, Simpson arranged a three-way Skype con-versation with Steele and Corn, something Steele was reluctant to do. The ground rules were the same: You could quote him as a former senior intelligence official, but you could not identify Steele's name or national-ity. In short order, Corn satisfied himself that Steele was the real thing and that the authorities were indeed taking his information seriously. Hours later, Corn went online with his story: "A Veteran Spy Has Given the FBI Information Alleging a Russian Operation to Cultivate Donald Trump."

That story would cause the FBI to cut Steele loose as a source. Gaeta called Steele after the story ran, and the two exchanged sharp words. Steele said he had been led to believe the story wouldn't be explicit about his relationship with the FBI, adding angrily that "any misstep by Orbis or Fusion pales in comparison to what Comey did in disclosing the Hil-lary investigation."

Referring to Steele by the acronym CHS (confidential human source), the FBI typed up a form FD-1040a, titled "SOURCE CLOSING COM-MUNICATION." Steele had "confirmed to an outside third party" that he had a confidential relationship with the FBI. That relationship now appeared to be over.

At this point, Steele didn't really care. Nor did Fusion. Comey had demonstrated bad faith in publicly reviving the FBI's investigation of the Clinton email server while burying an investigation of Russia's attempts to compromise a presidential candidate. "The public absolutely needs to be made aware of this information," Steele said.

Corn's story caused a minor stir, which was disappointing but not terribly surprising. Another potentially impactful story was posted by *Slate* barely a half hour later, at 5:36 P.M., written by Washington journalist Franklin Foer.

Foer recounted the efforts of some of the country's most renowned computer scientists to analyze Internet traffic they'd stumbled on linking a computer server sitting in Trump Tower with a politically connected bank in Moscow. The headline, "Was a Trump Server Communicating with Russia?," was a bit equivocal, but the facts were intriguing, at the least. According to *Slate*, the servers appeared to be specially configured to communicate with each other, the equivalent of a hotline.

The institution in question, Alfa Bank, was known to Fusion. Its owners were billionaire oligarchs close to Putin. One owner, Petr Aven, would later testify to special counsel Robert Mueller that he "met on a quarterly basis with Putin, including . . . shortly after the U.S. presidential election." Aven made clear that he took his orders from the Kremlin: As the Mueller report later stated, "Aven said that he took these meetings seriously and understood that any suggestions or critiques that Putin made during these meetings were implicit directives, and that there would be consequences for Aven if he did not follow through."*

Foer's story lit up Twitter. It was a complicated but deeply reported tale with authoritative sourcing. At a minimum, it called for further investigation. The Clinton campaign jumped on it instantly, taking to Twitter. They had hoped the big boys would follow up and rebalance the scales, post-Comey.

Fritsch knew the story would cause heartburn for other reporters in town, particularly at the *Times* and the *Post*. Both publications had been chasing the Alfa story, but Fusion had heard that senior editors had

---

*Another Alfa owner, German Khan, is the father-in-law of Alex van der Zwaan, a former Skadden Arps lawyer who pleaded guilty to lying to Mueller. Marshall Cohen, "Dutch Lawyer Who Pleaded Guilty in Mueller Probe Serving Sentence in Pennsylvania," CNN Politics, May 9, 2018.

killed the stories as too sensitive late in the campaign, over the strenuous objections of reporters. The *Times*'s Eric Lichtblau, in particular, was rumored to be furious with *Times* executive editor Dean Baquet for spiking a story he'd been working on for months on the supposed Alfa-Trump connection.

Fusion's partners were then shocked when, at 9:14 that evening, the *Times* posted a story that stomped on both Corn's and Foer's pieces. The headline basically declared as dead an investigation the *Times* had never reported on in the first place: "Investigating Donald Trump, FBI Sees No Clear Link to Russia." Sources told the *Times* that "none of the investigations so far have found any conclusive or direct link between Mr. Trump and the Russian government." And Russian hacking was simply aimed at disrupting the election, "rather than electing Mr. Trump," the story said. The piece also took pains to dismiss *Slate*'s server story, saying that FBI officials "even chased a lead—which they ultimately came to doubt—about a possible secret channel of email communication from the Trump Organization to a Russian bank."

That was that, then. Nothing to see here. Some cable networks decided to nix segments following up on the Corn and Foer stories. Even before anyone had reported on an ongoing FBI investigation of the Republican nominee's ties to Russia, the *Times* had deemed it moot. It was a journalistic travesty and led to a stunned and glum Halloween for the Fusion team.

And yet, news of intricate interactions between the Trump team and various Russians kept piling up. The next day, *Financial Times* Moscow reporter Catherine Belton posted a story that confirmed that Fusion was not the first to question Sergei Millian's possible ties to the Kremlin. Reporting that "questions are mounting over whether Mr. Millian was one of a number of people who could have acted as intermediaries to build ties between Moscow and Mr. Trump," Belton wrote that Millian had a history of arranging for Russian government officials to visit the United States, purportedly to discuss trade deals. She wrote that the Russian intelligence services had a history of using trade promotion as a front for intelligence operations.

Most surprising, Belton reported, "Mr. Millian came on to the FBI's radar after he participated in a 2011 trip to Moscow for 50 U.S. businessmen and offered to organize further trips." The trips, she added, had come up in the course of a major FBI espionage investigation into the Washington, D.C., branch of a Russian government cultural organization suspected of acting as a front for Russia's Foreign Intelligence Service, the SVR. The whole thing was run out of the Russia House, a bar and restaurant just a block from Fusion's Washington offices.

It was too late. In the wake of the devastating *Times* article, the *Financial Times* could have shown Millian ferrying love letters between Putin and Trump and still not made any impact.

Months later, after the dossier was published, the *Times*'s public editor wrote an eye-popping column taking the paper to task for being "too timid in its decisions not to publish the material it had" about the FBI investigation of Trump and the server issue. The column even disclosed that "the F.B.I. was so serious about its investigation into the server that it asked *The Times* to delay publication." The public editor was fired not long afterwards. Later, FBI general counsel James Baker told congressional investigators that the order to step on the *Times*'s Alfa story had come from the very top, and likely involved both Comey and McCabe.

Inside the *Times*, the Halloween Special (as Simpson later called it) generated incredible acrimony. Lichtblau was angry Baquet had gutted his story. Baquet suspected that Lichtblau had dished to the public editor about the *Times*'s lack of courage. That suspicion prompted Baquet to flame Lichtblau in an email. "Eric, I hope your colleagues tear you a new asshole," for publicly airing an internal dispute over coverage decisions. Later, Baquet told his staff, "You may find me less open, less willing to invite debate, the next time we have a hard decision to make." Lichtblau would later leave the *Times*.

The FBI's probe of the Clinton emails on Weiner's laptop would, in the end, turn up nothing new. But the damage had been done. Months later, polling guru Nate Silver would declare flatly, "Hillary Clinton would probably be president if FBI Director James Comey had not sent a letter to Congress on Oct. 28."

But Comey did do that. And he did nothing to warn the American public of the FBI's deep concerns regarding possible illicit dealings between the government of the Russian Federation and the campaign of the Republican nominee for president of the United States. In fact, the FBI went out of its way to do the opposite, helping turn the *Times* story on the FBI investigating Trump's Russia ties into a piece that suggested there was nothing there.

For Simpson and Fritsch, it really did feel like a conspiracy, with a hidden hand guiding Trump into the presidency.

CHAPTER TEN

"COURAGE, FOLKS"

ELECTION DAY DAWNED WITH A REPORT FROM ACROSS THE pond, via the not-always-reliable U.K. news stable of Rupert Murdoch. At 3:55 A.M., an insomnia-stricken Fritsch flagged a purported "World Exclusive" by a gossipy online site called Heat Street, claiming that the FBI had obtained a secret warrant under the Foreign Intelligence Surveillance Act to investigate the Trump campaign's ties to Russia—an extraordinary claim, if true, because it meant the government had convinced a judge there was something there.

The report's author was an eccentric former Tory member of the U.K. Parliament named Louise Mensch, later to become notorious among journalists for her fevered but unconfirmable reports on Trump's dealings with the Russians. The explosive FISA story made barely a ripple in the United States amid the crush of Election Day voting coverage.

"It's as if the Brits are the only people who believe this," Berkowitz said.

In any event, the national security threat posed by the Kremlin's efforts to capture Trump would soon be academic, the Fusion team figured. No one was expecting a landslide for Clinton, but everyone thought she would win. In the office pool, predictions of her popular vote share ranged from 46.3 percent to 48.7 percent and from 287 to 341 electoral votes. No one picked Trump as the winner of either the popular vote or the Electoral College.

As the polls began closing in the East that evening, a few friends gathered at Simpson's house for what everyone expected would be a long evening watching the returns. Instead, most of the guests slunk off early as the bad news for Clinton began to build.

Anxiety began to overrun an all-staff email chain. At 8:41 P.M. Simpson, fearing the worst, wrote, "Courage, folks. No matter the outcome we will do what we need to do."

Brave words, but mainly liquid courage. Six hours later, the Associated Press called the race for Trump.

The Fusion team tried to sleep in, but the swamp creatures were up early the morning after. Trump's victory was barely eight hours old when the city's legions of opportunists began peppering inboxes to hail the victor—and, of course, pitch their services. "Sphere Consulting's unparalleled stable of relationships and unique business model has been built for this day," wrote one lobbyist locally famous for his aggressive billing practices. "The old prototypes of lobbying and media affairs are in the past. . . . Now we are even better positioned to help our clients."

Business wasn't really on anyone's mind at Fusion. The team had just pulled hard on the oars for fourteen months straight and done its best to catalog and expose Trump's unfitness for office. The feeling in the office was that Fusion had come up short. What if Fusion's focus on the Russia story had had the perverse effect of diverting the attention of voters from the bread-and-butter issues they might have cared about more, the ones the team had originally targeted before Russia began its play to help Trump? Issues such as Trump's promises to fix a broken immigration system he personally profited from; his business relationships with the very same foreign countries he blasted on the campaign trail for stealing American jobs; his history of business failures; his established record of lies and fabrications.

Exhausted after more than a year of breakneck work, some employees felt despondent. Their efforts hadn't echoed as loudly as they might have. Complicated information about covert Russian influence operations was just never going to penetrate the brains of an electorate ready to take a sledgehammer to the establishment.

The Russian reaction to Trump's victory, on the other hand, was euphoric. The state assembly, the Duma, burst into applause upon learning of his victory. Sergei Ryabkov, deputy foreign minister, told the Interfax news agency that Russia had been in regular contact with the Trump campaign. "We are doing this and have been doing this during the election campaign," he said, adding that many of Trump's people "have been staying in touch with Russian representatives." Trump spokeswoman

Hope Hicks claimed the Trump campaign had had "no contact with Russian officials."

At a company meeting that afternoon intended to boost morale, Simpson veered off-script and predicted darkness ahead. "We're in for a pretty mean time," he said. Fritsch said the incoming one-party government under a vindictive person like Trump might well seek to use its powers against its critics. Maybe no one would ever find out about Fusion's work, but that seemed unlikely: Trump's victory meant that questions about his ties to Russia would continue to fester, which would power Washington's rumor mill. And thanks to the *Free Beacon* engagement, a number of Republican operatives who'd eventually gotten behind Trump were aware of Fusion's early work on the issue.

A pall hung over the office. Senior research analyst Jay Bagwell seemed to be taking the Trump victory particularly hard. A lawyer and former high school history teacher from Florida who had served as an army counterintelligence agent in Afghanistan, Bagwell had seen his share of horrors. He had spent years attempting to whittle his smoking habit down to just enough butts to keep the demons at bay. "Been through some rough spots in life, this is rougher than any," Bagwell wrote to his colleagues of Trump's victory. "Didn't think this country could sink this low."

Most of the staff hadn't seen Steele's reports and had little or no knowledge of his work with the FBI. But the gestalt of the moment escaped no one: There was something deeply troubling and unexplained about Trump's ties to Russia. Those worries were now no longer academic.

The question for Fritsch and Simpson was what to do about it. They had long known that Fusion's engagement with the Clinton campaign would end on Election Day. Whatever Fusion did next, it would be doing on its own.

Though both of them would later remember this time as one of paralysis, uncertainty, and fear, Simpson and Fritsch began reaching out immediately to prominent fundraisers and philanthropists to gauge whether there would be any financial support to keep up the fight. Fritsch emailed one friend on the West Coast on November 10 to let him know Fusion would soon be passing the hat.

"When we meet in person I will describe what we did over the past year and what we want to do next," Fritsch wrote. "We are going to need a real budget from a solid group of donors who really love this country." The early responses were encouraging.

Simpson and Fritsch felt certain there was an active FBI investigation of the president-elect and thought they had a responsibility to now go beyond the steps they had taken before the election. The national security community and the public needed to understand their concerns about Trump's possible compromise.

That's where Steele's mind was, too.

In its seven-year history, Orbis had twice stepped outside its role as private consultants to warn the government of a potential national security emergency. In 2014, it went to the German government with credible information indicating that ISIS was planting operatives among Syrian refugees headed to Western Europe. In 2015, Steele and Burrows helped a former MI6 officer in China make a discreet report to the U.K. government about an attempt by Chinese intelligence to recruit him.

During the 2016 campaign, they decided to hold off on reporting their concerns about Trump and the Russians to the U.K. authorities. "The FBI was against our doing that," Steele recalled. "We made the critical decision not to go to the U.K. government unless Trump was elected."

Steele and Burrows believed, however, that Trump's election had profound implications for U.K. security and decided to alert British authorities. On November 15, Steele went to the Wimbledon home of Sir Charles Blandford Farr, chairman of the Joint Intelligence Committee, a cabinet-level position roughly equivalent to director of national intelligence in the United States. Farr was himself a former spy who had served MI6 in Afghanistan in the 1980s and was friendly with Steele and Burrows. Steele gave Farr a summary of their findings.

"He took our reporting extremely seriously," Steele recalled. After the meeting, Farr wrote an executive summary of the reporting that, he told Steele, went in early December to Andrew Parker, head of MI5, Britain's domestic security and counterintelligence agency, and to the wider cabinet.

In Steele's view, the U.K. government eventually concluded that the contents of the dossier constituted as much a political problem as a counterintelligence issue. The United States is London's closest ally. The two countries stand together on nearly every issue of international significance. There was little chance the electoral outcome would be reversed. In that context, the political class came to the conclusion that it would be unwise to make a stink about Steele's intelligence reporting with an incoming administration it would have to deal with for at least four years. That appeared to be that.

What Steele didn't know, however, was that concern about Russia's influence on the incoming administration was building fast in Washington. Two days after the election, President Obama used a ninety-minute meeting with Trump to advise his successor against the appointment of Michael Flynn as his national security adviser, a warning reported only later, after Flynn's extensive contacts with Russia's U.S. ambassador became known.

On November 18, Trump named Flynn to the post.

That same day, some three hundred leading lights of the international security community arrived in Halifax, Nova Scotia, for a three-day annual conference. Among the attendees were Senator John McCain and Sir Andrew Wood, the former U.K. ambassador to Russia and mentor to Steele. During a break, Wood pulled aside McCain advisor David Kramer. Wood said he "was aware of information that he thought I should be aware of and that Senator McCain might be interested," Kramer later recalled.

The meeting wasn't pure coincidence. Weeks earlier, Steele had taken Wood into his confidence about the information in the dossier and sought his opinion on whether he should take more aggressive action to alert authorities on both sides of the Atlantic. Prior to going to Halifax, Wood had stopped by Orbis's offices in London and discussed the idea of approaching McCain.

"You don't have a choice. At least, you don't have an honorable choice," Wood told Steele, adding that he needed to loop in "the right sort of people."

McCain, a senior senator and a renowned Russia hawk, was the ideal messenger. As the chairman of the Armed Services Committee, he had the authority to call on the FBI director. He also had the respect of leaders in both parties and the clout to make bureaucrats jump. And he wasn't afraid of contradicting his own party's leadership if he felt strongly about something. Wood didn't know him personally, however, so he decided to approach Kramer, who he knew was close to McCain.

In Halifax, Wood told Kramer about the basic findings of the dossier and that the information came from Steele, a highly credible source. This was information McCain needed to hear right away, Kramer concluded. Later that afternoon, he and Wood briefed the senator in a small breakout room used for private meetings. Wood mentioned the possibility of a video showing the president-elect in a compromising situation in a Moscow hotel suite. "The senator listened very carefully. He didn't really have much in the way of a reaction," Kramer said. McCain then "turned to me and asked me if I would go to London to meet what turned out to be Mr. Steele."

McCain recalled the encounter in his book *The Restless Wave*: "Our impromptu meeting felt charged with a strange intensity. No one wisecracked to lighten the mood. We spoke in lowered voices. The room was dimly lit, and the atmosphere was eerie." Reassured by Wood that Steele was reliable, McCain concluded that "even a remote risk that the President of the United States might be vulnerable to Russian extortion had to be investigated."

Fusion didn't learn of this meeting until days after it occurred.

The Sunday after Thanksgiving, Kramer took an overnight flight from Washington to London, using his own frequent-flier miles. He gave Wood his cellphone number and boarded the flight, knowing only that he would be met upon his arrival at Heathrow. Once on the ground, he received a text message from Steele instructing him to look for a man in a blue coat holding a copy of the *Financial Times* (a bit hokey, perhaps, but sometimes life imitates pulp fiction). Kramer located Steele outside customs. Steele then drove Kramer to his home in Farnham, about thirty miles southwest of Heathrow.

Once they had settled in the living room, Steele handed Kramer the memos Orbis had produced to date and explained that they were field intelligence collected for a private client he did not name. The sources had proven extremely reliable in the past, and their information had checked out. "He explained again that the information he gathered was what he found, not what he thought the client might want," Kramer later said. "He stressed that point to me several times."

Steele explained his sourcing and provided Kramer with sufficient background information to explain how each person was in a position to know what they knew. Simpson and Fritsch had been similarly briefed during the election; the detail about the quality of the sources significantly increased the credibility of the reporting in their minds. Steele declined to give Kramer a copy of the memos; he worried that Kramer might be searched upon reentering the United States. He also hadn't had a chance to confer with Fusion.

Steele told Kramer that he had shared his information with the FBI but that the relationship had soured, and that he understood Kramer might be in a position to get his reports to Senator McCain for the express purpose of asking FBI Director Comey what was going on. Kramer said that, yes, he represented McCain in an unofficial capacity and he believed he could do that.

After they walked through the memos, Steele took Kramer to lunch and then back to Heathrow for a 4:20 P.M. United flight back to Washington. Steele said that, once Kramer was back in the United States, he could get him a copy of the reports from Simpson, who Steele said had hired him. Kramer had spent a total of about eight hours in the U.K.

Once Kramer was airborne, Steele checked in with Simpson and told him of his hastily arranged rendezvous with Kramer. Was Kramer as close to McCain as he claimed, and could he be trusted with a copy of the dossier? Steele asked.

"Yes," Simpson replied. "I've known David for a long time. . . . He's legit." He recounted the role Kramer had played as a confidential source for *Wall Street Journal* stories in 2007 and 2008 outing Oleg Deripaska's visa problems and his Washington lobbying activities.

"David loathes Putin and his oligarchs with a passion," Simpson told Steele. "I'm not really sure what accounts for the virulence of his animosity, but it might be because he saw disturbing classified information about Deripaska and Putin when he was at State. In any event, we definitely do not need to worry about where he stands on the Russians."

Steele asked Simpson to provide a copy of the Steele memos to Kramer so that he could pass them along to McCain, who Kramer said had promised to raise them directly in a private meeting with Comey. Simpson agreed.

The next day, November 29, Kramer made his way to the Fusion office in Dupont Circle for a 5 P.M. meeting with Simpson. Fritsch was out of town, so Simpson asked Berkowitz to join.

It had already turned into another hair-raising day. That morning, Orbis sent over a fresh memo (it was continuing its work pro bono) relating some chatter out of Moscow concerning Trump's recruitment of Mitt Romney to be his secretary of state. The choice struck many as odd, not just because Romney was a vocal critic of Trump but also because he had presciently stated in 2012 that Russia "is, without question, our number-one geopolitical foe. . . . They fight every cause for the world's worst actors."

Steele contributed a disturbing new snippet:

> Speaking on November 29 2016, a senior official working at the Russian MFA reported that a rumour is currently circulating there that US President-elect TRUMP's delay in appointing a new Secretary of State is the result of an intervention by President PUTIN/the Kremlin. The latter reportedly have asked that TRUMP appoint a Russia-friendly figure to this position, who was prepared to move quickly on lifting Ukraine-related sanctions and cooperation ("security") in Syria.

Steele had asked Simpson, who, he knew, planned to meet with Kramer later in the day, to pass along the latest memo, too. (Two weeks later, Trump abruptly decided to dump Romney in favor of oil executive Rex Tillerson, whom Putin had awarded the Russian Federation's Order of Friendship in 2013.)

Simpson and Kramer did a little catching up, then Simpson walked Kramer through Fusion's research into Trump's Russia ties. He also told Kramer, as Steele had, that there were indications the FBI had an active investigation of Trump and how it appeared the Bureau had deliberately thrown the *Times* off the scent in late October (as would later prove true). Maybe, he said, someone in the FBI was trying to suppress information about Trump's relationship with the Kremlin.

Those concerns, Simpson said, had been amplified by a story written by Trump's nemesis Wayne Barrett in *The Daily Beast* just a few days before the election, disclosing the existence of a pro-Trump faction within the FBI that appeared to be working closely with longtime Trump ally Rudolph Giuliani. The report was quickly confirmed by both the *Times* and *The Guardian,* with one anonymous agent telling *The Guardian* that the FBI was "Trumpland," while Hillary Clinton was "the antichrist personified to a large swath of FBI personnel."*

---

* While Republicans on the Hill would later warp Special Agent Strzok's concern about the potential threat posed by Trump to national security into a paranoid fantasy about a partisan inside the FBI working to advance his political beliefs, the Republican committee chairs would not raise a peep—let alone hold a single hearing—about the bias against Hillary Clinton within the ranks of the FBI.

Simpson and Kramer then recalled Russia's covert attempts to cultivate influence in Washington since the mid-2000s, along with Kremlin efforts to cozy up to some of the sleazier and more powerful members of the U.S. Congress. It appeared that the Russians had initially targeted the leading figures in *both* major political parties, Simpson said, adding that there were indications that the Russians also made efforts to influence Hillary Clinton and her advisers with suspicious business propositions and generous donations to the Clinton Foundation.

Eventually, though, the Russians appeared to have tilted toward the Republicans. There were circumstantial reasons to believe that top figures in the Republican Party—not just the Trump campaign leadership— were well aware that the Russians favored their party. There were credible news reports that top congressional leaders, including Senate Majority Leader Mitch McConnell, had been warned by the Intelligence Community about Russian cyberattacks on Democrats as far back as 2015, Simpson said.*

Russia's ambitions also appeared to go beyond the United States. Simpson said Fusion's research indicated that the Russians were conducting similar operations in Europe to destabilize the European Union and may have made comparable efforts in the U.K. to sway the Brexit referendum. Steele had made similar observations to Kramer based on the work Orbis did in early 2016, Project Charlemagne. That reporting examined Russian interference in the domestic politics of France, Italy, the U.K., Turkey, and Germany. It all made sense to Kramer, who recounted Putin's prolific human rights abuses and military adventures.

"His best export to the West is corruption," Kramer said, adding that he believed Putin was capable of doing "whatever he thinks is necessary" to defeat the West.†

Kramer, who had helped drive Paul Manafort out of the McCain presidential campaign in 2008 over Manafort's suspected ties to the Rus-

---

* Ten days after Simpson and Kramer met, *The Washington Post* reported that McConnell—after receiving a classified intelligence briefing in September outlining Russian efforts to boost Trump—told the Obama administration that he would publicly dispute those findings if the White House called out Moscow. Critics would later blame McConnell for putting party before country at a critical moment before the vote.

† Days before the 2016 election, Kramer made similar comments at a McCain Institute forum. "Campaign 2016 and Russia," C-SPAN, October 27, 2016, https://www.c-span.org/video/?417539-1/discussion-focuses-campaign-2016-russia&start=1318.

sians, did not need to be persuaded that the Kremlin had now successfully infiltrated his party. Kramer recounted his own efforts to alert the
Republican political establishment to what he'd long believed was an
insidious and unrecognized threat.

Simpson then told Kramer that Fusion's research had found a pattern of connections between Trump campaign figures and the Russians
that raised questions about a possible conspiracy. Steele's memos were
field intelligence, he added, and did not include any of Fusion's own research.

At the end of the meeting, Simpson handed over the memos in a
manila folder, emphasizing the extreme sensitivity of the material and
extracting a promise to provide the documents to McCain and no one
else.

Twenty-four hours later, Kramer met with McCain in his office on
Capitol Hill. After reviewing the memoranda, McCain asked for Kram-
er's recommendation. *Take it to the directors of the FBI and the CIA,*
Kramer said. McCain said he needed some time to think about how to
approach the agencies. Kramer said he would follow up with Christian
Brose, McCain's right-hand man and staff director of the Senate Armed
Services Committee. Brose had been in Halifax with McCain.

"The allegations were disturbing, but I had no idea which if any were
true," McCain later wrote. "I could not independently verify any of it, and
so I did what any American who cares about our nation's security should
have done. I put the dossier in my office safe, called the office of the director of the FBI, Jim Comey, and asked for a meeting." McCain's friend
and colleague Lindsey Graham later admitted that he had encouraged
McCain to turn the dossier over to the FBI. Months later Graham would
feign outrage over the dossier during congressional hearings.

The next day, December 1, Fusion management converged on the San
Francisco Bay Area for a year-end retreat. Fusion's newest hire, Neil
King Jr., a friend and former *Journal* colleague, had cadged access to a
house in the Sonoma hills for the weekend. The plan was to do some
hiking, drink some wine, and begin mapping out a strategy for the
Trump era. Should they continue with political work? Should they keep
working with Steele? If so, how could they pay for it? King, Simpson,
and Fritsch were joined by Fusion partners Tom Catan, from D.C., and
Jason Felch, from Los Angeles.

Felch knew about Fusion's fifteen-month investigation of Trump. He was not, however, aware of Steele's role or his memoranda. In Sonoma, Simpson told him about Steele and his reports while hiking the hills above Geyserville on Friday morning.

As it happened, *BuzzFeed* reporter Ken Bensinger was also nearby. He and Felch were friends who both lived in Los Angeles and were veterans of the *Los Angeles Times*.

Felch had introduced Bensinger to Simpson the previous month. Bensinger was working on a book about the corruption scandals engulfing FIFA. Felch thought he might benefit from an off-the-record conversation with Simpson, who might be able to help with the FIFA story's Russia angle.

In the course of that first conversation, Bensinger said he'd discovered that the FIFA scandal actually originated with an FBI investigation into the Russian Mafia's involvement in a successful Kremlin scheme to bring the 2018 World Cup to Russia. Two of the key figures in the case, he said, were an FBI agent named Michael Gaeta and some former British spy named Christopher Steele.

That's interesting, Simpson replied. Steele hadn't shared the identity of his FBI handler in Rome with Fusion or mentioned his work with the FBI in the FIFA case. *Gaeta must be Steele's FBI contact,* Simpson figured.

From what was online, Gaeta appeared to be the real deal, a relentless pursuer of Eurasian gangsters. Simpson found a 2014 news report about Gaeta's pursuit of a Russian mobster nicknamed Taiwanchik, who was accused of trying to meddle in the 2002 Salt Lake City Olympic figure skating competition. Fusion had been investigating Taiwanchik since the spring—he was under indictment for running an illicit high-stakes gambling ring out of Trump Tower and was a fugitive from U.S. justice. Despite that, Taiwanchik had surfaced in the VIP section of Trump's Miss Universe contest in Moscow in 2013.

Bensinger had unwittingly helped Fusion figure out just how plugged into the FBI Steele really was. It would later emerge that the FBI had even paid Steele as a contractor on the FIFA case.

As the Fusion team settled in for an afternoon of wine and shuffleboard on Friday, December 2, Felch sent Bensinger a message suggesting that he tear up his plans to go home that evening; instead, he should rent a car and make the drive to Sonoma to hang with the Fusion gang. Felch didn't explain why he should make the trip; he only promised it would be worth his while.

The Fusion team figured Bensinger might be in a position to tell them how deeply the FBI had relied on Steele in the FIFA case, something Steele himself didn't want to discuss. Simpson thought that, depending on how close Bensinger was to Gaeta, he might have an outside shot at confirming the active investigation of the president-elect's Russia entanglements.

By the time Bensinger got to the house it was late, and the rest of the Fusion team soon rolled off to bed. Simpson and Bensinger stayed up, and Simpson described—off the record and in general terms—the contents of Steele's reports and Fusion's relationship with the former spy. Simpson didn't show or give Bensinger any of Steele's reports but suggested that he reach out to Steele directly, given their prior contact on the FIFA story.

Bensinger had an early flight back home to L.A. the next morning. He was gone before any of his hosts arose, armed with a good lead and a source in London he knew to be highly reliable.

The next day, Steele was sitting with Burrows in London's Garrick Club, an ornate gentlemen's retreat whose past members include Charles Dickens, H. G. Wells, and Sir Laurence Olivier. They were there to brief their old boss, Sir Richard Dearlove, former chief of MI6. Dearlove was a legendary spy, who had served in Prague and Nairobi and ran the Washington, D.C., station before rising to run the agency from 1999 to 2004. Steele and Burrows desperately wanted to escalate their findings, and Dearlove, knighted by Queen Elizabeth in 2001, would be the man to do it.

They pulled out a copy of the dossier and the spy chief read it carefully. They walked him through some of the sourcing, in the most general terms. The reporting was credible, Dearlove said. He then surprised Steele and Burrows by indicating that he was already aware that the British government had suspicions about links between Russia and members of the Trump campaign. It seemed the British government had made a political decision to not push the matter further.

This news irritated Steele while at the same time reinforcing his view that his reporting was strong. If MI6 had reason to believe that the incoming head of state of Britain's top ally could, in fact, be compromised by Moscow, he asked himself, why would the government be willing to "kick it into the long grass?"

CHAPTER ELEVEN

"I NEED TO KNOW IF ANY OF THIS IS TRUE"

ONE TOPIC ON THE AGENDA AT FUSION'S SONOMA RETREAT WAS what to do with the trove of Trump information the firm had amassed over the previous eighteen months. While Fusion's research reports to clients were proprietary, the expertise it had developed on Trump was the firm's own intellectual capital. Virtually all of the documents about Trump the firm had acquired—tens of thousands of pages by this point—were public records. And many had still never been digested by the media.

In effect, Fusion was sitting on a kind of alternative Trump presidential library, one that could be of use to those seeking to dig deeper into Trump's past and hold the incoming administration to account. What to do with it was the question.

The idea that got the most traction initially was the creation of a free online digital archive of important documents about Trump and his business associates to support the many post-election Trump-related investigative journalism ventures that were popping up almost weekly. Fritsch and Simpson even drafted a structure for what they called the Trump Archive. The plan, which they hoped to raise money to support, called for a nonpartisan research effort that would be overseen and executed by former investigative journalists. The draft plan lamented that, too often, serious work critical of Trump or the GOP is pushed through partisan channels too closely associated with the Democratic Party and its proxies. That made the work easy prey for the purveyors of alt-right spin, who then dub it fake news.

The idea wasn't short on ambition: It called for a large budget to support a website and a sustained investigative examination of Trump, his businesses, and his Russia ties. But Fritsch and Simpson worried that the plan might come under attack as appearing too partisan, too focused on Trump and not on the bigger picture of Russia's broad campaign to disrupt democratic institutions around the world. In the end, the archive project was scuttled for a different model, which Fusion didn't fully hatch until January. For the remainder of 2016, Fusion continued its Trump research as pro bono work without the financial backing of a client.

On December 7, *Time* magazine named Trump its Person of the Year and ran an accompanying interview in which he was asked about Russian election interference. "I don't believe they interfered," Trump said. "It could be Russia. It could be China. And it could be some guy in his home in New Jersey."

No, it couldn't. The swift reply came two days later with twin stories in the *Post* and the *Times* reporting that the CIA had concluded in a secret assessment that not only had Russia hacked the DNC, but it had done so with the express goal of electing Trump. The assessment, an obvious leak, had been briefed to U.S. senators.

Later that same day, the senior senator from Arizona was taking matters into his own hands. McCain went alone to FBI headquarters at the J. Edgar Hoover Building on Pennsylvania Avenue. He sat with Comey for ten minutes and handed him Steele's memoranda. Later, McCain said he "did what duty demanded I do. . . . I discharged that obligation and I would do it again. Anyone who doesn't like it can go to hell."

Kramer had kept Steele and Simpson apprised of his effort to get the dossier to Comey via McCain, and reported that McCain had gone to see Comey. McCain, according to Kramer, said he'd handed the dossier to Comey and told him simply, "I need to know if any of this is true."

Steele was grateful and hopeful that something would come of it soon. Kramer said he was happy to have helped. Burrows, Simpson, and Fritsch were skeptical that it would have any immediate impact. A sophisticated counterintelligence investigation would take months or even years to bear fruit. Trump would take office in little more than five weeks.

Little did they know, but Kramer had the same concern—and planned to push it as far as he could.

———

One problem the FBI would have in following up on McCain's query was that the Bureau was no longer in contact with Steele; it had formally severed its relationship with him after he spoke to *Mother Jones* eight days before the election.

That's where Bruce Ohr came in.

Ohr had worked closely with Steele's FBI handler, Gaeta, and other FBI counterintelligence agents for years and had already begun to brief the agency about the work of Fusion and Orbis since August.

On December 8, the day before McCain met with Comey, Ohr had reached out to Simpson to request a complete set of the Steele memos, without explaining why he wanted them. Simpson, who wrongly assumed that Ohr was acting at Steele's behest, placed a copy of the dossier on a USB thumb drive.*

Ohr and Simpson met on Saturday, December 10, at a Peet's Coffee on 11th Street, about a block from the FBI building. The temperature was barely above freezing, and downtown Washington was dead, save for a few tourists. Ohr was his usual sunny and unassuming self, displaying not the slightest hint that Operation Crossfire Hurricane, the probe of the possible compromise of the president-elect by a hostile foreign power, was ongoing.

Simpson knew not to ask too many questions. He handed over the USB stick and briefly summarized the main points of the Fusion-Steele investigations: Manafort's dealings with Oleg Deripaska; Sergei Millian, the mysterious Russian linguist with business and campaign ties to Trump; the midsummer trip to Moscow by Carter Page, who ran an obscure firm called Global Energy Capital along with a Russian "energy executive" named Sergei Yatsenko; the still unexplained computer server connection between the Trump Organization and Russia's Alfa Bank. Simpson also mentioned Trump lawyer Michael Cohen, whose importance as the keeper of Trump's darkest secrets Fusion was only beginning to fully understand.

"[Simpson] identified Michael Cohen, a lawyer in Brooklyn w. Russian (Brighton Beach) clients, as the go-between from Russia to the Trump campaign who replaced Manafort and Carter Page," Ohr wrote in his notes of the meeting.

---

*Later, when Simpson mentioned the meeting to Steele, he was surprised to learn that Steele had had nothing to do with arranging it and hadn't spoken to Ohr in months.

Simpson also related Fusion's suspicions about Russian penetration of the National Rifle Association. Ohr took it all in with a stone-faced demeanor, nodding and jotting a few notes.

Simpson knew better than to ask a law enforcement official about an ongoing investigation, but he couldn't resist one or two questions: Why would Ohr need a copy of Steele's memos? Ohr demurred, muttering something about the FBI being unwilling to share documents with the Justice Department.

That seemed like an excuse designed to play on the notorious obsession of the FBI with guarding its turf. But the real reason was probably Steele's ruptured relationship with the FBI, which meant that any Steele memos produced after November 1 would likely not have been in the Bureau's possession. It later struck Simpson that the FBI may have wanted Steele's reporting—without the bureaucratic risks of further contacts with Steele himself.

Ohr implicitly lent support for that interpretation, asking Simpson about the circumstances behind the Steele interview with *Mother Jones* that had triggered his breakup with the FBI. Simpson explained that the article hadn't been Steele's idea or initiative. In fact, Simpson explained, he had been the one who urged Steele to speak with the *Mother Jones* reporter.

"Thanks," Ohr said. "That helps."

Reading between the lines, it seemed likely to Simpson that Ohr was in a dialogue with his colleagues in the DOJ and the FBI about whether Steele could be trusted and why Steele had gone off the reservation by talking to a reporter on the eve of the election.

Before leaving, Simpson could not help but raise something that was troubling him: What would happen to the Justice Department's investigation of Trump and the Kremlin once Trump installed his own hand-picked loyalist as attorney general? Ohr seemed a little surprised that Simpson would have such a concern and seemed confident that there was little risk of a successful assault by Trump on the federal government's law enforcement institutions.

"I'm not going anywhere," he said.

After leaving Simpson, Ohr took the USB drive over to the FBI, which formally entered it into evidence and transferred the contents onto a CD-ROM "for investigative use," according to FBI records.

Over the next few days, Simpson followed up with more information for Ohr about the NRA, including a call in which he briefed Ohr on the suspicious activities in Washington of a mysterious Russian gun activist named Maria Butina, whom he flagged to Ohr as a possible undeclared Russian agent of some sort who had obtained a U.S. visa in August 2016 by registering as a college student at American University. Ohr thanked him for the info.

In the first weeks of December, desperate Trump opponents launched a last-ditch effort to block Trump from the presidency by persuading the members of the Electoral College to vote against ratifying the election. Kramer and other die-hard opponents of Trump hoped the establishment would somehow awaken to the threat Trump represented, rise up, and stop him from taking office. McCain, Kramer hoped, would use his status—war hero, former GOP presidential nominee, Russia hawk—to lead a Republican Party mutiny and recruit fellow senators Lindsey Graham and Marco Rubio to the effort. Kramer shared his ambition with Steele, who hoped it might be possible but had no way of gauging whether it was realistic or a pipe dream.

Steele's sources, meantime, continued to feed him information, which he would immediately pass on to Fusion. No one was compensating Fusion or Orbis for their work.

The final Orbis memorandum, dated December 13, described a Russian-owned company called Webzilla that had allegedly been involved in carrying out the DNC hack, Steele's sources claimed. The report alleged that the company had been pressed into service, under duress, by the FSB.

No one at Fusion had ever heard of Webzilla or its owner, a Russian with Cypriot citizenship named Alexsej Gubarev. Very quickly, Fusion researcher Laura Seago was able to locate common malware blocklists that flagged Webzilla and its parent company, XBT Holdings of Luxembourg, for leasing server space—mostly in the Netherlands—to individuals and organizations involved in malware, spam attacks, and other cybercrimes. The company operated through a vast web of shell companies stretching from Panama to the Marshall Islands.*

---

* Much later, Fritsch would have to testify on Fusion's behalf in a defamation suit Gubarev brought against *BuzzFeed* for having published the dossier. Gubarev's case was dismissed on the grounds that the *BuzzFeed* report was about a government investigation.

The final Orbis memorandum also reported that Michael Cohen met with Russians in Prague in late August under the cover of the known SVR front Rossotrudnichestvo—ostensibly a cultural organization for Russians living abroad. According to a Kremlin source, "the agenda comprised questions on how deniable cash payments were to be made to hackers who had worked in Europe under Kremlin direction against the Clinton campaign and various contingencies for covering up these operations and Moscow's secret liaison with the Trump team more generally."

The Cohen allegations would also soon spark enormous controversy and litigation. While Cohen would always deny that he'd been to such a meeting in Prague, the truth or falsity of the memo's reporting about such a meeting has never been settled.

On the morning of December 15, the Fusion team was busy looking into Rossotrudnichestvo and Webzilla when Simpson received an email from an unexpected source, Eric Lichtblau of the *Times*. The news the previous week of the Intelligence Community's conclusion that Russia not only had interfered in the U.S. election but had done so for the express purpose of helping elect Trump was causing the paper to reassess things, it seemed.

"Hey Glenn," Lichtblau wrote. "Are you available to talk again about Russia-Trump in the next day or two? We want to go back over all the stuff we looked at pre-election in light of CIA's findings and see what might be there."

The email was copied to Lichtblau's colleague Steven Lee Myers, the former *Times* Moscow bureau chief who had worked with Simpson on the Manafort stories but had been skeptical about the prospect of a Kremlin plot to help out the Trump campaign.

Lichtblau had already met Steele at the Tabard in September and seemed impressed. But five weeks later, he and Myers both had bylines on the October 31 *Times* story that did more than anything to shoot down the notion of an active U.S. investigation of Russian efforts to infiltrate or influence the Trump campaign. Now they wanted to talk. And bring along the wider *Times* national security team.

Simpson and Fritsch felt strongly that the *Times* had been played by the FBI. Their anger about the "Halloween Special" had not abated, but this wasn't a time to nurse grudges. The *Times* was one of the few news outlets in the world that had the sources to follow up on the Steele reporting and Fusion's own work.

That afternoon, Simpson and Fritsch walked down Connecticut Avenue to the *Times*'s Washington bureau, a block north of Lafayette Park. Lichtblau brought them to a large conference room. They were eventually joined by Myers, Mark Mazzetti, and the national security beat reporters Matt Apuzzo and Scott Shane.

Simpson and Fritsch brought along a copy of the Steele dossier memos—redacted to protect source identifiers and other details. Depending on how the meeting went, they were prepared to leave a copy to help inform the *Times*'s reporting.

Lichtblau opened the meeting with a preamble that essentially reprised his email: Now that Trump had been elected president, the *Times* was interested in taking a deeper look at his relationship with Russia to see whether they'd missed anything.

From across the conference table, Fritsch could see Simpson's blood pressure rising.

Simpson dislikes in-person confrontations but had a hard time containing himself. "I think first of all you need to know what an abortion of a story you guys wrote on Halloween," he said, to a stunned room. Subtlety is not Simpson's strong suit. "You fucking blew it. We told you a lot about how the FBI was investigating the Trump campaign for its ties to Russia, but your story made it sound as if they found nothing to it. We're quite sure that is wrong."

This was not the ideal way to begin a sensitive, off-the-record briefing. Fritsch winced inside, but it definitely felt good to hear that said.

Standing by his paper's story, Lichtblau calmly explained that the Halloween story reflected the best information they had at the time. Fritsch and Simpson didn't buy it, and, as later events would show, neither did Lichtblau. But in the moment, there was little else Lichtblau could say in front of his colleagues. So the Fusion delegation let it go.

Later, one *Times* reporter with direct knowledge of the Halloween story said the piece had been gutted by *Times* editors late in the day after one of the paper's reporters talked to an unnamed FBI official who was "way high up." The official planted doubts with the *Times* about the possibility that the Trump campaign might be colluding with the Kremlin. For emphasis, the *Times* reporter raised his hand high over his head. "Way high up," he repeated. In later congressional testimony, FBI general counsel James Baker confirmed that senior FBI officials had intervened.

Fritsch and Simpson spent the better part of two hours walking the

Times reporters through Trump's business entanglements with Russia and the elements of the dossier. They also walked through Fusion's role in the research. They stopped short of identifying their two anti-Trump clients, other than giving some generalities that Simpson and Fritsch had previously agreed upon: *In the beginning, there was a Republican. Then, there was a Democrat.*

As the meeting wound to a close, Mazzetti asked if they might have a copy of the Steele reports, on a strictly off-the-record basis. It was not to be reprinted, shared, or published. The Fusion partners hadn't checked with Orbis, but they agreed and passed them across the table.

Little did the two Fusion partners know, but thanks to David Kramer, awareness of the dossier around Washington was spreading—far beyond the confines of the discreet confidential encounters they'd had with the *Times*.

At McCain's behest, Kramer briefed the dossier's contents to a pair of Obama administration Russia hawks: Celeste Wallander, senior director for Russian affairs at the National Security Council, and Victoria Nuland, assistant secretary of state for Europe and Eurasian affairs. Both, Kramer later said, knew of Steele and believed his work to be credible. But Simpson and Fritsch had never met or talked with either of them—and Kramer never asked them to.

By the turn of the year, Kramer had also given copies of the dossier to a Republican congressman from Illinois whom Kramer knew and to a top aide to Speaker Paul Ryan.

All that would become known only later. At the time, Fusion had no inkling of what Kramer was doing and would have objected strongly had they known. The deal they had made with Kramer was a simple one: He could have Steele's memos for the express purpose of giving them to McCain so that he could share with Comey. Period.

As the inauguration of Trump drew closer, Kramer's evangelizing for the Steele memoranda grew ever more frenzied and would take a fateful turn when *BuzzFeed* reporter Ken Bensinger reentered the picture shortly after Christmas.

Bensinger, who was based in Los Angeles, was a resourceful and energetic reporter eager to follow up on Simpson's tips from their California conversation in hopes of netting a juicy scoop for his FIFA book, at a minimum. He had previously arranged to meet with Steele in London on January 24 to do more reporting on his book. But Bensinger now knew about Steele's reports and had grown worried that Steele might be less willing to talk by that date, which was four days after Trump was scheduled to be inaugurated.

Bensinger texted Steele on December 23 to say that something had come up and he now wanted to come earlier. Steele asked what was so urgent—couldn't it wait until after the holidays? The next day, Bensinger texted that "people" were telling him about a dossier describing how Trump had been compromised by the Kremlin.

"Can we discuss?" he asked.

Steele, who knew nothing of Fusion's chance encounter with Bensinger in Sonoma, didn't reply.

On December 29, Bensinger hopped on a flight from L.A. to Washington.

Soon thereafter, Steele got a text message from Kramer saying he had spoken to Bensinger and given him "the broad picture." Kramer later claimed he'd done so at Steele's urging; Steele disputes that.

In any event, Bensinger was now hot on the trail of the dossier, pushing all his sources—none more so than Simpson, whom Bensinger implored to give him a copy of the rumored memoranda. Failing that, could he at least show him a copy? Simpson declined. He was not going to provide such sensitive written material to a reporter he barely knew.

Undeterred, Bensinger went to meet Kramer. He had learned from an unknown source—not Fusion and not Orbis—that Kramer had a copy of the Steele memos and arranged to meet with him. The two met at the McCain Institute's deserted offices near the State Department in Foggy Bottom. The offices were closed for the week, but Kramer was there and had the dossier sitting on a table in front of him. Russia was still very much in the news. Indeed, that very same day, President Barack Obama had expelled thirty-five Russian diplomats and announced other measures in retaliation for Russia's hack attacks and election interference.

How exactly Bensinger obtained page-by-page photos of the highlighted dossier from Kramer was later the subject of some dispute. Kramer initially claimed he had not known that Bensinger would photograph the documents. "He said he wanted to read them, he asked me if I could take photos of them," Kramer testified in a defamation case. "I asked him not to. He said he was a slow reader, he wanted to read it. And so I said, you know, I got a phone call to make and I had to go to the bathroom . . . and so I left him to read for 20, 30 minutes."

Bensinger photographed the dossier with his iPhone.

In journalism and politics, the old "I left the room for twenty minutes" is a familiar ruse by sources who want plausible deniability for sharing confidential information. Kramer had been a senior government official who was accustomed to speaking to the media under a cloak of anonymity; he had done so with Simpson himself a decade earlier. Kramer likely knew exactly what he was doing—despite the explicit conditions he'd agreed to with Simpson that the memos were for Senator McCain and no one else.

Indeed, Kramer later admitted to having given a copy of the memoranda to two reporters for McClatchy newspapers in early December 2016 and eventually to at least four other news organizations.

Bensinger later testified that Kramer had explicitly allowed him to photograph the dossier with his iPhone. Kramer was forced to clarify for the record and say that he "had no objection" to Bensinger taking the report with him.

Bensinger had dinner that night with Simpson at a trendy farm-to-table restaurant on Connecticut Avenue called Buck's Fishing & Camping. Over dinner, Bensinger informed Simpson that he would no longer need to pester him for a look at the Steele memos. He said he had taken care of that with a new source—someone in Foggy Bottom. Simpson assumed that Kramer had simply briefed Bensinger on the contents and that Bensinger had left satisfied.

On New Year's Eve, Simpson flew to Mexico on vacation. That same day, Bensinger texted Steele asking if he was available to meet in London on January 3. Based on Bensinger's Christmas Eve text, Steele was concerned that he would want to talk about the Trump investigation, but he took the meeting based on Bensinger's claim that he wanted to discuss FIFA.

Ever the intelligence officer, he also wanted to find out what Bensinger had learned in Washington. At their meeting, Bensinger gave no hint that he had a copy of the dossier. When Bensinger turned the conversation to the substance of the Trump reports, Steele grew more guarded, and Bensinger left soon after.

Unbeknownst to Fusion or Steele, by then the Steele memos were all over town, thanks to Kramer. *The Wall Street Journal* had a copy. So did

NPR. And just as Steele was meeting with Bensinger in London, Kramer was meeting with Watergate legend Carl Bernstein in New York. Bernstein, who consulted for CNN, was now also in possession of a copy of the dossier. It was only a matter of time before it all burst into public view.

CHAPTER TWELVE

"YOU ARE GONNA
GET PEOPLE KILLED"

WHEN IT WAS RELEASED ON JANUARY 6, 2017, THE U.S. INTELligence Community's fourteen-page report on Russia's election meddling was stark and unambiguous. It confirmed all the worst suspicions and fears haunting Fusion and Orbis. It also marked a stunning aboutface for the United States government.

Here was the combined might of the FBI, the NSA, and the CIA saying in the clearest terms that Moscow had not just sought to undermine the public's faith in democratic elections but had "developed a clear preference for President-elect Trump" and worked to "denigrate Secretary Clinton and harm her electability." And the orders, the report said, had come directly from Vladimir Putin himself. All three agencies had "high confidence in these judgments."

These conclusions closely echoed the alarms Christopher Steele had been raising going all the way back to July 2016, six months earlier. Before the election, even after the Obama administration finally declared that the Russians were behind the DNC and other hacks, officials still didn't want to take the next step and say Moscow was trying to elect Trump—not with the vote itself still weeks away and Trump bellowing about a rigged election. But much had changed since then.

The day before the intelligence report went public, FBI Director Comey and the entire brain trust of the U.S. Intelligence Community had traveled to the White House to present their findings in person to President Obama.

After they had walked the president through the report, Director of

National Intelligence James Clapper raised another, more delicate matter. As Comey described later in his memoir, Clapper explained that there was some "additional material" that "needed to be brought to Mr. Trump's attention."

That material, Comey wrote, "had been assembled by an individual considered reliable, a former allied intelligence officer, but it had not been fully validated."

He was speaking, of course, of Steele's memos.

The intelligence chiefs told Obama about the memos' most striking allegations: Russia had material on Trump "for the possible purpose of blackmail." They said that Trump himself needed to be informed of this, as the FBI had heard that the media would soon report on the dossier's existence. When Obama was told that Comey would perform that task alone, the outgoing president shot the FBI director a look, Comey recounted, that said, "Good luck with *that*."

The next day, just hours before the release of the DNI report, the heads of the intelligence agencies traveled to Trump Tower to brief the president-elect about their findings and the Steele allegations. They slipped into the building through a side entrance. "We were sneaking in to tell him what Russia had done to try to help elect him," Comey later wrote.

When it came time for the briefings on the Steele material, the Trump aides and the Obama officials all left so Comey and Trump could talk one-on-one. The FBI director didn't get far before Trump cut him off. He dismissed it all as patently untrue, Comey said.

The release of the Intelligence Community assessment later that afternoon caused an explosion within a Washington press corps that had largely begun to move on from the Russia story. It would also reorient thinking in a way that heightened the impact of the Russia news to come. Four days later, CNN broke the dossier story, followed quickly by *BuzzFeed*'s posting of the Steele memos.

Fusion's work since the late summer of 2015 was about to go public.

The minute he saw the *BuzzFeed* story, Simpson called Bensinger and urged him to take the memos down. Bensinger said it was out of his hands, and Simpson had no real recourse other than to appeal to Bensinger's boss, Ben Smith. He, too, was unmovable. Simpson suspected that McCain adviser David Kramer had leaked the documents to Bensinger, so his next call was to Kramer, and it wasn't a polite one. Kramer, after denying to Simpson that he had leaked the memos to *BuzzFeed*, then called Bensinger and begged him to take the documents off *BuzzFeed*'s website.

"You are gonna get people killed," Kramer said.

Bensinger separately told Kramer and Simpson that he had opposed publishing the dossier, had been overruled by his editors, and only now understood why publishing the memos would put anyone in danger. He told colleagues at the time that he felt like he had just killed somebody. *BuzzFeed*'s editors said the contents of the dossier were important to readers because the government was taking the dossier seriously enough to brief Obama about it. But the obvious corollary to that was that if the information in the dossier really was being taken seriously at the highest levels of the U.S. government, and did come from high-level sources in Moscow, the Kremlin would now undoubtedly seek to hunt down the Kremlin insiders who had spilled some of its most precious secrets— acts of high treason that Putin would undoubtedly punish with the ultimate sanction.

Kramer, meanwhile, had a more parochial concern: He might now be sucked into the story himself. So he called Bensinger a second time to make sure Bensinger wouldn't finger him as the leaker. Later, when Steele confronted Kramer about whether he gave the memos to Bensinger, Kramer denied it to him, too. "Initially I panicked," Kramer later explained.

Across Washington—around the globe, really—people pulled up the dossier on their phones in elevators, in bars, and walking down the street and attempted to digest a document unlike anything they had ever seen.

The PDF consisted of photos of numbered "company intelligence" reports, each under a header marked CONFIDENTIAL/SENSITIVE SOURCE. The material was presented in bullet points, some of which someone had highlighted in yellow. Some portions were blacked out altogether. Sprawled across sixteen memos and thirty-five pages were mentions of golden showers, warnings of a wave of cyberattacks, moles within the DNC, and secret channels for moving Russian cash into the United States. The text was sprinkled with obscure names (like the "Anunak" and "Buktrap" gangs) and employed an intelligence style ("Source B asserted") that seemed exotic or confusing to many readers.

Fusion woke to a starkly different world the next morning. Their little shop above a Starbucks and a consignment store had kept such a low profile, it barely warranted a page of mentions on Google. Its deliberately barebones company website featured little more than a one-paragraph statement of purpose and an email address, which fed an inbox that was largely empty.

Within hours, that comfortable sense of anonymity went up in a puff of headlines and cable hits as the people behind the dossier became known. First to fall was the shroud around Steele.

In London, *Wall Street Journal* reporter Alan Cullison began calling Steele's friends and workmates. Kramer had given Cullison a copy of the memos in December. Now Cullison was reaching out directly to Steele, who told him he'd be willing to talk one day but that at the moment it was "too hot." Circumstances had now changed: The *Journal* seemed intent on outing Steele as the dossier's author.

Orbis and Fusion grew concerned that the media frenzy over the memos would cause outlets to override previous promises of confidentiality, raising possible safety concerns for staff. That became a near certainty on January 10 when a young reporter for the *Journal* showed up at the home of Steele's business partner, Chris Burrows, some seventy miles southwest of London and explained that he'd just traveled about ninety minutes on the U.K.'s notoriously shoddy South West service.

"You poor sod, you've been on South West Trains!" Burrows said cheerily. "You'd better come in." As they stood in his kitchen, the reporter explained his mission and brandished a copy of the Steele memos. "Is this yours?" he asked. Burrows said he could neither confirm nor deny, sent the reporter packing, and immediately phoned Steele.

Steele suspected that Kramer was the leak and phoned him to try to figure out what was happening. Kramer denied he had leaked but volunteered to try to convince the *Journal* to protect Steele's identity. "They had already made up their mind, it was clear to me, although I spent a good hour or two talking to them, explaining why this was a terrible decision on their part," Kramer later recalled.

The story went up on the *Journal*'s webpage that evening. Steele had already taken his family and fled his house, so by 10 P.M., British tabloid journalists were outside the Burrows house. By the following morning, the TV trucks were there. There was also a large media scrum camped outside the Orbis office in London, near Victoria Station.

The British government swiftly issued a so-called DSMA-Notice—an informal, voluntary request asking newspaper editors to refrain from publishing information that would be harmful to national security. "The public disclosure" of Steele's name "would put the personal security of that individual directly at risk," read the statement by secretary of the Defense and Security Media Advisory Committee. It was a noble but futile gesture.

A few of the reporters who played a role in exposing Steele would later express regrets about the personal consequences for Steele. Among the first was *BuzzFeed*'s Bensinger.

"I am sorry this has been a difficult week," he texted Steele after the *Journal* story. "I was very upset to hear you were forced to go into hiding. For what it is worth, which I suspect is not much, I have not told anyone we met and do not plan to, and have not mentioned your name to anyone."

For weeks and from his various hiding places, Steele would phone Simpson and Fritsch around 11 or 12 at night in the U.K., which was the end of the working day in Washington and around the time the cable news networks began giving their wrap-ups of the latest developments. In a hushed and often strained voice, Steele would provide vague accounts of his whereabouts and ask for a read on what was likely to happen next—always with an eye toward whether his sources might be exposed in the coming investigations. The Fusion partners would do their best to hold his hand while explaining how hard it is under the U.S. legal system to keep even sensitive information under wraps. "You can expect for every detail of our work together to become known, sooner or later," Fritsch told him one night.

"Utterly outrageous that a government can't keep its secrets," Steele replied.

Next to be exposed was the firm that hired Steele.

In Washington, Simpson received a call from *Times* reporter Scott Shane, who said he was reporting on the origin of the Steele memos and wanted to review the history confidentially. Simpson walked him through some of the basics. Simpson then mentioned that he'd heard the website Gizmodo, at that very moment, was attempting to out Fusion as the firm that had commissioned the Steele memos. *Then why not go on the record with me?* Shane asked. Simpson declined, reminding Shane that the paper had agreed to keep Fusion's identity under wraps.

As the media frenzy reached a crescendo that night, Simpson grew concerned that Shane might not keep that deal. So he called a *Times* editor he knew in New York. "I have a feeling you're getting ready to out us," he said, protesting that such a move would be improper, since Fusion had honored its end of the confidential source agreement.

You should be outing your government sources instead, Simpson argued—the ones who, it now seemed clear, had deliberately misled the paper the previous October about the seriousness of the FBI's Trump-Russia investigation. The editor gave no promises on Fusion's fate, but readers, he said, hadn't seen the last of the October episode.

At 9:17 that night, the *Times's* story hit the Web: "How a Sensational, Unverified Dossier Became a Crisis for Donald Trump." It identified Fusion as the firm that had hired Steele, and described it as a firm "sometimes hired by candidates, party organizations or donors to do political 'oppo' work."

Fritsch and Simpson were furious. The *Times* had used information about Fusion it had learned off the record and put it on the record unilaterally. Fritsch fired off a couple of angry emails to *Times* reporters that he instantly regretted. The truth was that Fusion's identity was bound to come out—and the *Times* story wasn't unfair. The heated reaction was fueled as much by an anticipatory dread of what Fusion feared could happen next: angry attacks from Trump supporters; nervous clients wanting to ditch Fusion; retribution from the incoming administration.

"We are in for some serious shit now," Fritsch told Catan that night.

Simpson locked himself in a spare bedroom and watched as his phone vibrated every few minutes with another message—a TV station in Japan, an old college friend, a Trump supporter. Scenarios for what might happen next played out in his head. One thing was for sure: Fusion would come under investigation by the Republican-controlled Congress, which had already vowed to look into the Russian attack on the election. The moment reminded Simpson of how he had felt after the death of a close friend in a plane crash: Something awful had suddenly happened, but there was nothing to do about it.

The next day, the main topic of conversation in the Simpson and Fritsch households was security. Simpson's house was less than a mile from Comet Ping Pong, the local pizzeria that had been shot up three weeks earlier by a Trump supporter who was convinced the restaurant was operating a child sex abuse dungeon tied to the Clintons. Simpson and his wife began to discuss whether their home was safe and decided to spend thousands of dollars to replace their flimsy backyard fence with a stout wooden wall seven feet high.

Given what had happened to Orbis, it seemed like a safe bet there would be camera crews outside the office the next morning.

"Hey all," Fritsch emailed the staff. "May want to telecommute tomorrow."

Trump and his aides reacted to the twin stories with a fresh geyser of lies, the start of what would become a relentless campaign by the incoming president to disavow any ties to Russia and to portray all investigators as sworn enemies out to undermine his presidency and the validity of his election.

"FAKE NEWS—A TOTAL POLITICAL WITCH HUNT!" Trump fulminated on Twitter at 8:19 P.M. The next morning: "Russia has never tried to use leverage over me. I HAVE NOTHING TO DO WITH RUSSIA - NO DEALS, NO LOANS, NO NOTHING!" To Fusion, this seemed like an instant rival to "I am not a crook" and "I did not have sexual relations with that woman" in the pantheon of presidential lies.

Then Trump accused the intelligence agencies of leaking the information against him. "Are we living in Nazi Germany?" he asked.

The great counteroffensive was under way.

Within hours, wild theories about the provenance and true purpose of the dossier began to proliferate. As they spread, these theories would help feed an increasingly elaborate Trump defense designed to convince the public—or at least his supporters—that there had been no Russian effort to aid the candidate and no attempt by the Trump campaign to court Russian support. It was all a partisan political operation to undermine his presidency.

On the day after those stories broke, no one on staff had taken up Fritsch's offer to work from home. Instead, the entire Fusion team gathered around the big screen in the office as Trump took to a podium at Trump Tower to tear into the dossier and to compare those who reported on it to Nazis.

Trump hadn't taken questions from the press for five months, so the hunger to attend his first presser as president-elect was intense—and all the more so in the wake of the dossier news. Cameramen and reporters had started lining up outside Trump Tower at 4 A.M., seven hours before Trump spoke.

Trump spokesman Sean Spicer got things started, blaming the media for "this political witch hunt," even though the mainstream media that conservatives so detest had done little to trigger the controversy. Trump minced no words when he took to the microphones. A cabal of enemies had conspired to take him down. "It was a group of opponents that got together—sick people—and they put that crap together," he said.

He claimed to have no involvement with Russia whatsoever. "I have no deals, I have no loans, and I have no dealings," he said. Later it would become known that he had been negotiating a deal for a hotel complex in Moscow only months earlier.

As for the allegations of Russian hacking, yes, he did think Russia was involved. "But I think we also get hacked by other countries and other people," he said. On top of that, the DNC had defended its systems poorly and "was totally open to be hacked."

The counter-narrative that Trump and his allies would later make their main pushback against the Russia story was beginning to fall into place. In Trump's version, he was the victim of a diabolical plot—a witch hunt!—that began with Fusion and the Steele dossier and then found enthusiastic help from enemies within the intelligence agencies and the rest of the federal government.

Trump had spent months during the final stage of the campaign warning that the election could be rigged. If he lost, it would be because the system had conspired against him. Now, even in victory, just days from inauguration, he saw similar sinister forces at play. No matter what the facts, his enemies were out to get him.

Never mind that almost none of the dossier's assertions had made their way into the public eye before Election Day. Its findings in no way impacted the election itself, unlike Comey's handling of the Hillary Clinton email investigation and the multitude of leaks and dirty tricks perpetuated by Russian hackers and bots—later determined to be the most aggressive foreign attempt in modern U.S. history to swing a national election. In the critical final days before the election, voters were swamped with headlines about Hillary's emails and FBI-fed suspicions of wrongdoing by her and her campaign team. Hardly a word was said about an active FBI counterintelligence investigation of the Trump campaign's many ties to Russia.

And yet, in the telling of the president-elect and his defenders, the dossier and its enablers were now part of a giant conspiracy to delegitimize and undermine a presidency that even Trump himself doubted would ever come to pass. Fusion, still bound by its confidentiality obligations to its clients, made no attempt to respond to these increasingly wild theories and allegations.

Fusion's skimpy webpage got its first surge of traffic in the hours after the *Times* piece. Soon, its general email address, info@fusiongps.com, would become a portal to a dark world, vibrating to whatever strange and alarming things were happening out there beyond Fusion's walls. If Trump or one of his lieutenants let it rip, or Sean Hannity spewed some conspiracy theory about the dossier on Fox News, the mailbox would fill with invective aping those remarks, often with a few threats thrown in.

"I hope you get caught up in the Steele operation and they take you all down . . . and out," said the first hate-mail message, received in the early morning of January 12. The sender, from Plantersville, Texas, signed off, indecipherably, with this query: "Why did WTC7 fall down????!!!!!!" One Fusion hater correctly guessed Fritsch's email address. "How about you stop being a treasonous pig?" he wrote. "Hillary Clinton is a criminal and you back her? Treason's punishment is death and the war is coming scumbag." Fusion reported that one to the police. There were frantic messages from cable news producers looking to get in touch, requests for comment from various reporters, and offers of help from old acquaintances.

The next day, January 13, Britain's *Daily Mail* ran a sensationalist piece about Fusion under the headline: "Meet the espionage firm which ordered Trump 'dirty dossier'—a secretive D.C. firm which has aided Planned Parenthood and attacked Mitt Romney's friends."

The reporter who wrote the article had been in Fusion's office more than a year earlier asking for help with stories. The article was accompanied by three vaguely sinister snapshots of Simpson, Fritsch, and their partner Tom Catan. More helpfully, it also included a photo of the squat glass tower across the street from Fusion's office, which was described as Fusion headquarters; in fact, it was the building where *BuzzFeed* has its D.C. office. That would feed the conspiracy theorists while at least keeping the crazies looking in the wrong direction.

That same day, *Forbes* published one of the first pieces attempting to debunk the dossier, written by a seventy-six-year-old former economist at Stanford's Hoover Institution named Paul Roderick Gregory. Gregory described himself as a Russian expert who had traveled there "close to one hundred times," he wrote. "I sort of know how these things work."

His judgment? "I can say that the dossier itself was compiled by a Russian, whose command of English is far from perfect . . . a Russian trained in the KGB tradition." This theory that Steele had been duped by the Russians—or, in this case, had simply passed along a Russian document wholesale—would have many progeny in the months ahead. Gregory's only known qualifications were that he himself was the son of a Russian immigrant and had taken Russian language lessons from the wife of JFK assassin Lee Harvey Oswald.

William Browder, still irked over his loss in the Prevezon subpoena battle, was also quick to jump on the "disinformation" bandwagon. In one interview a couple of weeks after Fusion was outed, Browder accused Simpson of "working with a Russian spy" and "spreading knowingly false information based on payments from the Russian government." In another interview, with the right-wing website *The Daily Caller,* Browder called Simpson "a professional smear campaigner."

The vitriol from the far right was aided by a spate of articles that began appearing about Steele's long-standing relationship with the FBI and his role in the DOJ's FIFA corruption investigations. Simpson and Fritsch hoped some of that reporting would validate Steele's credentials as a legitimate law enforcement source and someone who had helped expose Kremlin-led corruption. But to the conspiracy-minded, the information only served to fuel suspicions that the FBI was the puppet of Steele and Democratic dirty tricksters.

The dossier's release coincided with a surge in aggressive reporting on Trump's Russia entanglements from a variety of serious journalists. The morning after Trump's first presser, *Post* columnist David Ignatius dropped a bomb about retired general Michael Flynn, Trump's pick for national security adviser: "According to a senior U.S. government official," Ignatius reported, "Flynn phoned Russian Ambassador Sergey Kislyak several times on Dec. 29 [2016], the day the Obama administration announced the expulsion of 35 Russian officials as well as other measures in retaliation for the hacking."

Flynn had been holding secret talks with the Russian ambassador to discuss dropping U.S. sanctions against Russia, and the FBI had overheard the secret talks because it was taping Kislyak's phone calls. Flynn swiftly assured Vice President–elect Mike Pence that no such conversation ever happened, a lie that would lead to Flynn's resignation a month later.

The day after the Ignatius column, the Senate Intelligence Committee announced it would open an investigation into the 2016 election, "including any intelligence regarding links between Russia and individuals associated with political campaigns."

Trump's attempts to squelch the Russia controversy did not get much help from Putin, who blasted the Steele memos in his own press conference a few days later as "obvious fabrications" but then mischievously undermined his own denial by bragging about the prowess of Russian prostitutes. "I find it hard to believe that he rushed to some hotel to meet girls of loose morals—although ours are undoubtedly the best in the world," he said. It was vintage Putin.

Representative Devin Nunes of California, who served on Trump's transition team, would soon use his chairmanship of the House Intelligence Committee to try to gut the inquiries into Trump's Russia ties and to create multiple diversionary smoke screens. But days after the dossier leaked, he shrugged, saying it "wouldn't be news" to know Russians were seeking to spread material to smear Hillary Clinton. Any ties between Russia and the Trump campaign, though, would be "hard to believe."

The resignation of Trump's national security adviser, Michael Flynn, on February 13, 2017, was a seminal moment in the early days of the Russia scandal, seeming to support the Steele dossier's allegations of surreptitious dealings between the Trump camp and the Russians. But it also opened a new avenue of attack for Trump's defenders, who quickly blamed his downfall not on Flynn's own reckless actions but on pernicious leaks by U.S. intelligence.

Flynn had met repeatedly with various Russian officials, and held multiple conversations about the lifting of Russian sanctions with Ambassador Kislyak in the weeks after Trump's win in November. Compounding his foolishness, he then lied about the content of those discussions to FBI investigators. U.S. intelligence officials knew the contents of several Flynn phone conversations with Kislyak because they had eavesdropped on those calls, a fact *The Washington Post* broke four days before Flynn stepped down.

Those disclosures rocked Washington and pulled the camera away from Fusion and the dossier. But instead of showing alarm over Flynn's actions, Trump allies such as Nunes turned their fire instead on the national security agencies, demanding to know how the information had become public and again hinting that Democrats working deep inside the government were out to get the president. Trump took the same line, tweeting that "the real story here is why are there so many illegal leaks coming out of Washington." Old hands recognized it as straight out of Richard Nixon's Watergate playbook.

Two days after the Flynn resignation, everyone at Fusion again huddled around the big-screen TV on the wall as Trump dismissed as "a ruse" any suggestion he or his team had ties to Russia. It was his first solo White House press conference, and he began by unspooling a long list of the highlights of his first few weeks in office—record highs in the stock market, rising business confidence. Companies, he claimed, were already moving factories back to the United States. "I don't think there's ever been a president elected who, in this short period of time, has done what we've done," he said. He was just over three weeks into his presidency.

Then he laid into the news outlets who were following and reporting on the Russia story. Something had to be done about it. The media had it all wrong. Trump was the real victim. "The level of dishonesty is out of control," he said. Once his opening rant wound down, Trump was swamped by a volley of Russia questions from the assembled press corps. The first question: "Did you fire Mike Flynn?" Again, the problem for Trump wasn't Flynn or any of his other aides who appeared to have sought counsel from the Russians or even offered assistance in return. No, the problem was that someone from the inside had leaked tidbits about all this to the press. "It's an illegal process, and the press should be ashamed of themselves," he said.

On the bigger questions, he couldn't have been more emphatic. "I have nothing to do with Russia. To the best of my knowledge no person that I deal with does," he said as reporters kept pushing on the allegations. Ever gifted in the art of the counterattack, Trump soon began lobbing back his own allegations. They were clearly flimsy (Paul Manafort "said that he has absolutely nothing to do and never has with Russia") and stirred incredulity ("absolutely crazy," said Shepard Smith on Fox News) and immediate fact-checks ("That's not exactly true," *USA Today* observed), but they adroitly fed the GOP hunger for a counter-narrative.

By March 1, both the Senate and House intelligence committees had launched inquiries into Russian interference in the 2016 election. The next day, Trump's attorney general, Jeff Sessions, recused himself from any involvement in DOJ's Russia inquiries. He failed, in response to a direct question about the subject at his Senate confirmation hearing, to disclose two meetings of his own with Russian ambassador Kislyak.

Two days later, Trump opened yet another front in the Republican counterattack.

"Just found out that Obama had my 'wires tapped' in Trump Tower just before the victory. Nothing found. This is McCarthyism!" the president tweeted.

During Watergate, Richard Nixon and his allies also effectively deployed the "witch hunt" defense. Time and again they blamed the growing furor on a cabal of snobby East Coast reporters and pernicious anti-Nixon leakers from within the administration. Many prominent Republicans eagerly echoed those charges, including the young senator Bob Dole, who served at the time as the party's chairman. *The Washington Post*, he charged, was in bed with the Democrats. In September 1973, he even introduced legislation to stop television coverage of the Watergate hearings. "It is time," he said, "to turn off the TV lights."

What the Nixon team lacked was the unwavering, uncritical, and ceaseless support of a major media outlet. What they lacked, in other words, was Fox News and its allies in conservative digital media, who in Trump's case amplified the Republican charges of a "deep state" conspiracy or seeded that ground themselves. On many occasions, one could plainly see Fox News, the White House, and congressional protectors like Nunes coordinating with allies in the print and online media.

A month after taking office, Trump deemed the so-called mainstream media the "enemy of the American people," but his band of supporters within the media—the big names like Sean Hannity and Tucker Carlson at Fox News; columnists like Kimberley Strassel at *The Wall Street Journal*; writers at *The Daily Caller*, *The Federalist*, the *Washington Examiner*, and *The Hill*—became vital co-creators and curators of the upside-down world. For this contingent, it was never particularly important whether Russia and the Trump campaign had attempted to form a dark electoral alliance. When the Russia allegations exploded in early 2017, these instant promoters of the counter-narrative did not pause to examine the multiple reasons for concern: Trump's longtime interactions with the Russian underworld; his reliance on Russian buyers for Trump commercial properties; the fact that a Russian oligarch overpaid by tens of millions of dollars to buy his Palm Beach property on the eve of the housing crisis; the abundant interactions between his campaign and Moscow—none of this was worthy of consideration or column inches.

Instead, what mattered was that liberals in the press and in Congress, aided by Trump opponents within the government, were doing all they could to tear Trump down and frustrate the conservative push to remake the judiciary, the federal regulatory system, and the U.S. tax code. The editorial page of *The Wall Street Journal* was a particularly stark example of this willful blindness.

The *Journal* editorial board had deep misgivings about the many ways Trump appeared to stray from Republican economic orthodoxy—his penchant for deficit spending and tariffs and his punitive approach to trade, for starters. But the same *Journal* editorial page, which had published hundreds of columns on the Clintons' Whitewater real estate investments, ran no exposés on Trump's Russian entanglements or his highly dubious land deal in Palm Beach or his long history of consorting with organized crime in New York. It evinced no alarm over the clear signs that Moscow had gone to great lengths to aid the Trump campaign.

What it did do, just days after the dossier was published, was join Trump on the attack. And that job fell largely to Strassel, who covers the Washington political scene for the editorial page from her home in Wasilla, Alaska. Liberals, she asserted in her column just days after the dossier broke, resorted to "underhanded tactics," "smear strategy," "shock troops," "dirt diggers," and "character assassination." To Strassel, the dossier was nothing but "a turbocharged example of the smear strategy that the left has been ramping up for a decade." Trying to figure out if there was any truth in the allegations put forth in the dossier, she wrote, "arguably isn't worth the effort." Neither she nor her colleagues on the *Journal* edit board ever tried.

Over the coming months and years, Strassel would become one of the right's most reliable messengers—inspiring, augmenting, and amplifying whatever line of attack was spilling out of the Oval Office or from the desk of Sean Hannity. Events later revealed numerous Strassel columns to be wrong. In one stark example, she lampooned Simpson—under the headline "Russia, the NRA and Fake News"—for having spread "a wild new tale" in congressional testimony that the FBI was investigating allegations that Russians close to Putin had sought to infiltrate the NRA. Four months later, the Justice Department unsealed a criminal complaint charging that the Russians had done just that.

In all, Fusion was the target of no fewer than fifty *Journal* editorials and Potomac Watch columns between January 2017 and July 2019, accusing Fusion of a litany of nefarious misdeeds. A big U.S. company like IBM or Microsoft likely would have recoiled under such a barrage and spent mightily on some big PR firm to beat back the attacks, but the *Journal* veterans at Fusion knew that the paper's editorial page was all in for Trump, and saw no benefit in rebuttals. Week after week, the partners at Fusion marveled at the latest shell lobbed their way. Some columns they snipped out and tacked onto the wall.

The columns offended Fusion's founders with their intellectual dishonesty and reflexive defense of Trump. But the Fusion team was also saddened by the paper's willingness to trash its own alumni. Fusion employed four *Journal* veterans who had collectively worked for the paper for nearly six decades, breaking news and sometimes risking their necks on dangerous foreign assignments.

To make himself feel better, Fritsch drafted several angry notes to editorial page editor Paul Gigot. He never sent them.

It would be months before Trump himself turned his Twitter account squarely on Fusion, but in the meantime, the flood of emails and tweets from his supporters could hardly have been more caustic.

Fusion had to decide what to ignore—extreme abuse being the new normal—and what merited action to protect the staff, who hadn't asked for any of this. Fusion flagged for potential legal follow-up messages that seemed to cross the line by inciting violence against them. One account on Twitter posted Fusion's street address, along with the message "If you want to visit Glenn, this is his office."

The author identified as a member of a far-right, conspiracy-minded militia group called the Oath Keepers. He had nearly twenty thousand followers, many of whom professed to be armed. He spun an elaborate tale on Twitter for his followers suggesting that Fusion was part of a sophisticated global conspiracy to undermine Trump. The operation, he wrote, was being run out of the basement of Obama's new house in Washington's Kalorama neighborhood, a fifteen-minute walk from Fusion's office. He termed it "the Obama/Valerie Jarrett #DeepState Command Center." He posted photos of the outside of Obama's house and suggested he was conducting nightly surveillance runs there.

Several followers answered his call, one self-professed Second Amendment enthusiast replying, "Uh, yeah can I talk to Glenn." Another user, pictured firing a weapon, replied, "He's going to have a heart attack to the back of the head."

The Fusion staff closely tracked tweets like these, which in turn fanned fears among family members that some armed nut might come barging into the office. In this case, Fusion alerted the Secret Service, and his account was shut down not long after.

It was easy to write off some of these threats as the products of unhinged minds. Others were more upsetting. Fusion's partners and staff began crossing the street when suspicious-looking people approached and grew wary of opening packages. Simpson installed security cameras at his home. Fritsch allowed his dog to roam free in the house at night rather than confining him to the back hall.

Coming to work could be a nerve-racking exercise in the weeks after the dossier was published. It didn't help that Fusion's modest office building had no security guard in the lobby or that it shared the premises with a podiatrist and a psychotherapy practice admitting a constant parade of unfamiliar faces. Reporters and camera crews staked out the front door. One particularly determined reporter waited outside for several hours until Simpson went home for the night and then followed him to the subway station.

Recent events had shown how seemingly harmless conspiracies cooked up on the fringes of the Internet could spill over into real life. During the election, to take one example, Trump supporters on sites like 4chan, 8chan, and Twitter took mundane conversations plucked from John Podesta's hacked emails and weaved them together with other random elements to create the bizarro-world conspiracy theory that Democrats were molesting children in the basement of Comet Ping Pong, a local D.C. pizzeria. They termed the resulting theory "Pizzagate." It all seemed slightly comical until Edgar Maddison Welch, armed with a military-style assault rifle and several other guns, drove up from North Carolina with visions of saving children from depraved Democrats. He walked into the restaurant, in Northwest D.C., and fired three shots into the ground, sending families running for the exits. The judge later said it was "sheer luck" the gunman hadn't injured anyone.

The info@fusiongps.com account bore harbingers of other threats, too. Soon company email accounts were receiving fake messages posing as urgent requests by their email provider to change their password, or as prompts from cloud storage providers to accept a supposed file from a client. A nonexistent hedge fund—complete with its own phony website—expressed interest in becoming a Fusion research client, asking for a meeting. On another occasion, an email with a request to a co-worker was spoofed to look as if it had come from Simpson. Other times the would-be hackers tried to pose as Fritsch.

The same "spear-phishing" efforts, which aim to trick a user into giving up their credentials, had been used by Russian intelligence agencies to hack the DNC and Podesta's emails. Fusion moved to bolster its digital defenses. One gruff former FBI man, with a career in cybersecurity, came in and dismissed most of what was commercially available as snake oil. The best thing one could do, he said, was train everyone to recognize a phishing email—and not click on it.

Fair enough. But Fusion thought it needed more than behavioral training. It hired a former National Security Agency employee and his firm to assess their defenses, set up a continuous monitoring system, and investigate attacks. The good news was that, in its own haphazard way, Fusion had already made substantial progress in securing its systems. The former cyber soldier said they were already ahead of the vast majority of U.S. companies, even some many times their size. That fact seemed only to underline how vulnerable most American companies were to attack.

By March 20, when FBI Director James Comey sat down for his first post-election hearing, before the House Intelligence Committee, the gap between how Democrats and Republicans saw the swirl of Russia allegations was already miles wide. That rift only widened when he announced, at the top of his testimony, that the FBI had embarked on a full-blown investigation into Russia's meddling in the 2016 election. The investigation included "the nature of any links between individuals associated with the Trump campaign and the Russian government and whether there was any coordination between the campaign and Russia's efforts."

It was now official: The nation's most powerful law enforcement agency was digging into whether the president's team had cooperated with a foreign power to win the White House.

The Democrats, led by Representative Adam Schiff of California, had a litany of barbed questions for Comey. Why did the Russians jump to assist Trump? Who among Trump's aides had contacts with Russian actors, and to what end? Why did Flynn lie about his contacts with the Russian ambassador?

Chairman Nunes and the Republicans didn't care about any of that. Their questioning focused on whether Obama holdovers in the Justice Department and intelligence communities were behind a systematic campaign of leaks intended to destroy Trump. Nunes expressed passing concern that the Russians may have interfered in the election, but his primary interest was whether U.S. spy agencies had snooped on the Trump campaign. Previously a little-known congressman from rural California, Nunes was about to stumble into the national spotlight with a set of blunders that would nonetheless make him a star of the pro-Trump right.

The night after the Comey hearing, Nunes took a furtive trip to the White House, where a Trump aide slipped him a file meant to buttress the claim that the Obama White House had run a secret surveillance campaign on the Trump team. Nunes then deployed that material the next day in two press appearances—first in the Capitol and later in the White House driveway—telling reporters he had evidence that U.S. spy agencies had "incidentally" swept up communications involving Trump and his campaign aides. He said his committee would investigate, and he vowed to follow up with the FBI, the CIA, and the NSA.

"What I have read bothers me, and I think it should bother the president himself and his team," Nunes said. In fact, the White House had given him the material.

It soon came out that the White House had engineered the whole show, sharing with Nunes classified documents about incidental surveillance of Trump campaign officials collected during the campaign so he could then act as if they had come from somewhere else. Even Senator Lindsey Graham, soon to be a sturdy Trump ally, scoffed at Nunes's ham-handed effort to change the subject, calling it an "Inspector Clouseau investigation." The House Ethics Committee opened an inquiry into Nunes's actions. While under fire days later, Nunes recused himself from directing the committee's Russia inquiry, a pledge he would water down with each passing month.

And yet, despite getting caught red-handed, Nunes had laid another foundational building block for the emerging upside-down world. The GOP-led campaign to investigate the investigators was officially under way.

CHAPTER THIRTEEN

"CAN YOU CALL ME PLEASE?"

WITH HIS FIRST PUBLIC UTTERANCE AS PRESIDENT, IN HIS INaugural speech overlooking the Washington Mall, Donald Trump didn't attempt to soothe or lift up the nation. He played to people's fears in dystopian language, vowing to stop the "carnage" being inflicted on Americans by dark forces overseas. In the days that followed, he lied about the size of his inaugural crowd, publicly flirted with Putin, and sought to impose a sweeping ban on foreign Muslims entering the United States. In all, strongman rhetoric and behavior that was deeply unsettling.

Like much of the nation, Fusion had ample reason to worry about the whiff of authoritarianism in the air. The firm had commissioned the now public intelligence memos that accused the would-be strongman, soon to hold the most powerful job in the world, of cavorting with Russian prostitutes and a litany of potential criminal offenses. Now that he was firmly in power, it seemed only a matter of time before Trump would do what he could to use the powers at his disposal against Fusion.

There was nowhere to turn in Washington for support or protection. Voters had just returned Republicans to control of both houses of Congress. The Justice Department would soon be under Trump's control. While everyone at Fusion longed to continue to investigate the many mysteries surrounding the 2016 election, the firm was likely to be spending much of its time dealing with investigations of Fusion by Trump's allies in Congress.

The congressional inquisitions into Fusion were likely to last for most of the next two years, until the midterm elections, when historically the opposition party often takes over at least one of the two houses of Congress. It promised to be a lengthy battle to survive open-ended investigations by hostile congressional committees with almost infinite resources. In the meantime, could Americans rely on Trump's Justice Department and a Republican-held Congress to dig into what had happened in the last election—and prevent it from happening again? Recent history suggested that was unlikely.

Instead of business drying up, however, things were surprisingly stable. Fusion's partners found themselves fielding calls from people wanting to organize or fund private efforts to defend the firm or, far more commonly, keep investigating Trump. Interest in a renewed investigative push soared after the release of the dossier and the joint report of the intelligence agencies. Everyone at the firm wanted to revive the Trump research, and the partners began to deliberate in earnest over how that might happen.

The Fusion partners knew that things could turn on a dime for the worse, however. What if the new administration and subpoena-toting Republicans came pounding at the door? Fusion's partners knew they would have no one to blame but themselves for that, having agreed with Steele to share the dossier with Senator McCain. One option would have been to simply drop the whole matter, as consultants routinely do when they lose a client. That would have meant destroying its communications and written reports, giving no more information to law enforcement, and spurning all press calls.

But given the inevitable Republican attacks on their credibility, the best defense—really, the only defense—was to go out and gather more evidence supporting the original research. In order to be effective, though, Fusion would need the help of a good lawyer to fend off whatever Congress might throw at it.

Simpson decided to reach out to William W. Taylor III, a reserved and soft-spoken septuagenarian with a pronounced North Carolina drawl who had defended scores of people in highly charged public matters. Simpson had first met Taylor in the late 1980s while covering the political corruption investigations that grew out of the collapse of the savings-and-loan industry.

After they started Fusion, Simpson and Fritsch would also occasionally run into Taylor on the banks of the Potomac River during the annual spring shad run, when thousands of the sleek anadromous fish make their way upriver from the ocean to spawn. Taylor was a fishing fanatic, as was Fritsch. Simpson saw fishing largely as an opportunity to sit on a river with a pole in one hand and a can of beer in the other.

Taylor, who didn't shy from political controversy and was not afraid to take on unpopular clients, invited Simpson over to his house in Cleveland Park. Taylor poured two cups of coffee and they sat down together in his cozy day room.

"I think we may be in a shitload of trouble," Simpson said. He then laid out the whole history of the Fusion investigations into Trump. Taylor agreed that, sooner or later, Trump and his Republican allies in Congress would likely decide that Fusion and Orbis needed to be discredited, even destroyed. "They will need someone to blame and we're going to be a leading candidate," Simpson said.

He then rang Steele at one of his hideouts in England and put him on speaker. Steele briefed Taylor on his own investigations into Trump's dealings with the Russians and the fallout from the dossier's publication. Reporters were still camped outside his house and office, Steele said, and he couldn't be sure the Russians wouldn't also come after him for exposing what might have been Putin's biggest covert operation ever. He and his family had been forced to move from place to place, sheltering with friends.

After the call, Simpson told Taylor that the coming turmoil could destroy the firm, and that defending Fusion could cost millions in legal fees. That was the bad news. The good news, he added, was that Fusion had done nothing wrong, had the facts on its side, and had ample reason to believe that what it had uncovered to date was just the start of the story. The Steele memos—based as they were on anonymous sources— were certain to come under withering attack. But Fusion had reams of other research on Trump and the Russians that no one knew about and that could not be easily dismissed.

On top of that, Simpson said, a small number of Americans seemed willing to help fund continued investigations into Trump's seedy past and Russia's election meddling. That could help cover legal fees while also keeping the investigation going. Taylor said that this sounded like a natural fit for his skills as a white-collar defense lawyer. Taylor also thought it was a clear case of defending Fusion's right to free speech, one that could become very high profile. "I'd be happy to help any way you need," Taylor said.

Fusion's problems weren't just legal. Its biggest worry of all: the risk now faced by the sources behind the dossier. Given the Republican reaction to the memos, it was a decent bet that they wouldn't be too worried about exposing Steele's sources, if they were ever to discover them. There wasn't anything Fusion could do to protect Steele's sources inside Russia. Steele managed those relationships and would have to decide how to proceed. In reality, there was little he could do for them, either.

But one of Steele's sources was a Russian who wasn't in Russia. Steele and Simpson discussed whether the Russian intelligence services would seek to track down this source and attempt an assassination. That was a valid concern, Steele said. He spoke from experience: One of the biggest cases of his government career was his investigation of the 2006 poisoning in London of former FSB agent Alexander Litvinenko by suspected Russian agents. In 2016, the British government publicly stated what Steele suspected from the start: that "the F.S.B. operation to kill Mr. Litvinenko was probably approved . . . by President Putin."

The source was someone Steele and Fusion might be able to help. Simpson didn't know the source's identity but lobbied Steele to introduce the source to the FBI. If the FBI or the Justice Department knew the source's pedigree and skill, the agencies might want to intervene to offer protection—should he or she be willing to accept it. Steele initially demurred, saying that this person didn't want to have any contact with the FBI and had been well aware of the risks when he agreed to pass information along to Steele.

Simpson decided to explore the question himself. He sent Bruce Ohr a single-sentence text on January 20, 2017, at 3:13 P.M., some three hours after Trump had been sworn in as the forty-fifth president of the United States: "Can you call me please?" Soon thereafter, his cellphone rang.

As reflected in Ohr's scribbled notes, taken down at the time of the call but made public much later, Simpson explained that he was concerned about a person "likely to be identified by the other side & will need protection." Eventually, he feared, "articles will make it clear to [the Russians] who this is."

"They can't reach [the source]," Simpson added—at least not quickly. But in time, they might try. Ohr pressed for more details, but Simpson said he didn't have many and was already freelancing. Steele himself hadn't heard from his source in the wake of *BuzzFeed*'s release of the dossier.

"Chris has the information that can help you find [the source]," he told Ohr. Maybe there was something the U.S. could do to help this person, maybe even with money? By now there was a very public investigation going on. This person was someone the FBI would want to interview and evaluate. Ohr was noncommittal but said he would follow up with Steele.

Steele and Ohr talked on Skype the next day. Steele said he and his family were "restabilizing" after a tumultuous few days and had successfully avoided the British media's manhunt. With any luck, he said hopefully, he would be able to come out of hiding the following week.

Ohr related his previous day's talk with Simpson about the source's personal safety. The Russian's security was "a serious potential issue," Steele told Ohr, but he'd finally heard from his source via a message on social media, and the person was "alive and well." Steele added that he did not have "clearance" from the source to reveal his identity to Ohr, and the individual was waiting to see if he "gets into a real pickle."

"His default position is to keep his head down," Steele said, "but he may need help quickly."

They continued the conversation in encrypted text messages a week later.

"Hi B! Our [person's] OK for the time being but I would like to keep our channel open on [this] situation if that's alright?" wrote Steele.

"Understood," replied Ohr. "We will be available if needed."

Steele wasn't eager to turn the Russian over to the Justice Department at such a tumultuous time. No one was sure what would happen once Trump and his team took over. In late-night calls after Steele's family had gone to bed, Steele and Simpson fed each other's anxiety about what a lawless new president might be contemplating doing with the Justice Department and the FBI.

Those concerns were greatly intensified when the White House abruptly fired Ohr's boss, acting Attorney General Sally Yates, just three days later. With the loss of his longtime friend, Ohr was now far more exposed to potential White House retaliation for his ties to Steele, should it ever find out about them. Steele worried that this might hamper Ohr's ability to intervene effectively on behalf of the source. "B, doubtless a sad and crazy day for you re SY," Steele texted Ohr. "Just wanted to check you are OK, still in situ and able to help locally as discussed, along with your Bureau colleagues, with our guy if the need arises?"

While the public explanation for Yates's firing was her unwillingness to instruct the Justice Department to make legal arguments that would justify Trump's Muslim travel ban, Steele couldn't help but wonder if that was a pretext for something darker going on behind the scenes. Fusion and Orbis suspected that Yates might be aware of Ohr's contacts with Simpson and Steele, and might have even authorized them. Had Trump somehow found out?

Ohr might soon also be fired, Steele feared. If that were to happen, Steele would need another contact at the FBI to help him manage the Russian. "We can't allow our guy to be forced to go back home," he told Ohr. "It would be disastrous all round."

Two days later, *The Wall Street Journal* disclosed the existence of a DOJ counterintelligence investigation into Michael Flynn, Carter Page, Roger Stone, and Paul Manafort, "due to their known ties to Russian interests or their public statements."

While Yates and the White House both denied that her role in the counterintelligence investigation of Flynn had any role in her firing, her disappearance prompted Steele to put the brakes on efforts to bring his source in from the cold.

In the U.K., Steele remained in hiding, but some of the Russians named in his memos began to come after him—not with thugs, but with lawyers. His last memo in December had contained allegations that companies owned by a Russian Internet mogul had been used in the hacking operations against the Democratic Party. The mogul's lawyers sent Steele a threatening letter, calling the memo "gravely defamatory" and demanding a complete retraction and apology as well as a promise to pay damages. Steele and Burrows, who had only ever worked in the shadows, were trying to cope with a type of threat they'd never experienced, and they worried their firm could be driven into bankruptcy.

Orbis was in chaos, and some of its staff were close to open revolt, Steele told Simpson. Key employees felt that their professional careers were now endangered by a project they hadn't even known about or worked on. Everyone at Orbis had been forced to take down their profiles on LinkedIn, for security reasons and to avoid press scrutiny. It was a little difficult to market your services to clients, some of their best investigators complained, when prospective customers can no longer examine your background or send you a message on LinkedIn.

A more immediate concern for Steele and Burrows was the bills rapidly piling up from their law firm. Seeking to reassure them and send a tangible signal of solidarity, Fusion wired Orbis $50,000 to help pay their lawyers, no strings attached.

Fusion's other concern was how to push ahead on the Trump work. It was time to move on from the post-election swirl and to determine how best to augment other lines of inquiry—in the press, in Congress, or among state and local prosecutors. But who would they be working for, and under what arrangement?

Ever since the November election, Fusion had funded all of its work on Trump and Russia itself, and that was getting expensive. In one costly episode, Simpson and Berkowitz flew down to the Virgin Islands to meet a potential source claiming to have information about Trump's relationship with Deutsche Bank—Val Broeksmit, the son of a former top Deutsche executive who'd apparently committed suicide in 2014, shortly after quitting. Broeksmit had been introduced to Simpson by a reporter in Europe. He claimed to possess a cache of potentially telling emails downloaded from his father's computer. On the off chance these emails would offer new insights into the bank's interactions with Russia and its many loans to Trump, Simpson decided it was worth giving Broeksmit, a penniless rock musician, an all-expenses-paid jaunt to the U.S. Virgin Islands to find out. Berkowitz joined them.

The three spent several days there in the last days of January, at a slightly shabby beach resort. Simpson agreed to pay Broeksmit $4,000 for a copy of his father's emails and Broeksmit's time for help reviewing them. The correspondence turned out to be revealing about Deutsche Bank's mismanagement but did little to illuminate the bank's relationship to the Kremlin or to Trump.

These kinds of dry holes are common in investigations. But the affair underscored the challenge Fusion was facing: The Trump-Russia mystery would be unraveled only by an ambitious, well-funded investigation. They needed to be able to pay last-minute international airfares at the drop of a hat and compensate people who might be able to contribute their expertise or vital information. Fusion couldn't afford to fund that kind of operation for much longer without going broke.

Fusion suspected its work was unlikely to be sought after by the Republican majority in Congress, whose efforts to investigate Russia's assault on the 2016 election were likely to be cursory and half-hearted. Nor did it seem likely, given the politically charged nature of the dossier controversy, that law enforcement would come asking for help anytime soon. By necessity, the main constituency for any future Fusion research into Russia's attack on the 2016 election—at least for the next two years—would be the press and the public at large.

The American media was now plunging wholeheartedly into the many strands of the Trump-Russia story. In the weeks after the dossier went public, Fusion's inboxes were receiving queries from big-name broadcast and print journalists looking to truncate the reporting process with help from Fusion's knowledge and archives. Many reporters were having trouble connecting the dots, or getting up to speed on the complex history of corruption in Russia and the many ties between the new generation of Putin oligarchs and political figures in the United States.

Putting together reliable background information about all the players and allegations and launching a new round of research would require resources. No traditional political client would likely finance a sprawling investigation involving a sitting president, especially one run by Fusion and employing Steele. But what about creating a coalition of the willing—a group of contributors—to get behind what was no longer a campaign but an exercise in public education, in the public interest?

Fusion toyed with various proposals and iterations before settling on the idea of a nonprofit group that could work to investigate and expose Russia's efforts to disrupt democratic institutions in the West and split the NATO alliance. The idea was a logical extension of Steele's Project Charlemagne, which had looked at Russian electoral interference in Western Europe. The nonprofit would have to be nonpartisan and document its work rigorously.

Fusion outlined the scope of the project as an extensive examination of foreign influence and espionage against the United States and its allies. The plan called for assembling an elite team of linguists, open-source researchers, and intelligence veterans—along with field operatives—to identify new sources and information. The investigations would look at the foreign travel and business dealings of key figures connected to Trump and inventory and analyze suspicious financing of the 2016 election.

In some respects, it was also a survival plan. If some of their clients fled for fear of being unfairly dragged into a government investigation or political controversy, that would leave the firm with a lot of capacity to do something else. And Russian meddling in Western politics was a subject they knew a lot about already.

Any new investigative nonprofit couldn't be owned or controlled by Fusion, a for-profit entity that by now was inextricably (albeit wrongly) linked in the minds of many to the Democratic Party. As a public interest project, it would have to have an independent board and a separate governance structure able to accept money from donors of any ideological persuasion. The organization also needed a leader with impeccable credentials as an investigator and communicator. Most important, that person needed to be prepared for withering political fire: Anyone working with Fusion and Steele was bound to come in for sustained Republican—and Russian—attack.

There weren't many people in Washington who fit that bill. But in the weeks after the dossier exploded, Simpson began kicking the idea around with an acquaintance, a former Senate Intelligence Committee investigator named Daniel Jones. If anyone had the chutzpah to run a public interest investigation of foreign election interference and the dark history of a sitting president, it was Jones. A decade earlier, in the final year of the Bush administration, Jones had parlayed four years as an FBI counterterrorism analyst into a job on the staff of the Senate Intelligence Committee. He had been on the committee for barely a year when news broke that the CIA had destroyed videotapes depicting the brutal treatment of post-9/11 terror detainees. He led the ensuing committee investigation, a seven-year effort that brought him into regular and heated conflict with CIA officials eager to whitewash the Bush-era torture program. Over the course of the case, Jones found himself being spied on by the CIA and falsely accused of breaking the law. His quest to fully expose what had happened led to frequent tussles with the intelligence community and even the Obama White House.

The Intelligence Committee ultimately completed a blistering 6,700-page account of the CIA's horrific treatment of suspected jihadists that pulled no punches. The report won wide acclaim as a powerful indictment of practices that it said were "more brutal—and far less effective—than the agency acknowledged either to Bush administration officials or to the public." Committee chairwoman Dianne Feinstein read a glowing tribute to Jones into the *Congressional Record* when he left the Senate staff about a year later, a rare honor that impressed Fritsch and Simpson.

When Fusion reached out to Jones in early 2017, he was unfulfilled, if not unhappy, working as a consultant in the private sector. He missed working on projects he believed could make a difference. He also had good contacts in Washington, including senators on the Intelligence Committee, and experience working with the media, which had covered his committee work extensively over the years. Simpson reached out and asked if the two could meet in private.

The two met in the conference room of Jones's downtown office on the Sunday after the inauguration. Simpson told Jones the whole story, from Fusion's initial assignment, in 2015, to the events of the final days of the campaign. Jones had worked on various Russia-related security issues at the Intelligence Committee. He agreed that the United States was as unprepared to counter the new Russian security threat as it had been to cope with al-Qaeda fifteen years before. Simpson raised the idea of setting up a new group that could work with Fusion and other investigators around the world to expose Russian subversion operations in the United States and other Western democracies. Jones said he thought it needed to be done—right away.

The next morning, Simpson recounted the meeting to Fritsch.

"Is he game?" asked Fritsch.

"Two hundred percent," Simpson replied.

Nine days later, Jones incorporated a new nonprofit and named it The Democracy Integrity Project (soon known in-house as TDIP). The name was not intended to be flashy or to command attention. The first order of business: finding funders to pay for it. The endeavor—a more aggressive set of inquiries spanning numerous countries and requiring the services of Fusion, Orbis, and players to be named later—wouldn't be cheap.

Jones said he had some good leads on the West Coast, while Fusion had already received unsolicited inquiries from high-net-worth individuals and people who managed their political giving. "Glenn: Been thinking about you a LOT lately," one old friend wrote to Simpson in January. A prominent political consultant out west, she continued, "has a benefactor looking to hire someone to do some digging." Fritsch had received similar feelers from other possible donors, mostly Democrats.

As it turned out, though, one of the first people to step forward with financial support was a wealthy Republican investor from Arizona who wanted to explore whether it might be possible to buy a copy of any tapes the Russians had of Trump. It was a bad idea that would surface over and over, requiring Fusion to patiently explain that every scam artist on the planet would soon be selling fake Trump sex tapes. He was persuaded to support a more realistic plan.

———

In 1968, a small group of multimillionaires led by General Motors heir Stewart Mott changed the course of American history when they decided to muster some $1.5 million ($11 million in 2019 dollars) to support anti-war senator Eugene McCarthy's quixotic bid to deny the Democratic presidential nomination to President Lyndon B. Johnson. McCarthy went on to shock Johnson in the New Hampshire primary, coming within seven points of beating the incumbent president. McCarthy soon faded, of course, but the intervention rattled Johnson, encouraged other competitors to run against him, and led the president to ditch his bid for re-election.

The role of big money in the U.S. political system has changed profoundly since then. The wealthy and powerful have always held great sway over legislation, but their clout has grown dramatically since the 2010 Supreme Court decision on *Citizens United* opened the spigots for independent campaign expenditures by corporations and super PACs.

Largesse from the super-wealthy can also be a powerful tool for the public good, as seen in the boom in support for independent investigative journalism, for instance. It can fund tasks that government should do but can't, or won't.

In that spirit, TDIP intended to tap the super-wealthy to fund work to protect the democratic system of government from a new and insidious assault. Over the next few months, TDIP embarked on a series of fundraising trips around the country—to Boston, New York, Philadelphia, Los Angeles. But it didn't take Jones long to figure out that if you want to raise a lot of money in a hurry, the world's most animated, unbureaucratic, and risk-loving billionaires reside largely within an hour of San Francisco.

In mid-February, and then again in early March, Jones—supported by Fritsch and Simpson—took prospecting trips in the West. They didn't know the tech community well, so before heading out, they sought some door openers and validators from the world they knew best.

One of the most helpful turned out to be John Podesta, a former White House chief of staff who founded the Center for American Progress after his years in the Clinton administration. From his perch at CAP and a brief stint as a counselor to President Obama, Podesta had earned a reputation as hard-nosed and fearless. Podesta had not worked with Fusion during the campaign, but he respected its desire to finish what it had started. He was also, of course, one of the biggest victims of the Russian hacking operation. Podesta agreed to contact some friends out west on Jones's behalf and told him to drop his name in talks with other potential supporters. It was a brave gesture: He could have easily chosen to stay out of it altogether, given the fact that he had served as Hillary Clinton's campaign manager.

Fusion's first trips west in support of Jones were full of tension, small triumphs, and quirky encounters. These were people who guarded their privacy ferociously. Hushed discussions took place in the backs of restaurants, in hotel bars, in plush family offices, and in boardrooms with jaw-dropping views of Alcatraz and the Golden Gate Bridge.

With the Trump era not yet a month old, the fear of where he might take the country hung palpably over session after session. A few potential donors, including some big names in the tech industry, begged off for reasons of personal safety. One centimillionaire, in black hoodie and sweatpants, said he'd been eyeing offshore outposts where he and his family might flee in a pinch. He pledged a generous donation that never came through.

The sheer lack of red tape was astonishing. The beginning of the year had been nightmarish, but Fusion's exposure did eliminate the need for more formal introductions and allowed the discussions to get right to business. Interest was high in talking to "the guys behind the dossier." At a few sessions where two or three potential donors had been expected, a whole conference room showed up. There were also a lot of merely curious window-shoppers.

Back east, where the money tends toward old and stodgy, one might spend days walking a persnickety board through a meticulous set of slides with itemized deliverables and monthly metrics. In San Francisco, many fortunes aren't yet ten years old. One adviser to an Internet billionaire took no notes during a rushed encounter. He had already done his due diligence. "I think I know what I need to," he said, before ending the meeting after half an hour. Days later, he approved a high-six-figure contribution. Other encounters could be highly frustrating. One young techie asked why he should invest in TDIP when Congress would surely act as a check on Trump.

"Is that a serious question?" replied an exasperated Fritsch.

Fundraising turned out to be a lot harder than Jones had expected, especially for a new nonprofit with no track record and no obligation to hire Fusion. At the end of the first trip, Fusion newcomer Neil King wrote up an after-action report that ascribed levels of confidence to the various sessions. One quick conclusion: The project would need to rely on people who "have an easy stomach for political risk." Within weeks, some of the cases deemed long shots stepped up with significant commitments, while others that seemed surer tiptoed away.

In the end, TDIP got started with the help of a small handful of donors from both sides of the political aisle. Keeping the circle small had the merit of intimacy and shared purpose, and the added benefit of minimizing the risk of leaks. Fusion and TDIP were eager to launch a fresh batch of research both in the United States and abroad and to disseminate their findings through established channels. But no one relished more publicity, which they all agreed would get in the way of doing the actual work.

Among the biggest early donors was a self-made billionaire who, in addition to his concerns about Russia's interference in American elections, believed that the president of the United States was basically the don of an organized crime family.

By the end of February, real money began flowing into TDIP's bank account. As later reported in its public filings with the Internal Revenue Service, the group eventually raised a little over $7 million in 2017. It was time to get things rolling.

On March 2, Jeff Sessions had just recused himself from the Russia inquiry, sending Trump into a fury. That evening, over dinner at Mar-a-Lago, the *Times* would later report, Trump begged Sessions to reverse that decision and reassume command over the investigation, a request Sessions turned down.

Fusion now figured it was more obvious than ever that neither the Justice Department nor Congress was going to make a real effort to get to the bottom of Trump's relationship with Russia, much less Moscow's interference in the 2016 election. By design, TDIP was not a "get Trump" project. TDIP also needed to look at Russian efforts to disrupt America's democratic allies. That would be a job for Steele and his network in Europe.

Without the deadline of an election, but with a public interest mandate and better funding than Fusion had ever had, TDIP had the luxury to roam into underexplored areas while also opening up entirely new inquiries. It could bring on specialists: linguists, accountants, campaign finance nerds, Web-scraping data gurus. It could also go deep on some sprawling international projects, mapping who bought what, and when, in dubious Trump projects like the towers in Panama City and Toronto that bore his name. Fusion knew veteran investigators with experience in many of these locales.

The advent of TDIP was a relief to Fusion's partners, because the new structure meant that they were no longer running the show. Every project had to have board approval and a public education purpose, and former Fusion subcontractors like Orbis now reported to TDIP.

Two days after Sessions's recusal, Jones and the Fusion team convened on a Saturday afternoon at Fritsch's house in Maryland to begin charting a research strategy going forward. Fritsch led the Project Bangor team to his basement. Using a big whiteboard Simpson had brought and fueled with fresh pots of coffee, they took turns scribbling down the investigative and research priorities for TDIP. Soon the board teemed with names, bullet points, and overlapping arrows and circles. Threads included Russia's efforts to co-opt Viktor Orbán in Hungary, Moscow's ties to the key financial backers of Brexit in the U.K., and Russian efforts to sow more chaos in Italy's already chaotic politics.

Berkowitz suggested that TDIP also look at Russian efforts to co-opt American technology and make inroads into Silicon Valley. The Russian government had made numerous major investments in U.S. tech, with several encroaching on matters of U.S. national security. The FBI had even warned tech companies in 2014 about the potential for infiltration and theft, but it seemed to have fallen on deaf ears. Maybe TDIP could highlight the issue.

Within weeks, many of the priorities sketched out that morning were well under way. The effort would come to dwarf the original work done for the Clinton campaign, both in budget and scope.

One of Jones's top overseas priorities was the question of Russian interference in French politics. The French national elections in the spring of 2017 were hugely consequential for the U.S. alliance with NATO. Jones tapped Orbis and other sources in Europe to map Russia's French relationships. Steele, who'd been stationed in Paris during his time in government, identified many likely Russian confederates working on the fringes and with the right-wing campaign of Marine Le Pen. The Kremlin was running its French influence operations through an NGO called the Institute for Democracy & Co-operation (IDC), a Russian-government-funded think tank in Paris that advocates for Putin's warped Orwellian versions of "democracy" and "cooperation" and appeared to be a thinly veiled front for Russian intelligence.*

Russian intelligence was using "plausibly deniable business oligarchs" to support Le Pen's far-right National Front, Steele found.

Across the English Channel, Steele and Fusion also began giving Britain's vote to leave the European Union the thorough scrub it so clearly needed. The vote to depart the EU faced many of the same questions of outside meddling and dubious funding streams as Trump's election, yet it was not getting much investigative attention. It was also populated with many of the same odd characters who had featured in the Trump campaign, from Steve Bannon and Robert Mercer to Cambridge Analytica.

Using network-mapping software designed for intelligence agencies, Steele's team compiled a chart that appeared to show strong links between the right-wing networks in France and the U.K.

A TDIP inquiry that would pay huge dividends in terms of press coverage as events unfolded over the next year was an examination of the complex and highly questionable career of Michael Cohen, Trump's trusted fixer and a person with a long and sketchy history in the New York and Chicago taxi industries. Fusion led that work, carried out in collaboration with various TDIP contractors in New York and elsewhere.

No donor-supported research effort, no matter how thorough, meticulous, or well funded, was ever going to replace a legitimate federal examination of what happened in 2016. TDIP, of course, didn't have the power to issue subpoenas to compel testimony, as Congress did. The House and Senate intelligence committees opened their investigations with at least a whiff of bipartisanship and a hint of ambition. They even held public hearings that dug into Russia's active measures and featured riveting testimony from the likes of Comey and top intelligence officials. The Senate panel, led by Republican Richard Burr and Democrat Mark Warner, plunged in a week before Trump's inauguration. "The Commit-

---

* The French elections turned out to be something of a rerun of the U.S. presidential election. Colonies of fake social media accounts plugged the populist right-wing candidate, while the front-runner, Emmanuel Macron, was hit at the last minute by a leak of sixty thousand hacked emails that came out on WikiLeaks. "Macron Campaign Emails," WikiLeaks, https://wikileaks.org/macron-emails.

tee will follow the intelligence wherever it leads," Burr and Warner said in a joint statement. "We will conduct this inquiry expeditiously, and we will get it right."

But as TDIP's inquiries got under way, the congressional investigations into Trump's Russia ties began to look increasingly wobbly, plagued by partisan divisions. Barely a month after the committee's statement, the White House enlisted Burr's help to shoot down media stories about Trump associates' ties to Russia. Burr dutifully complied. On the House side, Devin Nunes also took his talking points from the White House but went even further, issuing a statement in support of Trump's unfounded allegation that he'd been wiretapped by the Obama administration. He also canceled at least one big hearing, featuring former intelligence chiefs and the fired former acting attorney general, Sally Yates. It was becoming obvious that his committee's inquiries would descend into partisan rancor as Nunes himself sought above all to protect the president.

News of the FBI investigation, meanwhile, had dramatically raised the stakes for Trump and his defenders. The FBI was now seeking witnesses and preparing subpoenas. The congressional investigative efforts may have been looking increasingly dysfunctional, but real threats were emerging from the Justice Department.

CHAPTER FOURTEEN

A SENATOR ATTACKS

THE FBI INVESTIGATION OF RUSSIA'S EFFORTS TO HELP TRUMP win the presidency was now public. Flynn had resigned after misleading the White House about his contacts with Russia's ambassador. Attorney General Jeff Sessions had recused himself from any involvement in the matter, a product of his own Russia contacts, infuriating the president. A press corps that had largely overlooked the Trump-Russia story in 2016 was now dropping bombs almost daily. Republicans feared their new leader could fall. If they were going to keep his fledgling administration from disintegrating, they needed to start firing back—and quick.

So on March 24, two days after Devin Nunes's secret trip to the White House, Senate Judiciary Chairman Chuck Grassley sent Fusion a letter of inquiry that, on its surface, sought to get to the bottom of the genesis of the Russia inquiry. The pretext for this, he said, was his committee's oversight of the Justice Department.

"I am writing to inquire about Fusion GPS's opposition research efforts regarding President Trump, particularly the dossier compiled for your company by Mr. Christopher Steele," he wrote.

Grassley then gave Fusion two weeks to answer thirteen questions, including: *Who first hired Fusion to examine Trump? How much did they pay? When did Fusion hire Steele? Who did Fusion give information to once it was gathered? Did Fusion have interactions with the FBI? Did anyone from Fusion instruct Steele to go to the FBI?* He also requested copies of all contracts and records of any communications with the DOJ or the FBI. On it went for three pages.

At eighty-three and just re-elected to his seventh term in the Senate, Grassley had earned a reputation over the years as a curmudgeonly protector of whistleblowers and someone who was willing to cross his own party to defend his principles. That reputation was earned, however, a long time ago. Grassley was about to become a prime example of how far the GOP was willing to go to bend the truth in an effort to protect the party's new standard-bearer.

Some three weeks earlier, Grassley had sent a letter to FBI Director Comey, which immediately became public, asking whether the Obama administration had, during the presidential campaign, used law enforcement and the intelligence agencies for political ends in collaboration with Christopher Steele. The letter was politics disguised as oversight, and it wasn't designed to elicit an answer. Grassley wanted an excuse to fulminate about being stonewalled.

Three days after his March 24 letter to Fusion, Grassley followed up with a theatrical "DOCUMENT PRESERVATION NOTICE" instructing the firm to preserve all records and messaging related to the Trump investigation and warning that "it is very important you DO NOT destroy, remove, discard, modify or change any document." The threat to Fusion was clear: *I am coming for you.*

Grassley publicized his pursuit of Fusion in the hope that the press would jump on his bandwagon and start asking Fusion the same loaded questions about Steele and the FBI. The company greeted that move with a mix of alarm and derision. Simpson shot Fritsch a text when Grassley released his letter publicly, just three days after sending it—and eleven days before Fusion was due to respond: "What obvious bullshit," Simpson wrote. "I seriously doubt the media will fall for this crap," Fritsch responded.

And, for the most part, they didn't. Mainstream news outlets were familiar with Grassley's tactics and recognized his letter for the political stunt it was. It was catnip, however, for reporters at fringe, alt-right publications, whose job was to counteract the flood of real news coming from the likes of the *Post* and the *Times* with attacks on Democrats and public enemy number one, Hillary Clinton.

Grassley's attack, despite its transparent cynicism, was a major escalation Fusion could not ignore. Congress is vested with broad investigative powers and has the ability to compel testimony. Grassley was particularly aggressive in his use of those powers. Fusion had worked with people targeted by Grassley's committee in the past and knew that his staff played dirty, using leaks and spin to muddy up targets for political purposes. Fritsch and Simpson also knew you could quickly go bankrupt paying lawyers to answer and rebut all the accusations, no matter how specious.

Steele was unnerved by Grassley's attacks on Fusion and Comey, fearing it could have safety implications for his sources should the FBI cave in and reveal their identity to lawmakers loyal to Trump, who Steele suspected would happily make their identities public. He expressed those concerns to Ohr, who sent back assurances that the DOJ and FBI wouldn't let that happen. "Thanks for that, old friend. Please do fight our cause and keep in touch," Steele texted afterwards. "Really fundamental issues at stake here."

Steele's sense of worry deepened in mid-March when Russian agents traveled to the quaint English town of Salisbury to poison a former double agent for MI6, Sergei Skripal, with a Soviet-developed chemical weapon agent called Novichok. The Russians were clearly on a mission, Steele thought, to eliminate perceived traitors. His sources, if discovered, would be at the top of the hit list.

Outside of Fusion, news of the Trump camp's surreptitious dealings with the Russians kept shaking the country. The press was now going after the Russia angle full bore, and the big papers were competing ferociously to advance the story. Each new disturbing revelation would then be picked up and aired on the television news, night and day.

Just two days after Grassley sent his first letter to Fusion, the *Post* reported that Jared Kushner and Ambassador Kislyak had, in late 2016, discussed setting up a secret back channel between the Kremlin and Trump's transition team to discuss sensitive issues such as policy in Syria. They even discussed the use of Russian diplomatic facilities to avoid detection. This was astonishing. Why would the incoming administration need a back channel, and on Russian soil no less? The only plausible explanation was that they wanted to hide their communications from the U.S. Intelligence Community. The news only added to the mushrooming Russia narrative playing everywhere but on Fox News, which continued to rant about Clinton's emails.

"Just amazing," Ohr texted Steele on March 30.

The House and Senate intelligence committees had already announced that they would be investigating Russian interference in the 2016 election and the allegations against Trump. It was obvious that Grassley was trying to lay the predicate for a subpoena of Fusion that would force them to produce documents and appear at a hearing—a ploy to put Steele and his dossier on trial.

If Grassley could make a case that the entire Trump-Russia controversy arose from political "opposition research," that would go a long way toward delegitimizing other congressional and law enforcement inquiries.

It was hard to believe he could pull that off. For one thing, the FBI would likely resist sharing details of an active investigation. For another, Senate rules required Grassley to obtain the consent of his Democratic counterpart, California senator Dianne Feinstein, in order to issue any subpoenas. Why would Feinstein go along with a subpoena of Fusion when the far more serious questions had to do with the Russian connections of people like Carter Page and Paul Manafort?

Grassley's public attacks on Fusion presented a conundrum for Simpson and Fritsch. They wanted to defend themselves and their work, but they were bound to silence by their confidentiality agreement with Elias, the Clinton campaign's lawyer. If Grassley pressed the issue with a subpoena, Fusion would have no choice but to protect its duty of confidentiality to its clients, which they hadn't waived. If the Fusion partners started making statements to the media, Grassley could argue that they had waived their right to remain silent.

Elias's firm, Perkins Coie, made it clear that it expected Fusion to resist Grassley's probing. But the law firm also never offered to cover Fusion's legal costs. That put Fusion in a tough position and became a source of tension among the Fusion partners. Fritsch thought Perkins Coie and its clients had a moral responsibility to step up and defend Fusion against the Republican assault, given that Fusion and Steele had worked at Elias's direction and done the right thing by reporting a possible crime in progress. Simpson argued that Fusion had no right to expect help from Perkins Coie or the Democrats. After all, neither he nor Fritsch had asked their permission to share Steele's information with the FBI and McCain; as a legal matter, Fusion had no choice but to go it alone. That wasn't wrong, Fritsch agreed, but the reality of the situation rankled as the bills piled up. The various legal fights would cost Fusion nearly $2 million and counting.

There was another, more strategic reason for keeping Grassley at bay for as long as possible—one that had nothing to do with money. If it came out too soon that the dossier had been paid for by the Clinton campaign, that revelation would allow the Republicans to depict Steele's work as a partisan hit job that had hoodwinked the FBI. And that, in turn, could give Trump the political cover he needed to shut down the FBI investigation.

Time—or, in this case, delay—was of the essence.

Grassley had given Fusion until April 7, 2017, to respond to his initial March 24 letter. Not content to wait for a reply, however, he broadened his political assault with yet another letter on March 31—this time to the Justice Department. In it, he falsely accused Fusion of working with a "former Russian intel officer" to lobby against the Global Magnitsky Act, a bill that would stiffen sanctions on the Kremlin and others who abused human rights. The Russian was Rinat Akhmetshin, the Washington lobbyist who had worked to discredit Kremlin critic William Browder, the Magnitsky Act's primary promoter.

Grassley's pursuit of Fusion had somehow led him to Browder, the former financier who nursed a terrific grudge against Fusion for forcing him to testify years earlier in the Prevezon court case. Working for a U.S. law firm, Fusion had helped the lawyers serve three subpoenas on Browder, ultimately forcing him to testify at length about his own business dealings in Russia and the efforts he undertook with his lawyers and accountants, including Sergei Magnitsky, to avoid paying Russian taxes.

In early 2016, Prevezon—apart from its court case—had launched a lobbying campaign against the Global Magnitsky Act, working with Akhmetshin, in a backhanded effort to discredit Browder in the halls of Congress.

Browder had been trying for months to convince a few journalists around Washington that Fusion was part of that lobbying campaign. Unable to get anywhere, he wrote a letter to the Justice Department in July 2016 complaining that Akhmetshin had not registered with the government as an advocate for Prevezon. (That was not true. He had filed his paperwork with the U.S. Senate as required.) Nor, Browder complained, had Fusion ever registered as a lobbyist for Prevezon. That *was* true—but also a non sequitur: Fusion never registered because it never lobbied.

The political play under way was transparent—at least to Fusion. The

Justice Department had given no sign of having any interest in Browder's letter, and the matter had seemed dead until Grassley suddenly revived it, resurrecting Browder's eight-month-old attack under the pretense of his committee's DOJ oversight. If Fusion could be depicted as having also engaged in helping out Russians in Washington, that would help Trump by evening the score and cloud the Trump-Russia narrative. Grassley was trying to normalize the behavior of Manafort and the rest of the Trump brain trust by showing that everybody does it in Washington.

Fusion, the senator claimed in his letter, should have registered as a foreign agent under the Foreign Agents Registration Act for "their efforts to bring down a U.S. law on behalf of the Kremlin." Grassley linked to Browder's 2016 "complaint filed with the Justice Department," eliding the fact that Browder barely mentioned Fusion in his July 2016 letter.

Grassley poured it on thick, accusing Fusion of working with a "Russian gun-for-hire [who] lurks in the shadows of Washington's lobbying world."

It dismayed the ranks at Fusion to be accused by a U.S. senator of working for the Kremlin. Once again, reporters on the fringe were eager to promote Grassley's claims, none more so than Chuck Ross of *The Daily Caller*, the right-wing online publication co-founded by Fox News's Tucker Carlson. The headline on his March 31 story said it all: "Trump Dossier Financier Accused of Improper Work for Kremlin." Ross had an uncanny way of being on top of every Fusion-related development coming out of Grassley's office, almost as if he had a friend there. Ross would later be outed by *The Washington Post* for his past sexist and racist blog posts under the handle Gucci Little Piggy.

Despite all the noise coming from Grassley's office, no real legal threat had yet emerged. No one from the DOJ had ever reached out to Fusion for even so much as an explanation of its Prevezon work.

Fusion had decided in late March, when Grassley sent his first letter, to add the boutique D.C. law firm Cunningham Levy Muse to its legal team. Partner Josh Levy had worked on the Hill as counsel to Senator Chuck Schumer. He co-taught a class on congressional investigations at Georgetown and was respected by both parties on Capitol Hill. Levy's partner Bob Muse was a scrappy litigator who had been a staff attorney on the Senate Watergate Committee. Both were eager to help.

In the fights to come with congressional Republicans, they would prove adept at delivering brass-knuckle haymakers in a velvet glove.

———

Things might have been different had Grassley simply approached Fusion in good faith and asked Simpson or Fritsch to explain their past work. But given the way Grassley worked, that was unlikely. Grassley's chief investigative counsel, Jason Foster, was known for his ruthlessly partisan attacks on Democrats, particularly during the Obama administration.*

Grassley's decision to cast Fusion as a band of mercenaries who would do anything for money, even help Vladimir Putin, suggested to Fusion that Foster was pulling the strings. The attack was blatantly partisan and cynical: There was a logical disconnect in the notion that Fusion was working with Steele to research Trump's Russia connections at the same time it was supposedly lobbying Congress on behalf of Putin. To most neutral observers, it made no sense. That didn't matter in a world where one political party can safely ignore logic and facts and deliver its version of events directly to its base, unchallenged, on Fox News. It was relatively easy for Grassley to demonize Fusion without ever presenting actual evidence to back up his allegations.

Simpson, whom Browder had singled out for retribution, bore the brunt of the media attacks from Grassley's go-to reporters on the right. Personalizing the fight made sense for the Republicans: It's easier to demonize a person than an abstraction like a research consulting company.

It worked. Simpson was soon to be a star on Fox News and the opinion pages of *The Wall Street Journal*. It was helpful to have the attacks largely confined to a single partner, to draw fire away from the rest of the staff, but it was bruising for Simpson, who had never experienced this level of vitriol.

Before long, Fritsch and the other partners came in for personal attack, too. The *New York Post* ran an op-ed that highlighted Fritsch's

---

* During Obama's second term, Foster ran an investigation—done in conjunction with Representative Darrell Issa's staff in the House—of the so-called Fast and Furious program, in which ATF officials lost track of some two thousand guns that ended up in the hands of a Mexican drug cartel. *ProPublica* said Foster's probe was "marred by leaks of sensitive law enforcement information and allegations of partisan mischief directed at both Grassley and Issa. The probe seemed to generate outlandish accusations [against the Obama administration] unsubstantiated by evidence but aired publicly."

$1,000 donation to the Clinton campaign as evidence of his clear bias. Seeking to inject some Trumpian xenophobia into the mix, the column also incorrectly criticized Fritsch for having "married into a family with Mexican business interests" and said Fusion partner Tom Catan had "once edited a business magazine in Mexico." The racist dog whistle could be heard loud and clear: *These people are Trump's enemies.*

Family and friends urged Simpson and Fritsch to issue public statements pushing back against the smears. Others urged patience and silence. "Everything you say can—and will—be used against you," said one adviser. Besides, Grassley really had nothing to work with from a legal standpoint. Best to develop a thick skin.

On April 7, Grassley's deadline for a reply, Levy answered with a polite but firm rejection. Fusion's work was privileged and protected by the First Amendment, he explained. Fusion was contractually obligated to keep its work and communications with clients confidential.

The anxiety over Fusion's mounting legal fees was not idle. Simpson and Fritsch, in their years as reporters at *The Wall Street Journal,* had been in plenty of legal fights. But it's one thing to be sued for defamation over a story you wrote with a large media corporation standing behind you. It's quite another to face open-ended congressional inquiry and have to pay for it out of your own pocket. Fusion had business insurance, but that wasn't going to cover a congressional inquiry. If their corporate clients bolted en masse, the firm would be wiped out in a matter of months.

Many of Fusion's longest-standing clients weren't scared off, but others were wary of catching shrapnel from a politically charged fight with the administration and its congressional proxies. Fritsch and Simpson had to walk a number of clients through the big picture of Project Bangor. Yes, Steele was reliable, and the dossier was his work. No, he didn't pay people in Russia for information. Grassley would never be able to prove that Fusion was lobbying for Russia, because it wasn't.

The more sophisticated clients understood the partisan political cast of the moment and were well aware that Fusion's own work was grounded in arduous public records research. One client, whom Fusion called "the honey badger" for his aggressive style, urged Fusion to "keep up the good work," even as his company's CEO publicly supported Trump.

Slowly, though, some clients began to drift away. "Bad news," Fritsch told Simpson one day in March. "Project Aberdeen is dead." That client's upper management wanted nothing to do with Fusion. Ditto a major law firm Fusion had worked with for years. "We love you guys, you know that," said an executive who was one of the first to hire Fusion. For some clients with business before the U.S. government, cutting a check to the president's enemy #1 was just too risky.

Fritsch and Simpson wanted to reassure clients with public statements shooting down Grassley's accusations. Fusion partners drafted responses to media inquiries seeking to address congressional spin or outright misrepresentations. Those felt good to write, but they never saw the light of day. Not only could Fusion not tell its side of the story, it couldn't really cooperate with others wanting to do so. It turned down all interview offers.

Steele and Burrows, likewise, were a locked box. They weren't talking on the record to anybody, period. Steele had emerged from hiding in early March and told the television cameras outside his office that he would have nothing more to say. Orbis had legal problems of its own. Alexsej Gubarev of XBT Holdings—the company Steele's sources fingered for having a role in the hack of the DNC—had filed defamation cases against Steele in the U.K. and *BuzzFeed* in federal court in Florida soon after the dossier was published.

The threat of legal action took a turn for the worse on May 5 when lawyers for Alfa Bank's owners—three of Russia's wealthiest oligarchs, collectively worth tens of billions of dollars—wrote to Fusion, threatening to sue the company and Simpson individually for defamation related to "publication" of the dossier.

A decade earlier, Alfa had spent years pursuing a defamation case against the nonprofit Center for Public Integrity for reporting on allegations that one of its affiliates, Alfa Eko, "had been deeply involved in the early 1990s in laundering of Russian and Colombian drug money and in trafficking drugs from the Far East to Europe." The story had been extensively reported and was based on Russian and American government documents and interviews with former government officials, but Alfa managed to keep the case going for years, nearly bankrupting the group before a judge finally dismissed the case on the grounds that the CPI hadn't published the story with actual malice.

Fusion would now have to square off in court against the same Russian billionaires.

Luckily, a major infusion of donor money to Dan Jones's nonprofit meant Fusion wouldn't have to scramble to replace lost clients as desperately as it had feared; in fact, Fusion and Steele would have the budget to double down on their research.

The timing was good. Major news organizations were also expanding their coverage, launching major investigations into Russia and Trump's business record and global trail of failed partnerships. They, like Fusion, now had the budget and green light to go as deep as the story took them. The first stop, for some, would be Fusion's offices in Dupont Circle.

Fusion's researchers—particularly Berkowitz—were in demand among reporters who were new to the story and trying to get caught up. Did Fusion have the documents on Trump's golf courses in Scotland and Ireland? What about that ill-fated Trump project in Panama? Berkowitz had many of the answers already in his head; those he didn't he could pull out of the tens of thousands of pages of public records Fusion had collected over the past year and a half.

One of Fusion's research priorities in this period was following up on leads about what looked a lot like a Russian campaign to infiltrate the Republican establishment via the National Rifle Association. Many months earlier, Fusion researchers had identified the strange relationship between a Russian student at American University named Maria Butina and a former Russian central bank official close to Putin named Alexander Torshin, who was also a lifetime NRA member. Butina, too, was a big NRA fan and kept turning up in unexpected places on the American political scene. At the 2014 NRA convention in Indianapolis, she managed to get one-on-one photos with NRA chief Wayne LaPierre and then Louisiana governor Bobby Jindal. In April 2015, Butina and Torshin took a photo with presidential candidate and Wisconsin governor Scott Walker. Butina had even turned up at a Trump appearance in Las Vegas in July 2015, where she identified herself as Russian and asked Trump whether as president he would "continue the politics of sanctions that are damaging of both economy," prompting Trump to reply, "I believe I would get along very nicely with Putin."

Fusion had suspected since 2016 that Butina was acting as some sort of covert agent of the Russian government and eventually set out to expose her.

Born in 1988, Butina grew up in Barnaul, in the far-flung Altai territory, on Russia's border with Kazakhstan. She was a minor athlete, according to news reports, and her father appeared to be a modest furniture entrepreneur and her mother an engineer. That's about all you could find about her—until, that is, she joined forces with Putin friend Torshin to advocate for gun rights in Russia. That made no sense. Russia is a police state that brutally represses dissent; Putin is not in favor of a well-armed populace, and per capita gun ownership there is roughly a tenth of what it is in the United States.

On February 23, Simpson forwarded Bruce Ohr a new article about Butina from *The Daily Beast,* "The Kremlin and GOP Have a New Friend—And Boy, Does She Love Guns."

"Thank you!" Ohr responded.

In late March, Fusion—which had been investigating the NRA for private clients since shortly after the 2012 Sandy Hook Elementary School massacre in Newtown, Connecticut—began to look more closely at Butina's footprint in the United States. Research analyst Berkowitz noticed an odd connection between her and the Center for the National Interest, a Washington think tank known for being sympathetic to Putin's Russia. In June 2015, just as the 2016 presidential election cycle was getting under way, Butina had authored an article for the group's magazine, *The National Interest,* that waded directly into American presidential politics. "It may take the election of a Republican to the White House in 2016 to improve relations between the Russian Federation and the United States," Butina wrote. "As improbable as it may sound, the Russian bear shares more interests with the Republican elephant than the Democratic donkey."

"This is a small detail, but pretty crazy that Butina is getting stuff published in *The National Interest* as some unheard of 26-year-old," Berkowitz said in a note to his Fusion research colleagues. "The content is also insane. Again just one little suggestive thing, but how did that happen? Someone in conservative intellectual circles must have been pulling strings for her."

The CNI's board members included conservative grandee David Keene, a former NRA president, who also knew Butina's mentor, Torshin. Keene and Torshin had met in Moscow in 2015 on an NRA trip organized by Butina. The CNI, headed by a Russian émigré who frequently boasted of his close ties to Putin, also played a central role in the rollout of Trump's original foreign policy team in the spring of 2016, hosting a speech by Trump at the Mayflower Hotel in Washington at which Trump struck an unusually conciliatory tone with Russia. "Common sense says this cycle, this horrible cycle of hostility [between the United States and Russia], must end and ideally will end soon," Trump said. "Good for both countries."

The speech was written by Richard Burt, a Washington lobbyist representing Russia's Alfa Bank and a pipeline company owned by Russia's state-owned gas company, Gazprom. The event featured the Russian ambassador, Kislyak, in the front row; afterwards, the diplomat also attended a VIP event with Trump and several advisers.

It would later turn out that Berkowitz's suspicions were correct. Butina did indeed have a good friend helping her gain entrée to conservative circles. She was romantically involved with longtime Republican operative Paul Erickson, according to her 2018 guilty plea for having acted as an unregistered foreign agent. Erickson was a big GOP supporter and NRA booster from South Dakota who ran Pat Buchanan's 1992 presidential campaign. In 2019, federal prosecutors would charge him with fraud in an unrelated investment scam. He pleaded not guilty.

If Russian money did somehow enter the 2016 election, as some suspect, how exactly that happened has not been determined. But the accumulation of connections between the Russians, the NRA, and Trump raised increasingly pointed questions in Fusion's mind about whether this political alliance may have served as an easy conduit. Those suspicions were fueled, in part, by the NRA's record-setting $30 million outlay in 2016 in support of Trump, triple what it spent on Mitt Romney in 2012. The NRA has denied accepting donations from Russia for Trump.

Fusion had many other things on its plate by then. There were Trump deals, from Panama to the Dominican Republic to India, still to unravel. Fusion was working with Steele and a group of contractors in Europe to map Russian influence operations in European elections that mirrored Russian meddling in the 2016 U.S. election. Another priority was returning to some of the key characters from the 2016 research to see what Fusion might have missed.

Paul Manafort was at the top of that list.

Steele had said in many conversations that he suspected Manafort was channeling money through offshore companies that he and his agents had registered in the Mediterranean island of Cyprus.

Cyprus is a favorite bolt-hole for Russian money, and Fusion had some experience chasing down corporate records there. While authorities often coughed up little in response to document requests, a persistent Fusion staff member, Taylor Sears, kept at it. She compiled a detailed list of offshore companies possibly linked to Manafort and sent them to a Fusion source in Cyprus who, in turn, ran those names through the Cyprus company registry.

After a long string of strikeouts, Sears finally scored. Fusion's Cyprus source came back in the summer with documents that turned out to constitute the most damning evidence to date that Manafort was more than just a sleazy political consultant. A series of accounting reports filed with Cyprus corporate regulators showed that a Delaware entity belonging to Manafort, Jesand LLC, had received more than $10 million in funds from Cypriot entities whose sources of funding included the Russian oligarch Oleg Deripaska and a Ukrainian politician. That raised more questions about the kinds of people Manafort had been doing business with: Fusion had an old Austrian police report that described the Ukrainian as an associate of one of Russia's most notorious crime lords.

But the records also raised a new set of Manafort questions that were a lot closer to home. It now appeared that Manafort could be violating U.S. tax and money-laundering laws. The payments were described in the records as "loans," but Jesand didn't appear to have repaid any of them. Jesand also appeared in New York City real estate records as the buyer of a $2.5 million condo, along with Manafort's daughter Andrea and his wife, Kathleen.

"They moved more money to Jesand than what that New York City apartment cost," Sears noted to Simpson in mid-June. "Supposedly as 'loans.'"

"That Jesand stuff is a major find," Simpson said.

The Jesand loans and the New York condo deal were red flags for possible tax fraud, at a minimum. Many tax evasion schemes involve mischaracterizing profits and other types of income as loans, which allows the recipient to pocket the funds without paying any income tax.

"Taylor, can you put together a spreadsheet of every company around the world we have linked to Manafort? Just list company, jurisdiction, and suspected tie to Manafort," Simpson asked a few days later. She came up with a list of twenty-seven "Manafort Entities."

About $6.9 million of the Jesand loans, it turned out, came from another suspected Manafort company in Cyprus called Lucicle Consultants. But Lucicle itself had no assets and precious little cash in its own bank account. It in turn had received a loan of $6.9 million from a mysterious company in the British tax haven of Gibraltar, while another $2.4 million came from a company in the Caribbean tax haven of St. Kitts and Nevis. The memo listed a dizzying array of other convoluted transactions that reeked of money laundering and tax fraud.

"These are all places the Russians like to use to launder money," said Sears, an avid student of offshore finance schemes.

On a balmy day in early July, Simpson hopped an early-morning Acela train to New York to meet with some subcontractors. A former prosecutor for the Manhattan District Attorney's Office had also arranged for Simpson to have an informal sit-down with some local prosecutors interested in any information he might have relevant to possible wrongdoing by people related to Trump in New York. He brought a memo on Cyprus.

The meeting took place in a conference room at the state attorney general's offices in lower Manhattan. Simpson was expecting to meet one or two prosecutors. Instead there were more than half a dozen, including some from the New York Attorney General's Office.

Simpson laid out the story about how they'd first come across Felix Sater while investigating Trump for Fusion's Republican client, and then later Paul Manafort. Both had left a long trail of lawsuits and media coverage alleging that they may have engaged in serious crimes—and that trail crisscrossed New York. The prosecutors took notes but said little.

They did not let on that they were already working with the special counsel.

But Simpson spent most of the time talking about Manafort, describing how he'd been researching him on and off for years and was even trying to trace his assets for an anonymous client in London when Manafort suddenly surfaced at the Trump campaign. He sketched out the millions of dollars in suspicious loans to Manafort from shell companies in Cyprus that they'd recently discovered and how some of the money appeared to have been used by Manafort to buy a condo at 123 Baxter Street in Little Italy, a short ways from where they were meeting.

As things were wrapping up, though, the mood in the room seemed to shift when one of the prosecutors asked Simpson whether Fusion had any other clients who might present a conflict of interest for its Trump-Russia work. Somewhat baffled, Simpson said no.

"What about Russian clients?" the prosecutor pressed.

"Um, not that I can think of," said Simpson. "We don't currently have any."

It didn't occur to him that the prosecutor might be referring to the Prevezon case, which Fusion hadn't worked on since the year before. On that note, they thanked Simpson for his time and said they'd follow up.

Later, Simpson checked in with Mike McIntire, a *Times* investigative reporter looking at Manafort. They were acquaintances from journalism circles and had been chatting about Trump and Russia since April 2016, when McIntire published a scoop about an aborted criminal investigation by New York prosecutors into Trump's involvement with Bayrock and Felix Sater.

Simpson suggested he might want to dig a bit more on Manafort.

As it happened, by June, McIntire had already gotten onto some of Manafort's Cyprus companies. Simpson suggested the names of a couple more companies McIntire hadn't already found. On July 19, the *Times* published his groundbreaking story, "Manafort Was in Debt to Pro-Russia Interests, Cyprus Records Show." Never lacking in chutzpah, Manafort had his lawyer's PR man send an email to the *Times* demanding a retraction. It didn't work.

Months later, those Cypriot companies would become the cornerstone of Mueller's indictment of Trump's former campaign manager.

If there was ever any doubt that Grassley was in the tank for Trump, it was erased for good on Tuesday, May 9, the day Trump fired James Comey.

The FBI director's abrupt dismissal left little doubt that an aggrieved Trump was getting rid of the one person he thought could cost him his presidency; Trump even alluded to the ongoing Russia probe in his dismissal letter, thanking Comey for supposedly informing him that he was "not under investigation." The moment was seismic, raising the specter of presidential obstruction of justice and a constitutional crisis.

When the news broke, Steele immediately pelted Fritsch and Simpson with questions they couldn't answer, most important, whether the FBI would be forced to give up Steele's sources to Trump.

Steele was so worried, he had trouble sleeping. At around 3:15 in the morning U.K. time, Steele sent Ohr a text: "B, obviously it's chaotic with you over there right now but we should probably talk again over the next couple of days if you can. Do let me know what might work. Best."

They texted again at 7 P.M. the next day. "Very concerned about Comey's firing—afraid they will be exposed," Steele said, referring to his sources and adding that he'd also received a letter from the Senate Intelligence Committee seeking information about his dealings with the FBI. "Please let the FBI know," Steele asked. Ohr sought to reassure him once again, which wasn't easy.

Ohr followed up again over the weekend and the following week. When they weren't discussing Comey, Steele told Ohr about the broader investigations Orbis was now conducting on Russian interference in the elections in France, Germany, and the U.K. Asked if he'd be willing to share some of that information with U.S. officials, despite everything that had happened so far, Steele replied, "I would be inclined to do that. I need to check with my colleagues and my former employer. But I would like to do that."

Few bought Trump's pretext that Comey had been fired for botching the Clinton email investigation. Grassley, however, was one of them. "The handling of the Clinton email investigation is a clear example of how Comey's decisions have called into question the trust and political independence of the FBI," Grassley said. Public trust in Comey, he continued, "has clearly been lost."

Trump wasted no time making Grassley and his fellow Republicans look foolish. The next day, in a meeting in the Oval Office with Russian ambassador Kislyak and Moscow's foreign minister, Sergey Lavrov, Trump blithely acknowledged firing Comey to disrupt the FBI's Russia probe. "I faced great pressure because of Russia. That's taken off," Trump told the Russians. Details and photos from the meeting would trickle out nine days later—Russian state television network RT was the only media outlet in attendance. Comey was "crazy, a real nut job," Trump told the Russians, boasting that he had just fired him the day before.

It was an extraordinary breach. Here was the president of the United States, bragging to the Russians about having fired the head of the agency tasked with investigating his ties to the Russians. For Fusion, and many others, the president's alarming statements offered yet more evidence that the Russians had a hold over Trump.

Days later, Trump would repeat his boast in a nationally televised interview with NBC's Lester Holt.

Fritsch and Simpson understood those who made the argument that, in a sense, Comey had it coming. This was the guy, after all, whose FBI had torpedoed Clinton in the critical homestretch of the election and thrown journalists off the scent of the Russia probe in that ill-fated

Halloween story in *The New York Times*. He was self-aggrandizing and sanctimonious. But the White House's attempt to use Comey's fumbling of the Clinton email controversy as a pretext for firing him was too rich. Far more likely was that Trump had learned that a federal grand jury had just issued subpoenas regarding Michael Flynn.

"He decided that letting Comey proceed was worse than weathering the fallout from firing him," Catan said to Fritsch.

The Republicans seemed to see no problem in Trump's rash move to sack Comey, who was, after all, a fellow Republican. Grassley captured the prevailing sentiment on the right when he appeared on *Fox & Friends* and instructed Trump's critics to "suck it up and move on."

If Trump thought he'd settled the Russia matter once and for all, he was sorely mistaken. On May 17, 2017, Deputy Attorney General Rod Rosenstein, who had written a memo for the White House that gave Trump the legal cover to fire Comey, issued Order No. 3915-2017, appointing a special counsel "to investigate Russian interference with the 2016 election and related matters." Rosenstein was acting to restore public confidence in the Justice Department's Russia probe, though it seemed obvious that he was also reacting to Trump's firing of Comey. The one-page order even made reference to the FBI probe of links between Russia and the Trump campaign that Comey had publicly confirmed.

Leading the investigation would be former FBI Director Robert Mueller, a stern, stone-jawed Republican widely respected for his independence and rigorous investigative capabilities.

The Mueller appointment was a huge relief to Fusion. Trump's sacking of Comey had backfired, and badly. Rosenstein's order was broad and seemed to give Mueller the latitude to explore whatever he saw fit. At the same time, Simpson and Fritsch feared there would now be an even more ferocious effort by Republicans to undermine the foundation of the Mueller probe by arguing that the investigation had begun under false pretenses—that Trump was set up by Steele, Fusion, and the Democrats.

On June 7, Grassley sent Fusion a new broadside complaining that Levy had failed to adequately explain why its research on Trump in 2016 was confidential and protected by privilege. He gave Fusion a week to cough up documents and defend the legal grounds for withholding material.

Otherwise, he threatened, the committee could seek to compel testimony by subpoena.

To be sure, this was some serious saber-rattling, but it seemed unlikely that Grassley would be able to get the ranking Democrat on the committee, Dianne Feinstein, to agree to a subpoena, as required by Senate rules. That seemed especially true in the context of the moment. The same day Grassley sent his letter, former director of national intelligence James Clapper said the Watergate scandal "pales" in comparison with the alleged links between Russia and the Trump campaign.

The following morning, James Comey walked into a hearing of the Senate Intelligence Committee and took a seat alone before a phalanx of news and television cameras seated below a bank of senators. The nation was riveted over the next two and a half hours as Comey tore into the president, who was watching at the other end of Pennsylvania Avenue. Comey said there was "no doubt" Russia had hacked the DNC and attacked Trump for a lack of moral fiber, saying Trump had told "lies, plain and simple," about the reason for his firing the previous month. Trump, he said, had fired him to derail the Russia investigation, clearly implying the president had obstructed justice.

White House spokesperson Sarah Huckabee Sanders later responded: "I can definitively say the president is not a liar."

Comey's testimony was devastating. The former FBI director had notes of his interactions with Trump and was happy to share them with Mueller. Whatever the truth of Trump's dealings with Russia, Comey's testimony made clear that the president was desperate to cover it up. A week later, Trump himself let slip in one of his impetuous tweets that he was under investigation for the firing of Comey, a hint that the Justice Department could be pursuing an obstruction of justice case against a sitting president. This was Watergate territory.

Mueller's team quickly assembled some of the most aggressive criminal prosecutors in the country, drawing from the Justice Department and top law firms like WilmerHale. Lawyers for Trump and Kushner began scouring email and other records for anything that might hurt their clients. If there was something bad there, the lawyers didn't want to learn about it in an indictment.

It didn't take them long to come across a June 3, 2016, email from British publicist and music promoter Rob Goldstone to Donald Trump

Jr., purporting to have some hot information from his client Emin Agalarov, a Russian pop star and friend of the Trumps. The Agalarovs were close to Putin. They had teamed up with Trump to put on the Miss Universe pageant in Moscow in 2013; Trump had even made a cameo in one of Emin's music videos.

"The Crown prosecutor of Russia," Goldstone wrote to Don Jr., "offered to provide the Trump campaign with some official documents and information that would incriminate Hillary and her dealings with Russia and would be very useful to your father." Would Don Jr. and the campaign be willing to meet with these Russian representatives?

The offer prompted the now famous response from Don Jr.: "If it's what you say I love it especially later in the summer."

Goldstone's offer amounted to an official government overture offering its support to damage a U.S. presidential candidate. That didn't bother Don Jr.; he was all in. He, Manafort, and Kushner were ready to meet with "the Russian government attorney who is flying over from Moscow," even in the midst of a heated presidential campaign. A meeting was set for six days later.

The Goldstone emails, certain to come out one way or the other, made their way to reporters at *The New York Times* in what appeared to be a leak from the Trump camp in an effort to get out in front of and try to spin another damaging story about Trump's ties to Russia.

When news of that June 9 gathering broke in the *Times,* it sent shockwaves through official Washington and across the country. Here, for the first time, was ostensible evidence of Russian outreach to the highest levels of the Trump campaign, offering material that would damage Trump's opponent. And Trump's own son had gleefully said yes. It would immediately become known as "the Trump Tower meeting."

But there was a bizarre plot twist to the story—one that would pose enormous problems for Fusion.

CHAPTER FIFTEEN

NATALIA

IT WAS A TURN OF EVENTS ALMOST IMPOSSIBLE TO BELIEVE.

The delegation that appeared that day to sit with the Trump campaign brain trust was led by none other than Natalia Veselnitskaya, the lawyer for the Russian company, Prevezon, that Fusion had worked for indirectly in an unrelated court case. Suddenly she was at the epicenter of a mushrooming political scandal.

Veselnitskaya had somehow obtained a meeting with the top command of the Trump campaign in the middle of the 2016 race—at the same time that Fusion was working for Trump's opponent. For the Trump camp, it all made perfect sense. Here was Fusion working with dark unseen forces, to set Trump up, covering their tracks with the help of a buffoonish English publicist.

When the *Times* story on the Trump Tower meeting broke on July 8, 2017, identifying Veselnitskaya as "a Russian lawyer who has connections to the Kremlin," no one at Fusion knew quite what to make of it. Patrick Corcoran, the firm's director of research, polled the rest of the group.

"This is the same Veselnitskaya?" he asked, holding out hope there might be other Russian lawyers by that name.

"Pretty amazing," Simpson replied. "I mean, who knew?"

Within Fusion, the meeting marked a shocking overlap of events, one of those truly hard to fathom coincidences. The partners quickly recognized that to outside observers, this was all just more fuel for the conspiracy theories. Surely Fusion had engineered the encounter on behalf of its Democratic clients to taint the Trump campaign with connections to the Kremlin. The White House now had a story line to counter all the revelations about Flynn, Sessions, secret back channels, and undisclosed contacts with Russians.

Hours after the initial *Times* story posted, Trump's legal team produced a handy explanation: It was all Fusion's fault. While the exact identity of Fusion's Democratic clients was still a secret, it had been widely reported that the firm had taken on an unnamed Democratic sponsor after Trump secured the nomination.

"We have learned that the person who sought the meeting is associated with Fusion GPS, a firm which, according to public reports, was retained by Democratic operatives to develop opposition research on the President and which commissioned the phony Steele dossier," said Trump legal team spokesman Mark Corallo. "These developments raise serious issues as to exactly who authorized and participated in any effort by Russian nationals to influence our election in any manner."

The statement landed on a Saturday night in July, prompting a flurry of calls and texts among the Fusion partners, most of whom were off on weekend getaways.

"That statement is just silly more than anything," Fritsch said. "Complete nonsense," Simpson agreed. However, he added, they should probably clear the air. "The Sunday news programs will be all over this tomorrow morning, so we should probably have the lawyers issue a denial."

"It needs to be UN-lawyerly," Catan came back. "Like: *This makes no sense*, or, *What??*"

The problem was that, to a casual observer, it did look suspicious, and expressions of incredulity were not going to help.

On reflection, the basic facts *were* incriminating, at least circumstantially. The Trump Tower meeting appeared to have taken place the same day Simpson was in New York to attend a federal appeals court hearing with his client Veselnitskaya. Even more bizarre, Veselnitskaya was sitting down with the Trump campaign at the very moment in early June 2016 when Steele was beginning his assignment for Fusion that would result in his collection of a stream of information about alleged Russian collusion with Trump. It was all going to be difficult to explain, even to rational observers.

The truth was, Fusion did not know much about Veselnitskaya. Simpson had met her only a handful of times, sometimes only exchanging pleasantries. She was the Russian lawyer who'd hired the American lawyers for whom Fusion worked. Fusion mainly dealt with the Americans, and they were some of the firm's oldest clients—serious professionals.

Had the lawyers somehow missed something? Had Fusion? One or both of those interpretations now seemed possible. Veselnitskaya hadn't come across as some Kremlin power broker, and there was no reason to suspect that she had the political juice to get a meeting with the leadership of the Trump campaign. On the other hand, it was known to Russia watchers that the Kremlin's efforts to influence events in the West frequently involved Russian businessmen and other civilians with business in the West. Moreover, while the Prevezon case had started out as a dispute over some international banking transactions, it had evolved into a battle with Browder, Putin's bête noire. It certainly seemed possible that once Prevezon had begun to raise serious questions about Browder's financial machinations and unwillingness to testify in an American court, the Kremlin had taken an interest in the case.

The bottom line was that Fusion's role in the Prevezon case was more than a simple problem of optics. Simpson and Fritsch liked to think of themselves as savvy players, and yet here they were—apparently sucked into just the kind of Kremlin plot Steele reported had been going on for years.

Simpson wondered whether the Trump Tower meeting was a "chicken feed" operation, in which an intelligence service makes a broad promise of bringing useful information to a potential asset (in this case, Don Jr.) with the goal of determining how receptive he'd be to a more substantial relationship. The actual information exchanged at such a "dangle" meeting would be real, albeit relatively unimportant—or chicken feed—but would give Russia a window into where it could apply additional pressure down the line. In this case, the meeting attracted Trump's son, son-in-law, and campaign manager. That alone was valuable intelligence, and also potential blackmail material.

If that theory was right, it meant Veselnitskaya was more than just some corporate lawyer bumbling through a boring civil forfeiture case. She was playing a game of chess on another level. Once they got past their incredulity, the thought made the Fusion partners sick.

The truth about Fusion's role was far from nefarious but no less comforting: The firm *had* helped some Russians accused of money laundering defend themselves in federal court, for all to see. It was a civil case, not a criminal one, and the whole thing had been resolved with an out-of-court settlement after it became obvious that the government's evidence was shaky at best. Lawyers and investigators defend the accused every day; it is a role fundamental to the legal system. Steele liked to point out that Western courts are one of the only venues where Russians resolve their disputes without resorting to bribes or guns. In that sense, Fusion hadn't done anything wrong. But that wouldn't be obvious or matter to many people.

The truth was that legal work had little resemblance to the public interest investigative journalism the Fusion partners had practiced for much of their careers, and from which they derived their own self-image as basically good guys doing good things. They'd left that world behind years ago.

The media, prompted by Corallo's statement, had begun hounding Fusion to respond the following Sunday morning, July 9. The partners issued a straightforward public denial. "Fusion GPS learned about this meeting from news reports and had no prior knowledge of it," it read. "Any claim that Fusion GPS arranged or facilitated this meeting in any way is absolutely false."

Then Trump lent a hand, undercutting his own whitewash with a competing cover story issued while flying back across the Atlantic aboard Air Force One. In this version, which Trump himself dictated, the Trump Tower meeting was merely about reviving a bilateral program that enabled Americans to adopt Russian orphans. Fusion's denial and Trump's continued bumbling hastened the collapse of the White House cover story—at least in the mainstream media.

The sexier angle for the press was the Sunday follow-up in the *Times* revealing that Don Jr. had eagerly accepted the meeting with the Russians after they promised him dirt on Hillary Clinton. That fit with the rest of the building narrative of undisclosed Trump team contacts with the Russians. Corallo resigned from Trump's legal team a few days later.

As bad as the Trump Tower news was for the White House, it also undercut Fusion's efforts to put off the Senate Judiciary Committee, sucking the firm into a brutal episode of political attack and maneuvering. Now Grassley had a whole new avenue to explore: Just what did Fusion know about this Trump Tower meeting, and when did they know it?

On July 5, days before the *Times* story broke, Grassley had invited Simpson to testify before the committee at a hearing on compliance with the Foreign Agents Registration Act, a ploy to air Browder's grievances about Fusion's supposed lobbying for the Kremlin. Senator Feinstein, the committee's ranking Democrat and Grassley's most important counterweight, declined to sign the letter. That meant Simpson could safely decline the request. But he never got that chance.

In the wake of the Trump Tower explosion, Feinstein was becoming just as eager as Grassley to get in on the Russia scandal action. She responded to the news of the Veselnitskaya meeting at Trump Tower by proposing a committee subpoena to compel Manafort to testify about the encounter. That seemed to make sense on the surface, but it would turn out to play into Grassley's hands.

On Wednesday, July 12, Grassley put out a notice announcing his plan to hold a hearing about foreign agents, with just two nongovernment witnesses listed: William Browder and Glenn Simpson. A total PR stunt. Simpson had not agreed to testify, and Democrats had not agreed to subpoena him. As the Democrats quickly pointed out, why should the committee focus on Simpson when the most notorious alleged unregistered foreign agent in Washington was the former chairman of the Trump presidential campaign, Paul Manafort? And that was probably just what Grassley was hoping they would say. Behind the scenes, he began offering Feinstein what must have seemed like an irresistible deal: a subpoena of Simpson in exchange for subpoenas of Manafort and Donald Trump Jr.

By this point, Manafort had been under active federal criminal investigation for about a year. Given that, the likelihood that he would appear before the committee was low; if called, he would probably invoke his Fifth Amendment rights against self-incrimination or insist on a grant of immunity. (Manafort never did testify.) Trump Jr., whose central role in arranging the meeting meant that he, too, was obviously now going to come under scrutiny by the special counsel, was also unlikely to comply. Feinstein didn't seem to appreciate this.

The hearing—featuring Browder, Simpson, Manafort, and Trump Jr.—promised to be a major spectacle. Except for one thing: Grassley's staff cut a secret deal with Manafort and Trump Jr. to spare them the embarrassment of having to invoke the Fifth Amendment. Instead, Grassley would allow them to appear for a voluntary interview behind closed doors. Neither would have to explain the Trump Tower meeting in public.

Grassley's staff didn't clue Fusion in on this deal, instead applying intense pressure on Simpson and his lawyers to formally answer whether Simpson would testify publicly or invoke his Fifth Amendment rights. *Yes or no! Time's up! What will it be?* The Fusion partners and their legal team, given the confidentiality agreements in place with their clients, saw no option other than to notify the committee that Simpson planned to take the Fifth.

The optics of declining to appear, as bad as they were, were far better than Simpson getting badgered and battered by the Republicans in what was guaranteed to be a partisan show trial.

The trap sprung, it produced exactly the headline that Grassley wanted. "Co-founder of Firm Behind Trump-Russia Dossier to Plead the Fifth," blared Fox News.

The Fox report included a photo of Simpson taken surreptitiously at a conference he was attending at the time, the Aspen Institute's annual Aspen Security Forum, where many of the leading lights of the national security community had gathered to try to make sense of the Russian attack on the 2016 election. Fox News cameramen had shadowed Simpson, apparently trying to obtain video of him talking to former Obama national security officials.

The hate mail was pouring in again, too. "You are doing the wrong thing and will be caught," warned one message to Simpson on LinkedIn. "Hope your proud," said another. "You have sold out your own country. . . . The real Americans will never forget or forgive."

Only Browder would agree to appear at Grassley's show hearing on July 27. But the committee went ahead with it anyway, dedicating nearly four hours over two days to the supposedly underhanded deeds of Fusion GPS. What started out being framed as a high-minded exercise in oversight of the Foreign Agents Registration Act wound up as an extended bashing of Fusion for a litany of supposed sins having nothing to do with that law—or even lobbying, for that matter. The star of the show would be the Trump Tower meeting, an event Browder knew about only from news reports.

For the Fusion staff, watching it all unfold on C-SPAN, the hearing was quite the spectacle. Unscrupulous politicians and their allies can do pretty much whatever they want with a congressional hearing. Thanks to the separation-of-powers doctrine at the heart of the Constitution, an elected official can slander anyone with total impunity.

The Democrats did little to push back. Feinstein even made a show of guaranteeing that the Magnitsky Act would never be repealed. That had the effect, in a hearing about supposedly improper lobbying by Fusion that had never even occurred, of validating Browder's vehement but vague allegations that Fusion had somehow gone to bat for the Kremlin and lobbied against the act.

Even as Grassley and his allies bellowed on about the evils of Fusion and political opposition research, one of his own staffers, a longtime Republican operative named Barbara Ledeen, was getting ready to face the music from the Mueller team, which had secretly opened up an investigation into her activities.

Ledeen was the wife of Michael Ledeen, a conservative foreign policy activist who had a brush with fame during another Republican scandal, the 1980s Iran-Contra affair. Michael had been a consultant working with the National Security Council and was accused of transferring arms to Iran in the secret arms deals between the United States, Israel, and Iran—a lower-profile version of Lieutenant Colonel Oliver North. The Ledeens were known in Washington as peddlers of far-right propaganda and were good friends of Michael Flynn, Trump's disgraced former national security adviser. Michael Ledeen was also a Trump foreign policy adviser who the Mueller report notes was in contact with Flynn shortly before Flynn had his infamous telephone call with the Russian ambassador about dropping sanctions on Russia.

During the campaign, Trump had famously urged Russia to look for the thirty thousand "missing" emails Clinton said she had deleted from her private email server. Behind the scenes, as Mueller would later report, Trump had also tasked Flynn with the hunt for the missing emails, a job he undertook with Barbara Ledeen and a Republican financier and operative named Peter Smith.

Many months before Trump's entreaty, Barbara Ledeen had emailed Smith to say that the Chinese, Russian, and Iranian intelligence services could "reassemble the [Clinton] server's email content." Smith raised tens of thousands of dollars and hired security experts to track down the emails. He even claimed, according to the Mueller report, that "he was in contact with hackers 'with ties and affiliations to Russia' who had access to the emails, and that his efforts were coordinated with the Trump campaign."

The special counsel devoted several pages of its report to describing the activities of the Ledeens but never established whether any of that was true. Smith's effort, which he did communicate to Trump campaign co-chairman Sam Clovis, never found any Clinton emails. However, the report established that Smith appeared to have inside information late in the campaign about WikiLeaks's plans to publish John Podesta's hacked emails, reporting that the group "will save its best revelations for last."

In May 2017, Smith checked into a motel in Rochester, Minnesota, near the Mayo Clinic, and tied a plastic bag over his head. His death was ruled a suicide.

Many of the details of the role played by one of Grassley's own staff members in the Trump campaign's effort to procure Hillary Clinton's emails from the Russians would remain a closely guarded secret for another two years. There was much irony in Grassley's focus on Fusion at a time when a senior member of his team was being investigated for Russia ties by the law enforcement community he purported to oversee.

In the summer of 2017, of course, the public knew little about what Mueller and his team were doing. The political stakes of his probe were incredibly high, and his staff were under strict orders not to leak. And they didn't. Reporters would stake out the special counsel's office in Washington, trying to figure out who came and went, striking out more often than not.

Fusion was also keeping its secrets. After Mueller's appointment, Simpson again began pressing Steele to connect the FBI with one of his sources who was outside Russia. Sometime after Mueller was appointed, Steele told Ohr how to find the source, which Ohr then relayed to the Bureau.

With strong encouragement from Simpson and Fritsch, Steele and Burrows had also sat down in September 2017 with a team of prosecutors and FBI agents from the special counsel's office at a London hotel. Steele already knew one of the agents. There was a little chest-beating at the start: Steele and Burrows reminded the investigators that they'd spent their entire careers being loyal allies of the United States and had no intention of changing course. They had nothing to hide, Steele said, but he demanded assurances that any information they provided about sources would not leak and put them in physical danger. The interview lasted the better part of two days. While Simpson and Fritsch were curious to hear the details, they decided it would be better not to know, so they couldn't be forced to provide that information if asked under subpoena.

For Fusion, it was tempting to leak news of this meeting to the media or the Democrats as a way to throw Republicans off-balance and possibly take some of the heat off. News that Mueller's office was now working with Steele would prove Orbis had no fear of an honest, independent investigation.

Simpson and Steele also debated whether and how to help some of the congressional committees. Steele had no faith that the committees would honor pledges of confidentiality. It was an agonizing dilemma, as Steele told Ohr. "The congressional committees leak," Steele said. "I want to help. But I don't want to see it all played out in the press for political points."

Fusion and Orbis decided they had no choice but to keep quiet.

There were plenty of other clues that Mueller's probe was gathering steam.

An increasingly desperate Manafort had finally registered in June with the Justice Department as a foreign agent for Ukraine and disclosed more than $17 million in payments to his consulting firm—a filing that by his own admission was several years late. It was clear to the Fusion team that Manafort's lawyers were scrambling to limit his legal exposure.

The action was even more dramatic behind the scenes. Early one morning in late July, the day before Grassley's hearing about the evils of Fusion, FBI agents raided Manafort's home in Alexandria, Virginia. A day later, former Trump foreign policy adviser Papadopoulos was arrested by the FBI at Dulles Airport after stepping off a flight from Munich. The Mueller team wanted to talk to him about his knowledge of Russian offers to help the Trump campaign.

The president's men were in real trouble.

News of the FBI raid on Manafort broke in *The Washington Post* two weeks later, giving more urgency to the Republican bid to discredit Fusion. Now that Mueller was clearly gaining momentum, the Fusion partners were even more convinced that it was important to his probe that they delay appearing before any public congressional hearings for as long as possible. There was also the risk that Republicans would extract something in the hearings that could lead to the revelation that one of their clients had been the Clinton campaign—which Republicans would use to impugn the Mueller probe. The more time went by, they reasoned, the stronger Mueller's case would become and the weaker the White House case for firing Mueller would be.

After Grassley successfully goaded Simpson into stating his intention to take the Fifth, Levy raised hell with Grassley's staff. Levy worked out a deal for Simpson to sit for a voluntary, closed-door interview that would be extremely limited in scope and would allow Fusion to keep confidential the identities of its clients and sources. Grassley withdrew his subpoena.

Simpson's interview with Senate Judiciary staff was set for 9:30 A.M. on August 22. This was not an encounter to be taken lightly. What he said would be on the record: Any slipup, any misremembered fact, could come back to haunt Fusion. So for two weeks straight, Simpson made a beeline for the Dupont Circle offices of Cunningham Levy Muse to prepare for his testimony.

During one of these sessions, Simpson recalled an aspect of Steele's dealings with the FBI that they'd kept secret for so long he'd almost forgotten about it. During the Rome meeting, Steele's handlers at the FBI had let slip that the Bureau had information from inside the Trump campaign that supported Steele's reporting.

"Apparently, someone at the Trump campaign bragged to someone else that the Russians were providing information hacked from the Democrats to the campaign," Steele told Simpson. "Whoever heard it decided to blow the whistle to the FBI."

It sounded to Steele like that whistleblower was someone low down on the totem pole, a secretary or intern, perhaps. It would later turn out not be a whistleblower, but George Papadopoulos. While Simpson didn't know that at the time, he was confident enough in Steele's account of the Rome meeting that he decided to bring it up during questioning in an effort to bat aside the Republican premise that Steele and Fusion had cooked up the FBI investigation.

Grassley's show-trial FARA hearing the previous month meant there was no longer any question that his staff was bent on destroying Simpson's credibility. He searched his memory for every stupid thing he'd ever done, anything embarrassing in his background. There was plenty. He'd made his mistakes with alcohol. That didn't seem likely to be the kind of thing anyone would find particularly interesting many years later, but you never knew. If asked, best to fess up. There were also old libel cases against him at the *Journal* (which the *Journal* successfully defended) and countless investigations they'd run at Fusion that had sparked one controversy or another. Sleep came late, if at all, counting all the possible things that might come up.

Witness preparation is basically an exploration of the limits of memory. It's important to recall events as best you can; it's equally important not to speculate about events you can't recall precisely. Over many hours, Simpson sat with Levy and Muse going over the galaxy of questions they expected Simpson would get from both sides. The Republicans would be fishing for intel on Fusion's clients and seeking to portray Simpson as a partisan dumpster diver who worked for Russians.

The interview was supposed to be conducted without notice to the press, but someone on the committee made sure to leak the time and place to the networks, resulting in a stakeout by broadcast news camera crews.

Levy's insistence that Simpson be afforded the exact same ground rules as Manafort and Don Jr. meant that Simpson was sitting for a voluntary interview and could refuse to answer certain questions without invoking the Fifth. The identities of sources and Fusion clients, Levy warned, were both off-limits.

Things got off to a rocky start when the Grassley investigator began quizzing Simpson on whether he had any offshore bank accounts or controlled any foreign companies—a tactic intended to unsettle him. The answers were no and no. But the questions annoyed Simpson. When the investigator next asked whether Fusion had an account at TD Bank in Washington, D.C., Simpson was too quick to say yes to what seemed like a routine question. Levy tried to object, but it was too late. The Republicans had obtained a vital piece of intelligence that they would later seek to exploit to the fullest.

The Republicans managed to get through the whole nine-and-a-half-hour exercise without turning to Trump's involvement with the Russians. The Democrats, on the other hand, wanted to know everything—especially regarding how Fusion had come to hire Steele.

"That calls for a somewhat long answer," Simpson said, explaining in detail for the first time how Fusion had already conducted a lengthy investigation of Trump's business empire by the time Steele came along. Simpson recounted the circumstances of the engagement with Steele and the former spy's early judgment that there was a possible crime in progress, which he felt duty-bound to report.

The Republicans, from the testimony's start at 9:34 A.M. until it finally wrapped up at 7:04 P.M., fixated on scrounging up any scrap of information that could support Browder's allegations about the Magnitsky lobbying controversy or prove that Simpson was the real mastermind of the Trump Tower meeting. Simpson thought it best to avoid antagonizing them by pointing out the fatal (and obvious) flaw in the fevered Trump Tower–Fusion conspiracy theory: If Fusion had arranged or even heard about a meeting between the Trump campaign and the Russians to get dirt on Hillary Clinton, wouldn't they have told the FBI, the Democrats, the Clinton campaign, and the media *before* the election?

The Republicans kept returning to Browder's many allegations, so Simpson decided to tell them all about Browder: how he'd ducked three lawful subpoenas, once by changing his SEC filings and twice by running away; how he'd surrendered his American citizenship and paid no taxes to his native country on his millions in profits from Russia yet secretly owned a mansion in Colorado, how Fusion found offshore companies he controlled in the leaked money-laundering documents known as the Panama Papers. "William Browder talks a lot about the Panama Papers and the Russians who are in the Panama Papers without ever mentioning that *he's* in the Panama Papers," Simpson said.

The Republicans probed for any information that suggested Fusion had a record of manipulating the government and the media. Their questions all drew on the myth, perpetuated by the editorial page of *The Wall Street Journal*, that Fusion was some left-wing puppeteer of a pliant press.

Did Fusion bribe journalists? No. Did Fusion get paid to manipulate the government into opening investigations? No. Those were not the answers Grassley's investigators were hoping for. *What about the FBI?* they asked. *How many times did you talk to them during the campaign?* None. Discouraged, they dropped this line of questioning.

The Democrats were far more interested in Trump and the Russians, but woefully unfamiliar with the subject matter—unsurprising, given the Judiciary Committee's belated attempt to snatch the Trump-Russia turf (and limelight) away from their colleagues on the Intelligence Committee. So Simpson spent a lot of time explaining the basics about Trump, Putin, and subjects such as the Russian Mafia. He had to slowly spell out a number of Russian names they'd never heard.

During a round of questioning by Feinstein's counsel, Simpson disclosed the gist of his conversation with Steele following Steele's October 2016 meeting in Rome with the FBI. "Essentially," Simpson said, "what he told me was they had other intelligence about this matter from an internal Trump campaign source.... My understanding was that [the FBI] believed Chris at this point ... because they had other intelligence ... and that one of those pieces of intelligence was a human source from inside the Trump organization." The Republicans made no attempt to follow up.

When the interview finally ended, Simpson and the lawyers attempted to escape the building without having to do another perp walk in front of the cameras. A crew spotted them and came in hot pursuit. They foolishly attempted to hide in a bathroom. The crew followed. They tried hiding in a stall, and the cameras started shooting them over the top of the stall. Cornered, Levy struck a deal with them: He would make a statement in a more dignified setting outside the building, where he offered a bland summation noting that Simpson had patiently replied to every question put to him.

Afterwards, they repaired to a pub at Union Station. Levy's first call was to Fritsch. Fusion staff had heard nothing all day and were dying for news. "How did he do?" Fritsch asked. "Killed it," Levy said.

No sooner had Fusion put the Senate Judiciary testimony behind it than the action shifted back to the House. Devin Nunes's House Intelligence Committee had reached out to Fusion on August 18 with a vague request for documents about Russia and the election. The committee hadn't really articulated what it wanted to investigate, but it was clear that they intended to beat up on Fusion in one way or another. They also wanted to hear from Steele, so badly, in fact, that two Nunes committee staffers—unbeknownst to the Mueller team, committee Democrats, or Senate investigators—made a clandestine trip to London in a foolish gambit to find Steele and speak to him. They even showed up outside his lawyers' office, leaving their business cards before slinking off. This was partisan amateur hour masquerading as aggressive government over-sight.

The committee's outreach to Fusion was similarly ham-fisted. It took the Nunes team a month to spell out what it wanted. In Septem-ber, committee Republicans finally said they wanted all Fusion docu-ments related to "the Russian active measures campaign targeting the 2016 U.S. election." They asked questions they knew Fusion couldn't possibly answer, including "What possible leaks of classified informa-tion took place related to the intelligence community assessment of these matters?"

In the committee's haste to fire up its investigative machine, it ap-peared to have simply cut and pasted some language from a previous missive it had sent to the CIA or some other intelligence agency. Fusion, of course, had no knowledge of what went on inside the intelligence community.

Nunes, a former Trump transition adviser, had recused himself from any Trump-Russia inquiry after he was busted months earlier surrepti-tiously collaborating with the White House to surface classified docu-ments that he claimed showed improper "surveillance" of the Trump campaign. That partisan stunt was an ongoing matter of investigation by the House Ethics Committee. It seemed apparent from the attempted ambush of Steele in London and the committee's pursuit of Fusion, how-ever, that he hadn't really recused himself and didn't care about the out-come of the ethics probe.

Nunes's staff didn't really seem bothered by documents or a serious investigation of Russian interference in the 2016 election. It wanted a series of perp walks to create the impression of guilt, starring Simpson, Fritsch, and Catan. Fusion's lawyers engaged with the committee to try to figure out what specifically they wanted to know, pointing out that Simpson had already answered questions for ten hours before the Senate Judiciary Committee. Wouldn't it make sense to read that transcript to avoid redundancy and make any interview more productive?

Nunes's reply: *Tell us when you're showing up or we'll subpoena you to appear.*

The legal cloud enveloping Fusion darkened further on October 3 when the three oligarchs who owned Russia's Alfa Bank filed a defama-tion suit against Fusion in D.C. federal court for its alleged role in pub-lishing the dossier. One of Steele's reports had highlighted Alfa's closeness to Putin—a claim later substantiated by the Mueller report—and described alleged details of the owners' relationship to the Russian leader. The suit disputed the accuracy of Steele's reporting.

The next day, Nunes issued subpoenas to Catan, Fritsch, and Simpson. He did so unilaterally, without seeking the consent of Adam Schiff, the leading Democrat on the committee. This was a breach of committee rules, not to mention comity, and a clear message that the investigation had little to do with the committee's role overseeing the Intelligence Community. There was nothing Schiff could do to stop it.

Of course, the Nunes strategy all along had probably been to make Fusion an offer it could refuse—baiting them into taking the Fifth, as Grassley had done—to create the impression of guilt. Indeed, the Fusion partners had mixed feelings about doing so and worried that they were playing into Nunes's hands. Invoking the Fifth was a constitutional right, but few understood why an innocent person would take that course.

Fritsch tried to explain the nuances of what was happening to his elderly mother, hoping to prepare her for what was likely to be ferocious spin from Nunes and the White House, once the committee leaked Fusion's intention to take the Fifth.

"Well, Pete," she said, "I'm sure that if you just tell them the truth, they'll understand."

"I don't think so, Mom."

Normally, Congress will excuse witnesses from having to appear once they communicate their intention to exercise their Fifth Amendment rights. In the 1970s, the Senate excused the Watergate burglars from having to appear to plead the Fifth. And only months earlier, Nunes himself had excused Michael Flynn from having to appear to take the Fifth. The Fusion partners, however, were given no such consideration. Nunes wanted his moment. So, on the morning of October 18, Fritsch and Catan made their way to the House Intelligence Committee's secure hearing room in the basement of the Capitol. They took the Fifth and bolted before the handful of reporters assembled by Fox News and the other pro-Trump media knew they were there.

Nunes himself didn't even bother to show up. He got what he wanted out of the supposedly confidential encounter: a spate of headlines that all blared some version of the people behind the dossier taking the Fifth. Nunes's biggest fan, Trump, weighed in quickly on Twitter with the first of what would be a steady stream of tweets attacking Fusion: "Workers of firm involved with the discredited and Fake Dossier take the 5th. Who paid for it, Russia, the FBI or the Dems (or all)?"

Fusion staff would later set those tweets in gaudy gilt frames—an homage to Trump's own taste for schlock—and hang them as an exhibit in the office entryway.

The Fifth Amendment wasn't going to stop Nunes, however. Behind the scenes, his staff was working with Grassley's to continue peeling the Fusion onion in an attempt to answer Trump's tweet. Who, indeed, had paid for it?

CHAPTER SIXTEEN

CAPTAIN AMERICA

FUSION LEARNED OF THE REPUBLICANS' NEXT, MOST UNDER-handed attack in early October, thanks to a bit of emergency preparedness.

Nunes had secretly served a subpoena on TD Bank for every transaction in Fusion's corporate account for the prior two years. Neither the committee's Democrats nor Fusion knew of the move, which was just how Nunes wanted it. He gave the bank seven working days to reply and hoped he'd get the records before anyone could object.

His ploy was outed when Fusion's lawyers learned of it from TD Bank. The lawyers had feared such a move since Simpson was asked about TD Bank during his testimony in August. They had warned the bank in writing that it should immediately notify Fusion of any subpoenas. So notified, Fusion asked a federal judge to issue a temporary restraining order to stop any release, which it got, touching off a big legal fight with the House.

Nunes's move was an indication that something even more sneaky was afoot. Simpson had mentioned TD Bank only to the Senate Judiciary Committee, in supposedly confidential testimony. It seemed obvious, then, that Grassley's staff was back-channeling with Nunes's staff to get around Feinstein and her fellow Democrats on the Judiciary Committee, who were no longer interested in pursuing Fusion. The bank records would give Nunes a granular view into Fusion's business operations, including payments from Perkins Coie, who served as lawyers for the DNC and the Clinton campaign.

"This is existential stuff here," Fritsch said to Simpson. "We can't let all our clients be exposed because [Perkins Coie] couldn't be bothered to pull their heads out of the sand" and admit it had hired Fusion—which was what Nunes was really after.

It was inevitable that their Trump research clients would be un-masked at some point, but the Fusion partners had all agreed that it was important to protect them for as long as possible. Upholding Fusion's reputation for protecting clients and denying Trump any ammunition to use against Mueller and the FBI were paramount.

Fusion filed suit against TD Bank asking a federal court to prohibit the bank from complying with the subpoena on the grounds that the bank had no right to violate the company's privacy to comply with an improper and overly broad subpoena that aimed to rummage through all of Fusion's records, not just those related to the Trump research. The filing accused Nunes and his colleagues of waging a campaign of illegal leaks against Fusion and violating the constitutional rights of both the firm and its clients. There was little hope of winning: The courts are not inclined to challenge the powers of Congress. But there were legitimate questions about the validity of a subpoena issued by a chairman under ethics investigation and without a proper committee vote, especially a subpoena written to scoop up records of innocent third parties with no relation to the Russia investigations.

The House's lawyers insisted to the court that everything the Re-publicans had done was completely proper. But when the judge indi-cated that she was not going to simply reject Fusion's concerns, they blinked and agreed to a court-approved "protective order" to narrow their demands and prohibit public disclosure of the records—a legal victory for Fusion that put off the day of reckoning for at least another month.

As the fight dragged on, the political and financial pressure on Fu-sion mounted, and tensions over how to proceed arose within its ranks. Clients and the press were pelting the firm with queries about what was happening. Death by legal fees was not out of the question.

Fritsch and Simpson staked out different positions. Fusion should not be spending untold sums, Fritsch said, to protect Perkins Coie and the *Free Beacon* when neither had stepped forward to help Fusion. They should be encouraged to either contribute to the cause or relieve Fusion of the obligation to protect them any longer.

Simpson argued that Fusion had no right to expect help from their clients since they hadn't asked their permission to share Steele's information. Having the clients essentially out themselves was unlikely to satisfy Nunes, he said. And there was a higher purpose to continuing the fight, even if that meant battling all the way to the Supreme Court. Fritsch took to calling Simpson "Captain America" for his vows to protect the republic at all costs. The partners faced an unappealing choice: loyalty to former clients or loyalty to the partners and employees of Fusion.

The media made the choice for them. On October 24, *The Washington Post* reported that Fusion and Steele had been paid by the Clinton campaign and the Democratic National Committee through Perkins Coie, a fact that Fusion had managed to keep secret in the nearly eleven months since the dossier broke. Perkins had finally fessed up in the *Post* story. Simpson was annoyed and accused Fritsch of leaking the story to the *Post*, a charge he denied. In fact, reporters had been zeroing in on Perkins Coie for days after a *Times* story said Elias had helped "lead research into Russian efforts to help Donald J. Trump and damage Mrs. Clinton during the 2016 presidential campaign."

The story was going to break no matter what Fusion or anyone else did. But the stress of the situation was beginning to cause suspicions and rifts to build between two old friends and partners.

The news about Perkins Coie meant that Trump's favorite foil, Hillary Clinton, had now resurfaced to give him a delicious public relations reprieve. The news was red meat for the "lock her up" crowd, prima facie evidence that the dossier was a political hit.

Fox & Friends jumped on the news. Their viewer in chief followed up on Twitter, decrying the DNC funding of the "Fake News Dossier." Lost in all the expressions of faux outrage on the right was one question: Why would Fusion or the DNC pay for a phony document it presumably could have made up for free? And if the dossier was such a dastardly political hit piece, why had so little of it filtered into the news before the election?

Trump's attempt to lay his troubles at the feet of Democrats was once again short-lived. Three days later, the Republican-funded *Washington Free Beacon*—a publication widely associated with billionaire and megadonor Paul Singer—confirmed that it had been Fusion's first client for the Trump research. The revelation baffled many of the capital's partisans and underscored what a strange animal Fusion was in the hyper-partisan world of twenty-first-century Washington.

The *Free Beacon* revelation was quickly swamped by even worse news for the White House. The following Monday, October 30, Mueller unveiled his first criminal charges against Trump campaign chairman Paul Manafort and his business partner Rick Gates—a twelve-count indictment for conspiracy to commit money laundering related to their work for a pro-Russian political party in Ukraine. Trump's pathetic reply on Twitter: "Sorry, but this is years ago, before Paul Manafort was part of the Trump campaign. But why aren't Crooked Hillary & the Dems the focus?????"

Also charged was the obscure former Trump campaign adviser George Papadopoulos, who admitted to lying to the FBI when asked about his contacts with people claiming to be in a position to arrange meetings with Russian officials.

The moment was sweet vindication for the Fusion team. Mueller, a Republican former FBI director, had handed down indictments that indicated a pattern of Russian efforts to compromise the Trump campaign and its senior officials—the core assertion the first memo in the dossier had made sixteen months earlier.

But by this time, what seemed obvious to Fusion and many mainstream journalists was no longer sufficient to clear the air of the idea that the firm was a political hit squad. Fusion was under daily assault by a now flourishing ecosystem of pro-Trump propaganda sites that appeared to be working closely with congressional Republicans to bury the facts of Trump's Russia connections and attack Fusion GPS.

At the forefront of this alt-right fog machine were Tucker Carlson's *Daily Caller* and a site called *The Federalist*. Many of *The Daily Caller's* articles about Fusion were attributed to the Daily Caller News Foundation, which appeared to be an oblique way of signaling that the news was sponsored by private donors. *The Federalist* had been founded by a young blogger who later resigned from the *Post* amid plagiarism charges, and had previously been exposed for taking cash from lobbyists for the government of Malaysia while writing articles helpful to their client. Still more attacks came from more established news organizations, like *Forbes*, that were also known to accept contributions from writers on the payrolls of PR firms.

The sites cranked out a steady supply of outlandish pieces accusing Fusion of various sleazy deeds, including bribing journalists to write articles helpful to Fusion's clients. It all seemed so absurd to everyone at Fusion that they would have ignored the noise entirely if it didn't have the pernicious effect of validating what some very powerful people in Congress and the White House were saying: Nunes and Grassley were also pushing the line that the allegations of sinister dealings between Trump and the Russians was all fake news cooked up by Clinton's goons at Fusion. The partners discussed options for dealing with the whole mess, including having Simpson leave the company, but decided that nothing would satisfy Trump and his defenders.

That was when an unexpected attack came from within the Fusion camp.

Before he became its biggest breach, Russell Carollo was one of Fusion's greatest assets.

Carollo was a former Pulitzer Prize–winning journalist with a rarefied and somewhat quirky talent: forcing reluctant bureaucrats to cough up information under the Freedom of Information Act. At its best, FOIA gives Americans more transparency into government and holds public servants accountable. Enacted in 1967, FOIA mandates the disclosure of previously unreleased federal records when they are requested by the public. But it takes an obsessive, relentless personality to stick with the fight and force compliance with open-records laws. Most of the time it is an exercise in frustration, leading many reporters to eschew the process altogether. Every so often, though, it yields priceless discoveries.

Carollo was something of a secret weapon and Fusion's longest-tenured contractor. Shortly after Simpson left *The Wall Street Journal* in 2009, he hired Carollo to file FOIAs on a couple of his first research contracts and never stopped. After Fusion was founded in 2010, the firm became Carollo's anchor client for a cottage business he built making FOIA requests for private clients from his home in rural Colorado.

He was a bit of an eccentric and a definite Luddite who required equal amounts of gentle persuasion and cash subsidies to ditch his Netscape browser and put in a new scanner—qualities that only endeared him to everyone at Fusion. And clients loved the results. After perusing some of Carollo's juicier product and hearing a bit of his backstory, one client dubbed him the "FOIA bomber" for the obsessive attributes he shared with Unabomber Ted Kaczynski. It stuck.

The FOIA bomber's emails, always eccentric missives filled with administrative arcana, began to take a turn toward the paranoid and conspiratorial in the fall of 2016. People were out to get him, he said. The other thing Carollo revealed to the Fusion partners was that he'd recently been diagnosed with Parkinson's disease. Informed by his doctors that his prospects for treatment were poor, Carollo announced in an email that he'd decided to sell his house and go off to Europe for some last adventures while he still had his health. Simpson set him up with some potential job leads and promised that Fusion would continue to give him work if he needed to support himself.

In December, he reappeared—in Sarajevo. "I am on the 9th floor of Radon Plaza, the largest hotel in Bosnia," he began in a rambling email. "I am in a suite reserved for the president of the country, or The President's Suite in case you call. The suite would cost $10,000 a night in New York, but I am paying a Motel 6 rate thanks to a friend I met here in 1994."

By the spring of 2017, mutual friends in Europe were expressing alarm at Carollo's behavior. Toward the end of September, at the height of the congressional investigations into Fusion, Fritsch and Simpson got a particularly distressing email. "Glenn: All you had to do was call me and say you needed help," Carollo wrote. "Instead, tracer files were put in my computer."

The note ended menacingly: Fusion would have to wire him 15,000 Swiss francs to buy back copies of all the FOIA files he'd executed on Fusion's behalf over the years, or else. As blackmail plots go, this was nothing to get suicidal over. After all, Carollo's job was looking for public records. He did, however, have about eight years' worth of email with Fusion that he also wanted to sell back—for another 5,000 francs. (A franc was roughly equivalent to a U.S. dollar at the time.)

"Poor guy, sounds like he may have dementia," said Catan. A quick check of medical websites showed that many early-onset Parkinson's victims were indeed prone to dementia. Fritsch wrote Carollo back, ignoring the extortion attempt: "No one here wants anything but the best for you, Russell. We had a great working relationship for a lot of years and see you as a colleague and friend."

His sense of reality dimming and with no promise of payment from Fusion, Carollo began trying to sell his material to newspapers from a perch in Switzerland. He sent Fusion an email recounting an unsuccessful effort to sell its proprietary data to *The New York Times*. Fritsch encouraged Carollo to seek help. His dementia was clearly getting worse. The threats were another absurd yet real problem: In the political environment now enveloping Fusion, even the most banal internal company material was liable to be spun in ways that would be damaging to the company's reputation and its clients. They debated filing a complaint with the Swiss police but couldn't bring themselves to do it.

By the end of October, Simpson and Fritsch thought the sad episode with Carollo had faded away, until they got a call one day from *The Washington Post*. The paper's reporters had worked closely with Fusion on some of its biggest Trump scoops and had largely ignored Republicans' efforts to create an alternative narrative about a rogue deep state in the Justice Department. But the bank records fight was in the news, and Fusion's clients had come forward. Now the paper needed a profile of Fusion, and fast. Fusion found out the *Post* reporters were working with Carollo and his email cache when Carollo mistakenly left a message on Fusion's voicemail intended for Shawn Boburg, the *Post* reporter working on the story.

"Hey, Shawn, it's Russell. I'm in Zurich," he said. "There's some other people interested in the story and I just wondered what's going on."

Fusion's partners could hardly complain about being investigated, and it certainly wasn't the first time. But the line the reporters were taking seemed to buy into some of the conspiracy theories swirling at the time. *Does Fusion pay journalists? Does Fusion routinely dig through divorce files? Does Fusion encourage its contractors to misrepresent themselves as journalists?* The answer to all of these questions was a simple no, and there was no evidence to the contrary in Carollo's files.

In the end, Carollo's trove of emails confirmed that Fusion did what it said it did—obtain public records and analyze them. To the editors of the *Post*, that didn't seem sexy enough. The paper's headline—"'Journalism for Rent': Inside the Secretive Firm Behind the Trump Dossier"—sounded sexier. Fusion, the story suggested, "operates with the secrecy of a spy agency," with almost mystical powers to mold the public debate according to its whim. The facts in the article weren't particularly concerning. But the sinister mood music employed by the *Post* set the tone and implied that Fusion's business model was to frustrate honest journalism on behalf of clients in crisis.

Fusion, the *Post* said, had worked to "blunt aggressive reporting" by the *Journal* on the embattled blood-testing company Theranos and its founder, Elizabeth Holmes. That was not right. Theranos had hired Fusion in early 2015 to research publicly available whistleblower cases filed against lab-testing competitors Quest Diagnostics and LabCorp in order to document cases in which they were alleged to have overbilled Medicare. It was a typical Fusion assignment: A startup wanted competitive intelligence on the market leaders. The assignment wasn't particularly sexy: a deep and mind-numbing document dive into years of court and regulatory records.

Fusion was in the midst of that work when *Journal* reporter John Carreyrou surfaced that spring asking tough questions about Theranos and Holmes. Fritsch happened to have worked at the *Journal* with Carreyrou, so Holmes and her lawyers asked Fritsch for advice on how to handle Carreyrou's queries. It wasn't what he signed up for, but Fritsch agreed. He urged Holmes to be totally transparent and engage with the *Journal*. Holmes ignored that advice and took a much more confrontational approach with the paper, as chronicled in Carreyrou's book *Bad Blood*. Her company eventually collapsed and Holmes was indicted for fraud.

The truth of Fusion's role in such cases was nuanced, and Fusion wasn't permitted to discuss those cases publicly, so it was hard to complain too much about the coverage. But the reporters writing about the company didn't know Simpson or Fritsch: Most of the reporters who dealt with Fusion over the years or during the 2016 election recused themselves from covering the controversies now enveloping the firm.

The easy assumption for journalists unfamiliar with Fusion to make was that its main line of business was a field known as "crisis PR," which is heavily populated by former journalists. Many crisis management professionals do indeed work to frustrate honest journalism. Reporters do battle with crisis PR guys all the time. That wasn't the line of work Fusion was in.

There was no arguing that Fusion wasn't fair game for a tough-minded journalistic examination, but the *Post* story was disappointing. Fritsch and Simpson thought the paper had exploited an old friend during the most precipitous part of his heartbreaking physical decline. The episode was one of the saddest moments of the whole post-dossier madness.

Russell Carollo died in Switzerland in December 2018, at age sixty-three.

The outing of the *Free Beacon* and Perkins Coie as Fusion's clients merely whetted the appetite of congressional pursuers, who soon came up with additional justifications for demanding Fusion's TD Bank records. These included the allegation that Fusion's nefarious methods included bribing journalists. "The Committee therefore seeks records related to Fusion's payments to journalists who have reported on Russia issues relevant to its investigation," the House argued in court. Fusion often hired freelance and former journalists to conduct research, not write stories.

After reviewing the records still being sought by the House, the Fusion partners realized that there was nothing in them likely to be of great interest to the House Intelligence Committee or to the media. The vast majority of Fusion's clients were ordinary companies and law firms—many of them supportive of Republicans—that retained Fusion for commercial research that had nothing to do with Fusion's political work. That was all the more reason to fight.

"Let's let the Republicans exhaust themselves chasing a rainbow that does not have a pot of gold at the end," argued Simpson.

Federal court was also an ideal venue for Fusion to shine a light on the Republican Party's quiet revival of some of the long-discredited investigative practices first used by Joseph McCarthy to sully and falsely incriminate innocent Americans. In a blizzard of filings in November and December, Fusion piled on new allegations accusing the House of additional violations of its own rules, of improper leaks, of trashing the Bill of Rights, and other abuses of power.

Central to this argument, Fusion believed, was that Nunes and his staff had found out that Fusion had an account at TD Bank from someone in Grassley's staff. The contents of Simpson's Senate testimony in August were supposed to be strictly confidential, but the information had somehow jumped the fence from Senate Judiciary to House Intelligence.

After Simpson testified before Grassley's committee, most of the committee's members had become reluctant to go along with further demands on the company. That meant Grassley's investigative counsel, Jason Foster, needed a new champion to pursue his case against Simp-

son and Fritsch. Grassley's office appeared to have found a willing partner in Nunes's office, whose chief investigative counsel, Kashyap Patel,
was one of the staffers who'd traveled to London over the summer in the
much-lampooned attempt to ambush and grill Steele.*

Fusion's suspicions about Grassley's underhanded dealings with
Patel and House Intelligence were all but confirmed when Foster appeared at a court hearing about the bank records and was seen confer-
ring with House lawyers.

As an anonymous blogger, Foster had once praised McCarthy and
accused liberals of "anti-American tendencies." His own tactics bor-
rowed directly from the methods of the disgraced Wisconsin senator. In
the 1950s, McCarthy had given himself unilateral subpoena power to go
after alleged Communists lurking in Hollywood and elsewhere. His
abuse of that power led the Senate to all but abandon the practice of
unilateral subpoenas. That was basically the state of affairs in the House,
too, until the 1990s, when Republicans in the House resumed the practice with the help of a young staff attorney named Jason Foster. Now
Foster had revived the McCarthy playbook in the service of Trump.

Throughout late 2017, Fritsch and Simpson were tending to multiple
fires a day. The Alfa Bank suit. The bank records fight with Nunes. Carollo's emails. Threats from Trump followers. Reporters wanting to know
how much Fusion was paid. Anxious calls with Steele about his security
and legal woes. And a budding legal fight with Fusion's insurance company, which didn't want to pay for any of the costs of fighting those battles. With the legal bills piling up, Fritsch worked with Fusion's lawyers
to create a legal defense fund, a low-key effort supported by a few donors. That helped, some.

Nunes still wanted his shot at Fusion. Having been spurned by Steele,
the Senate Intelligence Committee also wanted its interview with Simpson. He was due to appear before the House Intelligence Committee on
November 8 and its Senate counterpart a week later. Simpson had
planned to take the Fifth, as Fritsch and Catan had. But what was ex-

---

* Patel would go on to earn derision as the author of a widely criticized "secret"
Nunes report that accused FBI and Justice officials of bias against Trump. He now
serves as senior director of the Counterterrorism Directorate on Trump's National
Security Council.

pected to be a routine ten-minute appearance before House Intel turned out to be anything but, thanks to Adam Schiff, the committee's ranking member from California.

Nunes had hoped for another Fusion walk of shame before the Fox News cameras when Simpson appeared on the morning of November 8 to take the Fifth. But, while Nunes didn't manage to show up that morning, Schiff did. He wanted to know why the committee was compelling Simpson's testimony when it hadn't taken that step with Michael Flynn or Michael Cohen. If the Republicans withdrew the subpoena, Schiff asked, would Simpson be willing to sit for a voluntary interview under the same conditions that both Grassley and the House Intelligence Committee had granted to the president's men? Placed on the defensive by Schiff's articulation of their naked double standard, the Republicans backed down and agreed to offer equal terms for Simpson, who then agreed to an interview.

The House Intelligence Committee meets in a dimly lit chamber in the basement of the Capitol. The room was so cold that Schiff wore what appeared to be a leather trench coat that went down to his ankles. Simpson's lead interrogator was a former federal prosecutor from South Carolina, Representative Trey Gowdy, whose smooth, long face took on a lizard-like appearance under the poor lighting.

After a long back-and-forth over the Prevezon case, seemingly designed to coax Simpson into admitting he was a Russian agent, Gowdy handed the witness to Schiff, himself a former federal prosecutor. Schiff proceeded to elicit from Simpson a litany of sensational allegations against Trump and his associates for consorting with various known gangsters and engaging in possible fraud and money laundering on a massive scale.

Around 4 P.M., the proceedings broke so that members could go cast votes on pending legislation. To the great surprise of Simpson and his lawyers, when the hearing resumed, most of the Republicans, including Gowdy, hadn't returned. Instead, the Republicans handed off the questioning to Nunes staffer Patel, who resumed the monotonous attempts to fish out some sort of incriminating admission regarding the Prevezon case.

The Democrats, meanwhile, were having a field day. When their questions turned to the NRA, Simpson let it drop that "it appears the Russians, you know, infiltrated the NRA. . . . Broadly speaking, it appears that the Russian operation was designed to infiltrate conservative organizations. And they targeted various conservative organizations, religious and otherwise, and they seem to have made a very concerted effort to get in with the NRA."

Fusion would be ridiculed in the right-wing media for promoting this allegation—until mid-2018, when a federal indictment against Russian gun activist Maria Butina leveled exactly that allegation.

What seemed to be shaping up as a possible shutout for the Republicans took a turn when Patel began grilling Simpson about any dealings he might have had with the government. "You've never heard from anyone in the U.S. government in relation to those matters, either the FBI or the Department of Justice?" he asked. Lacking any wiggle room, Simpson disclosed his dealings with Justice Department prosecutor Bruce Ohr.

"We were, frankly, you know, very scared for the country and for ourselves and felt that if we could give it to someone else, we should, higher up. And so Chris suggested I give some information to Bruce, give him the background to all this. And we eventually met at a coffee shop, and I told him the story."

That honest answer from Simpson handed the Republicans a new cudgel in their search-and-destroy operation against the mythical deep state, resulting in severe professional and legal consequences for Ohr.

A week later, Simpson was back on Capitol Hill for a third appearance before a congressional committee.

The Senate Intelligence Committee's offices had the feel of a submarine or a weird terrarium out of a sci-fi movie. In these hermetically sealed spaces, the outside world becomes almost an abstraction and things like truth and reality are up for debate.

Here, in contrast to the stilted House proceedings, everyone sat around a conference table and pretended to be friends. At least until the questioning got going. Then it was the usual stuff about whether Fusion had wittingly or unwittingly been working for the Kremlin.

During a break, Simpson and the lawyers went down to the federal courthouse a few blocks away to watch the arguments between Fusion lawyers and the House over the bank records. None of it was fun.

Fusion eventually lost the bank records case. In early January, federal judge Richard Leon ruled that it wasn't his place to second-guess a congressional subpoena. Nunes would get Fusion's records after all. In one of the many delicious ironies of Fusion's fights with congressional Republicans, that ruling would later be cited in another momentous case—

this time when Trump tried, unsuccessfully, to stop Deutsche Bank from turning over records of its dealings with the Trump Organization in response to a subpoena from House Democrats.

Fusion had now furnished Congress with twenty-one hours of testimony and numerous investigative leads. Simpson and Fritsch knew the Republicans had little intention of chasing those leads. That would have to fall to Mueller's team, whose actions remained a complete mystery to Fusion, because no one there had ever reached out to them. Mueller's prosecutors had interviewed Steele over the summer, but Simpson and Fritsch didn't know what was said, and Steele was advised by his lawyers not to tell them. On one hand, it made sense that a politically charged inquiry already under Republican attack for supposed anti-Trump bias avoided Fusion. On the other, the Fusion partners were eager to share what they had learned from more than two years of Trump research. For that, they would have to content themselves with working with media contacts and Dan Jones's nonprofit.

In one of Fusion's most sprawling projects, it had been working for months with Reuters, NBC News, and the London-based NGO Global Witness to peel the onion of the Trump Ocean Club International Hotel and Tower, in Panama, the first international hotel venture launched under the Trump brand. The three organizations published the fruits of that investigation on November 17.

The core discovery in this consortium effort, at least for Fusion, was a long list of Trump condo buyers that investigators, deployed by Fusion, found in Panama real estate records. While many of the buyers were anonymous shell companies, it turned out to be possible to identify the people behind them by painstakingly cross-referencing the condo records with other records in Panama and other countries. The result was a rogues' gallery of international criminals, including a cell of Ukrainian and Russian gangsters from Toronto. The records also suggested Trump benefited from a scheme that resembled what happened with Bayrock and the Trump SoHo: A collection of fraudsters and money launderers were in the first wave of investors, putting up cash for what are known as "pre-sales." Using this sales data, the project was then promoted to ordinary American retirees, many of whom would end up stuck with lousy investments when the project (predictably) ran into financial trouble.

Panama is a steamy entrepôt famous for money launderers and scoundrels—and the characters in Trump's Panama project were cast to type. The sale of condos in the project fell to a Brazilian named Alexandre Ventura Nogueira, who partnered with a Colombian later convicted in the United States of money laundering in an unrelated case. Interviewed by NBC, Nogueira said he had sold a lot of Trump condos to Russians, including some tied to organized crime, but found out too late to do anything about it.

A Panamanian prosecutor who investigated the project described the Trump Tower to NBC News as "a vehicle for money laundering."

Nogueira would later be arrested by Panamanian authorities on charges of fraud and forgery unrelated to the Trump project. He jumped bail and fled to Brazil, where authorities were also investigating him for money laundering. He later fled Brazil and spent years on the run.

The Trumps disclaimed any recollection of dealing with Nogueira (despite the existence of photos of him with both Trump and daughter Ivanka) and said they were, as usual, just licensing their name. In 2018, amid the project's spiraling financial problems, Trump's name was scraped from the building; it is now a JW Marriott hotel. In June 2019, the private equity fund that bought the property accused the Trump Organization, in a lawsuit filed in Manhattan, of evading Panamanian taxes on project management fees. The Trump Organization denied the charges and countersued.

Days after the Trump-Panama stories ran, the Trump Organization agreed to remove its name from the failed Trump SoHo in New York and surrender management of the property—the latest signs that the president of the United States was either a sensationally reckless and incompetent real estate developer or a serial fraudster—or possibly both. The Panama story generated extensive follow-up coverage but did nothing to diminish Trump in the eyes of his followers.

On December 1, Trump's former national security adviser, Michael Flynn, pleaded guilty to lying to the FBI about his conversations during the presidential transition with Russian ambassador Kislyak. This was a direct hit to the administration, representing the first time a top Trump official had agreed to cooperate with the Mueller probe. What Trump himself knew about those contacts wasn't clear, but the *Times* reported that there was some sort of discussion of paring back U.S. sanctions on Russia.

None of this, of course, mattered to congressional Republicans. Trump himself cued his old standby, "Crooked Hillary Clinton." *Okay, so Flynn lied. But Hillary lies more,* went the presidential logic.

Nunes and company soon responded with more leaks designed to deflect the attention of Fox News viewers away from Flynn and back toward Fusion and the deep state. Jake Gibson, a Fox News producer, emailed Fusion late on the afternoon of December 11: "We have independently confirmed that Nellie Ohr worked for Fusion through the summer and fall of 2016"—information that could only have come from confidential records provided by Fusion to the House Intelligence Committee under subpoena and subject to a judicially ordered seal. The story published shortly thereafter said the information had indeed come from Nunes's committee.

The story was a follow-up to Gibson's "scoop" the previous week that Nellie's husband, Bruce, had been "demoted" within the DOJ over his contacts with Fusion in 2016, another handout from Nunes. The MAGA crowd on the Internet had a field day with that one and began circulating fevered conspiracy theories about the Ohrs. Within days, dozens of obscure websites with names like Thunder on the Right, American Thinker, and Liberty Unyielding had latched on to Nellie's publicly available May 2016 application for an amateur ham radio license as proof of the machinations of the Ohrs.

Aha! How better to communicate with Steele and those Russian handlers. This was up there with the D.C. pizza house that sat atop a secret Democratic child sex abuse dungeon.

Throughout 2017, Fusion had held its tongue in the face of Republican lies and leaks. The partners had declined all press interviews and invitations to appear on television, both in deference to its confidentiality agreements with clients and as a strategic decision not to engage in tit for tat. The consensus was that it would be wise to say what the firm had to say only at a time and place of its own choosing.

The Fusion partners felt it was time to clear the air.

They decided a newspaper opinion piece was the way to go. Fritsch and Simpson had had their ups and downs with the *Times* over the past year, but its opinion pages still constituted some of the most valuable real estate in journalism.

They began drafting an op-ed piece for the *Times* decrying Congress's investigations for the shams they were. Through the Christmas season, many drafts were circulated among the Fusion partners and their advisers, some of whom opposed the idea of going public. "Let's not lead with the chin," opined one. "This could get you another subpoena," warned another.

The result ran under a joint Simpson and Fritsch byline on January 2, just as everyone was getting ready to head back to work after the long New Year's weekend. Headlined "The Republicans' Fake Investigations," the piece was a fulsome defense of Fusion's Trump work and a call for honest congressional inquiry into Russia's efforts to help Trump become president. It ended with a plea for transparency. "The public still has much to learn about a man with the most troubling business past of any United States president. Congress should release transcripts of our firm's testimony, so that the American people can learn the truth about our work and most important, what happened to our democracy."

After a year under sustained fire, Fusion was on its front foot for a change.

CHAPTER SEVENTEEN

"WHAT I'M GOING TO DO TO YOU . . ."

FIGHTING BACK FELT GOOD, VERY GOOD.

The *Times* op-ed triggered a large wave of positive media coverage—as well as limp denials and denunciations from Republicans. "Herograms have temporarily replaced threats" in messages landing in Fusion's general email account, Catan told the partners.

The uplift was short-lived.

Two days later, a federal judge rejected Fusion's effort to block the House Intelligence Committee from obtaining more of its bank records. "Federal Judge Obliterates Fusion GPS' Attempt to Hide Info from Investigators," screamed one right-wing website. The next day, Grassley and his new wingman, Lindsey Graham, launched a counter-offensive against Fusion and Orbis, announcing they'd sent a letter to the Justice Department demanding a criminal investigation of Christopher Steele for supposedly lying to the FBI. The FBI was fully capable of referring for criminal prosecution any individual it believed had knowingly lied to or misled them. That had not happened. The Graham-Grassley referral was a transparent political stunt. On Friday, TD Bank dispatched a copy of Fusion's account records to the House.

It made for a lousy, wintry weekend. Of all the accusations leveled against Orbis and Fusion in the year since the dossier became public, the accusation by Grassley and Graham against Steele was perhaps the most outrageous. Steele phoned Simpson and Fritsch, distraught by these developments.

"I have served my country loyally for twenty years and only did what I thought was right," he told Simpson. "This is how I am thanked? These people have no shame."

Fritsch and Simpson spent the weekend reassuring Steele and Burrows that this was just politics. The Justice Department and the FBI would be hard-pressed to pursue a criminal case against someone outside of the country, let alone a British citizen who'd helped them repeatedly and honestly. "At least I hope that's still the case," Simpson told Fritsch privately.

Fritsch's and Simpson's words were small consolation to Steele. The Grassley accusation was all over the U.K. press, and Steele thought no one there would appreciate the political context of it—especially since Grassley had lobbed the charge for maximum publicity while refusing to make public any specifics. What was it that Steele had lied about? Grassley wouldn't say.

The unhappiness only deepened the following week when *The New York Times* published a less-than-flattering profile of Simpson, describing him as "brash, obsessive, occasionally paranoid, perhaps with cause." That's fair enough, they guessed, but the story also dredged up a tragic incident from Simpson's high school years, one that had haunted him for years. After a night of drinking at Simpson's house in the spring of 1982, a friend stumbled into the road and was killed by a car. Simpson's mother was arrested and charged with allowing her son to throw a party with alcohol. (The charges were later dismissed.) The anecdote felt like a cheap shot, and it landed. Simpson and his mother had to relive the horrible episode all over again.

"Well, that was gratuitous," Simpson told Fritsch. "Yeah," he replied. "Really uncool."

The wind then shifted again, this time for the better. A day after the *Times* story ran, Dianne Feinstein, the normally reserved Democratic senator from California, abruptly released the confidential transcript of Simpson's testimony before the Judiciary Committee—just as Fritsch and Simpson had called for in their op-ed a week earlier. She had had enough of Republican spin. "The innuendo and misinformation circulating about the transcript are part of a deeply troubling effort to undermine the investigation into potential collusion and obstruction of justice," she said.

For the first time, the press and the public now had a firsthand account of the long history of Orbis's and Fusion's investigations into

Trump, and saw Simpson's categorical denial that Fusion had played a role in setting up the notorious Trump Tower meeting.

After reading the transcript, Steele called Simpson. He'd worried for months that Simpson might have inadvertently said something in the interview that would give away the identities of his sources, and he was happy to see that hadn't happened. Steele was also grateful for his defense of his reputation and professionalism but teased Simpson for labeling him "basically a Boy Scout."

"That's laying it on a bit thick, don't you think?" he asked.

Trump was not pleased to see his narrative disrupted. "The fact that Sneaky Dianne Feinstein, who has on numerous occasions stated that collusion between Trump/Russia has not been found, would release testimony in such an underhanded and possibly illegal way, totally without authorization, is a disgrace," he tweeted.

At Fusion, it felt like a possible turning point.

Democrats who seemed wary of defending Fusion suddenly found their voices and denounced their Republican colleagues for attacking the messengers. "They have pushed to discredit Steele. They have pushed to discredit Fusion," Senator Richard Blumenthal said on the Senate floor. Republicans were well aware, he said, that the genesis of the FBI investigation of Trump was neither Orbis nor Fusion. "This has all been known for months, but the narrative about Fusion GPS and the FBI grinds on, unhinged from fact."

The media now began observing what had seemed obvious to Fritsch and Simpson all along: If Fusion had so much to hide, why did Simpson sit for twenty-one hours and answer the Republicans' questions? *Washington Post* columnist Dana Milbank faulted Grassley for "attempting to paint Simpson as a leftist contract killer" and noted Simpson's journalistic history of tough stories about both Republicans and Democrats.

The Republican effort to paint the Trump-Russia scandal as a Democratic hoax was beginning to wear thin.

Fusion's researchers pored over the newly released Judiciary testimony, curious about the jousting between Simpson and the lawmakers. Grassley's staff had refused to provide Fusion with a copy of the transcript. And while several staff members knew discrete parts of the Project Bangor story, Fritsch and Simpson shared information only on a need-to-know basis. Several researchers took turns doing dramatic readings of key exchanges.

In the middle of that exercise, a ripple of gasps and chuckles coursed through the office when up popped a news alert: Michael Cohen, the president's pit bull personal lawyer, had filed a defamation lawsuit in U.S. federal court accusing Fusion and Simpson of spreading false allegations, via the dossier, about Cohen's alleged interactions with various Russians. These reports had done "harm to his personal and professional reputation," the suit claimed. Cohen wanted to defend his honor in a trial by jury. His complaint, along with another against *BuzzFeed*, was filed one day shy of a year after the website had published the dossier, barely beating the buzzer on the statute of limitations for defamation.

No one at Fusion relished another depleting wave of legal fees and the distraction of another court battle—the fourth in a year. But there was the potential for getting court-ordered access to Cohen, his records, his friends and associates—even potentially the president himself. "He's going to lose this suit," Fritsch said. "Yeah," Catan replied, "but hopefully not before we get discovery."

Fusion could easily draw up a long list of things they would like to extract from Cohen—his whereabouts during the summer of 2016, when Steele's reporting placed him at a meeting with Russians in Prague; his passport and travel records; his emails; any recordings or notes of conversations with Trump or his campaign team. And that was even before delving into the reputational issues around Cohen's colorful history as a mob lawyer and would-be casino operator.

Fusion, it turned out, knew a lot about Michael Cohen—more by then, probably, than any news or law enforcement organization. It was information they'd accumulated and dug up over many months, ever since Steele spotlighted Cohen as a central player in the Trump-Russia relationship in 2016. All that work established that no incoming president in recent U.S. history had worked so closely with a person of such obvious ill repute. Cohen had been a bright-red warning signal flashing in plain sight. And yet no one paid him much mind until well after Election Day.

Cohen had surfaced early in the Bangor assignment, but only peripherally. At first, he seemed to be merely another brash New Yorker and loyalist working for Trump. He was the guy who would call gossip columnists to slip them some scoop favorable to Trump, or political reporters to scream about a story the boss didn't like. Oddly, he was also the person who fielded reporters' questions about Russia. Political reporters knew that Cohen was central to Trump's more recent forays into politics and had played a big role in his boss's brief flirtation with running for president in 2012. Cohen had gained a certain viral fame in July 2015 when he was caught on tape threatening a *Daily Beast* reporter ("What I'm going to do to you is going to be fucking disgusting") and insisting that Trump couldn't legally have raped his former wife Ivana, because she was his spouse. It was vintage Cohen, and no surprise to any of the reporters who had crossed him in the past. But very few at that point considered him more than another colorful Trump lackey.

Fusion's own interest in Cohen changed in September 2016, when the firm came across evidence suggesting that he had been a key link between Trump and various Russians of interest. Fusion noticed that Cohen had apparently served as the Trump Organization contact with the Belarusian émigré and suspicious Trump hanger-on Sergei Millian, who claimed to have partnered with the Trump Organization in making tens of millions of dollars in condo sales to Russians. Berkowitz found a message on Twitter from Cohen to Millian in August 2016 asking him if he'd seen Trump's standing in the polls. And Cohen was friends with Felix Sater—going back to high school. A review of open-source records showed Cohen's father-in-law was a Ukrainian émigré who owned New York taxi medallions and had once admitted to a felony money-laundering charge. Cohen's brother had also married into a Ukrainian family and gotten Cohen into potential business deals in Ukraine shortly before he joined the Trump Organization.

From a preliminary survey of published reports, Fusion saw that, since joining the Trump Organization in 2007, Cohen had been involved in a portfolio of Trump's sketchiest overseas projects. He worked on the failed Trump Tower project in the Republic of Georgia and sponsored mixed martial arts events with Russian fighters under a Trump MMA brand. He pursued a catering hall on Long Island that would carry Trump's name. The project stalled, but Cohen knew this world well. His uncle Morton Levine owned a Brooklyn club and catering hall called El Caribe, notorious throughout the city as a mob hangout.

Fascinated by these strands, Fusion asked Steele in the fall of 2016 to see whether Cohen rang any bells among his sources in Russia. On October 18, Steele filed a memo with the first mention of Cohen. "Kremlin insider highlights importance of TRUMP's lawyer, Michael COHEN in covert relationship with Russia." The memo stated cryptically that Cohen was playing "a key role in the secret TRUMP campaign/Kremlin relationship." Steele didn't know much more than that. Simpson and Steele's theory was that when Manafort resigned from the campaign in August, Cohen likely became an important liaison for contacts in Russia.

At the time, Trump was denying any business interactions with Russia, and no one outside the Trump Organization knew that Cohen had actually been pursuing a major Moscow tower project since late 2015, a quest that lasted at least into the early summer of 2016. Nor did anyone, back in the United States, realize how closely he was working with Trump and the *National Enquirer* to bury negative stories that involved Trump's alleged history of adultery, spousal abuse, and other sordid matters. As Trump's Mr. Fix-it, Cohen was putting out myriad fires all the way up to Election Day, sometimes with big cash payments.

At Fusion's urging, Steele kept pushing his sources for more information on Cohen. Two days after his first memo mentioning Cohen, he came back with more: In August, Cohen had held a secret meeting with "Kremlin officials" in Prague, Steele's source said.

It was a stunning report. While there was no way to immediately verify Cohen's whereabouts, other aspects of the Prague reporting fit with information coming in at the time from independent sources. One of the Russians who Steele said was at the meeting ran the Prague office of a Russian government cultural organization that the U.S. authorities believed was a front for Russian intelligence.

Cohen largely faded from view in the post-election scramble. He hung on for a few months with his Trump Organization job but then, after being rebuffed for an administration post, sought to cash in on his ties to the incoming president.

Fusion had long believed that Cohen shouldn't be forgotten so easily. A month after the election, Simpson raised his concerns about Cohen with Bruce Ohr during their December 10 meeting at Peet's Coffee. "Simpson identified Michael Cohen, a lawyer in Brooklyn, NY as having many Russian clients in the Brighton Beach, NY area," an FBI summary of the meeting recounted. "Cohen may have attended a meeting in Prague, possibly in September, regarding the Trump Campaign and the Russians."

Most Americans first heard of Michael Cohen one month later, on January 10, 2017, when *BuzzFeed* published the Steele dossier and its allegation that Cohen had had one or more secret meetings with Russian representatives in Prague the summer before. It was a simple, tangible, and shocking allegation, and one that Cohen swiftly rebutted on Twitter. "I have never been to Prague in my life. #fakenews," he posted that same evening, along with a photo of the cover of a passport. He appeared live the next day on both Sean Hannity's radio show and Fox News, laughing off suggestions that there were photos of him with Russian oligarchs. He thanked Trump for savaging the dossier in a press conference that afternoon. "Where do you go to get your reputation back? You go to Donald Trump," he told Hannity. This did little, however, to put to rest the swirl of accusations about Cohen's role as a liaison to the Russians.

A month later, Cohen was in the headlines again. In February 2017, news broke that he had tried to back-channel a secret Russia-Ukraine peace deal that would have paved the way to lifting sanctions on Moscow. His cohort in this secret diplomacy? None other than Felix Sater. By May 2017, both Congress and the special counsel had begun to investigate Cohen.

Despite stories about his dubious business past, Cohen was still something of a puzzle to Fusion in early 2017. Here was a guy with a history of working with suspected organized crime members who was still acting as Trump's personal lawyer and would soon move on to positions as a top RNC fundraiser and a rainmaker for a fancy D.C. lobbying shop. His was a profile you don't often see for someone in close contact with a sitting president.

Fusion set out to dig more deeply into his past.

As the Trump-Russia drumbeat grew, Fusion began working with a small but experienced investigative firm based in New York City to start pulling old public court and business records involving Cohen to get a better sense of where he came from. This was a team of sleuths with a track record of unearthing documents and leads in obscure and hard-to-find places. They were also skilled interviewers with deep contacts in law enforcement and the courts.

Sure enough, there were organized crime ties everywhere they looked: among his early legal clients and his Facebook friends, within his taxi medallion business, even in his political fundraising. The New York team set out to amass all archived records in New York, Florida, Illinois, and New Jersey involving Cohen and his business partners. It was no small task—thousands of pages in all. The records showed that Cohen had racked up a significant personal fortune. He had several Trump-branded apartments and even invested in his own side real estate projects, including several with mysterious LLCs as partners.

The Fusion team found that, over time, Cohen had built up significant taxi medallion holdings in New York City and Chicago, a onetime booming asset class that had begun to slip during the emergence of Uber and other ride-shares. They knew that, beginning as far back as the early 1980s, the FBI believed that Soviet émigré taxi operators based in Brighton Beach (and Chicago) belonged to "a loosely knit organized criminal community" with possible links to Russian intelligence.

Cohen had partnered through the early 2000s with two major ex-Soviet taxicab magnates to manage the taxi business, one of whom had faced convictions for assault, burglary, and criminal possession of a weapon. Cohen was even on the paperwork for a taxi company in Russia.

Stranger still, Cohen built up his taxi ventures while working as a personal injury lawyer out of a ramshackle office in a storefront on Long Island. The Fusion team discovered that the world surrounding Cohen's own legal practice was small and suspicious. His first boss in the industry was arrested for bribery. The taxi office Cohen worked in was run by a man named Simon Garber, a Ukrainian American known as the Taxi King of New York. Several of Cohen's legal partners in Garber's company were disbarred for filing false personal injury cases against rival cab companies.

The Fusion team pieced together the various records and found that some of the people Cohen represented in his legal practice, as business clients, were caught up in a major insurance fraud scheme that prosecutors pursued through 2016. After weeks of often mind-numbing work, the New York investigators figured out that Cohen had registered medical companies for several Brighton Beach doctors who had then collectively bilked Medicare for questionable medical claims for well over a decade—a story that had yet to be told. Cohen was never charged in the scheme, but many of his doctor clients were.

In 2006, Cohen made the leap to a white-shoe law firm in New York. Less than a year later—and for reasons that were never entirely clear—Cohen was working for Trump. A decade after that, Cohen was helping to get Trump elected to the White House. And now, in early 2017, he was setting himself up as a corporate lobbyist to profit off his proximity to the president.

Reporters were fascinated by Cohen's backstory but had a hard time justifying spending a lot of time reporting on a guy who was no longer in the Trump Organization and not in the administration, especially with all the Trump-Russia news then breaking on an almost daily basis. As a result, through much of 2017, reporters had a hard time telling the full story of Michael Cohen.

Cohen splashed back into the picture in late summer, when news broke of his work with Sater on the Trump Tower project in Moscow. Trump had scoffed throughout the campaign, and after the dossier emerged, at suggestions that he had anything to do with Russia. "I have no deals that could happen in Russia, because we've stayed away," he said at a news conference a day after the dossier came out. That denial became a mantra for Trump, repeated over and over without qualification on Twitter and in press appearances for all of 2017. But here was an internal Trump Organization document from October 2015, backed by emails and other records, that showed Cohen and Sater had pursued a Trump Tower Moscow deal during the presidential campaign—a deal that would have netted Trump millions.

Still, it wasn't until early 2018—right around when Cohen decided to sue Fusion for defamation—that the storm clouds finally began to open up over the president's personal lawyer.

When Cohen filed his lawsuit on January 9 claiming "significant financial and reputational damages," he was still serving as the president's personal attorney, as a deputy finance chairman for the RNC, and as a highly paid consultant to Squire Patton Boggs, a storied Washington lobbying shop.

Cohen's lawsuit against Fusion was yet another instance of the Trump team's terrible timing. Three days after he called attention to himself as the putative victim of a Fusion smear campaign, Cohen got hit by a story in *The Wall Street Journal* showing that he had arranged a $130,000 payoff to the porn star Stormy Daniels—a line of inquiry Fusion hadn't pursued. The Cohen payment had been made just weeks before the election, to keep Daniels quiet about an affair she'd had with Trump. There was no direct connection between the alleged Cohen hush money operation and the Fusion allegations, but the *Journal* report buttressed Steele's contention that Cohen was Trump's go-to man for clandestine assignments in the months leading up to the election.

Cohen fumed at the *Journal* for "raising outlandish allegations against my client," but dodged any reference to the payoff. The bluster lasted barely a month. In March, the *Journal* unearthed documents marked HIGHLY CONFIDENTIAL PROCEEDING that tied the payment to Daniels directly to the Trump Organization—credible evidence that Trump's company, working with his personal attorney, had sought to skirt federal election laws. Cohen then switched up his story, conceding that he had made the payments, but insisted it was without Trump's knowledge or involvement, another lie that would not hold up for long.

As Cohen struggled to stay afloat, Fusion became more taken by the idea of using his defamation suit to pry some information out of the secrecy-obsessed Trump World. Cohen's case was a flimsy one to start with, but the avalanche of accusations now swirling around him made it even weaker. Both Simpson and Fritsch began to relish the thought of answering Cohen's lawsuit with a motion to proceed immediately to discovery.

Months and months of depositions and exchanges of records, though, would mean big money in legal fees—certainly well north of a million dollars. So the Fusion partners put out feelers among a few past supporters. Who might be game to back a full discovery campaign against President Trump's now famous personal attorney? A couple of arms shot up, and one made a pledge to cover the entire tab.

Despite the legal setbacks and the continued congressional entanglements, Fusion was riding a wave of goodwill in early 2018 as developments affirmed the company's work on the Russia front.

A report in *The New York Times* had identified a chatty Trump campaign aide, George Papadopoulos, as the initial trigger for the FBI's Russia investigation. The story made clear that Simpson was right in telling the Judiciary Committee that the FBI had an additional source for its Russia allegations. The tide of the overall Mueller investigation had also markedly shifted in Fusion's favor in the wake of some prominent indictments. Mueller brought charges against thirteen Russian nationals and three Russian entities on charges of interfering in the 2016 election. Mueller also filed a raft of new financial charges against Manafort based on evidence provided by his longtime partner, Rick Gates.

Also helpful had been the release of a second transcript of Simpson's congressional testimony, this one from his time before the House Intelligence Committee.

The transcript outlined Fusion's suspicion that the Russians had conducted a larger operation in 2016 to compromise and gain sway over not just the Trump campaign but the Republican Party and the conservative movement. It appeared, said Simpson, "that the Russian operation was designed to infiltrate conservative organizations," including the religious right and the NRA. The Russians had also targeted Democrats over the years, he added, describing "a pretty elaborate attempt by the Russians to target and infiltrate our softer institutions" that took place over many years and included the famous FBI case in 2010 against a team of Russian spies including Anna Chapman, inspiration for the television show *The Americans*.

Simpson also ran through Trump's many business activities that smacked of money laundering. "There were a lot of real estate deals where you couldn't really tell who was buying the property," he told the committee. "Sometimes properties would be bought and sold, and they would be bought for one price and sold for a loss shortly thereafter, and it really didn't make sense to us." Most suspicious of all were Trump's golf courses in Ireland and Scotland, where "hundreds of millions of dollars" seemed to disappear. "They're sinks," he said. "They don't actually make any money."

The *Journal* stories on Stormy Daniels rekindled interest in Fusion's accumulated Cohen research. Reporters were now seeking to explore some of the dingier back alleys of his past. Building on what Fusion had gleaned over the past year, they would produce a flurry of deep examinations of Cohen's career, in print, TV, and radio. The picture that emerged was of a man who sought his fortune first among a wide array of underworld operators and seamy lawyers, and finally with a man who would become president of the United States.

Things came to a boil on April 9, when FBI agents swooped into Cohen's Rockefeller Center office, a Park Avenue hotel room, and his apartment, carting off boxes of records, cellphones, and recordings. Word quickly got out that they were investigating possible bank fraud.

It was an extraordinary moment. Few men had worked more hand in hand with Trump for the past decade, or been closer to the seamier side of his business and personal life. And now, more than a year into Trump's presidency, the FBI had multiple search warrants to dig through all the correspondence and legal records of his personal attorney and cleanup man. Even more worrisome for Trump, the orders had come from the Justice Department proper, not from the special counsel's office.

Hours after the raid, Trump went on a tirade. "A total witch hunt," he fumed on Twitter. "Attorney-client privilege is dead!" He called the search "an attack on our country in a true sense" and suggested that he would fire Mueller over the incident, even though the search was conducted by a team outside Mueller's orbit.

Cohen's woes only got worse. He tried to look resolute through the firestorm, saying right after the FBI raid that he would "rather jump out of a building" than turn on Donald Trump. But Trump soon began downplaying Cohen's importance to the Trump Organization, making it all the more likely that Cohen would crack and seek to protect his own interests.

With his reputation in tatters, and facing likely federal prosecution on several fronts, Cohen dropped his lawsuits against *BuzzFeed* and Fusion on April 19, ten days after the feds raided his office and residences. The dismissal deprived Fusion of the months of discovery it relished, but no one mourned the demise of another lawsuit.

By mid-May, Cohen's multiple lies were catching up with him on all sides. Trump's new personal attorney, Rudolph Giuliani, blurted out on Sean Hannity's show that Trump had in fact known about the Stormy Daniels hush payment and had actually paid Cohen back for it, undercutting months of denials. Investigators also found Cohen texts and emails showing that his work on the proposed Moscow Tower project had gone well into the late spring of 2016, at least five months longer than he originally told Congress.

Then came the revelations of Cohen's unexplained consulting contracts with corporate America, a true window into the unseemliness of Trump's Washington.

Cohen's Essential Consultants had even received nearly $600,000 for investment consulting from a company connected to Viktor Vekselberg, a Russian oligarch with close ties to Putin. Cohen had met with the billionaire businessman at Trump Tower eleven days before Trump's inauguration, shortly before he left his post within the Trump Organization. The monthly payments began twenty-two days later, just as Cohen was embarking under his own shingle, and continued into the summer of 2017.

With the pressure mounting, Cohen flashed the first sign that he was going to crack on June 13, when he fired his legal team and resigned his post at the RNC. Trump's sturdiest of loyalists—his pit bull, his Mr. Fix-it, his version of *The Godfather* consigliere Tom Hagen—was getting ready to flip.

CHAPTER EIGHTEEN

WAITING
FOR MUELLER

BY THE LATE SPRING OF 2018, LIFE AT FUSION FELT LIKE IT might be returning to a sort of normal again. The harsh post-dossier spotlight of the past sixteen months was beginning to dim—even as Trump himself escalated his denunciations of the firm on Twitter and in interviews and press availabilities.

The House Intelligence Committee had found nothing much in Fusion's bank records other than the identities of a few companies who were big donors to many GOP lawmakers—a bit of political insurance Fusion knew would frustrate committee Republicans. There were no leaks from the Republicans about these records, as they would only have angered their own supporters and demonstrated what Fusion had claimed all along: The firm was not an appendage of the Democratic Party. The silence further revealed Nunes's court fight for what it was. The GOP lawmakers had fought for access to the names of Fusion's clients, claiming that was critical to the investigation. But none of the third parties in those records were mentioned in Nunes's report, or ever again. The House's demand for those documents was punitive. Nunes wanted to put Fusion out of business, but he failed.

Efforts by Grassley and his allies to gin up a criminal investigation of Orbis and Fusion had similarly gone nowhere. The core theses of the dossier were only getting stronger with time. There were still lawsuits to defend and right-wing media attacks afoot, but the worst of it seemed to be over. Congress would soon be preoccupied with the midterm elections, and, farther over the horizon, the Mueller report loomed.

"Amazing to think, but it does seem like we just might survive this, touch wood," Catan said to Fritsch over drinks one evening in late May. "The weight of the evidence is making it just too hard for people to blame the messengers anymore."

Steele agreed with that assessment. He took the news that Cohen had been talking with Moscow during the 2016 election about a Trump Tower deal as a major vindication of his work. Didn't the Trump Tower Moscow revelation lie at the crux of the dossier's argument that Putin was trying to buy off Trump, and that Cohen was a central player? "Can anyone seriously doubt the thrust of the dossier now?" Steele told Fritsch. "Such a deal would only occur with official sanction. It is prima facie evidence of a compromised relationship."

Mueller, meantime, appeared to be closing in on more of the president's men: Indictments of Cohen and others now looked like a sure bet. Even the news pages of *The Wall Street Journal* were dogging every development of Cohen's mounting troubles and seemed convinced of the criminality at the heart of the Trump enterprise.

People were also beginning to realize that Trump was only a part of the Russia story. The broader theme of Putin's plan to destabilize America's European allies, a core focus of Fusion's nonprofit client, was also beginning to catch on in the media.

"Rather than simply concentrate its efforts on spreading subversion on Europe's vulnerable periphery, Moscow appears to have concentrated on destabilizing the West's most powerful countries," a Reuters columnist wrote.

The successful Brexit vote in 2016 and Britain's pending departure from the European Union continued to roil European politics, much to Putin's delight. Steele and the Fusion team had spent much of the past year delving into links between Trump and a group of Britons with curious ties to Russia who had backed Brexit.

That group was led by Arron Banks, a minor insurance executive with a Russian-born wife who had spent more than $10 million supporting the Brexit campaign. Where did that kind of money come from? It wasn't clear. Banks was close to Russians and had often boasted of a "boozy" lunch he had with the Russian ambassador to the U.K. in late 2015, eight months before the Brexit vote. In June 2018, leaked emails revealed that at the same time, Banks and one of his top advisers were in secret talks with contacts in the Russian embassy to pursue lucrative deals in Russian-owned gold and diamond mines. Banks ultimately did not invest, but those talks looked like a possible Kremlin plot to co-opt the Brexiteers—an eerie echo of the Trump Tower Moscow tease Cohen had chased (and lied about). The *Times* reported that Mueller's team, too, was interested in Banks and the ties the Brexit leaders had built to the Trump campaign. Banks had met with Trump in Trump Tower just days after the presidential election, a visit he recounted upon his return to London over a lunch with the Russian ambassador to the U.K.

The sum of those developments suggested to Simpson and Fritsch that Mueller was on it, as deep in the weeds of the possible collusion story as Fusion and Steele had been but with one key difference: Mueller had the power to compel people to talk. "These guys do not seem to be messing around," Simpson told Steele. "And it looks like they are closing in."

Trump himself, of course, remained the biggest obstacle to a real reckoning of his relationship with Russia. He unleashed a barrage of Twitter attacks on Mueller after the FBI's raid on Cohen, a sign that the president was afraid of what the feds might turn up. Powerful committee chairmen in Congress like Nunes dutifully followed, renewing their claims that the Russia probe was a hoax cooked up by Fusion, Steele, and Democrats inside the FBI. He and his colleagues were sure to back Trump if the president made good on his repeated threats to fire Mueller and the "Angry Democrats" he claimed populated the special counsel's office.

These attacks significantly raised the stakes for the midterm elections now flickering just over the horizon in November. If Republicans held on, that could spell disaster for the Mueller investigation. And even if Mueller survived the onslaught from Trump and the Nunes crew, any findings suggestive of high crimes and misdemeanors were likely to go nowhere without a change in control of the House. Mueller was not likely to defy Office of Legal Counsel opinions and indict a sitting president. The job of acting on his report, then, would be left to Congress. And there was no hope a Republican-controlled House would ever bring articles of impeachment against Trump or proceed with tough investigative hearings, no matter what Mueller found.

Democrats had good reason to be fired up for the midterms. Trump was deeply unpopular, and many voters seemed eager to punish the Republicans for abetting the president's racist and misogynist rhetoric, inertia on gun control, and ruthlessness toward immigrants and their children. The Democrats had strong candidates lining up to compete for seats once presumed to be safely Republican, and many incumbent Republican representatives had announced their decision to retire rather than face the voters again.

Fusion ordinarily didn't work on congressional races, but as the election drew closer, the firm began to mull a few ways it could have an impact. Later, it would decide to design and launch a more systematic cyber-monitoring campaign, but first it went small, focusing on a single congressional district in California's heavily agricultural Central Valley. That solidly red seat happened to have been occupied since 2003 by one Devin Nunes.

Nunes's hometown paper, *The Fresno Bee,* had endorsed him in every election since he first ran for Congress, in 2002. But after his jaw-dropping performance running interference for Trump in the Russian probe, sentiment had begun to turn against him. The *Bee* endorsed his opponent, a little-known county prosecutor, and even reliably conservative outlets like RedState.com were calling for him to go.

Fusion had no illusions about being able to topple Nunes, but the notion of digging into his record made many at the firm salivate. His bumbling investigation of Trump-Russia was amusing, in some respects, and Fritsch had taken up Senator Lindsey Graham's reference to him as Inspector Clouseau, after the incompetent police inspector in the Pink Panther movies. But there were far more serious issues at stake here, too: In his fiercely partisan stewardship of the Russia investigation, Nunes had also undermined the intelligence and law enforcement agencies and inflicted damage on dedicated crime fighters like Bruce Ohr. And he was a threat to Mueller's ability to do his job. When Fritsch asked Fusion staff for volunteers to look into Nunes, every hand shot up.

Through a friend, Fusion obtained a copy of the Democratic Party's research book on Nunes to see what kind of opposition research work had already been done. It was disappointing: an exhaustive review of his voting record on hundreds of bills and a smattering of random facts about his top donors and finances. In short, a 661-page collection of "votes and quotes" that lacked a coherent narrative or explanation of how Nunes had gone from the son of a proud family of Portuguese dairy farmers to a rabid conspiracy theorist who turned the crank on the GOP's anti-Mueller fog machine.

Fusion set to work, pulling public records from across the country and digging into Nunes's role in California's water wars, the defining issue for his agribusiness constituents. It turned out that Nunes had accomplished little on the one issue he was hired to champion: water rights. Farmers in his district were withering under a prolonged series of droughts. With little snowmelt flowing off the Sierras, farmers had drilled deep into the soil and drained the valley's lush aquifer in an effort to feed their thirsty groves of almond, citrus, and pomegranate trees. Now those aquifers were threatening to go dry, and many felt their way of life was imperiled.

Nunes blamed his constituents' plight on a Communist conspiracy to promote elaborate fairy tales about global warming to drive farmers off the land. "When you look at the radical environmental fringe, there's no question they are tied closely to the Communist Party," Nunes told reporters in 2009. "I have the documents that can prove it."

Now facing his first contested re-election bid in the 2018 midterms, Nunes didn't have much to show for his fifteen years in Congress. While he described himself as a farmer on the midterm ballot, Nunes hadn't been one for a decade. Three years after he was first elected, he had quietly sold off his shares of the family farm and invested the proceeds in a Napa Valley winery nearly two hundred miles from his district. He started spending more of his time hobnobbing at political fundraisers in Washington, with his campaign committees racking up more than $388,000 in expenses at the Capitol Hill Club, a private haunt for congressional Republicans where politicians and lobbyists gather to strategize and fundraise.

Some of his spending appeared to violate campaign finance rules. Fusion discovered "fundraising" trips to Las Vegas and Boston during which Nunes spent more than $130,000 on high-end hotels, meals, and NBA tickets, at the expense of his campaign committees. The Boston fundraisers appeared to have been outings to see his favorite NBA team, the Boston Celtics. (Nunes idolized Larry Bird.) In March 2018, Fusion found, Nunes charged more than $11,000 to his campaign for a private plane charter, despite House ethics rules that generally forbid noncommercial travel.

Nunes also spent tens of thousands of dollars in PAC money on wine from the wineries in which he held stakes. While dairy farmers had brought him to office, he was now a vocal proponent of government subsidies benefiting the Wine Institute, the industry trade group that represented both of his wineries. Collecting wine, he told a reporter in 2010, was his "one and only hobby."

In short, Nunes had become a D.C. swamp creature pushing the envelope of campaign finance law, maybe even breaking it. But that narrative, as clear as it was, was unlikely to capture the imagination of the public, or move the needle electorally.

In the end, Fusion found an obscure bit of litigation that lit up the race.

In May, weeks after that discovery, Nunes's ownership stake in the Napa winery Alpha Omega became national news when *The Fresno Bee* reported on a lawsuit filed in California state court by a young woman who had worked serving wine at a 2015 tasting event aboard the winery's sixty-two-foot yacht.

The booze cruise, she alleged, had dissolved into a drug-fueled orgy, with a dozen men snorting cocaine and carousing with prostitutes, whose performances were later rated by the group. The server said she feared she would be raped, and later sued the winery, alleging that management had knowingly subjected her to a hostile environment.

The young woman believed the party boys were investors in the winery, though both the winery and Nunes denied that. It didn't keep the lurid story from exploding on social media. Nunes was apoplectic. His anger only gave more oxygen to the story. Nunes spent tens of thousands of dollars on television, radio, and Facebook advertisements attacking the *Bee* for its coverage of the lawsuit, drawing more attention to the case. In the end, Nunes would win re-election in November with 52.7 percent of the vote, his lowest margin of victory ever.

Long after the election, Nunes remained apoplectic. In March 2019, Nunes sued Twitter and Republican political consultant Liz Mair for $250 million, claiming they had defamed him. He sued the *Bee*'s parent company, McClatchy, for defamation in April for reporting on the booze cruise lawsuit. He sued a farmer and several other constituents in his own district for questioning the ballot's description of Nunes as a farmer. In September 2019, he sued Fusion, accusing the company of "racketeering," for what was in fact public records research. The lawsuits were widely ridiculed, with a parody Twitter account claiming to speak for Nunes's cow gaining hundreds of thousands of followers in a few months.

———

Midsummer 2018 marked the beginning of the Waiting for Mueller period. Enterprise reporting on Trump and Russia had slowed to all but a trickle. There were still many leads for reporters to follow, but there wasn't much of an incentive to chase down stories Mueller's team could probably get to first. Besides, people were exhausted from the daily grind of the Trump-Russia story.

"It's Mueller Time," one television correspondent told Fritsch over the July 4 holiday. "Time to chill a bit and see what he comes up with."

Then, just days before Trump planned to meet with Putin in Helsinki, Finland, Mueller struck with an indictment of twelve Russian intelligence officers he alleged were behind the hacking of the Democratic National Committee and the Clinton campaign. The move confirmed in painstaking detail what the Intelligence Community had already said publicly, and had the effect of cornering Trump.

Three days later, on July 16, Trump stood next to Putin at a press conference in Helsinki and said he didn't "see any reason why" Russia would have been responsible for interfering in the 2016 election. It was a stunning slap at the U.S. Intelligence Community and a very public show of fealty to Putin. "Absolutely, utterly appalling" was all Steele could say when he called later that day. Even Cohen, Trump's blindly loyal lawyer, would later say the Helsinki moment was when he stopped believing once and for all in Trump's loyalty to his country.

The Helsinki summit quickly became an extraordinary political debacle—even for a president who seemed to engineer political debacles on a weekly basis. The episode took place just as the U.S. national security community was descending on the Colorado ski resort of Aspen for the annual Aspen Security Forum. Simpson found a very different atmosphere there from the previous year, when he'd spent much of his time on the defensive over Grassley's allegations. This time the Trump administration was on its heels, with the president's own intelligence leadership expressing shock and amazement at his behavior.

Speaking at the conference, Trump's own handpicked FBI director, Christopher Wray, publicly distanced himself from Trump's statements. "The Intelligence Community's assessment has not changed, my view has not changed, which is that Russia attempted to interfere with the last election and that it continues to engage in malign influence operations to this day," Wray told NBC's Lester Holt before dozens of top intelligence officials, military leaders, and journalists.

Meantime, the hits would keep on coming. The same day Trump stood by Putin in Helsinki, the Justice Department indicted Maria Butina, the Russian who had worked to get inside the GOP by cozying up to groups like the NRA. Prosecutors alleged that Butina had tried to set up a secret meeting between Trump and Putin during the election. Butina, according to Trump's own Justice Department, had come to the United States bent on "infiltrating organizations having influence in American politics, for the purpose of advancing the interests of the Russian Federation." The indictment said she worked to steer Republicans toward a more Russia-friendly policy through contacts she had made inside the National Rifle Association—precisely the thing Simpson had told House investigators she appeared to be doing eight months earlier. At the time, a column by Kimberley Strassel in *The Wall Street Journal* had ridiculed Simpson's House testimony about Butina as "another wild tale from Fusion GPS."

"THIS IS SOOO GREAT," Simpson messaged Fritsch, linking to the column as a reminder of its total wrongheadedness.

"Beyond glorious," Fritsch agreed.

Another Republican canard—that Carter Page had been unfairly maligned by Steele's reporting—collapsed in late July when the FBI released more than four hundred pages of redacted documents detailing why, in October 2016, agents thought Trump adviser Carter Page was a possible asset of Russian intelligence. It turned out that they had reams of intelligence on Page going back years that had nothing to do with the dossier or Fusion's research on Page. Russian intelligence had tried to recruit him as early as 2008.

As Congress broke for August recess, Trump's hardcore defenders were still scrambling to discredit Steele and find hard evidence of the Democratic deep state conspiracy at the heart of the FBI investigation.

With all eyes diverted by the twin courtroom dramas playing out in New York (where Cohen would plead guilty to campaign finance violations for paying off Stormy Daniels on Trump's behalf) and Virginia (where Manafort was convicted of tax fraud), Nunes made a secret trip to London to try to get the lowdown on Steele. He wanted to know what the British government knew about Steele's contacts with the DOJ. Like Trump, Nunes had also latched on to the fact that Nellie Ohr had worked for Fusion at one point and was married to Bruce Ohr of the Justice Department.

Nunes figured his status would help him get an audience with the heads of Britain's spy agencies—MI5 and MI6—as well as the GCHQ, Britain's equivalent of the National Security Agency. Normally, that might be the case. But this was amateur hour of the highest order: The agencies flatly refused to meet with him. He did, however, meet with a junior national security official, who very politely told him nothing, according to Steele's sources.

"This Nunes is a proper clown," Steele told Fritsch. "It's stunning he thought that would work."

Nunes had hoped to lay the groundwork for the upside-down world's other big event that month, Bruce Ohr's testimony before a joint, closed session of the House Judiciary and Oversight committees, which was set to take place August 28. Republican investigators would grill Ohr about his wife's work with Fusion and his meetings with Steele and Simpson.

Ohr recounted how, over many years as one of the U.S. government's top Russian organized crime experts, he had "become acquainted with both Chris Steele, Glenn Simpson, and other people. And from time to time, these people would give me information about Russian oligarchs and other Russian organized crime figures, and then I would pass that to the FBI."

He ran through his encounters with Steele and Simpson in 2016 and 2017 in detail, including the one meeting he had with Simpson before the election. During and after the election, he said, he'd passed along information from Simpson and Steele directly to the Justice Department's top criminal prosecutors and the FBI's top leadership, as well as its Russian counterintelligence division. When his testimony later became public, this would come as a revelation to Fusion, which had never asked what Ohr was doing with the information the firm provided.

Ohr also provided some context for why Orbis's and Fusion's reporting on Trump's dealings with Russian oligarchs had created so much concern: "The Russian state often uses oligarchs and criminals for government ends, to an extent which I think is not well understood by most people in the West."

Republicans strained to belittle that reporting, suggesting that Ohr was wrong to trouble the FBI with mere hearsay that would never be admitted in court. "But this is *not* evidence in a courtroom," Ohr pointed out. "This is *source* information. And most FBI investigations involve source information, at least in the early stages." Moreover, Ohr added, his main concern was not making a criminal prosecution. "If the Russian government was attempting to influence the Trump campaign in some way, I would think that would be a national security threat," he said. "I was very concerned when I got the information. It seemed to have very serious national security implications. . . . Any time a citizen gets information about a crime or a national security threat, it's appropriate to convey it to the FBI."

Ohr also disclosed that he had brokered the follow-up meeting between the FBI and Steele in the summer of 2017, which he said was undertaken at the FBI's request, not Steele's. Steele was "certainly very skilled" and "provided information that did help specific cases."

It didn't take long for word of Ohr's confidential interview to reach the tweeter in chief. Two days later, Trump went after the Ohrs: "Wow, Nellie Ohr, Bruce Ohr's wife, is a Russia expert who is fluent in Russian. She worked for Fusion GPS where she was paid a lot. Collusion! Bruce was a boss at the Department of Justice and is, unbelievably, still there!"

In fact, Ohr had already been stripped of both of his leadership titles, because, he said, DOJ officials "did not want me in a position where I would be having contact with the White House."

Back in the real world, a federal judge, on September 7, sentenced former Trump adviser George Papadopoulos to two weeks in jail, plus a year of probation and a $9,500 fine, for having lied to the Mueller team. The Fusion partners thought this was incredibly lenient, given the circumstances. Papadopoulos's lies had deprived prosecutors of the ability to extract more from Joseph Mifsud, a London-based Maltese professor suspected of being a Russian operative, who had first told Papadopoulos in April 2016 that Moscow had thousands of emails damaging to Clinton. James Comey, in an opinion piece in the *Post*, bluntly described Mifsud as "a Russian agent." Mueller would later write in his report that Papadopoulos's falsehoods had "hindered investigators' ability to effectively question Mifsud when he was interviewed in the lobby of a Washington hotel on Feb. 10, 2017."

Mifsud left the United States the next day and appears to have vanished.

Two weeks after the Papadopoulos sentencing, a curious Ukraine thread emerged that fed into yet another attempted counter-narrative to the Trump-Russia story. In this version, nefarious forces in Ukraine had cooked up the whole Russia saga in a bid to smear Trump. Months earlier, Fusion had received information from Ukraine that Republican operatives were making the rounds in Kiev, seeking information about

Orbis, Fusion, and the origins of the corruption allegations against Paul Manafort.

In one of these efforts, an American freelance political operative with links to the Republican right visited Kiev in early 2018 and allegedly offered to pay for information about this supposed smear campaign. Then in mid-September, a former Fusion contractor named Graham Stack published an article in the *Kyiv Post* repudiating his own work on Manafort's money laundering and arguing that Manafort owed no loyalties to Russia. "This narrative was developed by Washington commercial intelligence firm Fusion GPS in 2016, as part of their now famous dossier on Trump, distributed widely among major media outlets," he wrote. The piece was picked up by *The Daily Caller* and other pro-Trump outlets.

This campaign to seek an origin of the Russia meddling story in Ukraine became a favorite hobbyhorse of Rudolph Giuliani and of Trump himself, leading eventually to the commencement of an impeachment inquiry against Trump in September 2019.

In late September 2018, congressional Republicans served yet another subpoena on Simpson, demanding he be questioned a *fourth* time before Congress. Sweetening the invitation to testify was the public accusation, from Republican Matt Gaetz—infamous for inviting a Nazi sympathizer as his lone guest to Trump's State of the Union address—that either Simpson or Ohr was lying to Congress about the timing of their meetings. Simpson, through counsel, invoked his constitutional privilege not to testify and asked to be excused from appearing. The Republicans refused. Simpson appeared the next day and invoked his privilege, and no contempt proceeding ever occurred.

The Republican inquisition would soon be over—so long as the Democrats reclaimed the House.

With their last-ditch efforts to frame Simpson for perjury and destroy the careers of top law enforcement officials, the Republicans had made clear that they would be gunning for both Mueller and Fusion if they retained power. Continued GOP control of the House would also probably mean that Trump's ties to the Kremlin would never be seriously investigated by Congress, which instead would subject Fusion and its allies to at least two more years of frivolous subpoenas and baseless allegations.

More important, Fusion was also worried that Putin could again intervene to help the Republicans win. The Trump administration had done little to reassure anyone that it was ready or able to repel another Kremlin cyberattack. As early as February, the Intelligence Community warned that the Russians would be back in the fall. "There should be no doubt that Russia perceives its past efforts as successful and views the 2018 U.S. midterm elections as a potential target for Russian influence operations," Director of National Intelligence Dan Coats said at one hearing. In mid-July, executives at Microsoft disclosed that they had uncovered hacking attempts by the Russians against three Senate campaigns—incidents that were news to top U.S. officials.

Simpson worried that something unexpected would happen in the late stages of the election to radically change the picture. Steele's sources, meanwhile, were telling him that Moscow's Internet Research Agency would be deploying disinformation via its bot armies in support of vulnerable Republican candidates.

So, quite apart from the smaller-bore Nunes work, Fusion decided to launch a wider, more systematic effort to monitor and protect the election. It formulated a plan with Dan Jones at The Democracy Integrity Project to monitor battleground congressional districts for election interference and uncover and expose botnets and bogus websites pushing fake news. It began an effort, starting in early September, to sift through the traffic across thousands of websites to detect and flag any suspicious, nonorganic content.

Sure enough, the Russians were once again trying to fire up Trump's base by spewing anti-immigrant propaganda. Fusion, TDIP, and their partners at the cyber research firm New Knowledge eventually identified more than ten thousand posts on the Internet traced to known Russian influence operations. Even more troubling was the fact that much of the Russian disinformation was also now being circulated or mimicked by domestic sources.

Another threat to Democratic chances seemed to emerge in early October when a large caravan of asylum-seeking migrants formed in Honduras with the intention of eventually crossing into the United States. Trump quickly seized on the development, tweeting about the dangers of the caravans—"Great Midterm issue for Republicans!"—and threatening to mobilize the military to repel the approaching caravan. News of the caravan echoed across the Web, often augmented by dubious and inflammatory posts.

The caravan appeared to be another instance of desperate people fleeing poverty and gang violence in their home countries and banding together for safety. But this caravan was unusually large. A group of some five thousand migrants trudging toward the southern border of the United States created the perfect image to pair with Trump's closing argument to Republican voters before the midterms: *We must win to build the wall and keep these invaders out!*

The whole thing just seemed too perfectly timed to the elections to be totally random. Russia's intelligence services were known to instigate immigrant crises in Europe as a way to inflame public opinion and boost the political fortunes of far-right politicians. Could something like that be going on here?

As the final days before the election ticked by, Trump made the caravan the centerpiece of his campaign message, whipping up hysteria over the specter of an invasion by alien hordes. For a while, it seemed to be working. Polls showed the Republicans coming within five percentage points of the Democrats in voter preference for control of Congress, an ominous swing since early October. At that margin, Republicans had a shot at narrowly retaining control of the House. Suddenly the nightmare of 2016 was starting over again, where unexpected late-breaking events and a wave of cyber dirty tricks could cost Democrats the election.

And sure enough, the final days of the campaign saw shocking events—although not quite what Trump and his friends had been aiming for.

On October 24, the New York offices of CNN were evacuated after a pipe bomb was found there. Over the next forty-eight hours, additional bombs from a mentally disturbed Trump supporter named Cesar Sayoc were found at other news organizations and at the homes and offices of prominent Democrats, including Hillary Clinton and President Obama, whom Trump had repeatedly blasted as America's true enemies.

The national conversation suddenly shifted from talk of an alien invasion to the implications of the president's fearmongering and hateful rhetoric. Trump bitterly complained that, just when Republicans had begun bouncing back in the polls, "now this 'Bomb' stuff happens and the momentum greatly slows."

On October 27, Simpson was in Pittsburgh dropping his son off at college when he heard a chorus of emergency sirens. A far-right extremist had walked into a nearby synagogue with an AR-15 semiautomatic rifle and three pistols and murdered eleven Jewish worshippers.

Trump, who two weeks earlier had rousted the military to deal with the invaders, suddenly stopped mentioning the caravan. The demagoguery had backfired on Trump, as the president himself tacitly admitted on the eve of the election, complaining that "we did have two maniacs stop a momentum that was incredible. . . . It stopped a tremendous momentum."

With Trump's caravan talk suddenly silenced, Democrats dramatically widened their leads in the polls in the final days of the election and wound up beating the Republicans in the fight for the House by the largest margin of votes in a midterm since Watergate.

Maybe now, Fritsch and Simpson thought, they would be left alone. At least by Congress.

With their new majority in the House, the Democrats might finally have a chance to investigate what really happened between Trump and Russia. Incoming Democratic chairmen wasted little time announcing their intentions to do just that. Nunes would lose his prized seat as chair of the House Intelligence Committee—and, with it, his power to harass the Mueller probe, the FBI, and Fusion GPS.

Trump responded to the drubbing by firing his embattled attorney general, Jeff Sessions, whom the president had long criticized for having recused himself from the Russia investigation. In his place, Trump named as acting attorney general Matthew Whitaker, an ardent loyalist who had repeatedly echoed the president's gripes about the unfairness of the Mueller investigation, even adopting Trump's "witch hunt" epithet in a column for CNN three months earlier.

Whitaker was a former prosecutor from Iowa whose primary claim to fame was having caught a pass in the 1991 Rose Bowl as a backup tight end for the Iowa Hawkeyes.

Sometimes Fusion would jump on a case, with no client or marching orders, just because it looked tantalizing and fun—a sort of blend of public service, pro bono work, and staff entertainment. Whitaker was one of those cases. The moment Trump named him, Fusion dug in.

Within hours, Fusion researchers had burrowed deep into Whitaker's past as a board member for a fraudulent invention-marketing firm called World Patent Marketing. Whitaker had held the post from 2014 to 2017 and had used his résumé as a former U.S. attorney to try to intimidate WPM customers who complained they'd been cheated. In March 2017, the Federal Trade Commission filed fraud charges against the firm, a case that later led to a $26 million fine.

On the day the Trump announcement was made, Fusion researcher David Michaels found a number of brief video testimonials stored on Vimeo in which Whitaker had touted some of WPM's dubious inventions, even citing Trump in one clip as an inspiration for the company's entrepreneurial flair. Other WPM materials offered up gems such as the marketing launch of a "MASCULINE TOILET," with an elevated seat designed to accommodate "well-endowed men." The promotion for the toilet came on the same PR announcement as Whitaker's appointment as a board member and adviser to the firm.

Before announcing the Whitaker pick, Trump officials had made no effort to scrub the Web of any of this. The clips were taken down within hours, but not before Fusion had downloaded them and created an informal repository for all things Whitaker. It added to that in the days ahead with other facts that pointed to the flimsiness of his legal career. The stories lit up the Internet and the late-night comedy shows for well over a week. Whitaker was never likely to last in any job requiring confirmation, but his days were all the more numbered now. He was gone from the administration three months later.

The headlines of late 2018 and early 2019 seemed to be building to a likely crescendo in the Mueller report: "Mueller Revokes Manafort Plea Deal, Saying He Lied" (November 26); "Cohen Pleads Guilty, Saying He Also Lied to Mueller" (November 29); "Cohen Sentencing Memo Indicates He Is Cooperating Fully with Mueller" (December 7); "U.S. Attorney in NY Says Cohen Paid Off Stormy Daniels at Direction of Trump" (December 7); "Cohen Sentenced to Three Years in Prison" (December 12); "Maria Butina Pleads Guilty to Being a Russian Spy" (December 13); "Mueller Indicts Trump Ally Roger Stone for Lying, Obstruction and Witness Tampering" (January 25).

One by one, Mueller was winning convictions against people Fusion had been raising questions about for almost three years now. And he was methodically working his way up the food chain to Trump himself; a classic conspiracy case appeared to be in the works. The speculation now became not whether Mueller would find evidence that the president had committed a crime, but just how many crimes—and whether he would actually be charged.

To Steele and Fusion, Cohen's admission that he had lied about his negotiations with Moscow over a Trump Tower project represented an important milestone on the dossier's road to wider credibility. Here was proof of secret business dealings between Trump and the Russians of just the sort that Steele's sources had described. The admission also raised expectations that Mueller would at the least deliver evidence that the Trump team had been compromised by the Russians, though Simpson and Fritsch harbored doubts that Mueller's verdict would be all that clear.

They weren't alone in that assessment. "What the Steele dossier showed was how easy it was to see the basic narrative of what was going on," John Sipher, who once ran the CIA's Russian operations, said on Twitter at the end of November. "That was one guy's take using several existing informal sources. . . . Just think what real intelligence and investigative agencies can find."

"Correct," replied his former CIA Russia colleague Steven L. Hall. "Steele dossier was one small part, tip of the iceberg. Mueller is looking below the surface."

In response to the gathering gloom, Trump's defenders cranked up their standard what-about-this, what-about-that arguments. *Fusion set up the Trump Tower meeting! Cohen was never in Prague! The FBI spied illegally on the Trump campaign! The dossier was a setup, paid for by Hillary Clinton!*

Off in the wings, however, a more serious defense strategy was forming with the pending Senate confirmation of William Barr as Trump's next attorney general. Barr was no Matthew Whitaker. He was a serious lawyer who had already done a stint as the nation's top law enforcement officer under George H. W. Bush. Yes, Barr had written an unsolicited letter in June to Rod Rosenstein challenging Mueller's ability to go after Trump for obstruction of justice. "Mueller should not be permitted to demand that the president submit to interrogation about alleged obstruction," he said. But he would be fair, the thinking went. He was a solid member of the Washington legal establishment.

Few predicted just how fierce a partisan warrior he would become.

After Barr was confirmed by the Senate on February 14, all attention in Washington turned to the coming testimony of Cohen before the House Oversight Committee. Trump had called his former consigliere a "rat" for his willingness to cooperate with Mueller and Congress. Cohen's testimony at the end of the month was must-watch television: A blindly loyal servant who had done the boss's bidding and was now paying for it with a three-year prison sentence was out for revenge.

Cohen had nothing to lose, his credibility already gone. Cohen called

Trump a "racist," a "con man," and a "cheat" who had directed him to lie to Congress and had been well aware that WikiLeaks planned to publish stolen emails in an effort to hurt the Clinton campaign. He listed numerous examples of Trump's knowingly inflating the value of various properties to deceive lenders. He painted a picture of a petulant promoter who cared only about pimping his own brand through the presidency. Cohen delivered a lot of smoke, if not yet a gun. Backup, presumably, would come in the Mueller report.

Trump's defenders were determined that Mueller not get the first word. His report couldn't drop onto an expectant Washington without proper context and advance PR. So, in an extraordinary stroke of political legerdemain, Trump's new attorney general, Barr, moved to color the public's view of Mueller's work well before they could read it themselves.

On Friday, March 22, Mueller submitted his report to Barr. Two days later, midway through a hazy Sunday afternoon, Barr sent to Congress a four-page letter "to advise you of the principle conclusions reached by special counsel Robert S. Mueller III." The cable news networks went into overdrive. All the news outlets raced to post the letter online immediately. This was the moment the country had been waiting for.

Barr's letter listed the size of the FBI team devoted to the investigation, the 2,800 subpoenas issued, the nearly five hundred search warrants executed, the five hundred witnesses interviewed. Then he got to what mattered most to the White House: "The Special Counsel's investigation," he wrote, "did not find that the Trump campaign or anyone associated with it conspired or coordinated with Russia in its efforts to influence the 2016 U.S. presidential election."

Thus, according to Barr: No collusion.

Yes, there was massive evidence to support the allegation that the Russians had interfered in an unprecedented way in the 2016 election. But they had done so, Barr wanted to make clear, without the involvement of the Trump team.

On the issue of obstruction, Barr said that Mueller had "ultimately decided not to make a traditional prosecutorial judgment." Instead, Barr said, the special counsel had deferred that matter to him, the attorney general, and Barr had concluded that there was no grounds to criminally charge the president for obstruction, irrespective of any constitutional protections that might accrue to a president.

And so: No obstruction.

Clearly attuned to what was coming, Trump began the day with a cheery tweet: "Good Morning, Have A Great Day!" One minute later: "MAKE AMERICA GREAT AGAIN!" And then, shortly after Barr's letter went public, as though they had been in cahoots all along, Trump blasted the tweet he so wanted: "No Collusion, No Obstruction, Complete and Total EXONERATION. KEEP AMERICA GREAT!"

Barr's letter was intended to deflate, to prick the balloon in advance of the report itself. It was intended to get the simple message straight to the public that Mueller hadn't found all that much, and people could move on with their lives. In that, it largely succeeded.

At Fusion, the ploy stirred instant suspicions of a whitewash, as it did with most anyone who had followed developments closely. Trump's obstruction of justice was as plain as day. He had fired Comey to stop the Russia investigation and even admitted as much to Lester Holt on national television. That Mueller had fallen short of gathering evidence to support a single conspiracy charge also seemed astonishing, given the mass of contacts and attempts to egg the Russian efforts along. Then again, conspiracy is notoriously hard to prove beyond a reasonable doubt, and it seemed plausible that Mueller wouldn't have gambled on pursuing a charge he couldn't substantiate in court.

Based on Barr's letter, Mueller's inquest at first blush appeared to have been a bust. The press coverage reflected the anticlimax, with many reporters acting as though Barr's four-page letter was itself a worthy distillation of Mueller's entire report.

The chicanery at the heart of Barr's letter began to sink in over the coming days. Mueller himself wrote to Barr three days later, saying the summary "did not capture the context, nature and substance of this Office's work and conclusions." Barr had omitted reams of damaging information and context. The clamor for release of the full report increased.

When Mueller's report was finally released to the public on April 18, its 448 redacted pages provided, for the first time, a dense, detailed, blow-by-blow walk through the sordid twists and turns of the 2016 campaign, as well as the many Trump efforts afterwards to block Justice Department efforts to investigate what had happened.

In all, it was a devastating indictment of a campaign and a presidency. Had people received the full force of these findings for the first time, Trump's political career might have ended. As it happened, Mueller in many instances was simply confirming the litany of huge scoops the press had delivered since January 2017. The story was long. It was complicated. It involved a huge cast of characters that was hard to keep straight. It had all played out over several years. It was hard to see all the threads in the Russia picture. Many people were tired of it all. The nation had exhausted its capacity for outrage.

The more astute observers had warned all along that Mueller's final report would likely lack the cathartic finale many wanted. Mueller was a cautious man. He stayed within his prescribed lines and stuck religiously to the rules. His report was unlikely to stray beyond findings of fact already memorialized in the many indictments he had handed down. These skeptics were right, to a point. The report was a measured take on events, but it did furnish Congress with more than enough ammunition to pursue impeachment, if it so chose. Its pages very pointedly did not exonerate Trump. They described a leader obsessed with ending a federal investigation that could hurt him, an administration that repeatedly changed its story and told its members to lie, and a campaign that was in repeated contact with Russian officials and lied about it.

These same outlines held true when Mueller finally went before Congress to testify on July 24, a day long anticipated and duly trumpeted for days in advance by all the cable networks. In all, Mueller failed to impress. He was cautious, hesitant, at times bumbling. He offered no new revelations into what had happened in 2016, or how Trump tried to block his efforts in the years after.

The Republicans, predictably, brought the script back to two of their favorite bogeymen: Glenn Simpson and Fusion GPS. Simpson was mentioned no fewer than thirty-five times before the two House committees. Fusion GPS got fifty-four mentions.

For Devin Nunes, now merely the ranking member of the House Intelligence Committee, it was all about Fusion. "Welcome, everyone, to the last gasp of the Russia collusion conspiracy theory," he said, kicking off his opening statement, often with phrases taken straight from Sean Hannity's own spiels on Fox News.

"There is collusion in plain sight—collusion between Russia and the Democratic Party," Nunes said. "The Democrats colluded with Russian sources to develop the Steele dossier. And Russian lawyer Natalia Veselnitskaya colluded with the dossier's key architect, Fusion GPS head Glenn Simpson."

For all that the press had reported over three years, and all that Mueller had laid out in his report—the Russian bot armies; the indictment of multiple Russian actors; the varied efforts by Trump aides to connect with multiple Russian officials; the secret bid in 2016 to get a Trump Tower project under way in Moscow; Trump's many encouragements of Russian help; his bizarre obsequiousness around Putin; his steady campaign to hinder and obstruct any investigation of these actions—for all of that and more, Nunes wanted to cast the brightest light on Fusion.

"Fusion GPS, Steele, and other confederates," Nunes said, "fed these absurdities to naive or partisan reporters and to top officials in numerous government agencies."

The Republican construction of the upside-down world was now complete. The Russia investigation was all an elaborate ruse, created first and foremost by a little band of consultants called Fusion GPS.

The Democrats, determined and detailed in their questioning as the day wore on, did get Mueller to state publicly his most damning findings: That Trump had not, in fact, been exonerated. That Trump had lied repeatedly. That he had sought the aid of WikiLeaks to damage the Clinton campaign. That "it was not a witch hunt." That the Russians had very blatantly interfered in the election. And that they were preparing to do so again.

In the end, the Mueller probe sidestepped the question that so unnerved Fusion GPS and Christopher Steele in the summer of 2016: Was the president of the United States under the influence of a foreign adversary?

As the dust settled on Robert Mueller's work and his desultory testimony before Congress, several realities became clear.

First, the main lesson of Watergate wasn't heeded. Mueller did not—or was not allowed to—follow the money. There is no indication in his report that the investigation looked at Trump's taxes, his outstanding debts, his curious relationship with Deutsche Bank, or his long history of financing real estate projects with foreign cash of unknown origin— precisely the places where Russian influence efforts were most likely to surface. Over the years, projects from Trump Tower to Trump SoHo to Sunny Isles Beach, Florida, had all taken in millions in cash from Russian buyers. The special counsel's report did not address the possibility that Trump had used these properties to launder money, or that these deals left him susceptible to Russian manipulation when he ran for president.

Second, Justice Department policy ensured that the president would not be held accountable, regardless of what Mueller found. The report made clear that, were Trump anyone else, he would have been charged with multiple counts of obstruction of justice. On that, hundreds of former prosecutors agree. But two prior Justice Department opinions held that it was unconstitutional for a sitting president to be criminally charged while in office, and Mueller did not challenge those opinions.*

Third, Trump's sweeping efforts to obstruct Mueller's probe—and the lies that landed several of Trump's top deputies in jail—ultimately succeeded in preventing investigators from learning what took place between Trump and Russia. Time and again, the special counsel's report says that prosecutors were not able to answer some of the most pivotal questions. Why did Manafort share polling data from key swing states with Konstantin Kilimnik, a man with ties to Russian intelligence? Who tipped Trump off to the impending leaks from WikiLeaks? Did Roger Stone coordinate the release of hacked DNC emails with Russian intelligence and Julian Assange? Whom did Carter Page meet with in Moscow in June 2016? Did the Maltese professor Joseph Mifsud and Trump's Russian business associate Sergei Millian work on behalf of Russian intelligence? Why did Jared Kushner try to set up a secret back channel through the Russian ambassador?

Mueller never found out. And on several of these fronts, it is not clear how hard he tried.

It slowly became clear in the summer of 2019 that Mueller never investigated whether the Kremlin had turned President Trump or members of his administration into agents of Russian interests, witting or unwitting. Was Russia using economic or other leverage to manipulate Trump? Did that explain Trump's bizarre coddling of Putin and his reluctance to impose sanctions or say a harsh word about Russia's illegal seizure of the Crimea, its use of chemical weapons in England, and its attempts to hack the U.S. election system?

That central question—whether Russia had Trump under its thumb—was the focus of a secretive counterintelligence investigation that, according to Mueller, was hived off from his duties early on. Its findings—if any—remain buried deep in the bowels of the FBI's spy-

---

* An opinion memorandum from the DOJ's Office of Legal Counsel concluded in 1973, and again in 2000, that the indictment of a sitting president would "unconstitutionally undermine the capacity of the executive branch." While the opinion did not have the force of law, it was considered DOJ policy. As a DOJ prosecutor, Mueller would have had to request that the OLC opinions be revisited and overturned in order to criminally indict Trump. Such a move would likely have been challenged inside the DOJ and the courts. See Randolph D. Moss, Office of Legal Counsel, "A Sitting President's Amenability to Indictment and Criminal Prosecution," October 16, 2000, https://www.justice.gov/sites/default/files/olc/opinions/2000/10/31/op-olc-v024-p0222_0.pdf.

hunting unit, where they will likely remain. Some of those inquires quietly continue, Mueller told Congress in his June 2019 testimony. Given the sensitive nature of such investigations, the results are rarely disclosed, meaning the American people may never know what comes of them.

None of this is to suggest that Robert Mueller failed at his job. His team probed diligently within the Justice Department's narrow guidelines, leading to criminal indictments of thirty-four individuals, including six members of Trump's inner circle as well as a dozen Russian intelligence agents behind the hack of Democrats and thirteen individuals and three companies tied to Russia's Internet Research Agency, which ran propaganda efforts on social media. He finished his work in less than two years, avoiding the errors of past independent counsels like Kenneth Starr, who became a semi-permanent presidential inquisitor. As important, Mueller's team conducted itself with dignity and discipline amid the political maelstrom whipped up by Trump and his Republican allies, giving the nation a symbolic bulwark against those norm-destroying forces.

But Mueller's cramped mandate and his determination to wrap up expeditiously meant that key questions about Trump's relationship with Russia would have to be answered by Congress, other federal or state prosecutors, and the courts. Unfortunately, none appeared particularly suited to the task.

When Democrats retook the House of Representatives in 2018, they used its investigative authority to renew the inquiries Republicans spent two years blocking. But the Trump administration only intensified its campaign of open obstruction—ignoring subpoenas, citing legal privileges that don't exist, and refusing to produce documents even when ordered by the courts. The tactics worked, and congressional inquiries got bogged down in legal squabbling as the 2020 elections loomed. Democrats were bitterly divided by the demands of their base to hold Trump accountable in an impeachment proceeding, with many of the party's leaders wary of the reality that, post-Mueller, Russia had become a tricky political issue. Trump's Russia entanglements were hardly mentioned in the early rounds of the 2020 Democratic primary debates.

The federal courts proved to be the last bastion of the reality-based world, with federal judges unflinching in their handling of the criminal cases spinning out of the Mueller investigation. But while the Russia probe tangled the Trump administration for two years, White House officials quietly managed to remake the courts. By the summer of 2019, nearly one in four federal appeals court judges were Trump appointees. The impact of their lifetime appointments may hamstring future efforts to hold Trump accountable.

Ultimately, the job of finding answers to those questions Mueller left dangling fell to the fourth estate, private citizens, and researchers like those at Fusion GPS.

So just what did happen in the run-up to the election?

For Simpson and Fritsch, the extraordinary events of 2016 triggered early alarms because of the overlap between those events and their work as journalists in the 2000s, investigating the emerging nexus between post-Soviet kleptocracy and American politics. What at first seemed a colorful vein of reporting on the globalization of lobbying and corruption gradually became a far more troubling inquiry into how a rogue state—Russia—seemed to be attempting to infiltrate and subvert the American political system.

The story begins not with Trump but with Vladimir Putin, who for more than a decade aggressively pursued ways to covertly influence and disrupt the domestic politics of the United States and numerous other Western democracies he blamed for stripping Russia of its rightful role as a superpower. After the Cold War, Moscow's goal became one less focused on stealing state secrets than on cultivating support abroad for its political priorities, especially recognition of its territorial claims over parts of the former Soviet Union.

Before Trump, Putin's biggest "get" in this sense was former German chancellor Gerhard Schröder. After losing to Angela Merkel in 2005, Schröder became an ardent Putin supporter while earning riches sitting on the boards of companies led by Russian state energy giant Gazprom. Asked in 2004 if he thought Putin was a "flawless democrat," Schröder said, "I am convinced he is."

Like Schröder, Trump was more of a target of opportunity than a Manchurian candidate who was somehow brainwashed by Putin. He's simply the latest and most powerful politician to look past the crimes of an autocrat when there's possible money on the table. Trump's long infatuation with making deals in the former Soviet Union, combined with his craven desire for an economic comeback after years of bankruptcy, made him the most susceptible among a number of American political figures from both parties whom the Russians targeted for cultivation over many years.

The Russians invested in various other prospects, often by cultivating political figures through Putin's network of captive oligarchs, who have a history of backing large lobbying efforts, supporting Washington think tanks, and making politically strategic investments. These efforts mostly came up short. In the 2008 campaign, for example, the Russians appear to have attempted to infiltrate the McCain presidential campaign with the help of none other than Oleg Deripaska and Paul Manafort. The 2008 operation failed when it was partially exposed in the media.

Russia's political influence efforts in the United States surfaced again in 2010, when the FBI exposed and arrested a network of sleeper Russian agents in Operation Ghost Stories, better known as the Anna Chapman case. Intercepts and other evidence showed that the ring was more preoccupied with getting close to American political figures than in stealing state military secrets, an approach the media misread as some weird relic of the Cold War.

The agents were engaged in an elaborate exercise to identify people who might one day ascend to positions of political influence and power. It was the same Soviet intelligence tactic used in Britain in the 1930s to spot talent inside Cambridge University. That led to the recruitment of the Cambridge Five, whose most famous member, Kim Philby, became and MI6 officer and acted for decades as a double agent for Moscow.

At some point in the past decade, Putin decided to augment his foreign influence project with new propaganda technologies that would enable Russia to manipulate public opinion and even elections in the United States and other countries through social media, such as Twitter trolls.

Russia's targeting of democratic political systems was ingeniously opportunistic: While the intelligence and defense establishments of NATO countries are well defended against traditional espionage, their wide-open political systems make for soft targets. Politicians hate being monitored by their own security services and retaliate when such investigations come to light. This makes it difficult for the FBI and its counterparts to conduct counterintelligence investigations without getting sucked into precisely the sort of damaging political controversies that have erupted since Trump took office.

In Trump, Putin found the perfect opportunity to exploit Russia's newfound propaganda powers with a long-shot bid to install an ally in the White House. Falling short of that, Russia would at least sow distrust among Americans in their electoral system. As it turned out, Putin succeeded on both counts.

Was Trump a witting accomplice in all this? Mueller concluded that there wasn't sufficient evidence to say he was. But it is abundantly clear that Trump has shown an extraordinary fealty toward Putin as toward no other world leader. Trump's economic revival over the past fifteen years came about in large part because of a conduit of cash from the former Soviet Union into his various stumbling enterprises. And a vast number of his aides and advisers have had close ties to Moscow and welcomed Russia's help in what it did to twist the 2016 electoral outcome.

To deny that Russia intervened in the 2016 election with the express purpose of helping Trump win—given all the evidence presented by Mueller and the Intelligence Community—requires a staggering degree of willful blindness. Worse, however, is to support that position with silence.

Today's Republican leadership has much to answer for in that regard. There is strong circumstantial evidence to believe that Republican leaders in Congress either knew or suspected much more about what Russia was up to in 2016 than they let on. It is now known that Senator Mitch McConnell intervened almost two months before the election to stop the Obama White House from publicly calling out Putin's crimes. In 2019, McConnell has also repeatedly blocked bills aimed at protecting state voting systems from foreign hackers, earning him the epithet "Moscow Mitch" from critics and a shiny new aluminum factory back home in Kentucky courtesy of Oleg Deripaska's company.

Americans learned in September 2019 that just a day after Mueller's congressional testimony, Trump repeatedly pressed Ukraine's president to revive an investigation into unsubstantiated corruption allegations potentially damaging to Vice President Joe Biden, his most potent Democratic rival in 2020. Here was Trump, now acting as president, using the levers of U.S. foreign policy to enlist a foreign leader to help him undermine a domestic political rival. Feeling impunity from the outcome of an investigation into his conduct in one election, he was turning his sights to the next—this time even more brazenly, and again with only muted reactions from Republicans in Congress.

Like McConnell, the Republican establishment has proven itself extremely susceptible to foreign electoral blandishments. As the Republican Party's base of white voters has shriveled, there has been an increasing willingness on the part of its leaders to pursue win-at-all-costs electoral strategies, such as the deliberate disenfranchisement of minority voters and covert alliances with foreign regimes similarly fearful of demographic demise.

A handful of documents in recent times have bent the course of history deeply enough to merit their own sobriquet. The Pentagon Papers. The Warren Report. The Starr Report. Time will tell whether the Steele dossier—that collection of intelligence snapshots from a former British spy's source network—deserves to take its place among them. As a touchstone for the Trump-Russia scandal, it is already perhaps the most famous work of opposition research in American politics.

Yet as opposition research, the dossier's impact before the election was negligible. Republican efforts to portray the dossier as a hoax or a political dirty trick ignore the fact that it emerged publicly *only after the vote*. Because Fusion and Steele quietly provided their most alarming information to law enforcement, questions about the Trump campaign's cooperation with Russia had no sway over voters before the election. If the dossier had been created to swing the election, as many Republicans still suggest, it would have been released before Election Day.

The dossier's true impact was not as opposition research, but as a timely warning to the world about Russia's ability to deploy powerful new tools in a coordinated attack on Western democracies, and about very real concerns regarding the man whom the United States had just elected. These concerns have only grown over time.

The dossier's publication—something that, it is worth stressing again, Fusion never wanted or anticipated—helped thrust the Russian attack to the front of public consciousness from the first days of Trump's tenure and cast his intentions as president in a starkly different light. The document gave meaning and urgency to a closely held FBI investigation into Trump's Russia ties and set in motion a cascade of events that, when amplified by a newly aggressive news media, led to the appointment of Robert Mueller.

Had that collection of intelligence reports *not* exploded onto the world stage in January 2017, the Trump presidency—and possibly many global events—may have taken a dramatically different path. Among other things, the dossier appears to have derailed a plan by the incoming Trump team to reorder the post–World War II Western alliance through a rapprochement with Russia that would transform U.S. relationships with Europe, the Middle East, China, and beyond. Domestically, it helped fuel an investigation that landed several of Trump's closest allies in jail and tied his administration in knots.

Fusion GPS foresaw none of this when it hired Steele to make discreet inquiries in the summer of 2016. Steele's memos were one piece among dozens of research feeds that were intended to supplement and expand upon Fusion's own investigation, which focused on records available in the open source. These various threads of research would normally be distilled, analyzed, and—if deemed credible—passed along to the Clinton campaign.

That process was upended by an extraordinary historical event captured in the dossier itself: the Russian government's unprecedented attack on the American electoral system. Steele's first report arrived at the end of June 2016, just as news of those hacks was becoming public, and the dossier described aspects of the attack almost in real time. In the eyes of Fusion and Steele, that transformed a thread of opposition research into critically important evidence of a crime in progress.

Historic intelligence failures such as Pearl Harbor and September 11, 2001, have often been attributed to "failures of imagination." The same could be said of the Russian attack on the 2016 presidential elections. Neither the U.S. government nor the media nor the public were prepared to grapple with a sweeping foreign intrusion into our fragile electoral system. The efforts by Steele and Fusion to raise the alarm initially struck many as wide-eyed paranoia.

But by raising the alarm when they did, Steele's memos played a critical role in helping to alert the U.S. government—and eventually the media and the public—to Russia's sinister efforts and the Trump campaign's openness to them. It offered an explanation for much of the strange activity that had occurred over the previous year, from the RNC's platform change on the Ukraine conflict to Trump's incessant flattery of Putin. Events that seemed disconnected suddenly made sense to ordinary people in the light of the dossier's stark warnings.

The dossier also helped focus greater attention on broader dangers the United States is still grappling with: manipulation via social media, Putin's ambition to dismantle the Western alliance, and the nascent kleptocracy of the Trump administration.

In that sense, the dossier served a vital purpose: sparking the collective imagination like a bonfire on a mountaintop, awakening people to the previously unimaginable threats of the day.

While the dossier's impact on the events of the past few years is beyond debate, the veracity of all its claims is not.

After three years of investigations, a fair assessment of the memos would conclude that many of the allegations in the dossier have been borne out. Some proved remarkably prescient. Other details remain stubbornly unconfirmed, while a handful now appear to be doubtful, though not yet disproven.

For anyone familiar with human intelligence reports, that assessment should come as no surprise: A spy whose sources get it 70 percent right is considered to be one of the best. But that context was lost on many readers, who were befuddled by its staccato presentation of information from sources identified only by letter in a "company intelligence report." As journalists scrambled to corroborate or refute the startling allegations, they focused quickly on its salacious contents and minor details, such as the spellings of transliterated Russian names and whether there was a Russian consulate in Miami.

As a result, they tended to miss the central message, which, in hindsight, Steele got strikingly right. ·

In his first report, on June 20, 2016, Steele stated that Russian election meddling was "endorsed by Putin" and "supported and directed" by him to "sow discord and disunity with the United States itself but more especially within the Transatlantic alliance."

Six months later, the U.S. Intelligence Community's assessment determined that Steele was right. "Russian President Vladimir Putin ordered an influence campaign in 2016 aimed at the U.S. presidential election," the U.S. Office of the Director of National Intelligence stated. "Russia's goals were to undermine public faith in the U.S. democratic process" and "undermine the U.S.-led liberal democratic order."

The U.S. assessment also concluded that Steele was right about something top FBI officials appear to have been slow to admit or recognize: Putin wasn't merely seeking to create a crisis of confidence in democratic elections. He was actively pulling strings to destroy Hillary Clinton and elect Donald Trump. It is worth noting that, months earlier, in the run-up to the election, the FBI was either wrong about this fact or lying to the press.

In September 2019, U.S. officials confirmed that the Central Intelligence Agency had a human source inside the Russian government during the campaign, who provided information that dovetailed with Steele's reporting about Russia's objective of electing Trump and Putin's direct involvement in the operation. This may help explain why both

Obama and Trump were briefed on Steele's reporting weeks before the inauguration.

The first Steele memo also reported that the Russian effort to cultivate Trump included "various lucrative real estate development deals in Russia." Trump categorically denied having any ties to Russia, much less any lucrative business deals in the works. More than two years later, however, court records confirmed that throughout the election, Michael Cohen and Felix Sater communicated with Putin's top aides while working to secure permits for a Trump Tower in Moscow that would earn Trump an estimated $300 million. Steele's sources may have been vague, but they were ultimately correct.

A July 2016 memo by Steele reported, "Russians apparently have promised not to use 'kompromat' they hold on TRUMP as leverage, given high levels of voluntary co-operation forthcoming from his team." We now know the Russians kept their knowledge of the Trump Tower Moscow deal secret, and Trump has been inexplicably deferential to the Kremlin both as a candidate and as president. After a lengthy Helsinki meeting with Putin in July 2018, for example, Trump sided with the Russian leader over his own intelligence agencies, saying he "didn't see any reason why" he should believe Russia was responsible for hacking the DNC.

It is sometimes hard to credit the dossier for its prescience because so many of its claims are today accepted as common knowledge. But the dossier first introduced to the public a cast of characters that would later become central figures in the investigation. Carter Page, Michael Cohen, and the Agalarov family were all obscure names before their appearance in the dossier, yet they would prove to be key to the Mueller investigation. For example, the Agalarovs burst onto center stage only a year later, when *The New York Times* discovered in July 2017 that they had arranged the Trump Tower meeting with a Russian attorney to discuss Russian dirt on Hillary Clinton.

The dossier also correctly identified the figures at the center of the Trump campaign's secret dealings with Russia, including Paul Manafort and Michael Flynn. The Mueller report showed that Manafort was in contact with a Russian intelligence operative and several other Russians closely linked to the Kremlin during the 2016 campaign. Starting in the spring of 2016, Manafort began sharing internal Trump campaign polling data with an associate tied to Russian intelligence. The data focused on Rust Belt swing states that would later prove pivotal to Trump's election. Because Manafort and the associate lied to investigators, Mueller said his team could not determine how that data was used.

The dossier named Michael Flynn as a pro-Russia intermediary on the campaign and said the Kremlin believed it had successfully recruited him. Media investigations later found that Flynn was paid $68,000 by the Russians for a trip to Moscow, and he admitted to lying about several conversations with Ambassador Sergey Kislyak during 2015 and 2016.

Media also later reported that in intercepted phone conversations, Russian officials reportedly "bragged . . . that they had cultivated a strong relationship with former Trump adviser retired general Michael Flynn and believed they could use him to influence Donald Trump and his team."

The role of Trump foreign policy adviser Carter Page as a key intermediary with Russian officials was another central revelation of the dossier. Steele's sources said Page had privately met with senior Kremlin officials in Moscow in July 2016 to discuss Western sanctions. He was also said to have met with officials of the state-owned oil giant Rosneft so that he could earn broker fees on the forthcoming sale of company's shares.

That sale was little known at the time Steele described it, but it later came to pass as he described. Page adamantly denied the claims made in the "dodgy dossier," but records later revealed that soon after his trip, Page sent emails to the Trump campaign reporting on "incredible insights and outreach I've received from a few Russian legislators and senior members of the Presidential Administration here." According to the Mueller report, those contacts included "a private conversation" with the Russian deputy prime minister.

And in testimony before the House Intelligence Committee in November 2017, Page reluctantly acknowledged that he had also met with a Rosneft executive about sanctions and the company's sale of shares in the deal. His categorical denial was ultimately reduced to a quibble: The dossier was wrong, he complained, about *whom* he met with—it was the Rosneft head of investor relations, he said, not the CEO.

Steele's allegations about Trump fixer Michael Cohen remain unresolved. Steele's sources stated that Cohen had played an "important role" as a "secret liaison with Russian leadership," particularly after Manafort was forced to resign as campaign chairman in August 2016. Most notably, they alleged that Cohen had attended a meeting with Russians in Prague in late August or early September 2016. At the meeting, the memos said, the two sides discussed how to cover up the extensive co-operation between the two sides, including "deniable cash payments" to the hackers involved in the effort.

There is no doubt Cohen played a central role in dealing with Russians in the Trump Tower Moscow deal, but the explosive Prague allegation in the Steele reports was undermined—though not disproven—by Cohen's continued denials after his plea bargain with Mueller's team. In the Mueller report, the special counsel appeared to endorse those denials in a section describing Cohen's false testimony to Congress about Trump's ties to Russia. The report states, "Cohen had never traveled to Prague and was not concerned about those allegations, which he believed were provably false." A footnote cites Cohen's own testimony to Mueller as the evidence of this.

It is certainly possible that Cohen was mistakenly identified as one of the attendees of the meeting by Steele's source. It could also be that the whole story of the Prague meeting was misinformation fed to Steele to discredit him, something the former spy knew to be a risk anytime he collected information from sources. Yet Cohen has never publicly produced a concrete alibi concerning his whereabouts during the period in question, and there are still unexplained aspects of the alleged incident, such as reports of cell signals from Cohen's phone in the region and reports of his presence picked up by foreign intelligence agencies. In this age of relentless phone tracking, ubiquitous video cameras, and credit card use, the truth shouldn't be too hard to determine. But the facts, like so many others raised in the dossier, remain frustratingly beyond reach.

Other claims in the dossier have been corroborated. Steele alleged that the billionaire Russian bankers Mikhail Fridman and Petr Aven were "giving informal advice to Putin, especially on the US." The Steele memo also reported allegations about the history of their business activities in the 1990s. The Mueller report didn't address that history, but disclosed that Aven had meetings with Putin on a quarterly basis, including in 2016, where they discussed U.S. relations. Aven said he took Putin's suggestions or critiques as directives that could not be ignored without consequence.

In another memo, dated December 2016, Steele's source identified an obscure Russian firm called XBT/Webzilla as having used "botnets and porn traffic to transmit viruses, plant bugs, steal data and conduct 'altering operations' against the Democratic Party leadership." Webzilla's owner vehemently denied the claim, saying it didn't control what content traveled across its servers. It sued *BuzzFeed* for defamation after it published the dossier—a case *BuzzFeed* eventually won. The *Miami Herald* reported that Webzilla was used by the Russian troll farm, the Internet Research Agency, for "meddling operations" in the United States during the election.

While these threads were being slowly borne out, the media and the public tended to fixate on the lurid claim contained in Steele's first report: that Russian intelligence had recorded Donald Trump in 2013 cavorting in the Moscow Ritz-Carlton with prostitutes who urinated on a bed once slept in by Barack and Michelle Obama.

When the allegation surfaced, Orbis weighed whether to remove it from its reports, for fear that it would distract from the other reporting. They ultimately decided against doing so—Steele felt the allegation was important from a counterintelligence perspective. Russian *kompromat* against Trump would give them leverage over a future U.S. president. Fusion also had misgivings about being a conduit for such a tale. But when the decision was made to give the dossier to the authorities, Fusion saw value in keeping Steele's reporting separate from its own work and decided not to edit it in any way.

So is the Ritz-Carlton allegation true? The answer still isn't known, but some evidence supports the possibility.

Trump told FBI Director James Comey at a private dinner on January 27, 2017, that he had never even spent the night at the Ritz-Carlton when he visited Moscow in 2013 to host the Miss Universe pageant with the Agalarovs. It has since been established that he did spend the night. Trump's bodyguard Keith Schiller recalled the offer of prostitutes in congressional testimony. Schiller said he turned down the offer and eventually left Trump alone at his room in the Ritz-Carlton that night.

A final tantalizing clue about the possibility of a "pee tape" came in a footnote buried deep within the Mueller report: "On October 30, 2016, Michael Cohen received a text from Russian businessman [Giorgi] Rtskhiladze that read: 'Stopped flow of tapes from Russia but not sure if there's anything else. Just so you know. . . .' Rtskhiladze said 'tapes' referred to compromising tapes of Trump rumored to be held by persons associated with the Russian real estate conglomerate Crocus Group." The Crocus Group is the real estate company of the Agalarov family, Trump's partner in the Miss Universe contest.

Mueller's report is silent on the significance of this exchange, whether it involves the Moscow Ritz-Carlton or some other incident, and whether the existence of these tapes was ever verified. It is yet another piece of vital information stubbornly beyond reach for now.

Steele remains confident that the Ritz allegation is not disinformation, a hoax, or the fabrication of a fantasist. Ultimately, whether the incident detailed in the dossier is true or not is likely not of paramount importance. The Russians had ample *kompromat* against Trump and his top aides with or without any pee tapes.

One of the biggest sources of confusion over the dossier, Steele always complained, was the erroneous assumption that the memos were based on spontaneous encounters with random Russians. "What people don't know is that this is not an isolated group of sources, it is a network of tried and tested sources that have been proven up in many other matters," Steele would complain. While the public and many in the media did not understand that, it was *not* something the FBI was ignorant of. Indeed, that is exactly why he was taken so seriously, and helps explain why so much of what Steele reported turned out in the long run to be correct. It is ironic that many journalists, of all people, failed to appreciate this, given their own dependence on well-placed sources to deliver the news out of Wall Street and Washington.

Another line of attack that galls Steele is the tendency to dismiss the dossier as "disinformation," in part or in full.

"These people simply have no idea what they are talking about," he said to Simpson. "I've spent my entire adult life working with Russian disinformation. It's an incredibly complex subject that is at the very core of my training and my professional mission."

In his view, one of the most important criteria for disinformation "is whether there is a palpable motive for spreading it, and whether that motive outweighs the downside effects of putting it out. The ultimate Russian goal was to prevent Hillary Clinton from becoming president, and therefore, the idea that they would intentionally spread embarrassing information about Trump—true or not—is not logical."

The idea that they would be using such tactics merely to discredit Steele is even more absurd. "The stakes were far, far too high for them to trifle with settling scores with me or any other civilian. Damaging my reputation was simply not on their list of priorities. But helping Trump and damaging Hillary was at the very top of it. No one denies that anymore."

Steele has told associates that he remains confident that at least 70 percent of the assertions in the dossier are accurate. On that he hasn't wavered.

———

Perhaps the most consequential claim in Steele's memos is the description of a "well-developed conspiracy of co-operation" between the Trump campaign and the Russian leadership.

Mueller's report offers mountains of intriguing evidence of such a conspiracy, including more than 140 contacts—many of them surreptitious—between the Trump campaign and Russians. But he ultimately concluded that the evidence of a criminal conspiracy was insufficient for proving the case in court beyond a reasonable doubt.

That legal conclusion should not be mistaken for an exoneration. There is ample evidence amassed over the past three years to show that the Trump campaign and the Russian government repeatedly sought to work together to swing the 2016 election—and that they succeeded.

There is no other plausible explanation for Trump's ongoing subservience to Putin's agenda and the continuing campaign of obstruction and coordinated lies, in which several of Trump's closest aides have opted to go to prison for long prison terms rather than tell the truth to investigators. Not only has Trump failed to respond to an attack on the United States by a hostile foreign power—he welcomed it and used it to achieve power. He continues to publicly support and praise the author of that attack while dismantling the American institutions he took an oath to defend.

The Trump campaign's conspiring with Russia may not be a crime provable in federal court, but it amounts to one of the most significant betrayals in American history.

That, at its core, was the warning sounded by Fusion and Steele in 2016, a warning that remains as urgent today as it was then.

ACKNOWLEDGMENTS

This book is a product of the some of the finest investigative work we've ever been associated with—and we've worked and competed with a lot of terrific investigators over the course of our careers at *The Wall Street Journal* and beyond. Our colleagues at Fusion stand alongside the best of them. They don't get headlines or share their work on Twitter, but the Fusion team is among the most dedicated and creative group of writers and researchers working today. This book is theirs too.

Our point man on Project Bangor was, and is, Jacob Berkowitz. We dare say there is no one out there who knows more about the many business entanglements of Donald Trump. The late *Village Voice* muckraker Wayne Barrett, the first reporter to take Trump seriously, would have loved comparing notes with Jake. Research aces Patrick Corcoran, Laura Seago, Jay Bagwell, and David Michaels made important discoveries too numerous to mention. Taylor Sears, our in-house expert on offshore shell companies, helped unpack the many secrets of Paul Manafort. Thanks to Erica McMillon, who always keeps the trains running on time.

There were many people outside our company, in the United States and overseas, who also made valuable contributions to our understanding of Trump's record. We won't name them here, for obvious reasons. We do, however, want to single out the work of Nellie Ohr and her fellow Russian linguist and researcher Edward Baumgartner. Donald Trump and the right-wing commentariat he apes have portrayed Nellie as some sort of partisan warrior. In truth, she is an incredibly accomplished Russia expert who is meticulous in her research—and a person of impeccable character. We're proud to know her.

Chris Steele and Chris Burrows are gentlemen of grace and good humor. History will remember them for acting out of a sense of duty when many others dithered, and doing so without the expectation of recognition or thanks. The past few years have brought us closer as friends, and for that we are equally grateful. We thank them and their colleagues at Orbis. Daniel Jones was brave and foolish enough to step forward and work with us at precisely the moment when the political attacks on us were most intense. We won't forget that, nor will we forget those who stepped forward to support him and keep our work going.

Mary Jacoby, who partnered with Glenn twenty-five years ago when both were young reporters, has been an invaluable sounding board and supported Glenn through all of his endeavors.

We wish we didn't have so many lawyers to thank, but we do. Bill Taylor, Steve Salky, Bob Muse, Ted Boutrous, Rachel Cotton, Rachel Clattenburg, and their teams provided sage counsel and support in some very difficult times. Our old friend Stuart Karle painstakingly reviewed the manuscript. Joshua Levy deserves special recognition: lawyer, therapist, foxhole friend for life. Thank you.

We also want to recognize the great work of the many journalists on the Trump beat, both before the 2016 election and in its aftermath. As this book recounts, a lot of outstanding journalism was committed that got drowned out in the noise of a national election. It was out there, hiding in plain sight, if you looked closely enough.

Everyone needs a good editor. We were lucky enough to have three. Our partners Tom Catan and Jason Felch are great writers and thinkers, who made valuable contributions to the text (and helped keep our ship afloat through some very heavy seas). From the start, our old *Wall Street Journal* friend and Fusion colleague Neil King was this book's bureau chief, wrangling copy, resolving impasses, and contributing a significant share of the writing himself. We're getting the bylines on this one, but this book is as much Neil's as anybody's. We can't thank him enough.

Thanks to our editor Andy Ward at Random House. At one point, Andy described one draft chapter as a "goiter on the book." If you can't identify it, thank him. Our agent, Tina Bennett, was patient, kind, and encouraging throughout. Our in-house copy maven Holly Yeager let no error pass. The fastidious Halle Rudolf and Frances King, worked tirelessly to create our endnotes, index, and bibliography, catching many errors along the way. They'll soon be in the job market. Hire them.

Finally, thanks to our families and the families of everyone mentioned above. Only you know how strange and difficult the past few years have been. We thank you and love you.

A NOTE ON SOURCES

In some ways, research on this book began in Brussels in the mid-2000s, when we worked on stories for *The Wall Street Journal* highlighting the odd marriage of money and convenience between Republican political consultants and Putin's Russia. That work, and our own research in 2015 and early 2016, helped us recognize the importance of Christopher Steele's explosive source reporting.

But we had other good reasons to believe that Steele's sources were credible. We can only go so far in this book, unfortunately, in explaining why we thought that, and still do. Steele has explained to us how some of his sources were in a position to know what they reported and why he thinks their information is credible. In some cases, we know who these people are.

Ideally, we would have quoted extensively from internal and external communications. That wasn't always possible, because much of our communications on Project Bangor occurred over end-to-end encrypted messaging applications that do not store traffic. Those messages are gone. In some cases, people with whom we communicated saved our exchanges and allowed us to review them. We're grateful for their help in re-creating certain scenes and dialogue. Other dialogue we re-created from memory. Where possible, we checked our recollection of events against that of other participants and the public record, such as congressional testimony.

In our endnotes, we've done our best to cite source material to primary and official documents, such as published works, media accounts, court filings, documents released under the Freedom of Information Act, and official government and congressional transcripts.

The nature of our engagement with the law firm Perkins Coie prevents us from recounting our communications after we were retained. We described one meeting with Marc Elias that occurred before we were hired. Perkins has not released us from our obligations to keep our communications confidential, nor have other clients.

Under pressure from Republicans in Congress, some of our clients provided limited waivers to our confidentiality agreements so that various committees could question us and examine some of our records.

We generally don't talk about our dealings with reporters because those discussions are conducted on a confidential basis by mutual agreement. We avoided disclosing the details of our dealings with individual reporters unless those interactions had already come to light in congressional investigations or other public accounts. In some cases, we recount discussions with journalists with their express permission. There are several instances, however, in which we believe news organizations and individual reporters voided their confidentiality agreements with us by publishing details of their off-the-record communications with Fusion.

Finally, we relied on many outstanding books on Donald Trump and Russia under Vladimir Putin, which informed our understanding of these subjects and helped us make our own observations about the events of 2016 and beyond.

ENDNOTES

CHAPTER ONE: "I THINK WE HAVE A PROBLEM"

6 **Senator McCain, still many months from a dire brain cancer diagnosis, wanted to put a copy of Steele's memos in front of FBI Director James Comey:** Manu Raju, "Graham Encouraged McCain to Turn Trump-Russia Dossier Over to FBI," CNN, March 25, 2019.

6 **The story blew open:** Evan Perez, Jim Sciutto, Jake Tapper, and Carl Bernstein, *The Situation Room*, CNN, January 10, 2017.

6 **"Classified documents on Russian interference":** Ibid.

7 **"compiled by a former British":** Perez et al., *The Situation Room*, January 20, 2017.

8 **"potentially a crime in progress":** Testimony of Glenn Simpson, Senate Judiciary Committee, August 22, 2017.

9 **published Steele's reports to Fusion:** Ken Bensinger, Mark Schoofs, and Miriam Elder, "These Reports Allege Trump Has Deep Ties to Russia," *BuzzFeed News*, January 10, 2017.

9 **The dossier's shocking main thesis:** A series of raw intelligence reports from Orbis to Fusion GPS, June 20, 2016–December 13, 2016, now commonly referred to as "the dossier."

11 **Later that day, the paper:** Bradley Hope, Michael Rothfeld, and Alan Cullison, "Christopher Steele, Ex–British Intelligence Officer, Said to Have Prepared Dossier on Trump," *Wall Street Journal*, January 11, 2017.

11 **the FBI had looked into suspected Russia ties:** Eric Lichtblau and Steven Lee Myers, "Investigating Donald Trump, F.B.I. Sees No Clear Link to Russia," *New York Times*, October 31, 2016.

11 **the *Times* published a front-page story:** Scott Shane, "What We Know and Don't Know About the Trump-Russia Dossier," *New York Times*, January 11, 2017.

12 **Trump weighed in:** Donald Trump, news conference, New York, January 11, 2017.

13 **"a garbage document":** Bob Woodward, *Fox News Sunday,* Fox News, January 15, 2017.

13 **"Thank you Bob Woodward":** Donald J. Trump (@realDonaldTrump), Twitter, January 15, 2017, 12:04 P.M.

CHAPTER TWO: PROJECT BANGOR

14 **the first GOP debate:** Joe Flint, "GOP Debate Draws 24 Million Viewers, Making Cable History as Donald Trump Leads the Race," *Wall Street Journal,* August 7, 2015.

16 **led to a grand jury investigation:** "Supplemental Report on the Qualifications of Donald J. Trump," *Report of the Division of Gaming Enforcement to the Casino Control Commission* (Trenton, N.J.: State of New Jersey Division of Gaming Enforcement, December 1, 1992).

16 **"While I was reporting that book":** Wayne Barrett, "Inside Donald Trump's Empire: Why He Didn't Run for President in 2012," *Daily Beast,* May 26, 2011.

16 **By Labor Day weekend, Trump had carved out a solid lead:** "2016 Republican Presidential Nomination," Polling Data, May 6, 2015–May 5, 2016, RealClearPolitics.

17 **top Republican strategists and donors were combining efforts:** Nicholas Confessore, "Talk in G.O.P. Turns to a Stop Donald Trump Campaign," *New York Times,* September 4, 2015.

18 **The earliest article, published on B1:** Charles V. Bagli, "Real Estate Executive with Hand in Trump Projects Rose from Tangled Past," *New York Times,* December 17, 2007.

19 **Wayne Barrett had also penned a 2011 follow-up:** Barrett, "Inside Donald Trump's Empire."

19 **The feds had accused him of large-scale money laundering and stock manipulation involving Italian organized crime:** Bagli, "Real Estate Executive."

19 **He was Russian-born and grew up in the rough-and-tumble:** Petition for Writ of Certiorari, *Palmer v. Doe,* No. 14-676, U.S. Supreme Court.

19 **Simpson went back on Amazon and ordered a copy:** Salvatore Lauria and David S. Barry, *The Scorpion and the Frog: High Times and High Crimes* (Beverly Hills, Calif.: New Millennium Press, 2003).

Salvatore "Sal" Lauria was a co-conspirator and business partner of Felix Sater during the massive Mob on Wall Street scandal of the late 1990s. They were both named in a 2000 press release by Loretta Lynch, then district attorney of the Eastern District of New York, as major cogs in an organized crime racket involving the La Cosa Nostra Mafia family. Lauria and Sater were co-owners of a stock brokerage known as White Rock Partners & Co., which defrauded investors on behalf of the Italian Mafia.

Lauria's book is a detailed account of his years perpetrating stock frauds on Wall Street, with various unsavory Russian mobsters. Sater's name in the text is changed to "Lex Tersa," but it's easy to identify him as Sater. The book also contains passages about Mr. Trump. Sater established an office at Trump's 40 Wall Street building (page 209), among other interactions, such as his actions at a party with Sal and Lex on page 89:

"We joined Lex and his wife, Lori, a beautiful blonde like Lynn. The two of them attracted the attention of Donald Trump, who apparently was always on the lookout for new possible conquests.

"Soon, Trump's bodyguard walked over to speak to Lori and Lynn. 'Hi,' he said. 'You two ladies are gorgeous and my employer, Mr. Trump,' he nodded back over his shoulder and paused for a moment to allow the dramatic impact to sink in, 'would like your names and phone numbers.'"

19 **"never really understood who owned Bayrock":** Deposition of Donald J. Trump, *Taglieri v. SB Hotel Associates,* No. 08-35643 CACE (07), 17th Judicial Circuit Court, Broward County, Florida, November 16, 2011.

20 **At the Republican debate:** Donald Trump, "Republican Presidential Debate," *CNN Live,* CNN, September 16, 2015.

20 **For decades, Trump had shown a starry-eyed fascination with Russia:** Michael Oreskes, "Trump Gives a Vague Hint of Candidacy," *New York Times,* September 2, 1987.

21 **Sater also had a business card:** Matthew Mosk and Brian Ross, "Memory Lapse? Trump Seeks Distance from 'Advisor' with Past Ties to Mafia," ABC News, December 10, 2015.

21 **Trump's legally required candidate financial disclosure forms:** All presidential and vice presidential candidates are required to submit financial disclosure reports to the U.S. Federal Election Commission (FEC). The FEC forwards the reports to the U.S. Office of Government Ethics for review. The forms are available to the public at the FEC (http://fec.gov) and the OGE (http://oge.gov). The disclosures should detail to the public any financial holdings, any debt, and any sources of income.

21 **Trump University, a for-profit, unaccredited real estate training school that had drawn a raft of lawsuits and regulatory scrutiny:** *Low v. Trump University,* No. 17-55635, U.S. District Court, Southern District of California; *Cohen v. Trump,* No. 13-cv-2519, U.S. District Court, Southern District of California (filed October 18, 2013); *Makaeff v. Trump University,* No. 3:10-cv-00940, U.S. District Court, Southern District of California.

22 **There were numerous ongoing fraud cases:** Ibid.

22 **Trump's $5 billion libel suit:** *Trump v. O'Brien,* No. CAM-L-545-06, Superior Court of New Jersey, 2006.

22 **Notably, one of Trump's own witnesses:** Ibid.

23 **The forty-six-story hotel:** Jesse Eisinger, Justin Elliott, Andrea Bernstein, and Ilya Marritz, "Ivanka and Donald Trump Jr. Were Close to Being Charged with Felony Fraud," *ProPublica,* October 4, 2017.

23 **The plaintiffs had alleged:** Mike McIntire, "Donald Trump Settled a Real Estate Lawsuit, and a Criminal Case Was Closed," *New York Times,* April 5, 2016.

23 **A classic example was Trump's Fort Lauderdale project, in which Trump initially said he was an investor:** Deposition of Donald J. Trump, *Abercrombie v. SB Hotel Associates,* No. 08-060702, 17th Judicial Circuit Court, Broward County, Fla., November 5, 2013.

24 **Trump's criminal ties were explored:** Robert O'Harrow Jr., "Trump Swam in Mob-Infested Waters in Early Years as an NYC Developer," *Washington Post,* October 16, 2015.

25 **all of his projects were fabulously successful:** As self-reported on Donald Trump's presidential candidate financial disclosure forms, housed at the FEC.

26 **Fusion had acquired a set of court documents filed by a former Bayrock executive:** Complaint, *Kriss v. Bayrock Whitestone,* No. 4899, Delaware Court of Chancery, September 15, 2009. Kriss and his lawyers eventually sued Sater and Bayrock in various other jurisdictions, including the Southern District of New York. The sprawling litigation yielded thousands of public documents about the company. Trump was a defendant in various cases against Bayrock.

26 **FL Group folded shortly afterwards:** Eric Pfanner and Julia Werdigier, "Iceland, in a Precarious Position, Takes Drastic Steps to Right Itself," *New York Times,* October 7, 2008.

27 **a proposed Trump Tower in Moscow:** Carol D. Leonnig, Tom Hamburger, and Rosalind S. Helderman, "Trump's Business Sought Deal on a Trump Tower in Moscow While He Ran for President," *Washington Post,* August 27, 2017.

27 **Trump had hired Cohen in 2007 to act as his in-house enforcer:** Michael Falcone, "Donald Trump's Political 'Pit Bull': Meet Michael Cohen," ABC News, April 16, 2011.

27 **On October 13, 2015:** Philip Bump, "The Events That Led to Trump's Abandoned Moscow Deal and Michael Cohen's Latest Plea Agreement," *Washington Post,* October 29, 2018.

27 **The Russia coincidences continued to pile up:** Gavin Finch and Ambereen Choudhury, "Deutsche Bank Sets Aside $1.3 Billion, Mostly for Russia Probe," *Bloomberg,* October 29, 2015.

28 **Between 2008 and 2014 she:** Résumé, Nellie Ohr.

28 **Fusion had worked to expose the digital manipulation of abortion clinic sting videos:** Jackie Calmes, "Planned Parenthood Videos Were Altered, Analysis Finds," *New York Times,* August 27, 2015.

CHAPTER THREE: THE CHARLATAN

31 **Labor department records showing:** Fusion compiled a spreadsheet of publicly available work visa petition data. The data was available online from the Office of Foreign Labor Certification at the U.S. Department of Labor, http://dol.gov.

31 **Reuters published its own report:** Mica Rosenberg, Ryan McNeill, Megan Twohey, and Michelle Conlin, "Exclusive: Donald Trump's Companies Have Sought Visas to Import at Least 1,100 Workers," Reuters, August 2, 2015.

32 **A Trump Taj Mahal casino worker:** Indictment, *United States v. Gomez-Rua,* U.S. Department of Justice, November 29, 2013.

32 **nearly all of his U.S. facilities:** Joshua Partlow and David A. Fahrenthold, "At Trump Golf Course, Undocumented Employees Said They Were Sometimes Told to Work Extra Hours Without Pay," *Washington Post,* April 30, 2019; Miriam Jordan, "Making President Trump's Bed: A Housekeeper Without Papers," *New York Times,* December 6, 2018; Claudia Uceda, "Exclusive: Trump Vineyard Also Hired Undocumented Workers," *Univision News,* May 2, 2019.

32 **Trump had moved swiftly to demolish:** *Diduck v. Kaszycki & Sons Contractors,* No. 83-cv-6346, U.S. District Court, Southern District of New York.

32 **illegal labor practices had ended up in court:** Massimo Calabresi, "What Donald Trump Knew About Undocumented Workers at His Signature Tower," *Time,* August 25, 2015.

32 **"working off the books":** Testimony of Donald J. Trump, *Diduck v. Kaszycki & Sons.*

33 **Danny Sullivan, a mob-linked labor consultant, testified:** Dean Baquet, "Trump Says He Didn't Know He Employed Illegal Aliens," *New York Times,* July 13, 1990. Sullivan's own tangled history with the Mafia, the FBI, and Trump is chronicled in a 1981 FBI 302 report posted on the Smoking Gun on May 19, 1997, "Donald Trump: Worried About OC in AC." See also Robert O'Harrow Jr., "Trump's Ties to an Informant and FBI Agent Reveal His Mode of Operation," *Washington Post,* September 17, 2016.

33 **The court ultimately endorsed:** *Diduck v. Kaszycki & Sons.*

33 **illegal immigrants were among the construction workers:** Antonio Olivo, "At Trump Hotel Site, Immigrant Workers Wary," *Washington Post,* July 6, 2015.

33 **the Trump Organization placed the onus:** Ibid.

33 **Bovis and the Trump Organization had a long-standing business relationship:** Kerry Burke, Mike Jaccarino, and Tina Moore, "Worker Killed at Trump Construction Site," New York *Daily News,* January 15, 2008.

33 **Trump, of course, wasn't the only real estate developer in his immediate family:** Gabriel Sherman, "The Legacy," *New York,* July 10, 2009.

33 **The two men planned to finance:** Jesse Drucker, "Trump Tower Funded by Rich Chinese Who Invest Cash for Visas," *Bloomberg,* March 6, 2016.

34 **Kushner had partnered with a company based in Shanghai:** "The Story Behind the Hot Sale of the US Immigration Trump Tower II Project," China Business Press Release Newswire, December 4, 2013.

34 **His sister was actively marketing the scheme:** Emily Rauhala and William Wan, "In a Beijing Ballroom, Kushner Family Pushes $500,000 'Investor Visa' to Wealthy Chinese," *Washington Post,* May 6, 2017.

34 **"has called for a revamping"**: Drucker, "Trump Tower Funded by Rich Chinese."

34 **"People that have come into our country illegally"**: Donald Trump, "Republican Presidential Debate," *CNN Live*, CNN, December 15, 2015.

34 **The glaring contradiction**: Charles V. Bagli and Megan Twohey, "Donald Trump to Foreign Workers for Florida Club: You're Hired," *New York Times*, February 25, 2016.

35 **The confidential thirty-six-page report**: "Supplemental Report on the Qualifications of Donald J. Trump," *Report of the Division of Gaming Enforcement to the Casino Control Commission* (Trenton, N.J.: State of New Jersey Division of Gaming Enforcement, December 1, 1992).

35 **One section of the report was devoted to Trump's relationship to convicted narcotics trafficker Joseph Weichselbaum**: Ibid., 3.

35 **Trump had personally leased one of his own apartments to him**: Ibid.

35 **Another disturbing section**: Ibid., 6.

36 **"behind-the-scenes"**: Wayne Barrett, *Trump: The Deals and the Downfall* (New York: HarperCollins, 1992), 236.

36 **Trump instructed McGahn to broker**: *Report of the Division of Gaming Enforcement*, 6.

36 **McGahn reportedly had a paralegal from his firm purchase the plot from Philly gangster Salvatore Testa**: Sal Testa is the son of mob boss Phil "the Chicken Man" Testa, a Scarfo family associate. McGahn's nephew Donald F. McGahn II later became the Trump campaign's lawyer and President Trump's first White House counsel. See Ben Terris, "Trump's Own Beltway Establishment Guy: The Curious Journey of Don McGahn," *Washington Post*, April 11, 2016.

36 **McGahn was already a mover and shaker**: Wayne King, "A City with a Big Stake in Trump, the Debtor," *New York Times*, June 22, 1990.

36 **was once the subject of a state investigation**: Iver Peterson, "Patrick T. McGahn Jr., 72, Lawyer for Casinos," *New York Times*, August 3, 2000.

36 **In 1991, Trump was fined**: *State of New Jersey Division of Gaming Enforcement v. Trump Plaza Associates*, Opinion Docket No. 90-343, New Jersey Casino Control Commission, November 20, 1991.

36 **The Trump-LiButti relationship would be chronicled**: Michael Isikoff, "Video Shows Trump with Mob Figure He Denied Knowing," *Yahoo News*, November 2, 2016.

37 **Trump had been beset by allegations**: Robert O'Harrow Jr., "Trump Swam in Mob-Infested Waters in Early Years as an NYC Developer," *Washington Post*, October 16, 2015.

37 **The firm's principals included Sater, who claimed to have co-founded Bayrock**: Felix Sater's LinkedIn profile, accessed November 9, 2015.

37 **described as the company's majority owner**: Verified Complaint, *Kriss v. Bayrock Group*, No. 10-cv-03959, U.S. District Court, Southern District of New York, May 10, 2010, 7.

37 **it was a criminal enterprise used for money laundering and tax evasion**: Ibid.

37   **While Trump was trying to distance himself:** Greg B. Smith, "Trump's Inn Trouble, SoHo Hotel Firm Cited in Worker Deaths, the Donald Denies Ties to Concrete Catastrophes," New York *Daily News,* July 16, 2015; "Donald Trump May Have Reviewed Construction Contracts for Trump SoHo—Where Worker Fell to His Death," New York *Daily News,* July 26, 2015.

37   **New York's so-called Martin Act:** The Martin Act, passed in 1921, is a law specific to New York State. It has been used to prosecute false statements by members of the financial industry. The law very simply can apply to "all deceitful practices contrary to the plain rules of common honesty," making it one of the most stringent fraud laws in the country.

    For more information on the Martin Act, see District Attorneys Association of New York, "New York State White Collar Crime Task Force Issues Sweeping Recommendations for Modernizing Antiquated Fraud and Corruption Laws," press release, September 24, 2013; Nicholas Thompson, "The Sword of Spitzer," *Legal Affairs,* May/June 2004; and David Voreacos, "The Martin Act," *Bloomberg,* November 10, 2015.

37   **His father was a convicted extortionist:** Petition for Writ of Certiorari, *Palmer v. Doe,* No. 14-676, U.S. Supreme Court, January 12, 2015.

37   **In 1991, Felix got into a bar fight:** He was convicted in 1993 and served a year in prison. Charles V. Bagli, "Real Estate Executive with Hand in Trump Projects Rose from Tangled Past," *New York Times,* December 17, 2007.

38   **In 1998, he was charged:** Information Sheet, *United States v. Sater,* No. 98 CR 1101, U.S. District Court, Eastern District of New York.

38   **He had faced up to twenty years' imprisonment:** Cooperation Agreement, *United States v. Sater,* No. 98 CR 1101, U.S. District Court, Eastern District of New York.

38   **included attempting to buy missiles:** See Bagli, "Real Estate Executive," and Petition for Writ of Certiorari, *Palmer v. Doe,* No. 14-676, U.S. Supreme Court.

38   **had an intimate role in the Trump organization:** Felix Sater's profile on LinkedIn and his website, http://felixsaterweb.com, which can be viewed via http://www.web.archive.org.

38   **a December 2007 *New York Times* article:** Bagli, "Real Estate Executive."

38   **Trump took his name off the project:** Ryan Yousefi, "Failed Fort Lauderdale Beach Trump Project Will Finally Open as Conrad Hotel," *New Times Broward Palm Beach,* October 3, 2014.

39   **Arif was arrested in Turkey:** Rich Schapiro, "Donald Trump Associate Tevfik Arif Prostitution Ring Bust: Cops Caught Businessmen in Act—Report," New York *Daily News,* October 1, 2010.

39   **Among the others arrested:** Benjamin Harvey, "Bayrock's Arif Detained in Turkish Vice Raid on Yacht," *Bloomberg,* October 1, 2010.

39   **she had traveled to Kazakhstan:** Ivanka Trump, *The Trump Card: Playing to Win in Work and Life* (New York: Simon & Schuster, 2010).

39   **"who had access to cash accounts":** Verified complaint, *Kriss v. Bayrock Group.*

39 Trump praised Arif's "international connections": Deposition of Donald J. Trump, *Trump v. O'Brien,* Superior Court of New Jersey, December 19, 2007.

39 "Tevfik is my friend!": Bozena Rynska, "Counted Stars," *Izvestia,* June 20, 2005.

40 The suits were brought by condominium purchasers: Plaintiff's Motion for Leave to Amend, *Taglieri v. SB Hotel Associates,* 17th Judicial Circuit Court, Broward County, Florida, December 20, 2013.

40 "We never knew that": Bagli, "Real Estate Executive."

40 Trump had been deposed: Deposition of Donald J. Trump, *Abercrombie v. SB Hotel Associates,* Nos. 08-060702 and 09-01853, 17th Judicial Circuit Court, Broward County, Florida, November 5, 2013.

40 a story on Trump's dubious denials ran on *Good Morning America*: Matthew Mosk and Brian Ross, "Memory Lapse? Trump Seeks Distance from 'Advisor' with Past Ties to Mafia," ABC News, December 10, 2015.

41 "I will get along—I think—with Putin": Donald Trump, "Republican Presidential Debate," *CNN Live,* CNN, September 16, 2015.

41 "I think I would get along very well with him": Donald Trump, interview by Erin Burnett, *Erin Burnett OutFront,* CNN, September 28, 2015.

41 in a November 10 debate: Donald Trump, "Republican Presidential Debate," Fox Business Network, November 10, 2015.

41 Trump and Putin were never on *60 Minutes* together: Donald Trump and Vladimir Putin, *60 Minutes,* CBS, September 27, 2015.

41 he had donated $5,000 to RT: Ohr brought the articles to Fusion's attention. The articles had proliferated on various Russian-language websites, but Fusion was never able to verify the origin of the articles.

42 Trump said that Russians were his favorite customers: Alexander Sirotin, "Breakfast at Trump," *Chayka (Seagull)* magazine, September 1, 2008.

42 "I have a very good business relationship": Ibid.

42 The Russian buyer in Florida: Alexei Barrionuevo, "Divorce, Oligarch Style," *New York Times,* April 5, 2012.

42 Rybolovlev eventually emigrated to Monaco: Andrew E. Kramer, "A Russian City Always on the Watch Against Being Sucked into the Earth," *New York Times,* April 10, 2012.

42 he purchased a Palm Beach mansion: David Rogers, "Trump Mansion Closes for $95 Million to Russian Tycoon," Palm Beach *Daily News,* July 17, 2008.

43 "Before he was a presidential candidate": Josh Rogin, "Trump's Long Romance with Russia," *Bloomberg Opinion,* March 15, 2016. Rogin is now a columnist for *The Washington Post.*

CHAPTER FOUR: THE FIXER

44 "Hillary would beat him from jail": Glenn Thrush, interview with Tim Miller, Off Message podcast, *Politico,* April 11, 2016.

45   Deripaska, a Russian billionaire long banned from entering the United States: Deripaska and his companies were sanctioned by the U.S. Department of the Treasury in April 2018, pursuant to Executive Orders 13661 and 13662, in retaliation to Russia's hostile actions around the globe. See the press release and documents at treasury.gov. Part of the government's justification included that "Deripaska has said that he does not separate himself from the Russian state. He has also acknowledged possessing a Russian diplomatic passport, and claims to have represented the Russian government in other countries."

The sanctions announcement went on to say that he had been investigated for money laundering and had been accused of threatening the lives of business rivals, having links to a Russian organized crime group, and taking part in extortion, bribery, and racketeering.

Deripaska was banned from entering the United States in 2008 over ties to organized crime. See Misha Glenny, Robert Booth, and Tom Parfitt, "US Refused Oligarch Visa Over Alleged Criminal Associations," *Guardian*, October 30, 2008.

45   What soon became Washington's most mercenary lobbying firm: Thomas B. Edsall, "Partners in Political PR Firm Typify Republican New Breed," *Washington Post*, April 7, 1985.

45   "exuded the decadent spirit of the 1980s": Franklin Foer, "Paul Manafort, American Hustler," *Atlantic*, March 2018.

45   burnishing the reputations: Tom McCarthy, "Paul Manafort: How Decades of Serving Dictators Led to Role as Trump's Go-to Guy," *Guardian*, October 30, 2017.

45   For the past decade: Simon Shuster, "How Paul Manafort Helped Elect Russia's Man in Ukraine," *Time*, October 31, 2017.

46   "among the few political hands": Alexander Burns and Maggie Haberman, "Donald Trump Hires Paul Manafort to Lead Delegate Effort," *New York Times*, March 28, 2016.

46   For much of the 2000s, Putin's efforts to dominate Ukraine politically: This would include Dmitry Firtash and similar Ukrainian oligarchs. See Stephen Grey, Tom Bergin, Sevgil Musaieva, and Roman Anin, "Putin's Allies Channeled Billions to Ukraine Oligarch," Reuters, November 26, 2014.

47   Foreign Agents Registration Act: To read more about the history of FARA, visit the U.S. Department of Justice website, https://justice.gov/nsd-fara.

47   "nothing more nor less than a propaganda arm": House Special Committee on Un-American Activities, *Report on the Axis Front Movement in the United States: Nazi Activities*, 78th Cong. (1944).

47   His apparent failure to register: Glenn R. Simpson and Mary Jacoby, "How Lobbyists Help Ex-Soviets Woo Washington," *Wall Street Journal*, April 17, 2007.

48   Deripaska emerged from those fights with a fortune: Andrew E. Kramer,

"Out of Siberia, a Russian Way to Wealth," *New York Times,* August 20, 2006.

48 **"US Department of State visa policies":** Jim Wolf, "U.S. Revoked Deripaska Visa—State Dep't Official," Reuters, May 11, 2007.

49 **Manafort and his longtime consulting partner:** Jeffrey H. Birnbaum and John Solomon, "Aide Helped Controversial Russian Meet McCain," *Washington Post,* January 25, 2008.

49 **Manafort had secretly been hired:** Jeff Horwitz and Chad Day, "AP Exclusive: Before Trump Job, Manafort Worked to Aid Putin," Associated Press, March 22, 2017.

49 **Simpson and Jacoby broke the story:** Mary Jacoby and Glenn R. Simpson, "McCain Consultant Is Tied to Work for Ukraine Party," *Wall Street Journal,* May 14, 2008.

50 **Court records later showed:** *Surf Horizon v. Manafort,* No. 650130/2018, New York County Supreme Court, January 10, 2018.

50 **This was one of the places:** See: Derek Robertson, "Manafort's Clothing Tab: $1.3 Million," *Politico,* October 30, 2017, and Farnoush Amiri, "Paul Manafort's Lavish Suits and Jackets Are 'Ludicrous' and 'Excess,' Menswear Experts Say," NBC News, August 2, 2018.

51 **One Cayman Island filing:** Winding Up Petition, *Pericles Emerging Market Partners, LP,* Financial Services Division, No. 0131, Grand Court of the Cayman Islands, December 4, 2014.

51 *Politico* **ran a long piece:** Alexander Burns and Maggie Haberman, "Mystery Man: Ukraine's U.S. Fixer," *Politico,* March 5, 2014.

52 **It then offered a jokey multiple choice:** Ibid.

52 **blandly captioned filing:** Michael Isikoff, "Trump's Campaign Chief Is Questioned About Ties to Russian Billionaire," *Yahoo News,* April 26, 2016.

52 **it alleged in scorching detail:** Ibid.

53 **One document seemed to show that:** Winding Up Petition, *Pericles Emerging Market Partners.*

53 **A records search turned up:** Shareholder Disclosure Form, United Company Rusal, Hong Kong Stock Exchange, accessed online.

CHAPTER FIVE: NEW CLIENT

55 **Trump romped on Super Tuesday:** Shane Goldmacher, "Trump Takes 7 Super Tuesday States, Cruz Takes 3," *Politico,* March 1, 2016.

55 **On March 15:** Patricia Mazzei, Amy Sherman, and Lesley Clark, "Trump, Clinton Sweep Florida in Primary Rout; Rubio Drops Out," *Miami Herald,* March 15, 2016.

55 **The state's governor, Rick Scott, endorsed Trump:** Rick Scott, Facebook, March 16, 2016.

55 **"I think you'd have riots":** Donald Trump and Chris Cuomo, *New Day,* CNN, March 16, 2016.

56 **the *Beacon* posted a story:** Lachlan Markay, "Lawsuit: Trump Aide Fun-

neled Mob-Linked Ukrainian Oligarch's Fortune into U.S. Real Estate," *Washington Free Beacon*, March 31, 2016.

56 **Trump took the New York primary:** 2016 New York Presidential Primaries Poll, RealClearPolitics.

57 **Clinton, the Democratic Party, and related PACs would go on to raise over $1.2 billion:** "How Much Money Is Behind Each Candidate," *Washington Post*, accessed September 1, 2019, https://www.washingtonpost .com/graphics/politics/2016-election/campaign-finance/.

58 **Trump's affiliations with Russians:** Mark A. Uhlig, "Brooklyn Fuel Distributor Pleads Guilty in Tax Plot," *New York Times*, March 12, 1987.

58 **he took an all-expenses-paid trip:** Michael Oreskes, "Trump Gives a Vague Hint of Candidacy," *New York Times*, September 2, 1987.

58 **Trump tried again in 1996 to cook up a big Moscow project:** Jeff Grocott, "Trump Lays Bet on New Moscow Skyline," *Moscow Times*, November 12, 1996. He was brought to Moscow by close friend Howard Lorber, now a major patron of his candidacy. Lorber actually developed the property without the Trump name.

59 **Donald Trump Jr. was boasting:** Linda Hohnholz, "Executive Talk: Donald Trump Jr. Bullish on Russia and Few Emerging Markets," *eTurboNews*, September 15, 2008.

59 **Five years later, in Moscow:** Donald J. Trump (@realDonaldTrump), "@AgalarovAras I had a great weekend with you and your family," Twitter, November 11, 2013, 8:39 A.M.

59 **investigators uncover that his own representatives were trying to cook up a Trump project in Moscow even as he campaigned to be president:** Carol D. Leonnig, Tom Hamburger, and Rosalind S. Helderman, "Trump's Business Sought Deal on a Trump Tower in Moscow While He Ran for President," *Washington Post*, August 27, 2017.

59 **Fusion had been drawn into a defamation lawsuit:** Order Granting the Defendants' Motion for Summary Judgement, *VanderSloot v. Foundation for National Progress*, No. CV-2013-532, Idaho Seventh Judicial District Court, October 6, 2013.

CHAPTER SIX: CALLING AGENT STEELE

64 **Steele was born in Yemen:** Information gleaned from conversations with the source. For additional background information on Christopher Steele, see Jane Mayer, "Christopher Steele, the Man Behind the Trump Dossier," *New Yorker*, March 5, 2018.

67 **one of the Obama administration's most successful organized crime prosecutions:** See Ken Bensinger, *Red Card: How the U.S. Blew the Whistle on the World's Biggest Sports Scandal* (New York: Simon & Schuster, 2018), and Des Bieler, "The British Spy Behind the Trump Dossier Helped the FBI Bust FIFA," *Washington Post*, January 13, 2017.

68 **a disgruntled former MI6 colleague:** Warren Hoge, "Britain Closes Web Site with Spies' Names," *New York Times*, May 14, 1999.

71   **research for a team of American lawyers:** *United States v. Prevezon Hold-ings,* No. 13-cv-6326, U.S. District Court, Southern District of New York, 2013. The U.S. government opened the case in 2013 and eventually set-tled with defendants in May 2017.

71   **A prestigious firm with deep Republican ties:** Alexander Burns, "GOP Group Snared in Money Scheme," *Politico,* August 4, 2014; "Mark Braden Named 2014 Republican Lawyer of the Year," "News," BakerHostetler, July 1, 2014; Martin Well, "William Schweitzer, Law Firm Partner and Lobbyist for Baseball, Dies at 70," *New York Times,* March 4, 2015.

71   **On June 9:** Jo Becker, Matt Apuzzo, and Adam Goldman, "Trump Team Met with Lawyer Linked to Kremlin During Campaign," *New York Times,* July 8, 2017.

71   **This session between the Russian lawyer and the top brass of the Trump campaign would remain unknown:** Ibid.

72   **accompanied Veselnitskaya to the Trump Tower meeting:** Desmond Butler and Chad Day, "Russian-American Lobbyist Joined Trump's Son's Meeting, Too," Associated Press, July 15, 2017. This episode was con-firmed and then recounted by the special counsel's office in the Mueller report.

72   **a legendary former prosecutor:** Robin Finn, "No. 2 Prosecutor Heads for Private Practice," *New York Times,* January 18, 2005. For more details on the Bank of Credit and Commerce International fraud case, see Stephen Labaton, "Six B.C.C.I. Officials Are Indicted," *New York Times,* Septem-ber 6, 1991.

      Other cases he worked on include the $600 million Tyco racketeering case (see Andrew Ross Sorkin, "2 Top Tyco Executives Charged with $600 Million Fraud Scheme," *New York Times,* September 13, 2002) and the widely reported Bank of New York Mellon scandal involving Russian money laundering. For case highlights, see Timothy L. O'Brien and Ray-mond Bonner, "3 Face Indictments in Federal Inquiry into Russian Case," *New York Times,* October 6, 1999; O'Brien and Bonner, "Banker and Hus-band Tell of Role in Laundering Case," February 17, 2000; and Paul Beck-ett, Ann Davis, and Andrew Higgins, "Two Russian Bankers Seen as Key in Bank of New York Investigation," *Wall Street Journal,* February 18, 2000.

72   **He revealed that much of his information on Prevezon came from doc-uments supplied by William Browder:** Deposition of Todd S. Hyman, *United States v. Prevezon Holdings,* No. 1:13-cv-06326, U.S. District Court, Southern District of New York, March 3, 2014. Hyman was a spe-cial agent for the U.S. Department of Homeland Security, assigned to the Prevezon case.

72   **After working as an investment banker, Browder had moved to Russia in the 1990s:** Paul Crowney, "Seeing Red," *Institutional Investor,* Septem-ber 1, 2002.

73   **Along the way, he gave up his U.S. citizenship:** Joshua Yaffa, "How Bill

Browder Became Russia's Most Wanted Man," *New Yorker*, August 13, 2018.

73 **Long an outspoken Putin fan:** "An Enemy of the People," *Economist*, March 23, 2006.

73 **Browder eventually fell out with the Kremlin in a dispute over unpaid taxes:** Deposition of William F. Browder, *United States v. Prevezon Holdings*, No. 1:13-cv-06326, U.S. District Court, Southern District of New York, April 15, 2015.

73 **Russian authorities had accused Hermitage of tax fraud:** Ibid.

73 **At Browder's urging, Congress passed a law in 2012:** Julia Ioffe, "His Russian Lawyer Dead, a Former American Turns to Congress for Revenge," *New Republic*, November 16, 2012.

73 **Browder was always eager to testify:** Browder routinely avoided any deposition about his role in the Prevezon case by dodging lawful subpoenas. For an overview, see Letter from Prevezon Attorney to Judge Thomas Griesa re: Browder's Failure to Produce Responsive Documents, *United States v. Prevezon Holdings*, No. 1:13-cv-06326, U.S. District Court, Southern District of New York, May 13, 2015; "Signed Declaration of Craig Janis," *United States v. Prevezon Holdings*, No. 1:13-cv-06326, U.S. District Court, Southern District of New York, December 10, 2014, which claims, "After being presented with the subpoena, Mr. Browder—after initially reaching out to accept the documents—then turned to run away"; and "Bill Browder Served with Subpoena in New York," YouTube video, 1:22, posted by "Casale Associates," February 5, 2015.

74 **the expanded Magnitsky Act:** Global Magnitsky Human Rights Accountability Act, S. 284, 114th Cong. (2015).

74 **Veselnitskaya worked with BakerHostetler and Akhmetshin:** Michael Weiss, "Putin's Dirty Game in the U.S. Congress," *Daily Beast*, May 18, 2016.

74 **Akhmetshin eventually testified:** Testimony of Rinat Akhmetshin, Senate Judiciary Committee, November 14, 2017.

75 **the Democratic National Committee's computer systems:** Ellen Nakashima, "Russian Government Hackers Penetrated DNC, Stole Opposition Research on Trump," *Washington Post*, June 14, 2016.

75 **advocates for remaining in the EU:** Nico Hines, "Why Putin Is Meddling in Britain's Brexit Vote," *Daily Beast*, June 8, 2016.

77 **"We threw a line in the water":** Testimony of Glenn Simpson, House Intelligence Committee, November 14, 2017.

CHAPTER SEVEN: SAY SOMETHING

81 **Once confirmed as the nominee, Trump would become eligible to receive a national security briefing from the Intelligence Community:** For a good overview of the practice, see Michael J. Morell, "Intelligence Briefings for the Presidential Nominees," *Cipher Brief*, June 1, 2016.

81 **Putin told the St. Petersburg International Economic Forum:** Henry

Meyer, "Putin Sticks to Praise for Trump's Pledge to Mend Russia Ties," *Bloomberg*, July 17, 2016.

81 **Trump fired campaign manager Corey Lewandowski:** John Santucci, "Trump Campaign Announces Expanded Role for Paul Manafort," ABC News, May 19, 2016; Maggie Haberman, Alexander Burns, and Ashley Parker, "Donald Trump Fires Corey Lewandowski, His Campaign Manager," *New York Times*, June 20, 2016.

81 **On June 25, a hacker named Guccifer 2.0:** Raphael Satter, "Inside Story: How Russians Hacked the Democrats' Emails," Associated Press, November 4, 2017; subsequently confirmed by the 2019 Mueller report.

82 **He had changed his name at some point in the 2000s from Siarhei Kukuts:** Brian Ross and Matthew Mosk, "US-Russian Businessman Said to Be Source of Key Trump Dossier Claims," ABC News, January 30, 2017.

82 **The article carried a photo:** Putin converted RIA into a state-run propaganda paper in 2013; see Timothy Heritage, "Putin Dissolves State News Agency, Tightens Grip on Russia Media," Reuters, December 9, 2013.

83 **"keeping Moscow in his sights":** "Sergei Millian," RIA Novosti.

83 **As Simpson would tell Senate:** Testimony of Glenn Simpson, Senate Judiciary Committee, August 22, 2017.

84 **Gaeta's pursuit of Taiwanchik:** Ken Bensinger, *Red Card: How the U.S. Blew the Whistle on the World's Biggest Sports Scandal* (New York: Simon & Schuster, 2018).

84 **James Comey later revealed:** Public Testimony of James Comey, House Intelligence Committee, March 20, 2017. Transcript at "Full Transcript: FBI Director James Comey Testifies on Russian Interference in 2016 Election," *Washington Post*, March 20, 2017.

84 **her conduct had been "extremely careless":** FBI National Press Office, "Statement by FBI Director James B. Comey on the Investigation of Secretary Hillary Clinton's Use of a Personal E-Mail System," press release, July 5, 2016.

85 **Carter Page delivered an address:** "Carter Page at the New Economic School in Moscow," YouTube video of Page speech given July 7, 2016, posted by "Katehon Think Tank," November 4, 2017.

85 **It was a shock when Trump revealed:** Trump first revealed his small list of foreign policy advisers on March 21, 2016, during an interview with the *Washington Post* editorial staff. Post Opinions Staff, "A Transcript of Donald Trump's Meeting with the Washington Post Editorial Board," *Washington Post*, March 21, 2016.

85 **His only previous stint in politics had been a minor role with McCain's failed presidential bid in 2008:** Testimony of Carter Page, House Intelligence Committee, November 2, 2017.

85 **"Washington and other Western capitals":** Carter Page, "Carter Page at the New Economic School." In fact, according to the Mueller report, Page made two speeches at the school on back-to-back days (July 7 and 8, 2016).

85 **"has close ties to Gazprom":** Steven Mufson and Tom Hamburger, "Trump Adviser's Public Comments, Ties to Moscow Stir Unease in Both Parties," *Washington Post,* August 5, 2016.

85 **A subsequent Steele memo:** Orbis, Company Intelligence Report 2016/94, July 19, 2016.

86 **the Trump campaign had quietly intervened:** Josh Rogin, "Trump Campaign Guts GOP's Anti-Russia Stance on Ukraine," *Washington Post,* July 18, 2016.

86 **That same day, *Yahoo News* reporter Michael Isikoff:** Lt. Gen. Michael Flynn, interview by Michael Isikoff, *Yahoo News,* July 18, 2016; Alex Moe, Courtney Kube, Ken Dilanian, and Kasie Hunt, "Flynn 'Lied to Investigators' About Russia Trip, Says Top House Dem," NBC News, May 22, 2017.

86 **WikiLeaks released thousands of DNC emails:** Ellen Nakashima and Shane Harris, "How the Russians Hacked the DNC and Passed Its Emails to WikiLeaks," *Washington Post,* July 13, 2018; subsequently verified by the 2019 Mueller report.

87 **forced the resignation:** Jonathan Martin and Alan Rappeport, "Debbie Wasserman Schultz to Resign D.N.C. Post," *New York Times,* June 24, 2016.

87 **"Experts are telling us that":** "Full Interview: Clinton Campaign Manager Robby Mook," YouTube video of interview with Jake Tapper on CNN's *State of the Union,* 8:56, posted by "CNN," July 24, 2016.

87 **"The new joke in town is":** Donald J. Trump (@realDonaldTrump), Twitter, July 25, 2016, 4:31 A.M.

88 **middle of a Russian active measures campaign:** "Active measures" describes any clandestine measures taken by the Russian government's security services in order to influence political outcomes abroad, usually against a foreign policy adversary, such as the United States.

89 **The *Times* published its first big story:** Steven Lee Myers and Andrew E. Kramer, "How Paul Manafort Wielded Power in Ukraine Before Advising Donald Trump," *New York Times,* July 31, 2016.

90 **Hamburger was eager to learn:** Tom Hamburger and Ellen Nakashima, "Clinton Campaign—and Some Cyber Experts—Say Russia Is Behind Email Release," *Washington Post,* June 24, 2016.

90 **"I will tell you this: Russia, if you're listening":** "Trump Hopes Russia Finds Clinton's Deleted Emails," YouTube video, 3:02, posted by "ABC News," July 27, 2016.

91 **Five hours later:** *United States v. Netyksho,* No. 1:18-cr-00215-ABJ, U.S. District Court, District of Columbia, July 13, 2018.

CHAPTER EIGHT: BREAKFAST AT THE MAYFLOWER

92 **The executive summary on Steele's newest memo said it all:** Orbis, Company Intelligence Report 2016/97, July 30, 2016.

93 **Steele and Ohr had recently worked together:** Kenneth P. Vogel and

Matthew Rosenberg, "Agents Tried to Flip Russian Oligarchs. The Fallout Spread to Trump," *New York Times,* September 1, 2018.

93 **His father worked as a scientist:** Brittany Crocker, "Trump Target Bruce Ohr Remembered in Oak Ridge as Part of Special Family," *Knoxville News Sentinel,* September 18, 2018.

93 **Nellie was a specialist in the rural history of Stalinism:** Nellie Ohr's 1990 PhD thesis, "Collective Farms and the Russian Peasant Society, 1933–1937: The Stabilization of the Kolkhoz Order," is available at the Stanford University library and online through academic subscription services.

94 **"I view myself as part of a community":** Testimony of Nellie Ohr, House Judiciary Committee and House Committee on Oversight and Reform, October 19, 2018.

94 **"had Donald Trump over a barrel":** Testimony of Bruce Ohr, House Committee on Oversight and Reform, August 28, 2018.

94 **"aha moment":** Testimony of Nellie Ohr, October 19, 2018.

94 **Nine months earlier:** Richard Reeve and Stephen Tschida, "Former Putin Aide, Founder of Russia Today, Found Dead at Dupont Circle Hotel," WJLA ABC7 News, November 6, 2015.

95 **The coroner said it was a drunken accident:** Michal Kranz, "'Everyone Thinks He Was Whacked': New Evidence Has Emerged That a Russian Media Mogul Was Beaten to Death by Hired Thugs in Washington," *Business Insider,* March 27, 2018.

95 **Lesin's hotel bill was being covered:** Ashraf Khalil, "Ruling Revives Questions About D.C. Death of Ex–Putin Aide," Associated Press, March 12, 2019.

96 **"Hey if you discussed new case":** Peter Strzok texts, released by Senate Homeland Security and Governmental Affairs Committee, February 7, 2018.

96 **Lisa Page later said that the agents working:** Philip Bump, "What We Know About the Genesis of the Russia Investigation," *Washington Post,* April 1, 2019.

96 **"Crossfire Hurricane":** Greg Miller, *The Apprentice: Trump, Russia, and the Subversion of American Democracy* (New York: Custom House, 2018), 147.

96 **Bruce Ohr reported his conversation with Steele to McCabe:** Testimony of Bruce Ohr, House Committee on Oversight and Reform, August 28, 2018.

97 **Address records linked him to a Soviet émigré in Florida:** Rosalind S. Helderman and Tom Hamburger, "Sergei Millian, Identified as an Unwitting Source for the Steele Dossier, Sought Proximity to Trump's World in 2016," *Washington Post,* February 7, 2019.

97 **Like Brighton Beach in Brooklyn:** Sunny Isles Beach, Florida, is commonly referred to as "Little Moscow" due to the large influx of Russian immigrants. Trump has several branded properties along the beach in

this section of Miami. See Tom Hamburger, Rosalind S. Helderman, and Dana Priest, "In 'Little Moscow,' Russians Helped Donald Trump's Brand Survive the Recession," *Washington Post,* November 4, 2016.

97 **One Sunny Isles investor:** Popovyan owned Trump Casa 1102 LLC before transferring it to someone who appears to be his daughter. His ownership was first reported by Ilya Shumanov, " 'Our Miami': Why Russian Businessmen and Bandits Settle in Trump Towers," *Forbes* (Russian edition), November 7, 2016.

97 **Roman Sinyavsky, a realtor:** According to his own Miami FIP Properties website, https://famvp.com, accessed September 1, 2019.

97 **On July 29, Millian sat down:** Sergei Millian, interview, ABC News, July 2016. Transcript available on scribd.com, uploaded by Pete Madden, investigative reporter for ABC News.

97 **The "Trump team":** Ibid.

98 **he followed up with a Facebook message:** Robert S. Mueller III, *Report on the Investigation into Russian Interference in the 2016 Presidential Election,* March 2019, vol. I, 103. Hereafter, "Mueller report."

98 **"despite our repeated efforts":** Mueller report, vol. I, 102.

100 **CIA Director John Brennan emerged:** Miller, *The Apprentice,* 149.

100 **he testified later to Congress:** John Brennan, "Russia and the 2016 Elections," C-SPAN, user-created video, 2:11:15, uploaded May 23, 2017.

100 **Brennan held a call with Alexander Bortnikov:** John. O. Brennan, "John Brennan: President Trump's Claims of No Collusion Are Hogwash," *New York Times,* August 16, 2018.

100 **With President Obama's approval:** John Brennan, "Brennan Gang of Eight," C-SPAN, user-created video, 1:09, posted May 23, 2017.

100 **On June 15, the day that Guccifer 2.0 leaked internal DNC research on Trump:** "DNC Hacker Releases Trump Oppo Report," *Smoking Gun,* June 15, 2016.

100 **Republican House leaders gathered privately:** Adam Entous, "House Majority Leader to Colleagues in 2016: 'I Think Putin Pays' Trump," *Washington Post,* May 17, 2017.

101 **"There's two people, I think, Putin pays: Rohrabacher and Trump":** Ibid.

102 **"actually communicated with [WikiLeaks]":** Roger Stone, speech to the Southwest Broward Republican Organization, Pembroke Pines, Florida, August 8, 2016. The media watchdog Media Matters (https://media matters.org) posted an online clip of the video on August 9, 2016. Stone Cold Truth, Stone's media brand, uploaded the whole speech to YouTube on August 11, 2016.

102 *Bloomberg* **filed a story from Spain:** Esteban Duarte, Henry Meyer, and Evgenia Pismennaya, "Mobster or Central Banker? Spanish Cops Allege This Russian Is Both," *Bloomberg,* August 8, 2016.

102 **Halfway through the story:** Ibid.

103 **gun ownership is tightly regulated there, far more than in the United**

States: See Matthew Bodner, "Russians, Their Guns and the State," *Moscow Times,* April 27, 2016.

103 **Operación Dirieba:** A sweeping investigation into organized crime by the Guardia Civil prosecutor José Grinda Gonzalez, among others in Spain. The Spanish government collected wiretaps that implicated Torshin in the Taganskaya organized crime family's operations there. See José María Irujo, "Las pruebas que implican al aliado ruso de Trump con el crimen organizado," *El Pais* (Madrid), April 3, 2016.

103 **"democratic principles and election legislation":** "Senator Torshin Says Elections in Ukraine Are Held in Line with Democratic Principles," RIA Novosti, November 22, 2004, accessed via https://factiva.com.

103 **It would be a perfect cover:** Amber Phillips, "The NRA-ification of the Republican Party," *Washington Post,* August 14, 2015.

103 **The NRA had publicly opposed:** "Obama Administration Bans Import of Popular Russian Firearms," NRA Institute for Legal Action, July 17, 2014.

103 **promoted the brand in the United States:** Alexandr Torshin, "Torshin: Kalashnikov, the Man and the Weapon," op-ed, *Washington Times,* January 2, 2014.

103 **the *Times* produced the results:** Andrew E. Kramer, Mike McIntire, and Barry Meier, "Secret Ledger in Ukraine Lists Cash for Donald Trump's Campaign Chief," *New York Times,* August 14, 2016.

104 **muckraking former journalist in the Ukrainian parliament:** Elias Groll, interview with Serhiy Leshchenko, "The Ukrainian Who Sunk Paul Manafort," *Foreign Policy,* August 27, 2018.

104 **Manafort resigned as Trump's campaign chairman:** Nolan D. McCaskill, Alex Isenstadt, and Shane Goldmacher, "Paul Manafort Resigns from Trump Campaign," *Politico,* August 19, 2016.

104 **Stone started messaging with Guccifer 2.0:** Andrew Blake, "Roger Stone, Trump Confidant, Acknowledges 'Innocuous' Twitter Conversation with DNC Hackers," *Washington Times,* March 10, 2017.

104 **Strzok texted Lisa Page in all caps:** Peter Strzok, texts released by Senate Homeland Security and Governmental Affairs Committee, February 7, 2018, https://www.hsgac.senate.gov/imo/media/doc/Appendix%20C%20-%20Documents.pdf.

105 **He had also learned of Russian efforts to infiltrate the computers of state election systems:** Harry Reid to James Comey, August 27, 2016. Letter described in David E. Sanger, "Harry Reid Cites Evidence of Russian Tampering in U.S. Vote, and Seeks F.B.I. Inquiry," *New York Times,* August 29, 2016.

105 **Reid sent a letter to Comey:** Ibid.

105 **He texted Page a link to the *Times* account:** Peter Strzok, texts released by Senate. The text linked to the article by Sanger, "Harry Reid Cites Evidence."

105 **caused Obama to task Homeland Security:** Jacob Pramuk, "Jeh Johnson:

Cyberattacks 'Are Going to Get Worse Before They Get Better,'" CNBC, June 21, 2017.

105 **the effort broke down along party lines:** Miller, *The Apprentice*, 60.

106 **he would put out his own statement:** Scott Neuman, "Biden: McConnell Refused to Sign Bipartisan Statement on Russian Interference," NPR, January 24, 2018.

CHAPTER NINE: HAIL MARY TIME

107 **"Russians do have further 'kompromat'":** Orbis to Fusion, Company Intelligence Report 2016/111, September 14, 2016.

107 **Russian military intelligence officers:** Mueller report, vol. I, 42.

107 **The next day, the Russians reached out to WikiLeaks:** "On September 15, 2016, @dcleaks wrote to @WikiLeaks" via Twitter; Mueller report, vol. I, 46.

111 **Jane Mayer would later describe her session with Steele:** Jane Mayer, "Christopher Steele, the Man Behind the Trump Dossier," *New Yorker*, March 5, 2018.

111 **Isikoff published a story:** Michael Isikoff, "U.S. Intel Officials Probe Ties Between Trump Adviser and Kremlin," *Yahoo News*, September 23, 2016.

111 **Page told the *Post*:** Josh Rogin, "Trump's Russia Adviser Speaks Out, Calls Accusations 'Complete Garbage,'" *Washington Post*, September 26, 2016.

111 **the Foreign Intelligence Surveillance Court:** Verified Application, Carter W. Page, U.S. Foreign Intelligence Surveillance Court, Washington, D.C., October 2016. Declassified version accessible at nytimes.com.

112 **Russian intelligence had tried to recruit:** Ali Watkins, "A Former Trump Adviser Met with a Russian Spy," *BuzzFeed News*, April 3, 2017.

112 **The FBI had even asked him about his Russian contacts in March 2016:** Natasha Bertrand, "Carter Page Is a Very Unlikely GOP Hero," *Atlantic*, September 19, 2018.

112 **The lawyer and diplomat knew a lot of journalists in:** See Winer biographies/profiles at https://apcoworldwide.com, on LinkedIn, and on the U.S. Department of State archived site, https://2009-2017.state.gov.

112 **he acted as an informal pipeline:** Jonathan M. Winer, "Devin Nunes Is Investigating Me. Here's the Truth," *Washington Post*, February 8, 2018.

112 **in the interest of helping an ally:** Upon his retirement from government in 2016, Winer was given the State Department's highest award for service for, among other things, "extraordinary service to the U.S. government" in helping save the lives of more than three thousand Iranian exiles in Iraq. The Iranians belonged to a cultlike group called the People's Mojahedin, long considered a terrorist organization by both Iran and the United States.

113 **Shearer was, in fact, the author of the document:** Stephanie Kirchgaessner and Nick Hopkins, "Second Trump-Russia Dossier Being Assessed by FBI," *Guardian*, January 30, 2018.

114 **He provided a copy of the memo:** Fusion would also learn that the FBI had offered to bring Steele on for $50,000 to assist with its investigation, money that was never paid. The FBI also failed to reimburse him for his travel to Rome.

115 **"My understanding was that [the FBI] believed Chris at this point":** Testimony of Glenn Simpson, Senate Judiciary Committee, August 22, 2017.

115 **"She's saying Russia, Russia, Russia":** Donald Trump, "First Presidential Debate," NBC News, September 26, 2016.

115 **the Obama administration put out a statement:** Department of Homeland Security Press Office, "Joint Statement from the Department of Homeland Security and Office of the Director of National Intelligence on Election Security," press release, October 7, 2016.

116 **Trump had been caught on an *Access Hollywood* videotape:** Now commonly known as the *Access Hollywood* tape. See David A. Fahrenthold, "Donald Trump Recorded Having Extremely Lewd Conversation About Women in 2005," *Washington Post*, October 7, 2016.

116 **"locker room banter":** Trump Pence Campaign, "Statement from Donald J. Trump," press release, October 7, 2016.

116 **WikiLeaks released the trove of emails:** Amy Chozick, "John Podesta Says Russian Spies Hacked His Emails to Sway Election," *New York Times*, October 11, 2016.

116 **October surprises:** U.S. political term referring to a news story deliberately dropped late in the campaign for maximum effect.

116 **"Our standard is we do not confirm or deny":** "FBI Oversight," video of James Comey testimony. House Committee of Oversight and Reform hearing, 3:58:12, C-SPAN, September 28, 2016.

117 **Comey sent a letter:** James B. Comey to Richard M. Burr et al., October 28, 2016, https://www.nytimes.com/interactive/2016/10/28/us/politics/fbi-letter.html.

117 **"Lock her up, lock her up":** "Donald Trump Campaign Rally in Cedar Rapids, Iowa," video, 28:00, C-SPAN, posted October 28, 2016.

117 **"a surprise or two":** "Giuliani Responds to Reports the FBI Leaked Info to Him," *Kelly File*, Fox News, November 4, 2016.

117 **"explosive information about close ties":** Aaron Blake, "Harry Reid's Incendiary Claim About 'Coordination' Between Donald Trump and Russia," *Washington Post*, October 31, 2016.

118 **Referring to Steele by the acronym CHS:** "Records Between FBI and Christopher Steele," unclassified but redacted, publicly available via Freedom of Information Act, accessed online at http://vault.fbi.gov.

119 **"Was a Trump Server Communicating":** Franklin Foer, "Was a Trump Server Communicating with Russia?" *Slate*, October 31, 2016.

119 **"met on a quarterly basis":** Petr Aven, interview with the special counsel's office on August 2, 2018, as cited in the Mueller report, vol. I, 146.

119   **"Aven said that he took these meetings":** Mueller report, vol. I, 154.

120   **the *Times* posted a story that stomped:** Eric Lichtblau and Steven Lee Myers, "Investigating Donald Trump, F.B.I. Sees No Clear Link to Russia," *New York Times,* October 31, 2016.

120   **"even chased a lead":** Lichtblau and Myers, "Investigating Donald Trump."

120   **Catherine Belton posted a story:** Catherine Belton, "The Shadowy Russian Émigré Touting Trump," *Financial Times,* October 31, 2016.

120   **"Mr. Millian came on to the FBI's radar":** Belton, "The Russian Émigré."

121   **the *Times*'s public editor wrote:** Liz Spayd, "Trump, Russia, and the News Story That Wasn't," *New York Times,* January 20, 2017.

121   **James Baker told congressional investigators:** Testimony of James A. Baker, House Committee on Oversight and Reform, October 3, 2018.

121   **Baquet suspected that Lichtblau:** Maxwell Tani, "In Blunt Book on Media, Jill Abramson Dishes on the *Times,* Reveals Profane Dean Baquet Rant," *Daily Beast,* January 5, 2019.

121   **"Hillary Clinton would probably be president":** Nate Silver, "The Comey Letter Probably Cost Clinton the Election," FiveThirtyEight, May 3, 2017.

CHAPTER TEN: "COURAGE, FOLKS"

122   **"World Exclusive":** Louise Mensch, "Exclusive: FBI 'Granted FISA Warrant' Covering Trump Camp's Ties to Russia," *Heat Street,* November 7, 2016.

123   **"Sphere Consulting's unparalleled stable":** Sphere Consulting, post-election email to clients, November 9, 2016. Sphere Consulting LLC is a DC public relations and lobbying firm run by James Courtovich. Courtovich has courted controversy around Washington in the past; see Brody Mullins, "The Rise and Fall of a K Street Renegade," *Wall Street Journal,* February 13, 2017.

123   **The state assembly, the Duma, burst into applause:** Andrew Osborn, "Russia Says It Was in Touch with Trump's Campaign During Election," Reuters, November 10, 2016.

124   **Hope Hicks claimed the Trump campaign:** David Filipov and Andrew Roth, "Moscow Had Contacts with Trump Team During Campaign, Russian Diplomat Says," *Washington Post,* November 10, 2016.

126   **President Obama used a ninety-minute meeting:** Kristen Welker, Dafna Linzer, and Ken Dilanian, "Obama Warned Trump Against Hiring Mike Flynn, Say Officials," NBC News, May 8, 2017.

126   **Trump named Flynn to the post:** Bryan Bender, "Trump Names Mike Flynn National Security Adviser," *Politico,* November 17, 2016.

126   **Among the attendees:** 2016 conference details and attendee lists are available at https://halifaxtheforum.org.

126   **Wood said he "was aware":** Deposition of David Kramer, *Gubarev v. BuzzFeed,* No. 17-cv-60426, U.S. District Court, Southern District of Florida, December 13, 2017.

126 **"You don't have a choice"**: Tom Hamburger and Rosalind S. Helderman, "Hero or Hired Gun? How a British Former Spy Became a Flash Point in the Russia Investigation," *Washington Post,* February 6, 2018.

127 **"The senator listened"**: Deposition of David Kramer, *Gubarev v. Buzz-Feed.*

127 **"Our impromptu meeting"**: John McCain and Mark Salter, *The Restless Wave: Good Times, Just Causes, Great Fights, and Other Appreciations* (New York: Simon & Schuster, 2018).

127 **"He explained again that the information"**: Deposition of David Kramer, *Gubarev v. BuzzFeed.*

128 **"I've known David:** Testimony of Glenn Simpson, Senate Judiciary Committee, August 22, 2017.

129 **"is, without question, our number-one"**: Mitt Romney, interview by Wolf Blitzer, *The Situation Room,* CNN, March 26, 2012.

129 **Trump abruptly decided to dump Romney:** Reuters, "Trump Chooses Exxon Mobil CEO Rex Tillerson for Secretary of State," Reuters, December 13, 2016.

129 **a story written by Trump's nemesis:** Wayne Barrett, "Meet Donald Trump's Top FBI Fanboy," *Daily Beast,* November 3, 2016.

129 **the FBI was "Trumpland"**: Spencer Ackerman, " 'The FBI Is Trumpland': Anti-Clinton Atmosphere Spurred Leaking, Sources Say," *Guardian,* November 4, 2016.

130 **There were credible news reports:** Mark Hosenball and John Walcott, "Exclusive: Congressional Leaders Were Briefed a Year Ago on Hacking of Democrats—Sources," Reuters, August 12, 2016.

131 **Kramer met with McCain:** Deposition of David Kramer, *Gubarev v. BuzzFeed.*

131 **"The allegations were disturbing"**: McCain and Salter, *Restless Wave,* 238.

131 **Lindsey Graham later admitted:** Felicia Sonmez, "Sen. Lindsey Graham Says He Told John McCain to Give Trump-Russia Dossier to FBI," *Washington Post,* March 25, 2019.

132 **Gaeta's pursuit of a Russian mobster:** Cindy Galli, Patrick Reevell, and Brian Ross, "Russia Protects Alleged Mobster Accused of Olympic Judge Bribes," ABC News, January 28, 2014.

CHAPTER ELEVEN: "I NEED TO KNOW IF ANY OF THIS IS TRUE"

135 *Time* **magazine named Trump:** Michael Scherer, "2016 Person of the Year: Donald Trump," *Time,* December 2016.

135 **twin stories in the** *Post* **and the** *Times***:** Adam Entous, Ellen Nakashima, and Greg Miller, "Secret CIA Assessment Says Russia Was Trying to Help Trump Win White House," *Washington Post,* December 9, 2016; and David E. Sanger and Scott Shane, "Russian Hackers Acted to Aid Trump in Election, U.S. Says," *New York Times,* December 9, 2016.

135 **"did what duty demanded I do"**: McCain and Salter, *Restless Wave,* 239.

136 **had already begun to brief the agency about the work of Fusion and**

Orbis: Bruce Ohr, interview with FBI agents, November 22, 2016. Documented in FBI 302s, obtained via a Freedom of Information Act request by Judicial Watch Inc., available online at https://judicialwatch.org.

136 **"[Simpson] identified Michael Cohen":** Bruce Ohr, interview with FBI agents, December 14, 2016. Documents available at https://judicialwatch .org.

137 **After leaving Simpson, Ohr took the USB drive:** Ibid.

138 **The final Orbis memorandum, dated December 13:** Orbis to Fusion, Company Intelligence Report 2016/166, December 13, 2016.

139 **"the agenda comprised questions":** Cohen has repeatedly denied having ever been to Prague, and the Mueller report is vague on the point. Steele point outs that Cohen has never publicly documented his whereabouts in late August 2016, something it should be relatively easy to do with his digital footprint and things like credit card statements.

140 **FBI general counsel James Baker confirmed:** Testimony of James A. Baker, House Committee on Oversight and Reform, October 3, 2018, 110.

141 **Victoria Nuland, assistant secretary of state:** Deposition of David Kramer, *Gubarev v. BuzzFeed*, No. 17-cv-60426, U.S. District Court, Southern District of Florida, December 13, 2017.

142 **"the broad picture":** Ibid.

142 **The offices were closed for the week:** Ibid.

142 **"He said he wanted to read them":** Deposition of David Kramer, *Gubarev v. BuzzFeed*.

CHAPTER TWELVE: "YOU ARE GONNA GET PEOPLE KILLED"

145 **Here was the combined might:** Office of the Director of National Intelligence, *Assessing Russian Activities and Intentions in Recent US Elections*, Intelligence Community Assessment, January 6, 2017, https://www.dni .gov/files/documents/ICA_2017_01.pdf.

145 **FBI Director Comey and the entire brain trust:** James Comey, *A Higher Loyalty: Truth, Lies, and Leadership* (London: Macmillan, 2018).

145 **After they had walked the president:** Ibid.

146 **That material, Comey wrote, "had been assembled":** Ibid.

146 **"We were sneaking in":** Ibid.

147 **"You are gonna get people killed":** Deposition of David Kramer, *Gubarev v. BuzzFeed*, No. 17-cv-60426, U.S. District Court, Southern District of Florida, December 13, 2017.

147 **"Initially I panicked":** Ibid.

148 **"Is this yours?" he asked:** Bradley Hope, Michael Rothfeld, and Alan Cullison, "Christopher Steele, Ex–British Intelligence Officer, Said to Have Prepared Dossier on Trump," *Wall Street Journal*, January 11, 2017.

148 **"They had already made up their mind":** Deposition of David Kramer, *Gubarev v. BuzzFeed*.

148 **The British government swiftly issued:** The D-notice (defence and secu-

rity media advisory notice) offers "guidance on the public disclosure of the names of members of the UK Intelligence Agencies." Andrew Vallance, air vice marshal, put out the notice on January 11, 2017, advising members of the media:

"In view of media stories alleging that a former SIS officer was the source of the information which allegedly compromises President-Elect Donald Trump, would you and your journalists please seek my advice before making public that name. Irrespective of whether or not the stories are true, the public disclosure of that name would put the personal security of that individual directly at risk."

150 **At 9:17 that night:** Scott Shane, Nicholas Confessore, and Matthew Rosenberg, "How a Sensational, Unverified Dossier Became a Crisis for Donald Trump," *New York Times,* January 11, 2017.

151 **"FAKE NEWS—A TOTAL POLITICAL WITCH HUNT!":** Donald J. Trump (@realDonaldTrump), Twitter, January 10, 2017, 8:19 P.M.

151 **"Russia has never tried to use leverage":** Donald J. Trump (@realDonald Trump), Twitter, January 10, 2017, 7:31 A.M.

151 **"Are we living in Nazi Germany?":** Donald J. Trump (@realDonald Trump), Twitter, January 11, 2017, 7:48 A.M.

151 **Trump took to a podium at Trump Tower:** Donald Trump, news conference, New York, January 11, 2017.

151 **Cameramen and reporters:** Michael C. Bender, "A Look Inside Donald Trump's First Press Conference Since Election Day," *Wall Street Journal,* January 11, 2017.

152 **Trump minced no words:** Trump news conference, January 11, 2017.

153 **"Meet the espionage firm":** Alana Goodman, "Meet the Espionage Firm Which Ordered Trump 'Dirty Dossier'—a Secretive D.C. Firm Which Has Aided Planned Parenthood and Attacked Mitt Romney's Friends," *Daily Mail,* January 13, 2017.

153 **"I sort of know how these things work":** Paul Roderick Gregory, "The Trump Dossier Is Fake—and Here Are the Reasons Why," *Forbes,* January 13, 2017.

153 **"I can say that the dossier itself":** Gregory, "Trump Dossier Is Fake."

154 **he himself was the son of a Russian:** Paul Gregory, "Lee Harvey Oswald Was My Friend," *New York Times,* November 7, 2013.

154 **"working with a Russian spy":** William Browder, interview with Jacob Weisberg, "The Magnitsky Act and the Looming Russian Danger," *Trumpcast* podcast, *Slate,* April 31, 2017.

154 **"a professional smear campaigner":** Chuck Ross, "Exclusive: Oppo Researcher Behind Trump Dossier Is Linked to Pro-Kremlin Lobbying Effort," *Daily Caller,* January 13, 2017.

154 **David Ignatius dropped a bomb:** David Ignatius, "Why Did Obama Dawdle on Russia's Hacking?," *Washington Post,* January 12, 2017.

154 **Flynn had been holding secret talks:** Ibid.

154 **the Senate Intelligence Committee announced:** Senate Intelligence

Committee, "Joint Statement on Committee Inquiry into Russian Intelligence Activities," press release, January 13, 2017.

155   **"obvious fabrications":** Vladimir Putin, press conference, Moscow, January 17, 2017. Russian language transcript available at http://kremlin.ru/events.

155   **days after the dossier leaked:** Greg Miller, Rosalind S. Helderman, Tom Hamburger, Steven Mufson, and David Filipov, "Intel Chiefs Briefed Trump on Unconfirmed Claims Russia Has Compromising Information on Him," *Washington Post,* January 11, 2017.

155   **he then lied about the content:** Greg Miller, Adam Entous, and Ellen Nakashima, "National Security Adviser Flynn Discussed Sanctions with Russian Ambassador, Despite Denials, Officials Say," *Washington Post,* February 9, 2017.

155   **"the real story here":** Donald J. Trump (@realDonaldTrump), Twitter, February 14, 2017, 9:28 A.M.

156   **"I don't think there's ever been":** Donald Trump, press conference, White House, Washington, D.C., February 16, 2017.

156   **"The level of dishonesty":** Ibid.

156   **"It's an illegal process":** Ibid.

156   **"I have nothing to do with Russia":** Ibid.

156   **"Just found out that Obama":** Donald J. Trump (@realDonaldTrump), Twitter, March 4, 2017, 6:35 A.M.

157   **"enemy of the American people":** Amanda Erickson, "Trump Called the News Media an 'Enemy of the American People.' Here's a History of the Term," *Washington Post,* February 18, 2017.

158   **"underhanded tactics":** Kimberley A. Strassel, "Dumpster Diving for Dossiers," *Wall Street Journal,* January 12, 2017.

158   **In one stark example:** Kimberley A. Strassel, "Russia, the NRA and Fake News," *Wall Street Journal,* March 22, 2018.

158   **the Justice Department unsealed a criminal complaint:** *United States v. Butina,* No. 18-218, U.S. District Court, District of Columbia, July 14, 2018.

159   **"If you want to visit Glenn":** The Twitter profile has since been deleted.

160   **He walked into the restaurant:** Benjamin Freed and Jessica Sidman, "Man with Gun Arrested at Comet Ping Pong," *Washingtonian,* December 4, 2016.

161   **when FBI Director James Comey sat down:** Testimony of James Comey, House Committee on Oversight and Reform, July 7, 2016.

162   **Nunes then deployed that material:** Devin Nunes, "Representative Nunes on Russia and 2016 Elections," video of Nunes press conference in front of the White House, 13:34, C-SPAN, March 22, 2017.

162   **"What I have read bothers me":** Ibid.

162   **It soon came out:** Brian Barrett, "Devin Nunes: A Running Timeline of His Surveillance Claims and White House Ties, *Wired,* April 12, 2017.

162   **Even Senator Lindsey Graham:** Louis Nelson, "Graham: Nunes Is Running 'an Inspector-Clouseau Investigation,'" *Politico,* March 28, 2017.

CHAPTER THIRTEEN: "CAN YOU CALL ME PLEASE?"

166 **the British government publicly stated:** Alan Cowell, "Putin 'Probably Approved' Litvinenko Poisoning, British Inquiry Says," *New York Times,* January 21, 2016.

166 **As reflected in Ohr's scribbled notes:** Notes released by the U.S. Department of Justice in response to a Freedom of Information Act (FOIA) request by Judicial Watch Inc.

166 **"They can't reach [the source]":** Ibid.

167 **the White House abruptly fired Ohr's boss:** Evan Perez and Jeremy Diamond, "Trump Fires Acting AG After She Declines to Defend Travel Ban," CNN, January 31, 2017.

168 **"We can't allow our guy to be forced":** Notes released by the U.S. Department of Justice in response to a Freedom of Information Act (FOIA) request by Judicial Watch Inc.

168 *The Wall Street Journal* **disclosed:** Carol E. Lee, Devlin Barrett, and Shane Harris, "U.S. Eyes Michael Flynn's Links to Russia," *Wall Street Journal,* January 22, 2017.

171 **The Intelligence Committee ultimately:** Spencer Ackerman, "Senate Investigator Breaks Silence About CIA's 'Failed Coverup' of Torture Report," *Guardian,* September 9, 2016.

171 **The report won wide acclaim:** Mark Mazzetti, "Panel Faults C.I.A. Over Brutality and Deceit in Terrorism Interrogations," *New York Times,* December 9, 2014.

173 **McCarthy soon faded, of course:** Richard Cohen, "How Political Donations Changed History," *Washington Post,* January 16, 2012.

175 **the group eventually raised:** IRS Form 990 for the Democracy Integrity Project, FY 2017, form available on projects.propublica.org/nonprofits.

175 **Trump begged Sessions:** Michael S. Schmidt and Julie Hirschfeld Davis, "Trump Asked Sessions to Retain Control of Russia Inquiry After His Recusal," *New York Times,* May 29, 2018.

177 **They even held public hearings:** Office of Senator Richard Burr, "Senate Intel Chairman Burr on Committee's Review of Russian Intelligence," press release, December 16, 2016. One press release claimed, "We believe that it is critical to have a full understanding of the scope of Russian intelligence activities impacting the United States"; see Senate Intelligence Committee, "Joint Statement on Committee Inquiry into Russian Intelligence Activities," press release, January 13, 2017; Testimony of James Comey, House Intelligence Committee, March 20, 2017.

178 **He also canceled at least one big hearing:** Adam Schiff (@RepAdam Schiff), Twitter, March 24, 2017, 11:16 A.M.

CHAPTER FOURTEEN: A SENATOR ATTACKS

179 **"I am writing to inquire":** Charles E. Grassley to Glenn R. Simpson, March 24, 2017.

180 **Grassley had sent a letter:** Charles E. Grassley to James B. Comey Jr., March 6, 2017.

180 **"DOCUMENT PRESERVATION NOTICE":** Charles E. Grassley to Fusion GPS counsel Josh Levy.

180 **Grassley released his letter publicly:** Grassley to Simpson, March 24, 2017.

181 **"Thanks for that, old friend":** "Judicial Watch Uncovers DOJ Records Showing Numerous Bruce Ohr Communications with Fusion GPS and Christopher Steele," Judicial Watch, March 7, 2019.

181 **the *Post* reported that Jared Kushner:** Ellen Nakashima, Adam Entous, and Greg Miller, "Russian Ambassador Told Moscow That Kushner Wanted Secret Communications Channel with Kremlin," *Washington Post,* May 26, 2017.

181 **"Just amazing," Ohr texted:** Note from Ohr, March 26, 2017. Notes available on Judicial Watch website; released by the U.S. Department of Justice in response to a Freedom of Information Act (FOIA) request by Judicial Watch.

184 **Fusion, the senator claimed in his letter, should have registered:** Charles E. Grassley to Dana Boente, Acting Deputy Attorney General, March 31, 2017.

184 **"complaint filed with the Justice Department:** Ibid.

184 **"Russian gun-for-hire":** Ibid.

184 **The headline on his March 31 story:** Ross would later be outed by the *Post* for his past sexist and racist blog posts regarding African Americans, published under the handle "Gucci Little Piggy." His hate-filled Web posts were eerily similar to those of Grassley's chief investigative counsel, Jason Foster, the architect of the Fusion attacks. Foster had once blogged under the name "Extremist." In his posts, he had likened homosexuality to incest and expressed "worry about a Muslim takeover and whether Joe McCarthy got a bum rap." Those revelations, when aired in the press, would cost neither Ross nor Foster his job. See Erik Wemple, "Daily Caller Reporter Renounces Racist, Misogynistic Writings," *Washington Post,* September 14, 2017; Robert Faturechi, "A Partisan Combatant, a Remorseful Blogger: The Senate Staffer Behind the Attack on the Trump-Russia Investigation," *ProPublica,* March 28, 2018.

185 **The *New York Post* ran an op-ed:** Paul Sperry, "Sketchy Firm Behind Trump Dossier Is Stalling Investigators," *New York Post,* June 24, 2017.

186 **Levy answered with a polite but firm rejection:** Josh Levy to Charles E. Grassley, April 7, 2017.

188 **Born in 1988:** Butina profile on Live Journal, https://butina.livejournal.com.

189 **a new article about Butina:** Tim Mak, "The Kremlin and GOP Have a New Friend—and Boy, Does She Love Guns," *Daily Beast,* February 23, 2017.

189 **"It may take the election":** Maria Butina, "The Bear and the Elephant," *National Interest,* June 12, 2015.

189 **Keene and Torshin had met in Moscow:** Joseph P. Tartaro, "Civilian Arms Rights Advocates Meet in Russia," *TheGunMag*, December 10, 2013.

189 **hosting a speech:** "Transcript: Donald Trump's Foreign Policy Speech," *New York Times*, April 27, 2016.

190 **The event featured the Russian ambassador:** Michael Crowley, "Trump Fails to Impress Foreign-Policy Experts," *Politico*, April 27, 2016.

190 **She was romantically involved:** Sentencing Memo, *United States v. Butina*, No. 18-218, U.S. District Court, District of Columbia, April 19, 2019.

190 **Erickson was a big GOP supporter and NRA booster:** Indictment, *United States v. Erickson*, No. 19-40015, U.S. District Court, South Dakota Southern Division, February 5, 2019.

191 **twenty-seven "Manafort Entities":** Using the 2014 Pericles litigation in the Cayman Islands, Fusion was able to identify affiliated funds based in Cyprus. The Cypriot funds were all concentrated at the same registrar's office. Once they pulled relevant information available from the Cypriot Ministry of Finance, they saw a strange pattern. The Cypriot shell companies were lending millions of dollars to other shell companies. Some of these companies were even based in the United States. It appeared to be an elaborate tax fraud. Some of the Cypriot shell companies tracked back to Russian and Ukrainian oligarchs as well.

193 **The *Times* published his groundbreaking story, "Manafort Was in Debt":** Mike McIntire, "Manafort Was in Debt to Pro-Russia Interests, Cyprus Records Show," *New York Times*, July 19, 2017.

193 **Manafort had his lawyer's PR man:** Hadas Gold, "NYT Rejects Manafort's Retraction Request," *Politico*, July 20, 2017.

193 **those Cypriot companies:** Indictment, *United States v. Manafort*, No. 1:17-cr-00201, U.S. District Court, District of Columbia, October 30, 2017.

193 **The FBI director's abrupt dismissal:** Donald J. Trump to James B. Comey Jr., May 9, 2017; Jeff Sessions to Donald J. Trump, May 9, 2017; Rod J. Rosenstein to Jeff Sessions, May 9, 2017.

194 **"The handling of the Clinton email investigation":** Charles E. Grassley to Dianne Feinstein, June 13, 2017.

194 **Details and photos:** Matt Apuzzo, Maggie Haberman, and Matthew Rosenberg, "Trump Told Russians That Firing 'Nut Job' Comey Eased Pressure from Investigation," *New York Times*, May 19, 2017.

194 **Trump would repeat his boast:** Donald Trump, interview by Lester Holt, *NBC Nightly News*, NBC, May 11, 2017.

195 **Grassley captured the prevailing sentiment:** Charles Grassley, *Fox & Friends*, Fox News, May 20, 2017.

195 **Grassley sent Fusion:** Charles E. Grassley to Glenn R. Simpson, June 7, 2017.

196 **the Watergate scandal "pales" in comparison:** Colin Packham, "Watergate 'Pales' Compared with Trump-Russia: Former U.S. Intelligence Head," Reuters, June 7, 2017.

196 **"lies, plain and simple"**: Testimony of James B. Comey, Senate Intelligence Committee, June 8, 2017.

196 **he was under investigation**: Donald J. Trump (@realDonaldTrump), Twitter, June 16, 2017, 9:07 A.M.

197 **"The Crown prosecutor of Russia"**: Rob Goldstone to Donald Trump Jr., email message, June 3, 2016; see "Read the Emails on Donald Trump Jr.'s Russia Meeting," *New York Times*, July 11, 2017.

197 **"the Russian government attorney"**: Ibid.

197 **news of that June 9 gathering**: Jo Becker, Matt Apuzzo, and Adam Goldman, "Trump Team Met with Lawyer Linked to Kremlin During Campaign," *New York Times*, July 8, 2017.

CHAPTER FIFTEEN: NATALIA

198 **When the *Times* story**: Jo Becker, Matt Apuzzo, and Adam Goldman, "Trump Team Met with Lawyer Linked to Kremlin During Campaign," *New York Times*, July 8, 2017.

199 **"We have learned that the person"**: Statement by Mark Corallo, Trump legal team spokesman, July 9, 2017.

201 **was merely about reviving a bilateral program**: Becker, Apuzzo, and Goldman, "Trump Team Met with Kremlin."

201 **The sexier angle**: Matt Apuzzo, Jo Becker, Adam Goldman, and Maggie Haberman, "Trump Jr. Was Told in Email of Russian Effort to Aid Campaign," *New York Times*, July 10, 2017.

201 **Corallo resigned**: Josh Dawsey, "Spokesman for Trump's Legal Team Resigns Just Two Months After Starting," *Politico*, July 20, 2017.

202 **She responded to the news**: Seung Min Kim and Austin Wright, "Senate Judiciary to Call Manafort to Discuss Trump Jr. Email Chain," *Politico*, July 12, 2017.

202 **Grassley put out a notice**: Office of Senator Chuck Grassley, "Judiciary Committee Announces Hearing, Sends Invitations, Requests Documents," press release, July 19, 2017.

202 **Manafort had been under active federal criminal investigation**: Michael S. Schmidt, Matthew Rosenberg, Adam Goldman, and Matt Apuzzo, "Intercepted Russian Communications Part of Inquiry into Trump Associates," *New York Times*, January 19, 2017.

203 **The trap sprung**: Fox News, "Co-founder of Firm Behind Trump-Russia Dossier to Plead the Fifth," Fox News, September 27, 2017.

204 **Trump had also tasked Flynn**: Shane Harris, "Trump Campaign Attempted to Obtain Hillary Clinton's Private Emails," *Washington Post*, April 18, 2019.

205 **Smith checked into a motel in Rochester**: Katherine Skiba, David Heinzmann, and Todd Lighty, "Peter W. Smith, GOP Operative Who Sought Clinton's Emails from Russian Hackers, Committed Suicide, Records Show," *Chicago Tribune*, July 13, 2017.

206 **Manafort had finally registered in June with the Justice Department**:

Theodoric Meyer, "Manafort Registers as Foreign Agent," *Politico*, June 27, 2017.

206 **FBI agents raided Manafort's home:** Carol D. Leonnig, Tom Hamburger, and Rosalind S. Helderman, "FBI Conducted Raid of Former Trump Campaign Chairman Manafort's Home," *Washington Post*, August 9, 2017.

206 **Papadopoulos was arrested by the FBI:** Matt Apuzzo and Michael S. Schmidt, "Trump Campaign Adviser Met with Russian to Discuss 'Dirt' on Clinton," *New York Times*, October 20, 2017.

207 **Levy worked out a deal for Simpson:** Office of Senator Chuck Grassley, "Following Subpoena, Simpson Agrees to Committee Interview," press release, July 25, 2017.

210 **They even showed up outside his lawyers':** Ali Watkins, "Hunt for Trump Dossier Author Inflames Russia Probe," *Politico*, August 4, 2017.

211 **"the Russian active measures campaign":** House Intelligence Committee to Fusion GPS, September 20, 2017.

211 **"What possible leaks of classified information":** Ibid.

211 **improper "surveillance" of the Trump campaign:** Brian Barrett, "Devin Nunes: A Running Timeline of His Surveillance Claims and White House Ties," *Wired*, April 12, 2017.

211 **Alfa Bank filed a defamation suit:** Complaint, December 12, 2017, *Fridman v. Bean*, No. 1:17-cv-02041, U.S. District Court, District of Columbia.

211 **highlighted Alfa's closeness to Putin:** Orbis to Fusion, Company Intelligence Report, September 14, 2016. Also included in the Mueller report.

212 **weighed in quickly on Twitter:** Donald J. Trump (@realDonaldTrump), Twitter, October 19, 2017, 4:56 A.M.

CHAPTER SIXTEEN: CAPTAIN AMERICA

214 **Nunes had secretly served a subpoena:** *Bean v. Defendant Bank*, No. 1:17-cv-02187, U.S. District Court, District of Columbia

215 **Fusion filed suit against TD Bank:** *Bean v. Defendant Bank*, No. 1:17-cv-02187, U.S. District Court, District of Columbia, October 23, 2017.

216 **Fusion and Steele had been paid:** Adam Entous, Devlin Barrett, and Rosalind S. Helderman, "Clinton Campaign, DNC Paid for Research That Led to Russia Dossier," *Washington Post*, October 24, 2017.

216 **"lead research into Russian efforts":** Kenneth P. Vogel and Cecilia Kang, "Senators Demand Online Ad Disclosures as Tech Lobby Mobilizes," *New York Times*, October 19, 2017.

216 **"Fake News Dossier":** Donald J. Trump (@realDonaldTrump), Twitter, October 25, 2017, 7:21 A.M.

216 **the Republican-funded *Washington Free Beacon*:** Matthew Continetti and Michael Goldfarb, "Fusion GPS and the Washington Free Beacon," *Washington Free Beacon*, October 27, 2017.

217 **Monday, October 30, Mueller unveiled:** *United States v. Manafort*, No: 1:17-cr-00201, U.S. District Court, District of Columbia.

217 **"Sorry, but this is years ago":** Donald J. Trump (@realDonaldTrump), Twitter, October 30, 2017, 10:25 A.M.

217 **Also charged was an obscure former:** *United States v. Papadopoulos,* No. 1:17-cr-00182, U.S. District Court, District of Columbia.

217 **Still more attacks came:** Paul Roderick Gregory, "Is Russiagate Really Hillarygate?" *Forbes,* June 19, 2017. *Forbes* has been caught doing pay-to-play journalism before; see John Plunkett, "Forbes Investigates After 'Contributor' Asks PR for £300 to Write Online Profile," *Guardian,* March 26, 2016.

220 **"'Journalism for Rent'":** Jack Gillum and Shawn Boburg, "'Journalism for Rent': Inside the Secretive Firm Behind the Trump Dossier," *Washington Post,* December 11, 2017.

220 **"operates with the secrecy of a spy agency":** Ibid.

221 **"blunt aggressive reporting":** Ibid.

222 **Carollo died in Switzerland:** Obituary of Russell Carollo, accessible online at http://obits.nola.com. Carollo attended college in Louisiana and worked there for many years as a journalist.

222 **"The Committee therefore seeks":** Notice of Filing Redacted Versions of Documents, November 21, 2017, *Bean v. Defendant Bank,* No. 1:17-cv-02187, U.S. District Court, District of Columbia.

223 **one of the staffers who'd traveled:** Katie Rogers and Matthew Rosenberg, "Kashyap Patel, Main Author of Secret Memo, Is No Stranger to Quarrels," *New York Times,* February 2, 2018.

223 **As an anonymous blogger:** Robert Faturechi, "A Partisan Combatant, a Remorseful Blogger: The Senate Staffer Behind the Attack on the Trump-Russia Investigation," *ProPublica,* March 28, 2018.

224 **"it appears the Russians":** Testimony of Glenn Simpson, House Intelligence Committee, November 14, 2017.

225 **federal judge Richard Leon:** Memorandum Opinion, *Bean v Defendant Bank,* No. 1:17-cv-02187, U.S. District Court, District of Columbia, January 4, 2018.

225 **that ruling would later be cited:** Opposition of Intervenor-Defendants to Plaintiffs' Motion for a Preliminary Injunction, *Trump v. Deutsche Bank,* No. 1:19-cv-3826, U.S. District Court, Southern District of New York, May 10, 2019.

226 **The three organizations published:** Ned Parker et al., "Ivanka and the Fugitive from Panama," Reuters, November 17, 2017.

227 **Interviewed by NBC:** Aggelos Petropoulos and Richard Engel, "A Panama Tower Carries Trump's Name and Ties to Organized Crime," NBC News, November 17, 2017.

227 **He later fled Brazil:** Brad Brooks, "Former Broker in Trump Panama Project Under Investigation in Brazil," Reuters, November 17, 2017.

227 **Trump's name was scraped from the building:** Patrick Clark, "Former Trump Hotel in Panama Will Be Branded as a JW Marriott," *Bloomberg,* June 27, 2018.

227   **the private equity fund:** Heather Vogell, "Trump Companies Accused of Tax Evasion in Panama," *ProPublica*, June 3, 2019.

227   **the Trump Organization agreed to remove:** Jonathan O'Connell and David A. Fahrenthold, "Trump's Name Is Coming Off His SoHo Hotel as Politics Weigh on President's Brand," *Washington Post*, November 22, 2017.

227   **pleaded guilty to lying:** Michael D. Shear and Adam Goldman, "Michael Flynn Pleads Guilty to Lying to the F.B.I. and Will Cooperate with Russia Inquiry," *New York Times*, December 1, 2017.

228   **"Crooked Hillary Clinton":** Donald J. Trump (@realDonaldTrump), Twitter, December 2, 2017, 9:06 P.M.

228   **The story published shortly thereafter:** Jake Gibson, "Wife of Demoted DOJ Official Worked for Firm Behind the Anti-Trump Dossier," Fox News, December 11, 2017.

228   **follow-up to Gibson's "scoop":** Ibid.

228   **Nellie's publicly available May 2016 application:** Amateur License No. KM4UDZ, accessible at the U.S. Federal Communications Commission website, https://www.fcc.gov.

229   **"The Republicans' Fake Investigations":** Glenn R. Simpson and Peter Fritsch, "The Republicans' Fake Investigations," *New York Times*, January 2, 2018.

CHAPTER SEVENTEEN: "WHAT I'M GOING TO DO TO YOU . . ."

230   **The *Times* op-ed:** Glenn R. Simpson and Peter Fritsch, "The Republicans' Fake Investigations," *New York Times*, January 2, 2018.

230   **"Federal Judge Obliterates Fusion GPS' Attempt":** Mollie Hemingway, "Federal Judge Obliterates Fusion GPS' Attempt to Hide Info from Investigators," *The Federalist*, January 5, 2018.

230   **Grassley and his new wingman:** Office of Senator Chuck Grassley, "Senators Grassley, Graham Refer Christopher Steele for Criminal Investigation," press release, January 5, 2018.

231   **a less-than-flattering profile:** Matt Flegenheimer, "Fusion GPS Founder Hauled from the Shadows for the Russia Election Investigation," *New York Times*, January 8, 2018.

231   **"The innuendo and misinformation":** Office of Senator Dianne Feinstein, "American People Deserve Opportunity to Read Glenn Simpson, Fusion GPS Transcript," press release, January 9, 2018.

232   **"basically a Boy Scout":** Testimony of Glenn Simpson, Senate Judiciary Committee, August 22, 2017.

232   **"The fact that Sneaky Dianne Feinstein":** Donald J. Trump (@realDonaldTrump), Twitter, January 10, 2018, 10:00 A.M.

233   **filed a defamation lawsuit:** *Cohen v. Bean*, No. 1:18-cv-00183, U.S. District Court, Southern District of New York, January 9, 2018.

234   **he was caught on tape threatening:** Brandy Zadrozny and Tim Mak, "Ex-Wife: Donald Trump Made Me Feel 'Violated' During Sex," *Daily Beast*, July 27, 2015.

234 **a message on Twitter from Cohen:** Michael Cohen (@MichaelCo-hen212), "@SergeiMillian have you seen the polls that were announced formally today?," Twitter, August 18, 2016, 11:09 P.M.

234 **A review of open-source records:** Conspiracy to structure monetary transactions to evade currency reporting requirements; *United States v. Shusterman,* No. 1:93-cr-00186, District Court of New York, February 19, 1993.

234 **Cohen's brother had also married:** Josh Marshall, "Says Who—Piecing Together the Michael Cohen Story," *Talking Points Memo,* March 1, 2017.

234 **Steele filed a memo:** Orbis to Fusion, Company Intelligence Report 2016/135, October 19, 2016.

235 **secret meeting with "Kremlin officials":** Orbis to Fusion, Company Intelligence Report 2016/36, October 20, 2016.

235 **"Simpson identified Michael Cohen":** Bruce Ohr, interview with FBI agents, December 14, 2016. Documented in FBI 302s, obtained via a Freedom of Information Act request by Judicial Watch, available at https://judicialwatch.org.

236 **"I have never been to Prague":** Michael Cohen (@MichaelCohen212), Twitter, January 10, 2017, 8:21 P.M.

236 **He appeared live the next day:** Donald J. Trump, *The Sean Hannity Show,* Fox News, January 11, 2017.

236 **he had tried to back-channel:** Meghan Twohey and Scott Shane, "A Back-Channel Plan for Ukraine and Russia, Courtesy of Trump Associates," *New York Times,* February 19, 2017.

237 **Soviet émigré taxi operators:** Clifford D. May, "U.S. Officials Tell of Russian Émigré Crime Group in Brooklyn," *New York Times,* February 12, 1983.

238 **Cohen and Sater had pursued:** Gloria Borger and Marshall Cohen, "Document Details Scrapped Deal for Trump Tower Moscow," CNN, September 9, 2017.

238 **"significant financial and reputational damages":** Preliminary statement, *Cohen v. Bean,* No. 1:18-cv-00183, U.S. District Court, Southern District of New York.

238 **he had arranged a $130,000 payoff:** Michael Rothfeld and Joe Palazzolo, "Trump Lawyer Arranged $130,000 Payment for Adult-Film Star's Silence," *Wall Street Journal,* January 12 , 2018.

238 **"raising outlandish allegations":** Ibid.

239 **HIGHLY CONFIDENTIAL PROCEEDING:** Declaration of Jill A. Martin, *EC v. Peggy Peterson,* an alternative dispute resolution filing, February 22, 2018. The highly confidential court documents were posted by *The Wall Street Journal.* "Peggy Peterson" is a pseudonym used by Stormy Daniels.

239 **A report in *The New York Times*:** Sharon LaFraniere, Mark Mazzetti, and Matt Apuzzo, "How the Russia Inquiry Began: A Campaign Aide, Drinks and Talk of Political Dirt," *New York Times,* December 30, 2017.

239 **a raft of new financial charges:** Superseding Criminal Indictment, *United States v. Manafort,* No. 17-cr-00201, U.S. District Court, District of Columbia, September 14, 2018.

240 **"that the Russian operation":** Simpson, Senate Judiciary Committee, August 22, 2017.

240 **"There were a lot of real estate deals":** Ibid.

240 **FBI agents swooped into:** Matt Apuzzo, "F.B.I. Raids Office of Trump's Longtime Lawyer Michael Cohen; Trump Calls It 'Disgraceful,'" *New York Times,* April 9, 2018.

241 **"A total witch hunt":** Donald J. Trump (@realDonaldTrump), Twitter, April 10, 2018, 7:08 A.M.

241 **"Attorney-client privilege is dead":** Donald J. Trump (@realDonaldTrump), Twitter, April 10, 2018, 7:07 A.M.

241 **"an attack on our country":** Aaron Blake, "Trump's Tirade After the Michael Cohen Raid, Annotated," *Washington Post,* April 9, 2018.

241 **"rather jump out of a building":** Michael M. Grynbaum (@grynbaum) of *The New York Times,* Twitter, April 11, 2018, 1:13 P.M.

241 **Trump's new personal attorney, Rudolph Giuliani, blurted out:** "Rudy Giuliani Contradicts Trump, Says the President Knew About Michael Cohen's $130,000 Payment to Stormy Daniels and Reimbursed Cohen for It," Associated Press, May 2, 2018.

241 **Investigators also found Cohen texts:** Hunter Walker and Brett Arnold, "Michael Cohen's Efforts to Build a Trump Tower in Moscow Went On Longer Than He Has Previously Acknowledged," *Yahoo News,* May 16, 2018.

241 **Cohen's Essential Consultants:** William K. Rashbaum, Ben Protess, and Mike McIntire, "At Trump Tower, Michael Cohen and Oligarch Discussed Russian Relations," *New York Times,* May 25, 2018.

242 **he fired his legal team and resigned:** Brian Ries, Meg Wagner, and Amanda Wills, "What's in the Cohen Warrant Documents," CNN, March 19, 2019.

CHAPTER EIGHTEEN: WAITING FOR MUELLER

244 **That group was led by:** Billy Perrigo, "The Billionaire Who Bankrolled Brexit Is Now Under Criminal Investigation. Officials Suspect Foreign Money," *Time,* November 1, 2018.

244 **boasted of a "boozy" lunch:** Carole Cadwalladr and Peter Jukes, "Arron Banks 'Met Russian Officials Multiple Times Before Brexit Vote,'" *Guardian,* June 9, 2018.

245 **looked like a possible Kremlin plot:** David D. Kirkpatrick and Matthew Rosenberg, "Russians Offered Business Deals to Brexit's Biggest Backer," *New York Times,* June 29, 2018.

247 **sold off his shares of the family farm:** Ryan Lizza, "Devin Nunes's Family Farm Is Hiding a Politically Explosive Secret," *Esquire,* September 30, 2018.

248 **"one and only hobby":** Kris Kitto, "Meet the Lawmaker: Rep. Devin Nunes (R-Calif.), 21st District," *Hill,* February 1, 2010.

248 *The Fresno Bee* **reported:** Mackenzie Mays, "A Yacht, Cocaine, Prostitutes: Winery Partly Owned by Nunes Sued After Fundraiser Event," *Fresno Bee,* May 23, 2018.

248 **The booze cruise, she alleged:** Ibid.

248 **later sued the winery:** *Anase v. Alpha Omega Winery,* No. 16-cv-000134, Superior Court of the State of California, County of Napa, March 21, 2016.

248 **Nunes would win re-election:** "California Election Results," *New York Times,* January 28, 2019.

248 **Nunes sued Twitter and Republican political consultant Liz Mair:** *Nunes v. Twitter,* No. C49-1715, Henrico County Circuit Court, Virginia, March 18, 2019. As of late 2019, this case is still pending. See https://www.scribd.com/document/402297422/Nunes-Complaint-3-18-19.

248 **He sued the** *Bee's* **parent company:** *Nunes v. McClatchy Company,* No. CL19-629, Albemarle County Circuit Court, Virginia, April 8, 2019. As of late 2019, this case is still pending.

249 **Mueller struck with an indictment:** *United States v. Netysho,* No. 1:18-cr-00215, U.S. District Court, District of Columbia, July 13, 2018.

249 **"see any reason why":** "Trump Sides with Russia Against FBI at Helsinki Summit," BBC News, July 16, 2018.

249 **the Helsinki moment was when he stopped:** Testimony of Michael D. Cohen, House Committee on Oversight and Reform, February 27, 2019.

249 **the Justice Department indicted Maria Butina:** *United States v. Butina,* No. 18-218, U.S. District Court, District of Columbia, July 14, 2018.

250 **"another wild tale":** Kimberley A. Strassel, "Russia, the NRA and Fake News," *Wall Street Journal,* March 22, 2018.

250 **the FBI released more than four hundred pages:** Verified Application, Carter W. Page, U.S. Foreign Intelligence Surveillance Court, Washington, D.C., October 2016. Declassified version available at https://www.nytimes.com/2018/07/21/us/politics/carter-page-fisa.html.

250 **Cohen would plead guilty:** Plea, *United States v. Cohen,* No. 1:18-cr-00850, U.S. District Court, Southern District of New York, November 29, 2018.

250 **Manafort was convicted:** A federal grand jury found Manafort guilty of eight counts of tax fraud, bank fraud, and failure to file reports of foreign bank accounts, August 21, 2018. See https://www.justice.gov/sco.

250 **Nunes made a secret trip:** Mark Hosenball, "Congressman Nunes Sought Meeting with UK Spy Chiefs in London," Reuters, August 28, 2018.

251 **Republican investigators would grill Ohr:** Testimony of Bruce Ohr, House Committee on Oversight and Reform, August 28, 2018.

252 **"Wow, Nellie Ohr":** Donald J. Trump (@realDonaldTrump), Twitter, August 30, 2018, 8:54 A.M.

252 **sentenced former Trump adviser:** *United States v. Papadopoulos,* No. 1:17-cr-182, U.S. District Court, District of Columbia, September 7, 2018.

252 **Papadopoulos's lies had deprived prosecutors:** Mark Mazzetti and Sharon LaFraniere, "George Papadopoulos, Ex–Trump Adviser, Is Sentenced to 14 Days in Jail," *New York Times,* September 7, 2018.

252 **a London-based Maltese professor:** Eileen Sullivan, "Joseph Mifsud, Key to Russia Inquiry, Gets Moment in the Spotlight," *New York Times,* July 24, 2019.

252 **"a Russian agent":** James Comey, "No 'Treason.' No Coup. Just Lies—and Dumb Lies at That," *Washington Post,* May 28, 2019.

252 **"hindered investigators' ability":** Sentencing Memorandum, *United States v. Papadopoulos,* No. 1:17-cr-182, U.S. District Court, District of Columbia, August 31, 2018.

253 **"This narrative was developed":** Graham Stack, "Graham Stack: Everything You Know About Paul Manafort Is Wrong," *Kyiv Post,* September 17, 2018.

254 **"There should be no doubt":** Matthew Rosenberg, Charlie Savage, and Michael Wines, "Russia Sees Midterm Elections as Chance to Sow Fresh Discord, Intelligence Chiefs Warn," *New York Times,* February 13, 2018.

254 **executives at Microsoft disclosed:** Hannah Knowles, "Chairman of House Intelligence Panel Says He First Learned of Russian Attacks on Senate Campaigns at a Security Forum," *Washington Post,* July 22, 2019.

254 **identified more than ten thousand posts:** Jonathon Morgan and Ryan Fox, "Russians Meddling in the Midterms? Here's the Data," *New York Times,* November 6, 2018.

254 **much of the Russian disinformation:** New Knowledge (@NewKnowledgeAI), "There is a significant imbalance of user activity," Twitter, October 26, 2018, 1:21 P.M.

254 **"Great Midterm issue for Republicans":** Donald J. Trump (@realDonaldTrump), "Hard to believe that with thousands of people from South of the Border," Twitter, October 17, 2018, 6:45 A.M.

255 **Trump made the caravan the centerpiece:** Christopher Cadelago and Ted Hesson, "Why Trump Is Talking Nonstop About the Migrant Caravan," *Politico,* October 23, 2018.

255 **Polls showed the Republicans:** https://polling.reuters.com.

255 **Republicans had a shot:** Political scientists estimate that gerrymandering of House districts provides Republicans with a roughly 5-percentage-point advantage.

255 **the New York offices of CNN were evacuated:** Michael Gold, "CNN Found a Bomb at Its New York Office. Confusion and 'False Alarms' Followed," *New York Times,* October 24, 2018.

255 **Over the next forty-eight hours:** Shortly after the election, Simpson went to London to catch up with Steele and Burrows. As they sat together, Simpson saw an unfamiliar number from the 202 area code on his mobile phone and decided to pick up. It was the FBI. "Just a courtesy call," the agent said. Nothing to be alarmed about. By law, we're required to let you know: "We found your name in Cesar Sayoc's computer."

255 **"now this 'Bomb' stuff happens"**: Donald J. Trump (@realDonaldTrump), "Republicans are doing so well in early voting," Twitter, October 26, 2018, 7:19 A.M.

256 **"we did have two maniacs"**: President Donald Trump, political rally, Columbia, Missouri, November 1, 2018. Referenced in Allyson Chiu, "Trump Mourns Loss of 'Tremendous Momentum' for GOP Because of Pipe Bombs, Synagogue Shootings," *Washington Post*, November 2, 2018.

256 **wound up beating the Republicans**: Allan Smith, "Democrats Won House Popular Vote by Largest Midterm Margin Since Watergate," NBC News, November 21, 2018.

256 **firing his embattled attorney general**: Peter Baker, Katie Benner, and Michael D. Shear, "Jeff Sessions Is Forced Out as Attorney General as Trump Installs Loyalist," *New York Times*, November 7, 2018.

256 **"witch hunt"**: Matthew Whitaker, "Mueller's Investigation of Trump Is Going Too Far," CNN, November 7, 2018.

258 **"What the Steele dossier showed"**: John Sipher (@john_sipher), Twitter, November 29, 2018, 8:15 A.M.

258 **"Correct," replied his former CIA Russia colleague**: Steven L. Hall (@StevenLHall11), Twitter, November 29, 2018, 12:08 P.M.

258 **"Mueller should not be permitted"**: Bill Barr to Deputy Attorney General Rod Rosenstein and Assistant Attorney General Steve Engel, memorandum, June 8, 2018.

258 **Trump had called his former consigliere**: "Watch: Trump Calls Michael Cohen a Rat," video, *Good Morning America*, ABC, December 16, 2018.

258 **Cohen had nothing to lose**: Testimony of Michael D. Cohen, House Committee on Oversight and Reform, February 27, 2019.

259 **Mueller submitted his report to Barr**: Sharon LaFraniere and Katie Benner, "Mueller Delivers Report on Trump-Russia Investigation to Attorney General," *New York Times*, March 22, 2019.

259 **Barr sent to Congress**: William P. Barr to Lindsey Graham, Jerrold Nadler, Dianne Feinstein, and Doug Collins, March 24, 2019; available at https://www.nytimes.com/interactive/2019/03/24/us/politics/barr-letter -mueller-report.html.

259 **Barr's letter listed the size**: Ibid.

259 **"ultimately decided not to"**: Ibid.

260 **"Good Morning, Have A Great Day"**: Donald J. Trump (@realDonald Trump), Twitter, March 24, 2019, 5:01 A.M.

260 **"MAKE AMERICA GREAT AGAIN!"**: Donald J. Trump (@realDonald Trump), Twitter, March 24, 2019, 5:02 A.M.

260 **"No Collusion, No Obstruction"**: Donald J. Trump (@realDonald Trump), Twitter, March 24, 2019, 4:42 P.M.

260 **admitted as much to Lester Holt**: Donald Trump, interview by Lester Holt, *NBC Nightly News*, NBC, May 12, 2017.

260 **Mueller himself wrote to Barr:** Robert S. Mueller to William P. Barr, March 27, 2019.

261 **Mueller finally went before Congress:** Testimony of Former Special Counsel Robert Mueller, House Judiciary and the Permanent Select Committee on Intelligence, July 24, 2019.

261 **"Welcome, everyone, to the last gasp":** Nunes opening statement, Hearing, Former Special Counsel Robert S. Mueller III on the Investigation into Russian Interference in the 2016 Presidential Election, House Intelligence Committee, July 24, 2019.

261 **"There is collusion in plain sight":** Ibid.

262 **"Fusion GPS, Steele, and other":** Ibid.

262 **"not a witch hunt":** Robert Mueller, Hearing, Former Special Counsel Robert S. Mueller, July 24, 2019.

EPILOGUE

263 **hundreds of former prosecutors agree:** "Hundreds of Ex–Federal Prosecutors Sign Letter Saying Trump Deserved Obstruction Charge," Associated Press, May 6, 2019.

266 **nearly one in four federal appeals:** Carrie Johnson, "Trump's Impact on Federal Courts: Judicial Nominees by the Numbers," NPR, August 5, 2019.

267 **the FBI exposed and arrested:** Sealed Complaint, *United States. v. Chapman*, U.S. District Court, Southern District of New York, 2010.

267 **the ring was more preoccupied:** In one 2002 conversation, one of the spies boasted to headquarters that she was cultivating "an active fundraiser" for the Democrats who was "a personal friend" of Hillary Clinton. Yet another sought to cozy up to a Washington think tank with close ties to the Clintons, the New America Foundation.

269 **questions about the Trump campaign's cooperation:** Eric Lichtblau and Steven Lee Myers, "Investigating Donald Trump, F.B.I. Sees No Clear Link to Russia," *New York Times,* October 31, 2016. To the extent they did finally surface in the final days of the campaign, they were effectively snuffed out as a political issue by *The New York Times* a week before the vote.

269 **The dossier's true impact:** Ironically, the appearance of the first Steele memo at Fusion's offices in June 2016 may well have helped Trump. The alarming confirmation of Fusion's early suspicions led it to focus on the Trump-Russia relationship and not on other research threads that likely would have been more politically damaging, such as Trump's use of immigrant labor and his offshoring of jobs.

270 **Historic intelligence failures:** Errol Morris, "The Certainty of Donald Rumsfeld (Part 3)," *New York Times,* March 27, 2014.

270 **"failures of imagination":** Alec Russell, "9/11 Report Condemns 'Failure of Imagination,'" *The Telegraph,* July 23, 2004; Dana Priest, "Russia's Election Meddling Is Another American Intelligence Failure," *New Yorker,* November 13, 2017.

271 **A spy whose sources:** Jane Mayer, "Christopher Steele, the Man Behind the Trump Dossier," *New Yorker,* March 5, 2018. "In the intelligence business, you don't pretend you're a hundred per cent accurate. If you're seventy or eighty per cent accurate, that makes you one of the best."

271 **"Russian President Vladimir Putin ordered":** Office of the Director of National Intelligence, *Assessing Russian Activities and Intentions in Recent US Elections,* Intelligence Community Assessment, ICA 2017-01D, January 6, 2017.

271 **"Russia's goals":** Ibid.

271 **"undermine the U.S.-led liberal democratic order":** Ibid.

271 **the FBI was either:** Eric Lichtblau and Steven Lee Myers, "Investigating Donald Trump, F.B.I. Sees No Clear Link to Russia," *New York Times,* October 31, 2016. As late as eight days before the election, top FBI officials told *The New York Times* that investigators "have become increasingly confident, based on the evidence they have uncovered, that Russia's direct goal is not to support the election of Mr. Trump, as many Democrats have asserted."

271 **U.S. officials confirmed that the Central Intelligence Agency:** Julian E. Barnes, Adam Goldman, and David E. Sanger, "C.I.A. Informant Extracted from Russia Had Sent Secrets to U.S. for Decades," *New York Times,* September 9, 2019.

272 **secure permits for a Trump Tower in Moscow:** Hunter Walker and Brett Arnold, "Michael Cohen's Efforts to Build a Trump Tower in Moscow Went On Longer Than He Has Previously Acknowledged," *Yahoo News,* May 16, 2018. The deal reportedly also included a penthouse for Putin on the top floor. In Steele's account, there was no specific reference to Trump Tower Moscow, but there was a vague reference to the deal being "in relation to the ongoing 2018 World Cup." That likely refers to possible joint ventures that were explored between Trump and the Agalarovs, who at the time were planning construction projects related to the World Cup. But the notion of real estate projects being dangled by Russia as leverage over Trump was accurate.

272 **"Russians apparently have promised":** Orbis, Company Intelligence Report 2016/097, July 30, 2016.

272 **discovered in July 2017:** Jo Becker, Matt Apuzzo, and Adam Goldman, "Trump Team Met with Lawyer Linked to Kremlin During Campaign," *New York Times,* July 8, 2017.

272 **The dossier also correctly identified:** Flynn and Manafort were subsequently charged and convicted by the special counsel, in part for their dealings with Russians, while Page was the subject of multiple classified electronic eavesdropping warrants, an extraordinary measure that required extensive corroboration of Steele's claims to be submitted in court. Cohen, of course, also eventually admitted many of his lies about his dealings with Russia and ended up in prison.

272 **showed that Manafort was in contact:** *United States v. Manafort,*

No. 1:17-cr-00201-ABJ, U.S. District Court, District of Columbia, June 8, 2018.

273 **Flynn was paid $68,000:** Rosalind S. Helderman and Tom Hamburger, "Trump Adviser Flynn Paid by Multiple Russia-Related Entities, New Records Show," *Washington Post,* March 16, 2017.

273 **admitted to lying:** Chris Sommerfeldt, "Trump's Ex–National Security Adviser Michael Flynn Had Undisclosed Meet with Russian Ambassador in 2015," New York *Daily News,* April 27, 2018.

273 **"bragged . . . that they had cultivated":** Ryan Nobles, *New Day Saturday,* CNN, May 20, 2017.

273 **Page had privately met with:** Orbis to Fusion, Company Intelligence Report 2016/094, July 19, 2016.

273 **That sale was little known at the time Steele described it:** Katya Golubkova, Dmitry Zhdannikov, and Stephen Jewkes, "How Russia Sold Its Oil Jewel: Without Saying Who Bought It," Reuters, January 24, 2017.

273 **Page adamantly denied the claims:** Testimony of Carter Page, House Intelligence Committee, November 2, 2017.

273 **"incredible insights and outreach":** Ibid.

273 **His categorical denial was ultimately reduced:** Steele's timely reports on Page were part of the body of intelligence that led the FBI to initiate its own investigation into Russian meddling in the election, which included obtaining secret surveillance warrants against Page. The Justice Department later "provided additional information obtained through multiple independent sources that corroborated Steele's reporting," according to a January 2018 minority report from the House Intelligence Committee. "Steele's information about Page was consistent with the FBI's assessment of prior (but not public) Russian intelligence efforts to recruit Page in 2013 and his connections to Russian persons of interest." The Mueller report revealed that Carter Page had prior contact with Russian intelligence not once but twice—in 2008 as well as 2013.

273 **Steele's sources stated that Cohen had played an "important role":** Orbis to Fusion, Company Intelligence Report 2016/35, October 19, 2016.

273 **Cohen had attended a meeting:** Ibid. Prior to the publication of the Steele memoranda in January 2017, Michael Cohen was a relatively obscure figure in Trump's orbit and had few known connections to the Trump-Russia controversy. That changed in 2017 and 2018 as a steady trickle of revelations indicated that Cohen indeed had more dealings with Russia than he'd admitted. In April 2018, soon after his office was raided by the FBI, Cohen dropped a libel suit he had filed against Fusion GPS over the Prague claim. Then, in late November 2018, Cohen abruptly appeared in court to admit that he had indeed acted as a liaison to the Kremlin in 2016—regarding not the election hack but the Trump Tower Moscow project. He also said he had lied about it in testimony to Congress in a cover-up that was allegedly coordinated with the White House.

Mueller's prosecutors told the court that Cohen had provided important but unspecified other information "on core topics" of their Russia investigation.

274 **"giving informal advice to Putin":** Orbis to Fusion, Company Intelligence Report 2016/111, September 14, 2016.

274 **Aven said he took Putin's suggestions:** From Mueller report, vol. I, 146: "Aven told the Office that he is one of approximately 50 wealthy Russian businessmen who regularly meet with Putin in the Kremlin; these 50 men are often referred to as 'oligarchs.' Aven told the Office that he met on a quarterly basis with Putin, including in the fourth quarter (Q4) of 2016, shortly after the U.S. presidential election. Aven said that he took these meetings seriously and understood that any suggestions or critiques that Putin made during these meetings were implicit directives, and that there would be consequences for Aven if he did not follow through. As was typical, the 2016 Q4 meeting with Putin was preceded by a preparatory meeting with Putin's chief of staff, Anton Vaino."

274 **"botnets and porn traffic":** Orbis to Fusion, Company Intelligence Report 2016/166, December 13, 2016.

274 **Webzilla's owner vehemently denied:** *Gubarev v. BuzzFeed*, No. 1:17-cv-60426, U.S. District Court, Southern District of Florida, December 19, 2018.

275 **Webzilla was used by the Russian troll farm:** Kevin G. Hall, "Russian Trolls Pumped Out Malware Along with Pro-Trump messages. Venezuelans Helped," *McClatchyDC*, April 2, 2019.

275 **Trump told FBI Director James Comey:** "Donald Trump Press Conference," YouTube video, 1:02:33, posted by "CNBC," January 12, 2017. Trump has also sought to discredit the story by claiming he is a "germaphobe," yet the porn star Stormy Daniels claims he had unprotected sex with her.

275 **Schiller recalled the offer:** Adam Goldman and Nicholas Fandos, "Keith Schiller, Trump's Ex-Bodyguard, Says He Turned Down Offer of Women in Moscow," *New York Times*, November 10, 2017. After he left the White House in the midst of the Mueller investigation, Schiller landed a job at the Republican National Committee that paid $15,000 a month.

275 **"Stopped flow of tapes from Russia":** Mueller report, vol. I, 27n.

277 **Mueller's report offers mountains:** For example, the Kremlin's use of WikiLeaks as a proxy to distribute the hacked emails is well documented, as is the Trump campaign's belief that Russia possessed damaging information about Hillary Clinton and their prior knowledge that WikiLeaks would release hacked material harmful to Clinton. Manafort's alleged use of Carter Page as an intermediary wasn't specifically addressed by Mueller; Page depicted himself as an informal intermediary between the campaign and the Kremlin in emails cited by Mueller. The existence of Trump campaign or Russian moles within the DNC has never been addressed publicly by law enforcement or Congress, and may be a reference to sus-

picious efforts by the children of Russian oligarchs to attend Democratic fundraising events. Likewise, the alleged use of pension payments to fund Russian covert operations has never been addressed in public by Congress, Mueller, or the FBI, and the indictment of the Russian hackers describes their use of cryptocurrencies to conduct transactions in the United States.

SELECTED BIBLIOGRAPHY

Albats, Yevgenia. *The State Within a State: The KGB and Its Hold on Russia—Past, Present, and Future*. Toronto: HarperCollins Canada, 1994.

Andrew, Christopher, and Oleg Gordievsky. *Comrade Kryuchkov's Instructions: Top Secret Files on KGB Foreign Operations, 1975–1985*. Palo Alto, Calif.: Stanford University Press, 1994.

Atkins, Jordan. *Putin's Russia: Beyond Media Headlines; Why Knowing the Truth Will Protect Your Family*. Self-published, CreateSpace, 2016.

Bagley, Tennent H. *Spy Wars: Moles, Mysteries, and Deadly Games*. New Haven: Yale University Press, 2007.

Banks, Arron. *The Bad Boys of Brexit: Tales of Mischief, Mayhem and Guerrilla Warfare from the Referendum Frontline*. London: Biteback, 2017.

Barrett, Wayne. *Rudy! An Investigative Biography of Rudy Giuliani*. New York: Basic Books, 2000.

———. *Trump: The Deals and the Downfall*. New York: HarperCollins, 1992.

Barron, John. *KGB Today: The Hidden Hand*. New York: Reader's Digest Press, 1983.

Barsky, Jack. *Deep Undercover: My Secret Life and Tangled Allegiances as a KGB Spy in America*. Carol Stream, Ill.: Tyndale Momentum, 2018.

Bensinger, Ken. *Red Card: How the U.S. Blew the Whistle on the World's Biggest Sports Scandal*. New York: Simon & Schuster, 2018.

Bittman, Ladislav. *The KGB and Soviet Disinformation: An Insider's View*. Oxford: Pergamon, 1985.

Bullough, Oliver. *The Last Man in Russia: The Struggle to Save a Dying Nation*. New York: Basic Books, 2013.

Cherkashin, Victor, and Gregory Feifer. *Spy Handler: Memoir of a KGB Officer; The True Story of the Man Who Recruited Robert Hanssen & Aldrich Ames*. New York: Basic Books, 2005.

Comey, James. *A Higher Loyalty: Truth, Lies, and Leadership*. New York: Flatiron Books, 2018.

Cooley, Alexander, and John Heathershaw. *Dictators Without Borders: Power and Money in Central Asia*. New Haven: Yale University Press, 2017.

Dawisha, Karen. *Putin's Kleptocracy: Who Owns Russia?* New York: Simon & Schuster, 2014.

Epstein, Edward J. *James Jesus Angleton: Was He Right?* New York: FastTrack/EJE, 2014.

Ericson, Claes. *The Oligarchs: Money and Power in Capitalist Russia*. Stockholm: Stockholm Text, 2011.

Farage, Nigel. *The Purple Revolution: The Year That Changed Everything*. London: Biteback, 2001.

Felshtinsky, Yuri. *The Age of Assassins*. London: Gibson Square Books, 2008.

———. *Corporation: Russia and the KGB in the Age of President Putin*. New York: Encounter Books, 2008.

Felshtinsky, Yuri, and Vladimir Pribylovsky. *The Putin Corporation: The Story of Russia's Secret Takeover*. London: Gibson Square Books, 2012.

Finckenauer, James, and Elin Waring. *Russian Mafia in America: Immigration, Culture, and Crime*. Brattleboro, Vt: Echo Point Books & Media, 2018.

Freeland, Chrystia. *Sale of the Century: The Inside Story of the Second Russian Revolution*. Eastbourne, U.K.: Gardners Books, 2005.

Fridman, Ofer. *Russian "Hybrid Warfare": Resurgence and Politicization*. New York: Oxford University Press, 2018.

Friedman, Robert. *Red Mafiya: How the Russian Mob Has Invaded America*. Boston: Little, Brown, 2009.

Galeotti, Mark. *The Vory: Russia's Super Mafia*. New Haven: Yale University Press, 2018.

Golden, Daniel. *Spy Schools: How the CIA, FBI, and Foreign Intelligence Secretly Exploit America's Universities*. New York: Henry Holt, 2017.

Goldstone, Rob. *Pop Stars, Pageants, and Presidents: How an Email Trumped My Life*. New York: Two Many Hats/Oui 2 Entertainment, 2018.

Gould, Jennifer. *Vodka, Tears, and Lenin's Angel: My Adventures in the Wild and Wooly Former Soviet Union*. New York: St. Martin's Press, 1997.

Green, Joshua. *Devil's Bargain: Steve Bannon, Donald Trump, and the Storming of the Presidency*. New York: Penguin Press, 2017.

Gulko, Boris, Vladimir Popov, Yuri Felshtinsky, and Viktor Kortschnoi. *The KGB Plays Chess: The Soviet Secret Police and the Fight for the World Chess Crown*. Milford, Conn.: Russell Enterprises, 2010.

Gustafson, Thane. *Wheel of Fortune: The Battle for Oil and Power in Russia*. Cambridge, Mass.: Belknap Press of Harvard University Press, 2012.

Handelman, Stephen. *Comrade Criminal: Russia's New Mafiya*. New Haven: Yale University Press, 1997.

Harding, James. *Alpha Dogs: The Americans Who Turned Political Spin into a Global Business*. New York: Farrar, Straus & Giroux, 2008.

Harding, Luke. *Collusion: Secret Meetings, Dirty Money, and How Russia Helped Donald Trump Win.* New York: Vintage Books, 2017.

———. *Mafia State: How One Reporter Became an Enemy of the Brutal New Russia.* London: Guardian Books, 2012.

———. *A Very Expensive Potion: The Definitive Story of the Murder of Litvinenko and Russia's War with the West.* London: Guardian Faber, 2016.

Haslam, Jonathan. *Near and Distant Neighbors: A New History of Soviet Intelligence.* New York: Farrar, Straus & Giroux, 2015.

Haynes, John Earl, Harvey Klehr, and Alexander Vassiliev. *Spies: The Rise and Fall of the KGB in America.* Ann Arbor, Mich.: Sheridan Books, 2009.

Herpen, Marcel H., van. *Putin's Wars: The Rise of Russia's New Imperialism.* Lanham, Md.: Rowman & Littlefield, 2014.

Hettena, Seth. *Trump/Russia: A Definitive History.* Brooklyn: Melville House, 2018.

Hill, Fiona, and Clifford G. Gaddy. *Mr. Putin: Operative in the Kremlin.* Washington, D.C.: Brookings Institution Press, 2013.

Isikoff, Michael, and David Corn. *Russian Roulette: The Inside Story of Putin's War on America and the Election of Donald Trump.* New York: Hachette Books, 2018.

Jamieson, Kathleen Hall. *Cyberwar: How Russian Hackers and Trolls Helped Elect a President; What We Don't, Can't, and Do Know.* New York: Oxford University Press, 2018.

Johnson, Dennis W. *Democracy for Hire: A History of American Political Consulting.* New York: Oxford University Press, 2017.

Johnson, Juliet. *A Fistful of Rubles: The Rise and Fall of the Russian Banking System.* Ithaca, N.Y.: Cornell University Press, 2000.

Judah, Ben. *Fragile Empire: How Russia Fell In and Out of Love with Vladimir Putin.* New Haven: Yale University Press, 2013.

Kalugin, Oleg. *Spymaster: My Thirty-two Years in Intelligence and Espionage Against the West.* New York: Basic Books, 2009.

Kaplan, Fred. *Dark Territory: The Secret History of Cyber War.* New York: Simon & Schuster, 2016.

Kasparov, Garry. *Winter Is Coming: Why Vladimir Putin and the Enemies of the Free World Must Be Stopped.* New York: PublicAffairs, 2015.

King, M. S. *The War Against Putin: What the Government-Media Complex Isn't Telling You About Russia.* Self-published, CreateSpace, 2014.

Klebnikov, Paul. *Godfather of the Kremlin: The Decline of Russia in the Age of Gangster Capitalism.* New York: Mariner Books, 2001.

———. *How the Cold War Began.* New York: Carroll & Graf, 2005.

Knight, Amy. *Orders to Kill: The Putin Regime and Political Murder.* New York: St. Martin's Press, 2017.

Kolb, Larry J. *America at Night: The True Story of Two Rogue CIA Operatives, Homeland Security Failures, Dirty Money, and a Plot to Steal the 2004 U.S. Presidential Election—by the Former Intelligence Agent Who Foiled the Plan.* New York: Riverhead Books, 2007.

————. *Overworld: The Life and Times of a Reluctant Spy*. New York: Riverhead Books, 2004.

Krebs, Brian. *Spam Nation: The Inside Story of Organized Cybercrime—from Global Epidemic to Your Front Door*. Naperville, Ill.: Sourcebooks, 2014.

Kreiss, Daniel. *Prototype Politics: Technology-Intensive Campaigning and the Data of Democracy*. New York: Oxford University Press, 2016.

Krushelnycky, Askold. *An Orange Revolution: A Personal Journey Through Ukrainian History*. London: Harvill Secker, 2006.

Kuzio, Taras. *Putin's War Against Ukraine: Revolution, Nationalism, and Crime*. Self-published, CreateSpace in association with the chair of Ukrainian Studies, University of Toronto, 2017.

Laqueur, Walter. *Putinism: Russia and Its Future with the West*. New York: St. Martin's Press, 2015.

Lauria, Salvatore, and David S. Barry. *The Scorpion and the Frog: High Times and High Crimes*. Beverly Hills, Calif.: New Millennium Press, 2003.

Lucas, Edward. *Deception: Spies, Lies and How Russia Dupes the West*. London: Bloomsbury, 2012.

Magyar, Bálint. *Post-Communist Mafia State: The Case of Hungary*. Budapest: CEU Press, 2016.

Malloch, Theodore Roosevelt. *The Plot to Destroy Trump: How the Deep State Fabricated the Russian Dossier to Subvert the President*. New York: Skyhorse, 2018.

McCabe, Andrew G. *The Threat: How the FBI Protects America in the Age of Terror and Trump*. New York: St. Martin's Press, 2019.

McCain, John, and Mark Salter. *The Restless Wave: Good Times, Just Causes, Great Fights, and Other Appreciations*. New York: Simon & Schuster, 2018.

Mezrich, Ben. *Once Upon a Time in Russia: The Rise of the Oligarchs—A True Story of Ambition, Wealth, Betrayal, and Murder*. New York: Simon & Schuster, 2015.

Miller, Greg. *The Apprentice: Trump, Russia, and the Subversion of American Democracy*. New York: HarperCollins, 2018.

Myers, Steven Lee. *The New Tsar: The Rise and Reign of Vladimir Putin*. New York: Simon & Schuster, 2015.

Nance, Malcolm. *The Plot to Hack America: How Putin's Cyberspies and WikiLeaks Tried to Steal the 2016 Election*. New York: Skyhorse, 2016.

Ostrovsky, Arkady. *The Invention of Russia: From Gorbachev's Freedom to Putin's War*. New York: Penguin Books, 2017.

Papadopoulos, George. *Deep State Target: How I Got Caught in the Crosshairs of the Plot to Bring Down President Trump*. New York: Diversion, 2019.

Pomerantsev, Peter. *Nothing Is True and Everything Is Possible: The Surreal Heart of the New Russia*. New York: PublicAffairs, 2015.

Putin, Vladimir. *First Person: An Astonishingly Frank Self-Portrait by Russia's President*. New York: PublicAffairs, 2000.

Remnick, David. *Lenin's Tomb: The Last Days of the Soviet Empire*. New York: Random House, 1993.

———. *Resurrection: The Struggle for a New Russia*. New York: Random House, 1997.

Risen, James. *The Main Enemy: The Inside Story of the CIA's Final Showdown with the KGB*. New York: Random House, 2003.

Robinson, Peter. *It's My Party: A Republican's Messy Love Affair with the GOP*. New York: Warner Books, 2000.

Rogers, Douglas. *The Depths of Russia: Oil, Power, and Culture after Socialism*. Ithaca, N.Y.: Cornell University Press, 2015.

Satter, David. *Age of Delirium: The Decline and Fall of the Soviet Union*. New York: Knopf, 1996.

———. *Darkness at Dawn: The Rise of the Russian Criminal State*. New Haven: Yale University Press, 2003.

———. *The Less You Know, The Better You Sleep: Russia's Road to Terror and Dictatorship Under Yeltsin and Putin*. New Haven: Yale University Press, 2016.

Segal, Adam. *The Hacked World Order: How Nations Fight, Trade, Maneuver, and Manipulate in the Digital Age*. New York: PublicAffairs, 2016.

Serio, Joseph. *Investigating the Russian Mafia*. Durham, N.C.: Carolina Academic Press, 2008.

Shekhovtsov, Anton. *Russia and the Western Far Right*. New York: Routledge, 2018.

Shipman, Tim. *All Out War: The Full Story of How Brexit Sank Britain's Political Class*. London: HarperCollins, 2016.

Shirreff, Richard. *War with Russia: An Urgent Warning from Senior Military Command*. London: Coronet, 2017.

Shvets, Yuri. *Washington Station: My Life as a KGB Spy in America*. New York: Simon & Schuster, 1994.

Soldatov, Andrei, and Irina Borogan. *The New Nobility: The Restoration of Russia's Security State and the Enduring Legacy of the KGB*. New York: PublicAffairs, 2010.

———. *The Red Web: The Struggle Between Russia's Digital Dictators and the New Online Revolutionaries*. New York: PublicAffairs, 2015.

Stephenson, Svetlana. *Gangs of Russia: From the Streets to the Corridors of Power*. Ithaca, N.Y.: Cornell University Press, 2015.

Stone, Roger. *The Making of the President 2016: How Donald Trump Orchestrated a Revolution*. New York: Skyhorse, 2017.

Sudoplatov, Pavel, and Anatoli Sudoplatov. *Special Tasks: The Memoirs of an Unwanted Witness—A Soviet Spymaster*. Brattleboro, Vt.: Little, Brown, 1994.

Szabo, Stephen. *Germany, Russia, and the Rise of Geo-Economics*. London: Bloomsbury, 2015.

Trump, Donald, and Robert Kiyosaki. *Why We Want You to Be Rich: Two Men—One Message*. New York: Rich Press, 2006.

Unger, Craig. *House of Trump, House of Putin: The Untold Story of Donald Trump and the Russian Mafia*. New York: Dutton, 2017.

Varese, Federico. *Mafia Life: Love, Death, and Money at the Heart of Organized Crime*. New York: Oxford University Press, 2018.

Walker, Shaun. *The Long Hangover: Putin's New Russia and the Ghosts of the Past*. New York: Oxford University Press, 2018.

Ward, Vicky. *Kushner, Inc.: Greed. Ambition. Corruption. The Extraordinary Story of Jared Kushner and Ivanka Trump*. New York: St. Martin's Press, 2019.

Watts, Clint. *Messing with the Enemy: Surviving in a Social Media World of Hackers, Terrorists, Russians, and Fake News*. New York: HarperCollins, 2018.

Welch, Toby. *Vladimir Putin on Life, World Affairs and Russia*. Self-published, CreateSpace, 2016.

Williams, Phil. *Russian Organized Crime: The New Threat?* London: Routledge, 1997.

Wolff, Michael. *Fire and Fury: Inside the Trump White House*. New York: Henry Holt, 2018.

———. *Siege: Trump Under Fire*. New York: Henry Holt, 2019.

Woodward, Bob. *Fear: Trump in the White House*. New York: Simon & Schuster, 2018.

Wright, Tom, and Bradley Hope. *Billion Dollar Whale: The Man Who Fooled Wall Street, Hollywood, and the World*. New York: Hachette Books, 2018.

Zygar, Mikhail. *All the Kremlin's Men: Inside the Court of Vladimir Putin*. New York: PublicAffairs, 2016.

INDEX

ABOUT THE AUTHORS

GLENN SIMPSON is the co-founder of Fusion GPS. He is a former senior reporter for *The Wall Street Journal* who has specialized in campaign finance, money laundering, tax evasion, terrorism finance, securities fraud, and political corruption. He is also the author, with Larry J. Sabato, of *Dirty Little Secrets: The Persistence of Corruption in American Politics.* He lives in Washington, D.C.

PETER FRITSCH co-founded Fusion GPS. He is a former reporter and bureau chief for *The Wall Street Journal,* previously based in Mexico City, São Paulo, South and Southeast Asia, and Brussels. He finished his *Wall Street Journal* career as national security editor in Washington, D.C. He lives in Maryland.

ABOUT THE TYPE

This book was set in Minion, a 1990 Adobe Originals typeface by Robert Slimbach. Minion is inspired by classical, old-style typefaces of the late Renaissance, a period of elegant and beautiful type designs. Created primarily for text setting, Minion combines the aesthetic and functional qualities that make text type highly readable with the versatility of digital technology.